Robin Williams

Cool Mac Apps

Robin Williams
Cool Mac Apps

John Tollett

with Robin Williams

Peachpit Press · Berkeley · California

Robin Williams Cool Mac Apps
©2005 John Tollett with Robin Williams

Cover design: John Tollett
Production: John Tollett and Robin Williams
Index: Julie Bess
Editing: Nancy Davis and Ted Waitt
Prepress: David Van Ness

Peachpit Press
1249 Eighth Street
Berkeley, California 94710
800.283.9444
510.524.2178 voice
510.524.2221 fax

Find us on the World Wide Web at **www.peachpit.com**
To report errors, please send a note to errata@peachpit.com
Peachpit Press is a division of Pearson Education

ISBN 0-321-24693-4

10 9 8 7 6 5 4 3 2 1

Printed and bound in the United States of America

Contents

Cool apps, hot stuff

iLife

1 iPhoto

2 iTunes

3   iMovie   123

4 iDVD

.Mac apps

Mac OS X apps

16   Mail & Address Book

Mail

Address Book

17 iChat AV and Rendezvous

Index

Cool apps, hot stuff

A book about cool apps is really hard to write. I wondered if we would ever finish it. Not because the apps are hard to understand—they're incredibly easy to learn and fun to use. Here's the problem: These apps are such incredibly hot stuff that you can't stop playing with them. And they have the power to transform you. For example, when writing the GarageBand chapter, I realized for the first time that *I'm a brilliant musical composer*—I couldn't stop creating music. When Robin asked "How's that chapter going?" I couldn't even hear her because I had headphones on, and besides, I was concentrating on which drum effect sounded best under the Southern Rock piano. Then, while writing the iMovie chapter, I discovered that *I'm a genius video editor.* I had to force myself to stop importing video clips and editing them, experimenting with different sound tracks and effects. It only got worse when I was working on the iTunes chapter. I had an epiphany—*I'm a music connoisseur*—of all kinds of music, which just happened to be at my fingertips! The iChat chapter added to the problem because *I love to chat with buddies*. It's very hard to break off a chat with an old high school buddy in Germany just because you've got a book deadline.

Even with these obstacles, the day finally arrived when it was time to write this introduction. I'll make it brief, because I've got some movies that need editing and they'll be needing original sound tracks.

This book is divided into three main sections:

Section One, iLife apps covers the suite of five fabulous applications that will change your digital life. If you don't have a digital life, these apps will most likely persuade you to get one. Before iLife, we rarely used our digital camera or our video camera; we seldom bought music, and our existing music collection consisted of dust-covered, scratched CDs scattered around the house. Now we shoot photos, edit movies, create DVDs, buy songs and albums without leaving the house, and compose original music tracks for our movies and DVDs.

Section Two, .Mac apps tells all about the great software, features, and services provided with a .Mac membership (pronounced "dot Mac"). If you don't have a .Mac membership, you're missing out on some of the great advantages of being a Mac user.

Section Three, Mac OS X apps explains in detail the main productivity apps that are included as part of Mac OS X. If there's a Mac application or utility that's not covered here, it's in the *Robin Williams Mac OS X Book, Panther Edition.*

We don't just write about these apps. We use them every day. And every night. Even when we don't have to. Wow, it's fun being a Mac user.

John

Section *one*
iLife

What is **iLife** and what does the "i" mean?

When the iMac was originally introduced, Apple explained the "i" as symbolizing both *innovation* and the computer's built-in *Internet* capabilities. But that was many millions of web pages ago. Now the "i" represents the concept of a digital lifestyle and the software applications that can enhance that lifestyle. Your Mac is meant to be a *digital hub* that enables the various apps to work together as powerful, creative tools. At the core of the digital hub concept are five separate applications: **iMovie, iPhoto, iTunes, iDVD,** and **GarageBand.** As stand-alone applications, they're amazing— add the feature of built-in integration between them and the result is an increase in creativity and productivity that can only be described as *inspirational.* This special collection of applications is what's called **iLife.**

If you have a digital still camera, digital video camera, or a CD collection gathering dust, iLife will turn them into your most important creative tools. It's unofficial, but think of the "i" as a symbol for **inspiration** in your digital lifestyle. You're certain to find yourself thinking "iLove iLife!"

iPhoto

iPhoto makes managing, sharing, and enhancing your digital photos both easy and fun. You can effortlessly import photos straight from most digital cameras, as well as from digital card readers, CDs, DVDs, Zip disks, or any location on your Mac's hard disk.

Organize your photos, expertly retouch blemishes, get rid of red-eye, adjust contrast and brightness, make other adjustments, then share your photos with friends, relatives, or business associates in a number of different ways.

If you have a .Mac account, use iPhoto to create web photo albums and screensaver slideshows, order custom prints online, and create hardcover photo albums of your favorite digital photos.

If you don't own a digital camera, you can send your exposed film to companies that offer digital film service, then import those image files into iPhoto. These companies can process your film and put your photos on a CD or post them on the web for you to download. Visit **www.ofoto.com** or **www. shutterfly.com** to see what services are available.

For a list of **compatible** cameras, printers, and digital card readers, check the iPhoto web site **(www.apple.com/ support/iphoto/).** Look for the "iPhoto camera compatibility" link. If your digital device is not listed as compatible, there is still a chance that it may work—try it before you buy a new one.

In this chapter

iPhoto

Open iPhoto

Single-click the iPhoto icon in the Dock, *or* go to the Applications folder (click the Applications icon in the Sidebar of any open Finder window), then double-click the iPhoto icon. The iPhoto window (below) opens, although yours will be empty if this is the first time you're using it.

The **Photo Library** (top item in the Source pane below) stores all the photos you ever import. Create separate **Albums** (pages 16–17) to organize selections from the Photo Library into groups.

Photo Library:
Click here to
see your entire
collection of photos.

Recent Import albums.

Albums.
Select an album in
the Source pane to
see its contents in
the main window.

Resize buttons (drag).

File information
area.

Comments.
Play slideshow.
Create new albums.

Bottom pane.

File information:
Click to show file
info, click again to
show the Comments
pane. Click a third
time to hide the file
information and
comments.

Source pane.

Viewing area.

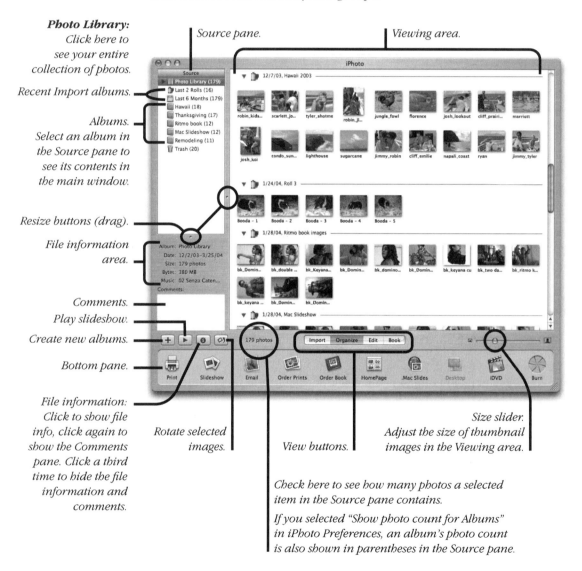

Rotate selected
images.

View buttons.

Size slider.
Adjust the size of thumbnail
images in the Viewing area.

Check here to see how many photos a selected
item in the Source pane contains.

If you selected "Show photo count for Albums"
in iPhoto Preferences, an album's photo count
is also shown in parentheses in the Source pane.

The iPhoto Main Window

Before you can use iPhoto's various features, you first have to **import** the photos into the Photo Library, as explained on the following pages. When you import photos, iPhoto considers each import session a "Film Roll." Each time you import, the photos are grouped beneath a film roll icon that shows the date of the import and the import session number (shown as Roll 29 in the example below). Each image is tagged with the name that your camera automatically assigned. You can **rename** any photo with a name that makes more sense, as shown below: Just select a photo, click on the "Title" text field to highlight it, then type in a new name.

When you import a folder of photos, the Film Roll contains the folder name, such as "Scarlett stills" shown above.

*Each import session is separated by a Film Roll icon. To select **all** the photos in a Film Roll, single-click this icon.*

If the import sessions in your Photo Library are not separated by a Film Roll icon, go to the View menu and select the "Film Rolls" item to place a checkmark next to it.

To rename a selected photo, type here.

Click on a photo to select it.

Click the disclosure triangle next to Photo Library to reveal automatically created "Smart Albums" that categorize your photos by year.

Import Your Photos to iPhoto

When a digital camera or a memory card reader is connected to the computer with a USB cable and recognized by iPhoto, the "Import" view button is automatically selected. The next few pages explain how to import your photos directly from a camera, a digital card reader, a CD, or a location on your hard disk.

Import photos from a digital camera

You can transfer photos directly into iPhoto if your camera has a USB port and if it is compatible with iPhoto (see page 3 regarding compatibility).

1. Turn your camera off.

2. To conserve your camera's battery power, we suggest you connect the camera's AC power adapter to the camera, then plug the adapter into a power outlet.

TRANSCEND

When you connect a digital camera to your Mac, an icon appears on your Desktop named with the brand of memory card that's in the camera.

3. Use the USB cable that came with the camera to connect the camera to your Mac's USB port. **Turn on your camera.** These things happen:

   ▼ An icon representing the digital card in your camera (shown to the left) appears on the Desktop, indicating it has been mounted.

   ▼ The Mac automatically recognizes the camera and opens iPhoto.

   ▼ iPhoto opens with the Import pane showing at the bottom of the main window (shown below).

   ▼ A camera icon (or its digital card icon) and the name of the attached camera (or its card) appear on the left side of the Import pane.

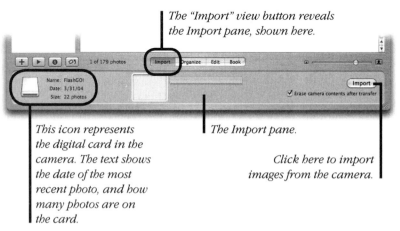

The "Import" view button reveals the Import pane, shown here.

This icon represents the digital card in the camera. The text shows the date of the most recent photo, and how many photos are on the card.

The Import pane.

Click here to import images from the camera.

4. **To delete all the images from your camera** after they've been imported to iPhoto, select "Erase camera contents after transfer" in the lower-right corner of the Import pane.

5. Click the "Import" button on the right side of the Import pane (shown on previous page). To stop an import, click the "Stop" button. The "Import" button changes to a "Stop" button during import.

6. After the photos have been imported, drag the digital card icon on the Desktop to the Trash to unmount it.

   Or Control-click the card's icon on the Desktop, then choose "Eject" from the contextual pop-up menu.

   Or click the Eject icon next to the card's icon in the Sidebar (shown to the right).

   If you do not unmount the card before disconnecting the camera, you'll get an error message warning that you could possibly damage any images left on the memory card.

7. Turn the camera off and disconnect it from your computer.

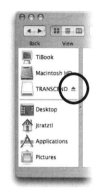

To unmount a digital card in a connected camera, click the Eject icon next to the digital card's icon in the Sidebar.

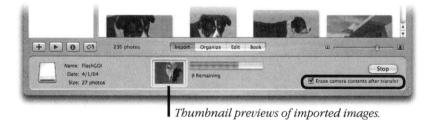

| Thumbnail previews of imported images.

If there are images left in your camera (or on your digital memory card) from the last import, iPhoto asks if you want to import the duplicate photo.

Select "Applies to all duplicates" to apply your answer ("Yes" or "No") to all duplicates found. Otherwise you'll have to answer "Yes" or "No" for every duplicate found during the import.

The imported photos are placed in the Photo Library. All of your newly imported photos will **always** go to the Photo Library. From there you can organize them, as described on pages 20–22.

Import photos from a digital card reader

You can import your photos from a **digital memory card reader,** even if your digital camera is not directly supported by iPhoto.

VIKINGFLASH

This icon appears on your Desktop, named for the card that's in the reader.

The most common types of memory cards are CompactFlash,™ SmartMedia,™ and Memory Stick.™ Some card readers can read only one type of memory card, while others can read two or more types of cards.

1. Make sure the card reader is connected to your Mac using a USB cable.

2. Take the digital memory card (CompactFlash, SmartMedia, SD card, Memory Stick, etc.) out of your camera and insert it into the card reader.

   The card's icon appears on your Desktop, as shown to the left, indicating it has been mounted.

3. iPhoto automatically recognizes the digital card and opens; if iPhoto is already open, it switches to the "Import" view. The card in the card reader is identified on the left side of the Import pane, as shown below.

4. **To erase the contents of your digital card** after importing the photos, select "Erase camera contents after transfer" in the Import pane.

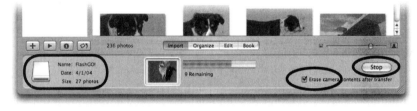

5. Click the "Import" button in the bottom-right. After you click "Import," the button becomes a "Stop" button, as shown above. The lower pane of the iPhoto window shows the import in progress, plus a thumbnail (small version) of the current image being copied to iPhoto.

6. Unmount the digital card when all is done: drag its icon from the Desktop to the Trash.

   Or Control-click on the digital card icon and choose "Eject" from the contextual menu that pops up.

The imported photos are placed in the Photo Library. They are also temporarily available through the *recent import* categories ("Last 2 Rolls" and "Last 6 Months") that appear in the Source pane, shown to the left and explained on page 10.

Import photos from a location on your hard disk or from a CD

You can import any photos that you already have stored on your hard disk or that might be on a CD.

1. Press the Eject Media key on the upper-right corner of your keyboard to open the CD tray. If your keyboard does not have an Eject Media key, try pressing the F12 key.

2. Place the CD that contains photos you want to import into the tray, and press the Eject Media key to close the CD tray. If your CD drive is slot-loading, insert the CD into the slot.

3. Open iPhoto if it is not already open.

4. From the File menu, select "Import..." to open the "Import Photos" window, shown below. In the window, find the CD you inserted, or choose a location somewhere on your hard disk where photos are stored that you want to import.

5. Select an entire folder of photos, an individual photo, or multiple photos, then click the "Import" button.

The selected photos are placed in the Photo Library. The imported photos also appear temporarily in the *recent import* categories ("Last 2 Rolls" and "Last 6 Months") in the Source pane, as explained on page 10.

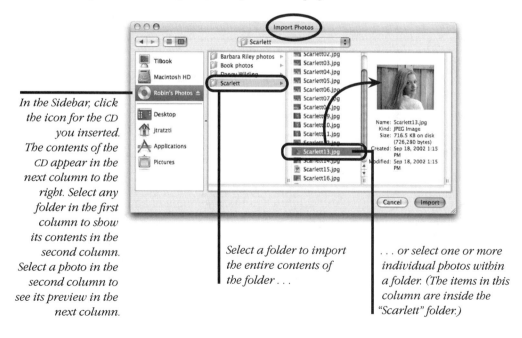

In the Sidebar, click the icon for the CD you inserted. The contents of the CD appear in the next column to the right. Select any folder in the first column to show its contents in the second column. Select a photo in the second column to see its preview in the next column.

Select a folder to import the entire contents of the folder . . .

. . . or select one or more individual photos within a folder. (The items in this column are inside the "Scarlett" folder.)

Viewing Your Photos

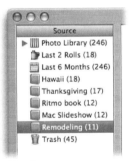

The Source pane.

Once you've imported photos to iPhoto, there are several ways to view them within the main viewing area.

▼ Single-click the **Photo Library** icon in the Source pane to view all photos that have been imported into iPhoto during your various import sessions.

▼ Single-click one of the **recent import** icons, **Last 2 Rolls** or **Last 6 Months,** in the Source pane to show only the most recently imported photos.

You can change the number of rolls or the number of months to be shown: *From the iPhoto application menu, choose "Preferences," then click the "General" icon.*

Enter new numbers in the "Sources" text fields, as shown to the right.

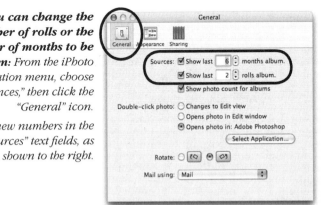

The checkmarks in the View menu indicate which descriptors you've selected to appear next to photos in the main View area.

▼ Single-click an **album** icon in the Source pane to show only photos that you've placed in that specific Album (how to create and use albums is explained on pages 16–17).

▼ From the **View menu,** shown to the left, choose **Arrange Photos,** then select one of the following views:

By Film Roll arranges photos into the groups in which they were originally imported.

By Date arranges photos by the date they were taken in the camera, **if** you set the date in your camera before you took pictures.

By Title arranges photos alphabetically.

By Rating arranges photos by your "star" rating, **if** you assigned ratings to photos. Rating photos is explained on page 19.

Manually lets you drag photos to rearrange them, but only in albums, not the Photo Library or the *recent import* categories.

File Information and Comments

iPhoto gives you file information about selected photos, such as title, date created, size in pixels (dimensions), size in bytes (how much space it takes up on your hard disk), and what music is currently selected for slideshows. Comments you type in will be used in albums, books, or web pages created by iPhoto.

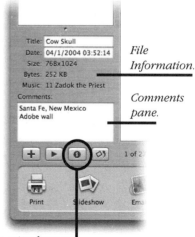

File Information.

Comments pane.

Information button.

1. Single-click on a photo to select it.

2. Click the Information button to display the block of File Information.

3. Click the Information button again to show the Comments pane. Type any comments you want in here.

4. Click the Information button once more to hide both the File Information and Comments pane.

The "View mode" Buttons

Each **View button** gives you access to various options and tools. Each of these views is explained in detail on the following pages.

Import button: Provides information and options for importing photos from a camera, a card reader, your computer, or a disc.

Organize button: Provides tools for organizing and sharing photos.

Edit button: Displays a large version of the selected photo in the main Viewing area, and the lower pane switches to image-editing and enhancement tools.

Book button: Provides tools for creating a hardbound book.

iPhoto Preferences

You can set basic characteristics that affect iPhoto's behavior and how you view your photos. Go to the iPhoto application menu and choose "Preferences…."

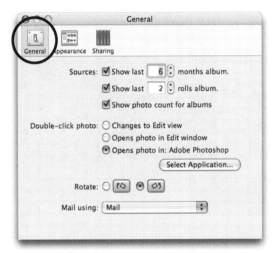

General Preferences

Click the "General" button to show the General Preferences pane.

Sources:

Select **Show last (number) months album** to set how many months of recent photos you'll see when you select the "Last Month" album in the Source pane. You can choose to show between 1 and 18 months of photos. To remove this album from the Source pane, *uncheck* the box.

Select **Show last (number) rolls album** to set how many recent rolls (import sessions) of photos you'll see when you select the "Last Roll" album in the Source pane. You can choose to show between 1 and 25 recent rolls. To remove this album from the Source pane, *uncheck* the box.

If you select **Show photo count for albums,** each album in the Source pane displays in parentheses how many photos it contains.

Double-click photo:

Choose a preferred behavior for when you double-click an image in the main View pane.

Changes to Edit view switches iPhoto to Edit view, the same as if you clicked the "Edit" view button located beneath the View pane.

Opens photo in Edit window opens the photo in a separate Edit window, complete with Edit tools. Choose this option if you want to have multiple photos open at the same time, along with iPhoto's editing tools. This option also provides a "custom" sizing option in the Toolbar that is not available in the standard Edit view. Learn more about the Edit window on pages 26–34.

Choose **Opens photo in** if you have some other image-editing application you want to open when you double-click a photo, such as Adobe Photoshop or Adobe Photoshop Elements. Click the **Select Application…** button, then, in the "Open" window that appears, select an image-editing application installed on your computer.

Rotate:

Choose a default direction for rotation when you click the Rotate button *in the main iPhoto window.* To rotate a photo in the opposite direction in the main window, press the Option key as you click the Rotate button.

Mail using:

From the pop-up menu, shown below, choose the email application you want to use when you use iPhoto's Email feature. Applications in the list that are not installed on your computer will be grayed out.

Appearance Preferences

Border:

Select the **Outline** checkbox to place a small black border around thumbnail images in the View area.

Select the **Drop Shadow** checkbox to add a drop shadow to thumbnail images.

Background:

Use the slider to change the color of the View area background to black, white, or any shade between.

Organize View:

Check the **Align photos to grid** checkbox to neatly organize thumbnail images in columns *and* rows.When this option is *not* selected, thumbnail images are organized in rows only, which saves a little space and may allow more photos to show at one time in the View pane, depending on the size you show them and how many photos are present.

Check **Place most recent photos at the top** to make it easier to find your most recent photos when you have a large collection of photos in your Photo Library.

Source Text:

From the pop-up menu, choose to use **Large** or **Small** text in the Source pane. The difference in text size is shown to the right.

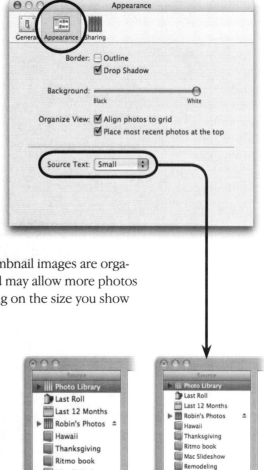

Sharing Preferences

iPhoto lets you **share your photos** with other people on your local network. When you check the **Look for shared photos** checkbox, iPhoto looks for other iPhoto users that have checked **Share my photos.**

When you choose "Share selected albums," you can add checkmarks to the albums you want to share.

This name will appear in the Source pane of other iPhoto users on your local network if they selected "Look for shared photos" in their iPhoto Preferences.

When you set iPhoto to share photos, you can then choose to **Share entire library** or **Share selected albums.**

If you choose *Share entire library,* all of the photos and albums in your Photo Library will be accessible to other iPhoto users on the local network.

Learn how to create albums on page 16.

If you choose *Share selected albums,* a list of your iPhoto albums (which were previously grayed out) becomes available for selection. Place check-marks next to the albums you want to make accessible to others on your network, as shown above.

Assign a **Shared name:** As shown below, the assigned name you choose will appear in the Source pane of another user's iPhoto, **if** that user selected the "Look for shared photos" option in their iPhoto Preferences.

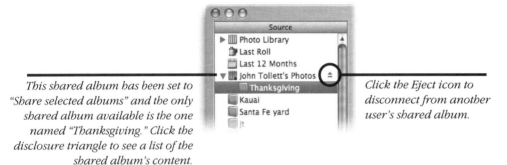

This shared album has been set to "Share selected albums" and the only shared album available is the one named "Thanksgiving." Click the disclosure triangle to see a list of the shared album's content.

Click the Eject icon to disconnect from another user's shared album.

Things you can do with shared photos: You can view them, import them, print them, create a slideshow, attach them to email, order prints, use them to create a .Mac HomePage web site, or create a .Mac Slides slideshow.

Things you cannot do with shared photos: You can't edit shared photos, use them to create a book (as described on pages 35–37), use them in an iDVD project, use them for your Desktop, or burn them to a disc. Of course, you *can* do all these things if you *copy* shared photos to your own computer. **To copy shared photos,** drag one or more shared photos on top of the Photo Library icon in your Source pane. **Or** drag shared photos into one of the album icons in your Source pane.

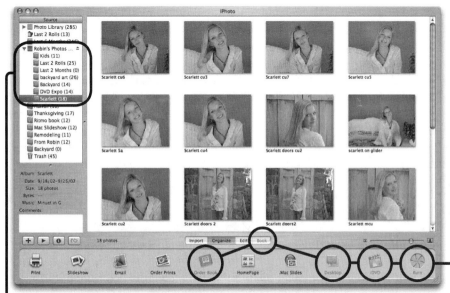

When viewing shared photos, notice that some buttons are gray, a clue that those features are not available for shared photos.

This shared album (Robin's Photos) contains Robin's entire Photo Library. A click on the tiny triangle reveals the separate albums that were created to organize photos into groups. A click on the title "Robin's Photos" would show every photo in Robin's Photo Library. In the example above, the "Scarlett" shared album is selected and shows in the Viewing area.

Select the **Require password** option to limit sharing to others whom you have given a password. Anyone on the network will be able to see your shared album in their Source pane, but when they click on it a "Photo Library Password" window will open that requires your password.

The current **Status** of iPhoto sharing (On or Off) is shown at the bottom of the Sharing Preferences window. To turn iPhoto sharing off, *uncheck* "Share my photos."

Create an Album and Add Photos to It

Create **albums** to help organize your photos, make them easier to find, and sort them in any order you wish.

You can put the same photo in any number of albums because iPhoto just "points" to the original photo stored in the Library (like aliases on your Desktop), which means you don't end up with multiple copies of the same photo taking up space on your hard disk.

To create a new album:

1. Click the "Add" button in the lower-left corner of the iPhoto window, circled below.

2. In the sheet that drops down, enter a name for the album and click OK. Your new album appears in the "Source" panel.

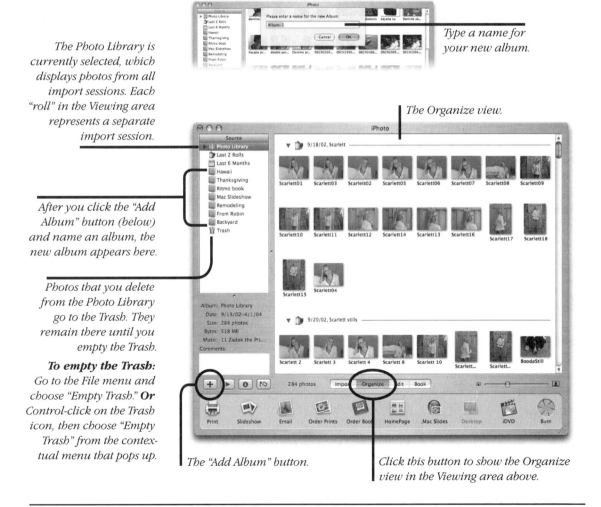

Type a name for your new album.

The Photo Library is currently selected, which displays photos from all import sessions. Each "roll" in the Viewing area represents a separate import session.

The Organize view.

After you click the "Add Album" button (below) and name an album, the new album appears here.

Photos that you delete from the Photo Library go to the Trash. They remain there until you empty the Trash.

To empty the Trash: Go to the File menu and choose "Empty Trash." Or Control-click on the Trash icon, then choose "Empty Trash" from the contextual menu that pops up.

The "Add Album" button.

Click this button to show the Organize view in the Viewing area above.

To add photos to the album:

Drag images from the Viewing area and drop them on an album icon.

To rename an existing album:

Double-click the album name to highlight it and type a new name.

To delete photos from an album:

If you delete a photo from an *album,* this will *not* delete it from the Photo Library—remember, the image in the album "points" to the stored image in the Library. **But** if you delete a photo from the *Photo Library,* it *will* disappear from the Library and every album that contained it.

1. Select an album from which you want to delete one or more photos.

2. Select one or more photos to delete.

3. Press the Delete key. **Or** Control-click on the photo and choose "Remove from album" from the contextual pop-up menu.

iPhoto provides a safety net in case you want to recover photos you've deleted. Click the Trash icon in the Source pane and your deleted photos appear in the Viewing area.

To recover photos from the Trash, Control-click them, then choose "Restore to Library" from the contextual pop-up menu. **Or** drag them back to the Source pane or to the Photo Library icon in the Source pane. **Or** select one or more photos in the Trash, then from the File menu, choose "Restore to Photo Library."

To permanently delete items from the Trash, from the File menu choose "Empty Trash." **Or** Control-click the Trash icon in the Source pane, then choose "Empty Trash" from the contextual pop-up menu.

To duplicate an album:

You may want to experiment with different arrangements of photos for a book project or a slideshow. You can duplicate an entire album. In the duplicate, you can rearrange the photos, delete some, add others, and it won't affect the original album or add significantly to the size of your Library (because duplicate albums just *refer* to originals in the Library).

1. Single-click an album in the Source pane to select it, then from the File menu, choose "Duplicate" (or press Command D).

   OR Control-click an album, then choose "Duplicate" from the pop-up menu.

2. Double-click the new album icon in the pane, then type a new name over the default name assigned by iPhoto.

Create Smart Albums

🔲 Flamenco photos

A Smart Album can be identified in the Source pane by the "gear" icon on it, representing automation.

Creating specific albums and dragging photos into them is a great way to organize your photos, but it gets a lot better than that. iPhoto lets you create "Smart Albums" that automatically find and organize photos that match certain conditions you've set. For instance, you can create a Smart Album that contains only photos to which you've assigned a five-star rating (see the next page). iPhoto will place all five-star photos in a separate album.

To create a Smart Album:

1. From the File menu choose "New Smart Album…."

2. In the sheet that drops down, type a name for the new Smart Album.

3. Using the pop-up menus, set the conditions that will qualify photos for this Smart Album. To add more conditions, click the plus button on the right side of the sheet. To remove a condition, click the minus button.

4. If you choose more than one condition, use the top pop-up menu to choose between "Match **any** of the following conditions" or "Match **all** of the following conditions."

You can set multiple conditions for Smart Albums, chosen from options in the pop-up menus.

*In this example, iPhoto will add any photo to the Smart Album that has a five-star rating, even non-flamenco photos, because it's set to match **any** of the conditions instead of **all** conditions.*

*To limit the Smart Album to only flamenco photos, we should have set it to "Match **all** of the following conditions."*

5. Click OK. The new Smart Album appears in the Source pane, automatically adding photos that meet the conditions you set.

To edit a Smart Album's settings:

From the File menu choose "Edit Smart Album."

Rate Your Photos

One way to organize your photos is by rating them on a scale of one to five stars. You can choose to hide or show the rating next to thumbnails in the Viewing area (see the bottom of this page). You can also arrange photos in the Viewing area by rating (learn how on page 10). And you can use your rating as a condition for Smart Albums (see the previous page).

To rate a photo:

1. Select one or more photos in the Viewing area.

2. Control-click on the selection, from the contextual menu choose "My Rating," then from the submenu choose a row of stars.
   Or, from the Photos menu choose "My Rating," then from the submenu choose a row of stars.

You can also use the Photos menu to rate selected photos.

Control-click on a photo to open this contextual menu and rate the photo.

Your photo rating is displayed beneath the photo **if** "My Rating" has been selected in the View menu, as shown on the right. To hide the rating, select "My Rating" again to remove the checkmark.

The Organize View

After you've imported all the photos from the camera to iPhoto, you can begin organizing, arranging, and sharing them. The **Organize view** lets you see and select many photos at once, and, in the Organize pane at the bottom of the window, provides all the tools you need to share your photos in many different ways. All of these powerful and fun tools are explained, starting on page 38.

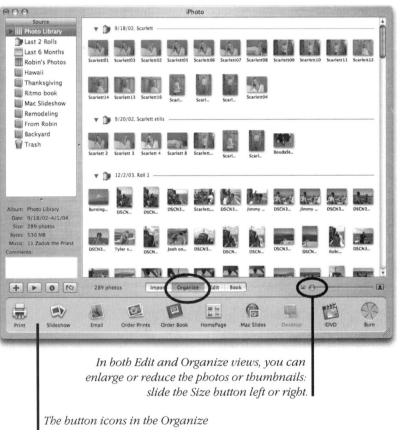

Double-click a thumbnail to display a large version of that photo in the Viewing area. This automatically switches iPhoto to the Edit view (depending on your Preferences settings; see page 12).

To return to the Organize view, click the "Organize" button.

In both Edit and Organize views, you can enlarge or reduce the photos or thumbnails: slide the Size button left or right.

The button icons in the Organize pane represent all the various ways of sharing your photos.

Organize into albums

At this point, for the sake of organization, you may choose to place selected images into an existing album or create a new album, as explained on the previous pages. (Briefly, to create a new album, click the "Add Album" button [the plus sign], name the new album, then drag photos into it.)

To delete unwanted photos from the Photo Library:

Note: If you delete a photo from the Photo Library, it *will* disappear from every album that contained it, and from iPhoto itself.

Tip: When you delete a photo from an album, it **will not** be deleted from the Photo Library.

▼ **To delete multiple photos that are next to each other** (contiguous), click on an image, then Shift-click on another image. All images between the two clicks are automatically selected. Press the Delete key to put all of the selected photos in the Trash.

▼ **To delete multiple photos that are NOT next to each other** (non-contiguous), Command-click on the images you want to select, then press the Delete key to put all selected photos in the Trash.

Photos deleted from the Photo Library are moved to the Trash icon in the Source pane. They are stored there until you go to the File menu and choose "Empty Trash." **Or** until you Control-click on the Trash icon and choose "Empty Trash" from the contextual menu.

To retrieve a photo from the Trash, click the Trash icon to display the images that are in it, then drag the photo from the Viewing area to the Source pane or to the Photo Library icon in the Source pane. **Or** Control-click on a photo and choose "Restore to Photo Library" from the contextual menu. **Or** select a photo, then from the Photos menu, choose "Restore to Photo Library."

The Trash icon appears below the albums in the Source pane. Click the Trash icon to see its contents in the Viewing area.

To arrange the order of the photos:

When you create a slideshow, book, or HomePage (see pages 38–49) iPhoto builds your project with your photos in the same order as the album they're in. So you might want to rearrange the photos in an album or in the Library. There are a couple of ways to do this.

▼ **To arrange photos in an album** (this doesn't work in the Photo Library), drag one or more photos to the location desired. As you drag, a black vertical bar indicates where the photos will be placed when you release the mouse button.

▼ **To arrange photos in the Library (or in an album)** by the date they were taken *(if you set your camera's date before you took the pictures),* by title, by rating, or by film roll (import session): From the View menu (shown left), choose "Arrange Photos," then from that submenu, choose "by Film Roll," "by Date," "by Title," or "by Rating."

Add titles and comments

The titles and comments that you type in the Information pane are used by the Book and HomePage features to add headlines and captions. When you create a web page or a book from these photos, you'll want them to have meaningful names instead of something like "DSCN0715.jpg." Meaningful titles also make it easier to conduct a search for photos based on titles.

1. Single-click a photo to select it.

2. If the Title field is not visible, click the Info button (the "**i**" beneath the Source pane) to show it.

3. Click in the "Title" field, then press Command A to select any existing text that might be in that field, such as "DSCN3054.jpg."

4. Type a new title into the "Title" field.

5. Click the Info button again to show the "Comments" field. Click inside that field, then type a comment for the photo.

Title: Booda the dog
Date: 12/24/2002 04:46:51
Size: 720x480
Bytes: 1.1 MB
Music: 11 Zadok the Priest
Comments:
A four-legged alarm clock. She knows when it's 5 pm (dinner time)

1 of

Info button.

Print   Slideshow   Em

Keywords and Searching

Searching for photos in iPhoto is fast and easy, especially if you previously assigned keywords or gave meaningful titles to your photos. You can create as many different keywords as you need and put them in the Keywords list.

To assign keywords to photos:

By assigning keywords to photos, you make it possible to search for photos based on those words. If you take the time now to assign keywords, you'll save a lot of time later when you're trying to find a certain photo.

1. From the Photos menu, choose "Keywords" to open the "Keywords" pane, **or** press Command K.

2. Select one or more photos in an album or in the Photo Library. (To select multiple photos, drag across a group of them, **or** hold down the Command key and click on individual photos.)

3. Single-click one of the preset keywords in the "Keywords" window ("Family," for instance).

4. Click the "Assign" button. That keyword is now attached to the selected photos.

To assign multiple keywords: Select the photo in the Viewer pane, hold down the Command key to select multiple keywords, then click "Assign."

To remove keywords from a photo: Select the photo in the Viewer pane, select the keyword in the Keywords list, then click the "Remove" button.

To add, rename, or delete keywords from the list, including the ones that Apple has already provided: Select a keyword in the list, then click on the pop-up menu in the "Keywords" window (shown above, on the right), and choose "New," "Rename," or "Delete." Of course, deleting a keyword from the list will also remove it from any photo it was assigned to.

To display the keywords in the Viewer pane, go to the View menu and choose "Keywords." Keywords will display underneath each photo that has a keyword assigned.

The checkmark

The checkmark in the list of keywords acts as a temporary keyword, useful for marking photos for which you haven't decided on a keyword or category. You can search for all photos that have a checkmark.

The "Keywords" window shows the keywords you can assign to photos. Choose "New" from the pop-up menu (above) to create a new untitled keyword (below). Type your new keyword in place of "untitled."

Photos that have been assigned a keyword "checkmark" have a checkmark in the bottom-right corner.

To search for photos by using keywords:

1. From the Photos menu, choose "Keywords" to open the "Keywords" window.

2. Click on the album you want to search, **or** click "Photo Library" to search your entire photo collection.

3. Single-click one of the keywords in the "Keywords" window. In the example below, we chose "Flamenco."

4. Click the "Search" button.

iPhoto displays all the photos that have been assigned that keyword.

This search of the entire Photo Library found all photos with the keyword "Flamenco" assigned to them. Some of the photos found in the search have also been assigned a checkmark.

To show all the photos in a selected album, click the "Show All" button located at the bottom of the "Keywords" window.

To search for titles and comments:

You can search for photos by searching for a word or phrase that you remember as part of the photo's title, or words that you typed into the photo's "Comments" field.

1. Select an album to search, **or** select the Photo Library to search all photos.

2. Create a new Smart Album (see page 18 for details). Set the conditions in the drop-down sheet to match a word or phrase used in the "Title" or "Comments" field of the photo you want to find.

3. Click OK.

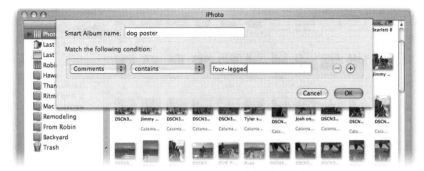

The new Smart Album appears in the Source pane and the results are shown in the Viewing area.

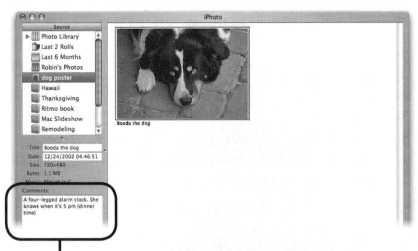

The Smart Album condition required that a photo's Comments field contain the phrase "four-legged." As shown above, the found photo's Comments includes that phrase.

The Edit View

In the Edit view you can perform basic image-editing operations, such as adjusting brightness and contrast, cropping, reducing red-eye, and converting an image from color to black and white or sepia. The Enhance wand and Retouch brush make image adjustment and retouching incredibly easy.

Editing tools

To view a photo for editing:

Select a photo, then click the "Edit" view button (beneath the viewing area). Two things happen:

- ▼ The selected photo fills the entire Viewing area.
- ▼ The lower pane displays iPhoto's editing tools.

To choose the previous or next photo in an album without leaving Edit view, click the "Prev" or "Next" button in the bottom-right corner.

To undo editing changes:

As you make the changes described on the following pages, you can use the Undo command (Command Z, or "Undo" from the Edit menu) to undo your steps, one at a time.

Once you quit iPhoto, you cannot use Command Z to undo any changes you made last time you used iPhoto. But you can go to the Photos menu and choose "Revert to Original," and the original photo will reappear.

Create a duplicate photo before you do anything drastic

When you drag a photo from the Photo Library into an album, iPhoto doesn't make a separate *copy* of that photo—it puts a "link" from the album to the original photo that's still stored in the Library. This prevents your hard disk from getting full of multiple copies of the same photo.

So when you edit a photo, you affect its appearance not only in the Photo Library *but in all other albums in which that photo appears.* If you want to avoid changing the photo's appearance in every instance, create a *duplicate* of the photo and edit the duplicate.

1. Select a photo in the Photo Library or in an album. When you duplicate a photo *in an album,* the duplicate appears in both the album *and* the Library; any changes you make will apply to both duplicates, since they're actually the same photo.

2. From the File menu, choose "Duplicate," **or** press Command D.

   Or *instead* of Steps 1 and 2, Control-click on a photo, then choose "Duplicate" from the contextual menu that pops up.

3. iPhoto automatically renames the duplicate by adding "copy" to the title, but you may want to change the name: select the duplicate, then enter a new name in the Title field.

4. Select the duplicate photo, then click the "Edit" button to show the photo in Edit view and make changes.

Warning: It's possible to duplicate an entire album (select the album name, then press Command D), but any editing changes you make to photos in the duplicate album will apply to the original photos!

Original photo.   *Duplicate photo.*

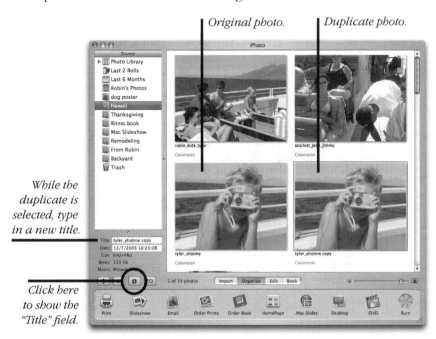

While the duplicate is selected, type in a new title.

Click here to show the "Title" field.

Crop an image

The Crop tool lets you select the most important part of a picture and delete the rest of it. Thoughtful cropping makes your photos stronger and more visually interesting.

1. Select a photo.

2. Click the "Edit" view button.

3. Select an option from the "Constrain" menu, shown to the left.

   The "Constrain" menu gives you common proportion ratios to apply to the Crop tool. Choose "None" if you want no restraints on your cropping so you can select any portion of the photo you want. Choose one of the other options to limit your cropping area to a specific ratio. For instance, if you plan to use the photo in an iPhoto book, select the "4 x 3 (Book)" option.

4. Position the pointer at one corner of the desired cropping area, then press-and-drag diagonally to select a cropping area, as shown below. When the desired area is selected, let go of the mouse.

   To move the crop selection, *press* inside the cropping area and drag.

   To resize the crop selection, position the tip of the pointer on any edge of the cropping selection, then press-and-drag the edge to a new position. **Or** click outside the crop selection and start over.

5. Single-click the "Crop" button.

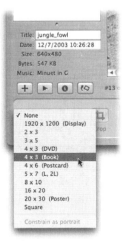

The Constrain menu.

Drag the arrow pointer diagonally to draw a cropping area within the selected photo. The "faded out" area will be deleted when you click the "Crop" button.

Constrain the shape and proportion of the cropped area by selecting an option from the "Constrain" pop-up menu.

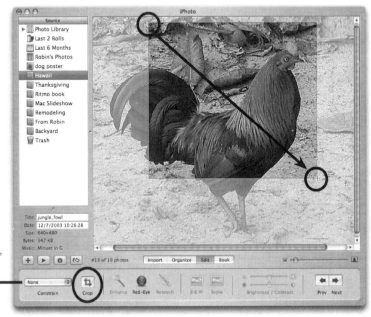

Jazz up photos with the Enhance wand

Sometimes images look pretty good because you don't have anything to compare them to. Colors may be dull and the contrast may be flat, but who notices? The "Enhance" wand analyzes an image and automatically adjusts the color and contrast. You might not always prefer the enhanced version, but it often makes dramatic improvements to photos.

To compare the "enhanced" photo to the original version, press the Control key. Release the Control key to show the current effect.

To use the Enhance wand:

1. Select a photo from an album or from the Photo Library.

2. Click the "Edit" button to fill the viewing area with the photo.

3. Click the Enhance wand once. Check the photo in the Viewing area to see if you like the changes.

    If you don't like the new version, undo the enhancement by pressing Command Z. **Or** from the Edit menu, choose "Undo Enhance Photo."

    If the enhancement is not dramatic enough, click the Enhance wand again.

To return to the original after several adjustments, press Command Z several times, **or** from the Photos menu, choose "Revert to Original."

Experiment with a combination of adjustments to find the best results. We often use the Enhance wand, then adjust the contrast with the "Brightness/Contrast" sliders (see page 32).

The Enhance wand can often make dramatic improvements in your photos.

The Enhance wand.

*This is the
Rotate button.*

Rotate an image

You can rotate a photo from any view mode. Just select a photo and click the Rotate button (shown to the left) to rotate the image 90 degrees counterclockwise (if counterclockwise is what you chose in Preferences, page 13). Additional clicks will continue to rotate the image in 90-degree increments.

Option-click the Rotate button to rotate the photo in the opposite direction indicated by the Rotate icon.

Reduce red-eye

Use the Red-Eye tool to eliminate or reduce the red glare in a subject's eyes caused by the flash. The results may vary with different photos.

1. Select a photo that needs red-eye reduction.
2. Click the "Edit" view button (if you're not already there).
3. In the Edit pane, choose "None" from the "Constrain" menu so you will be able to draw freely.
4. Press-and-drag a selection around the area of one eye. Select as small an area as possible. If necessary, zoom in on the photo before making your selection: drag the Size control toward the right.
5. Single-click the "Red-Eye" tool. iPhoto will remove all red from the selected area. Repeat Steps 4 and 5 for the other eye.

If you're not satisfied with the results, press Command Z (Undo), **or** from the Photos menu, choose "Revert to Original."

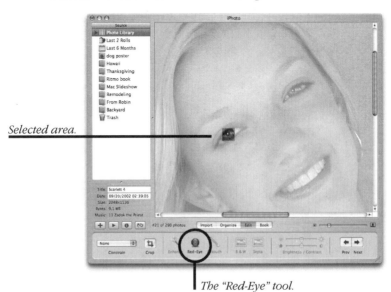

Selected area.

The "Red-Eye" tool.

Touch up photos with the Retouch brush

Even your best photos usually have some imperfections in them. If you scanned a photo, dust or scratches on the scanner glass may be visible, and digital images straight from a camera contain artifacts or digital "noise" that appears as oddly colored pixels in the image. There's also the possibility that the model or the background could have a blemish you want to remove.

The Retouch brush does an excellent job of fixing minor problems. Acting like a combination blur and smudge brush, it blends the pixels under the brush into the surrounding area.

Any retouching changes you make are applied to the original photo in the Photo Library, even if you selected the photo from an album instead of from the Photo Library. **The retouched version will replace all occurrences of the photo in all albums in which it appears.** If you want to prevent this, make a duplicate of the photo and make changes to the duplicate.

To use the Retouch brush:

1. Select a photo to retouch.
2. Click the "Edit" button to fill the viewing area with the photo. Use the Size slider to enlarge the area you want to retouch.
3. Click the "Retouch" icon in the Edit tools pane.
4. Press-and-drag the Retouch brush cursor (the crosshairs) on top of blemishes using short, scrubbing strokes.

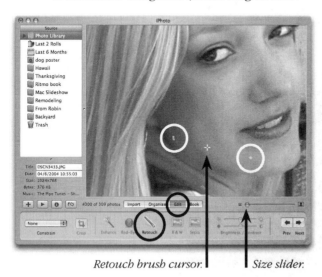

Retouch brush cursor.　*Size slider.*

The retouched photo, above, shows how expertly you can make repairs to an image.

Convert a photo to black and white or sepia

To convert a photo to black and white or sepia, select it, then click the "Edit" button. In the Edit tools pane, click the "B & W" or "Sepia" button.

Remember, this will affect how this photo looks in every album it appears in. If you don't want to affect other occurrences, first make a duplicate of the photo, rename it, and convert the *duplicate* to black and white.

Adjust the brightness and/or contrast

When a photo is a little too dark or too light, you can adjust the brightness and contrast. It's an easy way to juice up a flat photo.

To adjust the brightness and/or contrast, open a photo in Edit view. Drag the "Brightness/Contrast" sliders left or right until you're satisfied with the results. To undo the adjustment, press Command Z, **or** choose "Revert to Original" in the Photos menu.

The settings for this photo have not been altered.

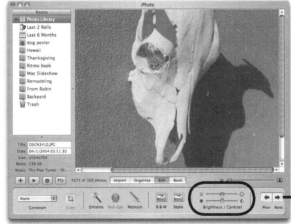

While in Edit view, you can move from one photo to another with the "Prev" and "Next" buttons.

In this photo, I increased the contrast (I moved the "Contrast" slider to the right). I also adjusted the brightness.

Even photos that don't need brightness and contrast adjustments can be manipulated to create different and unusual effects.

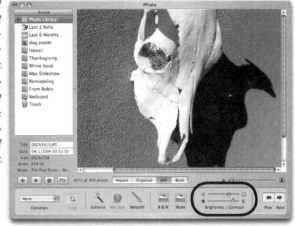

Open photos directly into another image-editing application

iPhoto's editing tools are fairly limited. For additional image editing, you might want to open a photo in another program, such as Adobe Photoshop (for professionals) or Adobe Photoshop Elements (for home users).

1. From the iPhoto menu, choose "Preferences...."
2. In the Preferences window, click the "General" button in the top bar.
3. In the General Preferences pane, click the "Opens photo in:" button.
4. Click the "Select Application" button.
5. In the "Open" window that appears, choose an image-editing application you want to use, then click the "Open" button.
6. Close the Preferences window.
7. Double-click on a photo in iPhoto's Viewing area. iPhoto will open the photo in the image-editing application you selected.

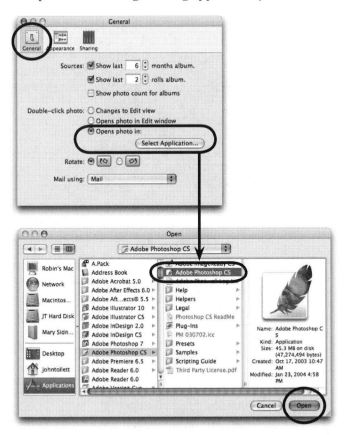

Tip: If you want photos to open into individual windows every time you double-click, choose "Opens photo in Edit window" in the Preferences; see page 12.

Edit a photo in a separate window

You can choose to edit a photo in its own, separate Edit window rather than in the iPhoto window. This lets you customize the window toolbar to display the tools you use most.

To open a photo in a separate window, hold down the Option key and double-click a photo. **Or** Control-click on a photo, then choose "Edit in separate window" from the menu that pops up.

The title bar shows the photo title and the viewing size (expressed as a percentage of the original image size).

Click this button to hide or show the toolbar.

This Edit window lets you edit the photo in its own window. You can open a number of separate windows— just Option-double-click on any number of thumbnails.

Click this icon to display the "Customize Toolbar" sheet, shown below.

The Edit window provides a "Custom" size tool not found in the main Edit view's tools.

Drag this corner to resize the Edit window.

Drag a tool to any location in the toolbar.

If you use a certain cropping constraint often, such as 8 x 10, drag that icon to the toolbar.

Before you crop a photo, click the constrain icon you put in the toolbar and the Crop tool will be constrained to that proportion.

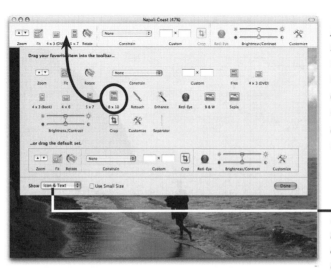

Drag toolbar items sideways in the toolbar to rearrange them.

Command-drag items off the toolbar.

Click "Done" to close the customize sheet.

Use the "Show" menu to change how icons are displayed in the toolbar.

The Book View

Through iPhoto, you can create a professionally printed hardbound copy of a book you design with your photos and captions. It might be a catalog, picture book, story book, portfolio, or any other sort of book you dream up. After you create it, you can order it with the click of a button and your beautiful book will be delivered to your door. A ten-page book costs approximately $30.

iPhoto books are great for personal keepsakes or for professional presentations.

Create a book with your own photographs

1. First create a new album (as explained on pages 16–17), **or** select an existing album. The order that photos appear in an album is the order in which they will appear in the book that you create, so rearrange the photos before you start building your book. The first page in the album will be the cover of your book.

2. With your album selected, click the "Book" view button to show the layout in the large viewing area, a scrolling thumbnails pane, and the Book layout tools in the lower pane.

3. Choose one of the design themes from the "Theme" pop-up menu.   *—continued*

Layout viewing area.

The scrolling thumbnails pane shows the book pages, made from photos that are in the selected album.

Book tools.

Choose a design theme.

Choose which elements to show on all pages.

Customize each page's layout. The options in this menu change slightly, depending on which theme you choose.

4. Select a thumbnail page in the thumbnails pane, then from the "Page Design" pop-up menu, choose a page layout style.

5. You can add titles and comments to most photo pages, depending on the theme style or page design you choose.

   To edit the text on a book page, select the text in the text box and type your changes.

   To add text directly to a book page, click inside any text box and the page will enlarge so you can see your text as you type.

   To choose a font, go to the Edit menu and choose "Font," then choose "Show Fonts."

6. Choose to show or hide "Titles," "Comments," and/or "Page Numbers" on the book pages by clicking (or not clicking) their checkboxes. These options affect the entire book, not individual pages.

7. Click the "Preview" button to see how your finished book will look.

If you need to **rearrange photos, add or delete photos,** or **edit individual photos,** click the "Organize" button to go back to your album. Your book for this album will stay as you left it; when you return to the book, it will reflect the changes you made in the album.

What is the yellow triangle?

When you create a book, some images may display a low-resolution warning (a yellow triangle containing an exclamation mark). iPhoto warns you if a photo has a resolution that is lower than that recommended for quality printing. Such photos will still print, but they may look pixelated and jaggy or appear to be of lower quality. If you plan to shoot photos for a book, set your camera to at least a medium-quality setting or even high-quality. You can often salvage a low-resolution photo by choosing a page layout that shows two or three photos on a page, making the photo smaller and its resolution less problematic.

If a caution sign appears on a photo in Book view, it means the photo will print at a very low quality. You'll get this warning when you try to order a book.

To order copies of this book with a single click, see the opposite page.

To order your book:

After you create a book (as explained on the previous pages), you can order hardbound copies of it using your Internet connection.

1. With the book open on your screen, click the "Order Book" button.

Click here to order your book.

2. Your Mac will connect to the Internet (if it isn't already) and open the "Order Book" window, shown below. A "Progress" window opens on the Desktop as the "Assembling Book…" process takes place.

3. If the button in the lower-right says "Enable 1-Click Ordering," click it. You will be asked to start an Apple account and provide your name, address, and credit card information (don't worry—this is safer than giving your card to an unknown waiter who takes it to the back room), as well as your shipping preferences. If you already have an Apple account, you will be asked to turn on "1-Click Ordering." Click OK.

4. In the "Order Book" window, choose a color for the cover, the quantity of books (they will all be copies of this one book), and the shipping options.

5. Click "Buy Now."

6. You'll see a "Transferring book…" progress window that indicates the files for your book are being transferred via the Internet to the publisher. Your book will arrive on your doorstep in about a week.

You'll receive a notice when the ordering process is finished.

Click here to set up a new account or to get account information.

The Organize Pane

The Organize pane is visible when you are in the Organize view. It contains tools that let you share your photos with others in a variety of ways. You can print your photos in various formats, create a slideshow to play on your computer, export a QuickTime slideshow for others, order professional prints over the Internet, order a professionally bound, hardcover book, create a web site and publish it with blinding speed, burn your photos to a CD or DVD, and more.

Print

Print your photos to your desktop printer

1. Select a single photo or multiple photos from an album or from the Photo Library.

2. Click the "Print" icon in the Organize pane.

3. In the Print sheet, click the "Style" pop-up menu and choose one of the options. Each option will display different parameters; check it out.

4. Enter the number of copies to print.

5. Put photo-quality paper in your printer and click "Print."

The "Style" pop-up menu offers these options.

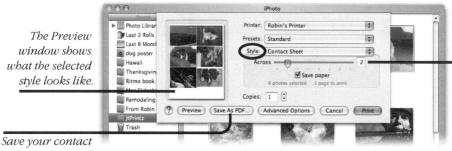

The Preview window shows what the selected style looks like.

Save your contact sheet as a PDF.

Use the slider to set how many pictures will fit in a single row.

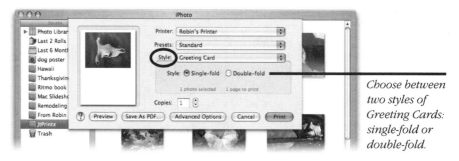

Choose between two styles of Greeting Cards: single-fold or double-fold.

Create a slideshow to view on your iMac

With the Slideshow tool in the Organize pane, you can quickly create a slide-show with a sound track that will play full-screen on your monitor.

Slideshow

1. Select an album, the Photo Library, or a group of photos within either collection. Or create a new album just for the Slideshow.

2. Click the "Slideshow" icon. The "Slideshow" window will open, as shown at the bottom of the page.

3. Click the **Settings** button at the top of the window and set a type of "Transition." Set a "Direction" for the transition if your selection offers directional options. Use the "Speed" slider to set the speed of the transition, and type a duration for each slide in that field.

4. Click the checkboxes of the other slide behaviors you want to set.

5. Click the **Music** button at the top of the window. Select the music you want to use for a sound track: From the "Source" pop-up menu select "iTunes Library" then choose any song that you've imported into iTunes. **Or** from the "Source" pop-up menu, select "Sample Music" to play one of the songs that Apple has provided for you, in case you haven't had time yet to import any of your own music.

   When you choose an iTunes playlist from the "Source" pop-up menu, all songs in the playlist are added to the slideshow, a nice feature for long slideshows. **To select just one song** from a playlist, click on the song in the window to highlight it. **To play a specific selection of songs,** create a new playlist in iTunes that includes just those songs, then select that playlist in the "Source" pop-up menu.

6. Click "Play" to start the slideshow.

An advantage of creating a separate album for a slideshow (or for any project) is that you can rearrange the photos in an album in the order you want them to appear.

If your computer is in an office, you may prefer that your slideshow be silent. In this case, uncheck the "Play music" checkbox.

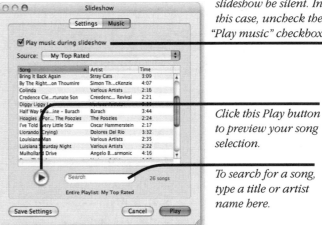

Click this Play button to preview your song selection.

To search for a song, type a title or artist name here.

To preview a "Quickplay" slideshow:

You don't have to go through the "Slideshow" window, explained on the previous page, to see a slideshow: Just select an album or a group of photos, then click the "Play slideshow" button.

Play Slideshow.

You can turn on Slideshow controls permanently. Open the Slideshow settings window (previous page) and click "Display slideshow controls."

This is a great way to preview the photos of an album. You not only get to see the images full-screen size, but you also can make some changes as you watch the slideshow, such as rotate left or right, assign a rating, or delete a photo. As the slideshow plays, you can use the controls shown below. If you don't see the controls, move your mouse to make them visible.

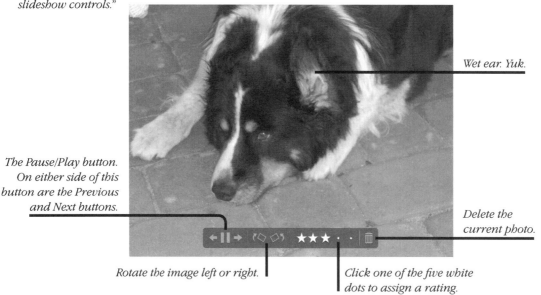

Wet ear. Yuk.

The Pause/Play button. On either side of this button are the Previous and Next buttons.

Delete the current photo.

Rotate the image left or right.

Click one of the five white dots to assign a rating.

You might have to wait a few seconds while iPhoto prepares the slideshow if a large number of photos are selected.

Slideshow keyboard commands

Use keyboard commands to control the playback of your iPhoto slideshow:

- ▾ **Up arrow:** Speeds up the slideshow.
- ▾ **Down arrow:** Slows down the slideshow.
- ▾ **Spacebar:** Toggles the slideshow between Play and Pause.
- ▾ **Left and right arrow keys:** Shows the previous slide or next slide.
- ▾ **Mouse:** Stops the slideshow.

Send your photos through email

One way to share your photos is to send them to someone through email. iPhoto makes it incredibly easy to do just that.

1. Select one or more photos in the Viewing area; you can choose photos from any album or from the Photo Library.

To select multiple photos, hold the Command key as you click on your photo selections.

Selected photos show blue borders.

Note: **If you use AOL,** go to the Preferences and choose "America Online" as your email application. The "Email" button in the lower pane will turn into an "AOL" button and you can send photos to anyone.

Note: **If you use any other email program,** people receiving your photos who use older versions of America Online may have trouble seeing the iPhotos you send this way.

2. Click the "Email" icon in the Organize pane to open the "Mail Photo" window (shown below).

3. In the "Mail Photo" window, choose a photo size from the pop-up menu, and choose whether to include titles and comments that you may have added to photos (as explained on page 11). Click the "Compose" button.

It's always a nice touch to type a personalized message in the Subject field instead of using iPhoto's automatic entry.

4. If you want, add text to the email message window that opens (shown to the right). Your photos are already sized and placed in the message area.

5. Enter an email address and click the "Send" icon in the email window Toolbar. Your Mac will connect to the Internet (if it isn't already) and send the photos along with your email. Amazing.

Order traditional prints of your photos

You can order regular, real, hold-in-your-hand prints of any photo or collection of photos. Your first **ten** 4x6 prints are **free!**

1. Make sure you're connected to the Internet.

2. Select an album or a group of photos within an album or in the Photo Library.

3. Click the "Order Prints" button in the Organize pane.

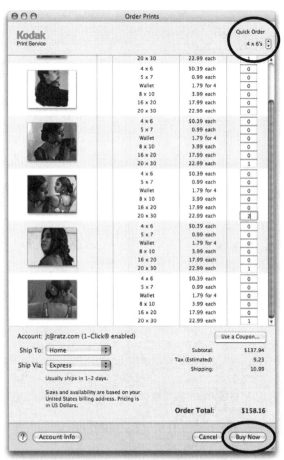

4. If the button in the lower-right says "Set Up Account" instead of "Buy Now" (as shown on the next page), click it. You will be asked to start an Apple account and provide your name, address, and credit card information, as well as your shipping preferences.

  If you already have an account set up, the "Set Up Account" window that opens lets you sign in with your Apple ID and password.

5. Select the size and quantity you want of each photo in the "Order Prints" window:

  In the top-right corner you can "Quick Order" 4x6 prints. Click the top arrow button to order one 4x6 of each photo in the list. Click again to change the order to two 4x6 prints of each photo. Every click adds to the order. To lower the quantity, click the bottom arrow button.

  You can also buy individual prints of any photo you selected in iPhoto, like a 16x20 or four wallet-sized prints.

  As you enter a quantity for each photo, the total amount is instantly calculated at the bottom of the window. To remove the order for a photo, type a "0" in the quantity field next to it.

6. Click the "Buy Now" button. Depending on the shipping option you chose in the "Ship Via" pop-up menu, you could have your prints in just a few days. Wow.

If you see a yellow triangle alert next to a certain print size in the "Order Prints" window, it indicates that photo's resolution is not suitable for a quality print at that size. A smaller size may be available without a warning.

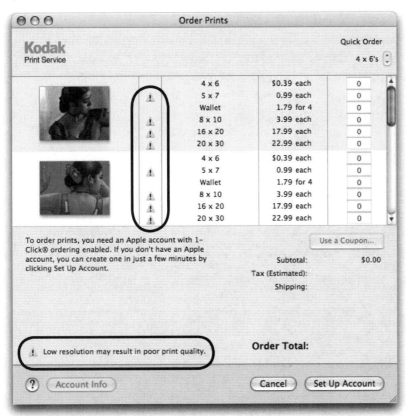

The photos above were optimized for a web page (72 pixels per inch), so they are not suitable for printing at larger sizes. They will be fine if you choose to print them as wallet-sized or as 4 x 6 prints.

HomePage

Tip: To create a web page with your photos that you can upload to a site you already own, see pages 52–53.

Build a HomePage photo album and publish it to the web

If you signed up for a .Mac account (as explained in Section 2), iPhoto will automatically create and publish a web site of your selected photos and store it on Apple's Internet servers. It's really incredible.

1. Select an album or a group of photos within an album. The order in which photos appear in the album determines the order in which they appear on the web page that iPhoto creates. To rearrange photos, drag them into new positions in the album.

2. While in the Organize pane, click the "HomePage" button. Your Mac will connect to the Internet and open the "Publish HomePage" window, as shown below. Your selected images are displayed on a web page template that you can customize.

All HomePage text is editable.   *The Themes drawer.*

Checkmark "Send Me a Message" to include a message button on the HomePage.

Check "Counter" to put a little counter icon on your page so you can see the number of visitors you've had.

From this pop-up menu, choose your .Mac account name.

Choose "2 Columns" or "3 Columns" for your layout.

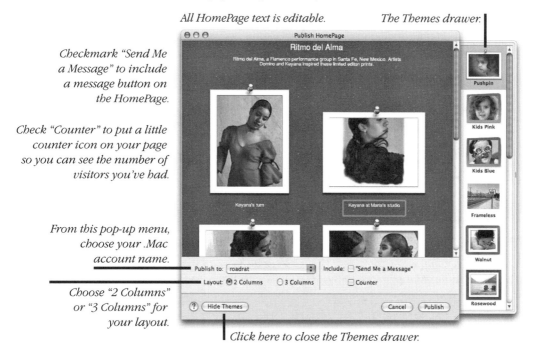

Click here to close the Themes drawer.

Tip: **To remove a HomePage photo album,** log in to your .Mac account, then click the "HomePage" button. You'll see a list of the albums you have posted. Single-click on the name, then click the minus sign right below the list.

3. Click one of the thumbnail images in the Themes drawer to choose an appearance for your HomePage background and photo frames.

4. Select the existing title and captions on the page (press-and-drag over the text) and type new text if you wish. If you have given titles to photos in iPhoto, those titles appear as captions in your HomePage layout.

5. From the "Publish to" pop-up menu at the bottom of the window (shown above), select your .Mac account name.

6. Click the "Publish" button. After the files have been transferred to Apple's .Mac server, a notice will appear telling you the web address of your new web site; this notice has a button called "Visit Page Now." Click it to open your brand-new HomePage photo album.

This notice gives you the web address for your HomePage photo album. Click the "Edit Page" button if you want to make changes.

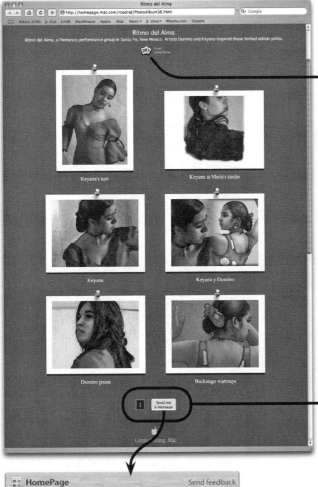

Click this icon or any photo to start a slideshow.

These two items appear on your page if you checked the boxes called "Counter" and "Send Me a Message" in the "Publish HomePage" window shown on the previous page.

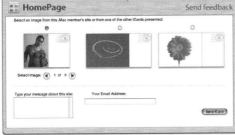

When a visitor clicks the "Send me a message" button (above), a window opens from which she can send you an iCard. She can choose an image from your photo album for the card.

Publish your slideshow on the Internet with .Mac Slides

If you have a .Mac account, the .Mac Slides option lets you publish a slideshow to your iDisk (storage space on Apple's servers). Anyone who uses Mac OS X version 10.2 (Jaguar) or later can view the slideshow on the Internet.

To create a .Mac slideshow:

1. Click the "Organize" button.

2. Select photos to use in the .Mac slideshow.

   Photos must be selected *individually,* not by clicking on an album in the Source pane. Command-click on individual photos in the Viewing area, or drag a selection around the desired photos.

3. Click the ".Mac Slides" button in the Organize pane.

4. In the window that opens (below), click the "Publish" button.

When you publish a .Mac slideshow, it replaces any other slideshow you may have previously published to that .Mac account name.

Click "Publish" to upload photos to your iDisk.

5. After your photos have been uploaded to your iDisk, click the "Announce Slideshow" button to send an email announcement. The automatically generated email contains instructions for viewing your .Mac slideshow. Address the email to one or more friends, then click "Send."

See Chapter 12 for more information about .Mac Slides Publisher. See Chapter 6 for information about iDisk.

Use a photo as your Desktop background

Desktop

Select one of your photos to use as a Desktop image. It's a great way to personalize the appearance of your Mac. Any photo you choose will fill the Desktop space.

1. Single-click **one** photo in any album or from the Photo Library.
2. Click the "Desktop" icon in the Organize pane. The selected photo displays instantly on your Desktop.

Select a photo that doesn't interfere too much with the visibility of folders and icons you may have on your Desktop.

Send photos to iDVD

If you have a SuperDrive in your Mac (a drive that can read *or write* DVDs), you can send a selection of photos to the iDVD application to make a DVD slideshow, which you can then burn to a DVD. In iDVD you can add music to play with the slideshow. To learn more about iDVD, see Chapter 4.

To send photos to iDVD:

1. Click the "Organize" button.

2. Select an entire album, or a group of photos from an album or from the Photo Library.

3. Click the "iDVD" icon in the Organize pane. (You won't see an "iDVD" icon unless your Mac has a SuperDrive.)

4. iDVD opens and automatically creates a menu with a title and a "text button" that links to a slideshow of your photos. You can customize the iDVD menu in all sorts of ways, change the design theme, the font style, the music, the slide duration, and more (see Chapter 4).

Use your arrow keys or the virtual controller to control the slideshow.

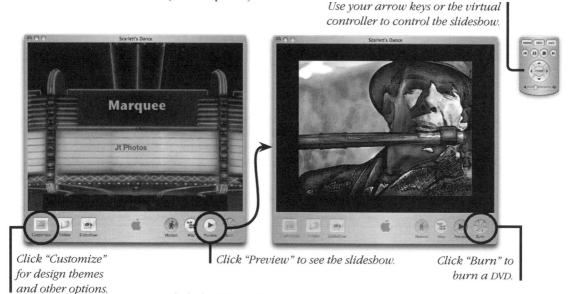

Click "Customize" for design themes and other options.

Click "Preview" to see the slideshow.

Click "Burn" to burn a DVD.

5. Click the "Burn" icon in the lower-right corner of the iDVD window to burn the slideshow to a DVD. **Or** just save the project so you can work on it later (from the File menu, choose "Save").

Burn a CD or DVD-R of selected photos

To burn your photo collections onto a CD or DVD, your computer must have an Apple-supported CD or DVD drive. If your computer has a SuperDrive, it can burn CDs or DVDs. The advantage of burning a DVD-R disc is that it holds much more than a CD (4.7 gigabytes of data, compared to 650 megabytes).

The "Burn" button looks like this before you click it.

To burn photos onto a disc:

1. Select a collection of photos to burn to a disc (one or more albums, individually selected photos, or the entire Photo Library).

2. Click the "Burn" icon in the Organize pane.

3. Insert a blank disc. Depending on the kind of drive in your computer, the disc can be a CD-R (CD recordable), a CD-RW (CD rewritable), or a DVD-R (DVD recordable). Click OK.

A disc icon appears in iPhoto's information panel. The green color on the disc icon shows how much of the disc space is required to burn your photo selection (shown on the right).

4. After you insert a disc, click the "Burn" icon in the Organize pane again.

5. In the "Burn Disc" window that opens, click the "Burn" button.

The darker color on the disc shows how much disc space the selected photos take.

6. The disc ejects when the burning is finished.

This process does not allow multiple burning sessions. After you burn a disc, the disc is "closed" and you can't put additional data onto it.

Export Photos in Various Formats

There are still more ways to share your photos with iPhoto. You can save photos into various file formats, export them as a web page, or use them to create a QuickTime slideshow.

Export copies or convert photos to other file formats

You might want to export photos to a different project folder or convert them to another file format. This does *not* remove the photos from the Photo Library. The converted or exported photos will be *copies* of the originals; any changes you make to those copies will not affect the originals.

To export or convert photos:

1. Select a single photo, an album, or a group of photos within an album or the Photo Library.

2. From the File menu, choose "Export...."

3. In the "Export Photos" window that appears, click the "File Export" tab.

4. From the **Format** pop-up menu, select a file format in which to save photos: "Original" saves photos in whatever format they currently use. The other options are "JPG," TIF," and "PNG." If you're not familiar with file formats, "JPG" is a safe choice that anyone can use. Most digital cameras create photos in this format, and it's the most common format for photos destined for web pages. If you plan to place the exported image in a page layout application for a printed project, "TIF" would be the correct format.

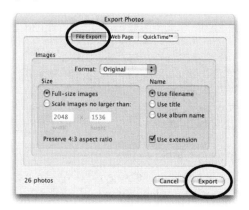

5. **Size:** "Full-size images" exports photos the same size as the original. **Or** you can enter specific dimensions in pixels.

6. **Name:**

   Use filename: The exported photos will have the default names your digital camera assigned (such as "DSCN0715.jpg"), unless you've renamed them.

   Use title: The photos will display the titles you gave them in iPhoto.

   Use album name: The photos will display the album name and a number for each image ("Kauai-07," for example).

   Use extension: The file format extension will appear at the end of the file name ("Kauai-07.jpg," for example).

7. Click the "Export" button. In the sheet that drops down, choose a location on your computer to save the exported files.

   If you want to put your exported photos into a new folder, click the "New Folder" button. In the "New Folder" window that appears, type a name for the new folder. Click the "Create" button to close the "New Folder" window.

8. Click OK to export the photos.

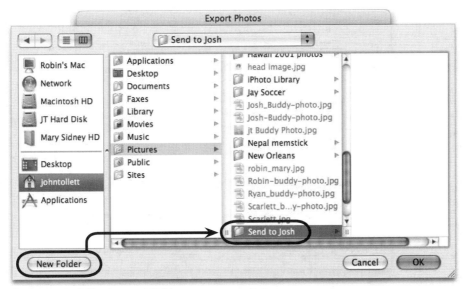

Save exported files into any folder on your computer or create a new folder in any location.

Export your photos as a web site

The Web Page option of the "Export Photos" window is very different from the HomePage feature as explained on pages 44–45. This Web Page tool creates a slightly plainer web site and saves it on your computer—it does not post this site on Apple's server. You can upload this site yourself to a server of your choice, or you may want to burn the site to a CD to share with others.

To export your photos as a web site:

1. Select an album or a group of photos within an album. The order the photos appear in an album is the order they will appear in the web page you create.

2. From the File menu, choose "Export...."

3. In the "Export Photos" window that opens, click the "Web Page" tab.

4. Make the following choices:

   Title: Enter a title for the web page.

   Columns and Rows: Choose how many columns and rows of thumbnail photographs to create on the start page (the first page of the web site).

   Background: To choose a background color, click the **Color** radio button, then click the color box for the palette. To choose a background image for the page, click the **Image** radio button, click "Set...," then from the "Open" dialog box, choose an image.

   Text Color: Click the box to choose a color for the text on the page.

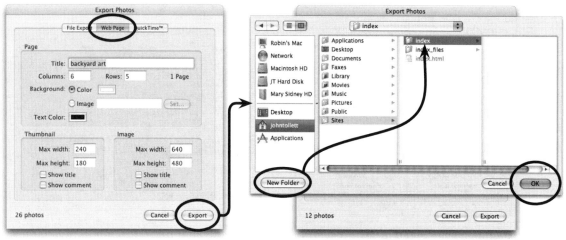

See the sidebar and Step 6 on the next page to learn why we named our new folder "index" (above).

Thumbnail: Set the maximum width and height for thumbnail images (the small photos on the "start page" or first page).

> **Show title:** Place the title you assigned to photos under the thumbnail version on the start page.

> **Show comment:** Show comments associated with photos.

Image: Same as "Thumbnail" settings, but this applies to the large photo pages to which the thumbnail images are linked.

5. Click "Export," shown on the previous page.

6. In the sheet that drops down, iPhoto may automatically choose the "Sites" folder to store your web page. You can choose any location you prefer, but you need to create a new folder *within* the selected folder to hold all the files that will be created during this export.

So click the "New Folder" button (previous page) and name it **index**. Why? Because, unfortunately, the Web Page feature names the start page the same as the folder into which it's saved. For a web page to work correctly on the Internet, the start page needs to be named "index.html." *After* the photos are exported to the new folder, you can manually change the name of the *folder* to something unique.

Click OK (shown on the previous page). Your new web page and all its related files will be stored in this new folder.

If the folder we export into is named "flamenco," iPhoto names the start page (the page with all the thumbnails on it) "flamenco.html." An HTML start page needs to be named "index" to work on the Internet, but if we manually change the name of the start page (after it has been created by iPhoto) to "index," the "Up" link on the secondary pages (the link that takes you back to the start page) will not work because it's programmed to link to a page named "flamenco.html." So, to make your web pages actually work on the Internet, export them to a folder named "index."

To see your new web page (which is really a web *site,* not an individual web *page*), find the new folder you just made (it's in the Sites folder in your Home window, unless you put it somewhere else) and open it.

Double-click the file named **index.html.** The site will open in your default web browser, *but it's not online!* You're actually just opening files on your own hard disk. This Web Page feature just builds the site for you—it's your responsibility to upload it to a web server if you want it online.

This is a finished web page shown in a browser.

Web Page creates a "start page" that contains thumbnail versions of your selected photos. Single-click any thumbnail to open a page that displays a full-sized version of that photo and navigation links for "Previous," "Up," and "Next" ("Up" means back to the start page).

Export your photos as a QuickTime slideshow you can give to friends

You can export photos as a QuickTime slideshow that plays in the QuickTime player or in a program that supports QuickTime, such as a web browser. The QuickTime slideshow can be put on a CD and sent to friends, posted on a web page, inserted into a PDF, or placed in other software that recognizes QuickTime (such as the presentation module in AppleWorks).

To export as a QuickTime slideshow:

1. Select an album, a group of photos within an album, or photos in the Photo Library. (The order that photos appear in an album is the order they will appear in the QuickTime movie.)

2. From the File menu, choose "Export...."

3. In the "Export Photos" window that opens, click the "QuickTime" tab.

4. **Images:** Set the maximum width and height for the slideshow images; 640 by 480 pixels is a standard measurement that works well (it's rather large). In the "Display image for" box, set the amount of time that each image will stay on the screen.

5. **Background:** Choose a background color or a background image. If some of your photos have unusual dimensions, the empty background area will be filled with the color or image you choose.

6. **Music:** Click "Add currently selected music to movie." The slideshow will play whatever piece of music you previously chose in the Slideshow "Settings" window, as shown on page 39 (click the "Slideshow" icon in the Organize pane, select a song, then click the "Save Settings" button).

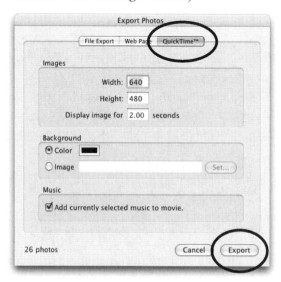

7. Click "Export."

8. In the sheet that drops down, name the file and choose a location to save the file (shown below). iPhoto automatically selects the "Movies" folder to save the slideshow in, but you can choose any location, then click OK.

To help locate the folder you want to use, click this button to reveal a Finder window, as shown to the right.

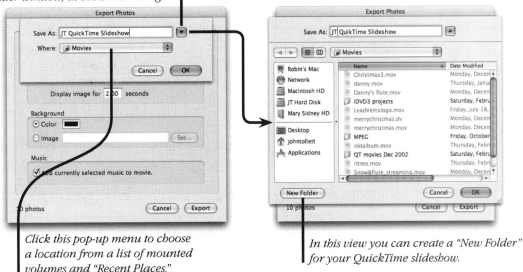

Click this pop-up menu to choose a location from a list of mounted volumes and "Recent Places."

In this view you can create a "New Folder" for your QuickTime slideshow.

The exported slideshow, shown in the QuickTime Player.

To open your QuickTime slideshow, locate the QuickTime movie file wherever you saved it on your hard disk, then double-click it to open it in the QuickTime Player.

To play your QuickTime slideshow, click the Play button on the QuickTime Player.

The Play button.

Extra Tips and Information

JPEG and JPG are the same thing. TIFF and TIF are also the same thing.

Most digital cameras store photos in the **JPEG format,** which combines a high-quality image with effective compression to economize file size. iPhoto works best with JPEG formatted photos, although it recognizes most common formats such as TIFF, PICT, BMP, TARGA, and PNG (but not EPS).

iPhoto Library

iPhoto provides a window where you can edit and organize your photos, but the actual photos themselves are stored in a folder on your hard disk named **iPhoto Library.** To find this folder, open your Home window, then open the Pictures folder; the iPhoto Library is inside Pictures. The Library folder also contains a folder of the **albums** you created in iPhoto. But these album folders don't really contain photos, even though you placed photos in them while working in iPhoto! Instead, they contain "references" to photos that you imported into the Photo Library. This way, you have the same photo in many different albums without overloading your computer with multiple copies.

Back up your iPhoto Library folder regularly by copying it to another disk or burning a CD or DVD so just in case your hard drive fails (which it will one day), you won't have lost all your photos!

Search the Internet for iPhoto scripts and plugins

You'll find some very interesting freeware and shareware that makes iPhoto even better. Search Google (or any search site) for "iPhoto scripts," or go to VersionTracker.com and search for "iPhoto." Some very useful add-ons are:

When you download and use software from freeware and shareware developers, be aware that you're doing so at your own risk and that the developers do not take any responsibility for unexpected hardware or software problems that may occur.

iPhoto Diet: When you edit photos, such as cropping or making color and contrast adjustments, iPhoto keeps a copy of the original in the iPhoto Library folder so you can choose to revert back to the original later. A convenient feature, but at the cost of using a lot of storage space. iPhoto Diet is an AppleScript droplet that slims down your iPhoto Library folder by moving unwanted duplicates to the Trash. Just drop your iPhoto Library folder (located in the Pictures folder, in your Home folder) on top of the iPhoto Diet droplet. Find it at **www. VersionTracker.com.**

BetterHTMLExport: This iPhoto plugin creates web pages, but gives more control over the appearance of the pages than iPhoto's built-in Web Page feature. After installation, the plugin appears as an extra tab in the "Export Photos" window (from the File menu, choose "Export..."). Visit **www.DroolingCat.com** to download.

Last but not least, perhaps even best: Apple's web site has a page dedicated to iPhoto scripts. Go to **www.apple.com/applescript/iphoto/** to download an entire collection of truly amazing iPhoto scripts, plus other goodies.

iTunes

Use **iTunes** to organize your music into playlists, burn your own music CDs, and connect to dozens of Internet radio stations offering a wide variety of music and talk radio. In the iTunes Music Store, preview more than 700,000 songs; purchase and download single songs, entire albums, or audiobooks with the click of a button. Check the top music charts for the Billboard 100 and for more than 1000 radio stations. Synchronize an iPod with your iTunes playlists, and carry up to 10,000 songs around with you. And watch dazzling visual-effects shows synchronized to your music selections.

This chapter covers version 4.6 of iTunes. Keep your version updated so you can take advantage of the newest features of both iTunes and The iTunes Music Store.

In this chapter

The iTunes Interface

A quick overview of the iTunes interface is shown here and on the next page. Most of the controls you need are located directly on the **iTunes interface.** Almost every control is explained in detail elsewhere in this chapter.

In the example below, the **Library** is selected in the **Source pane** (the section on the left side of the window) and the Library's contents are shown in the Detail window (the section to the right of the Source pane). When you select another item in the Source pane, its contents show in the Detail window.

Source pane,
page 78. To resize the Source pane, drag the tiny dot. **To eject** *a CD or to unmount an iPod, click the Eject symbol next to the item.*

Show mini-graphic equalizer, *page 91.*

Status display, *page 91.*

Search field, *page 72 (Music Store) and 83 (iTunes).*

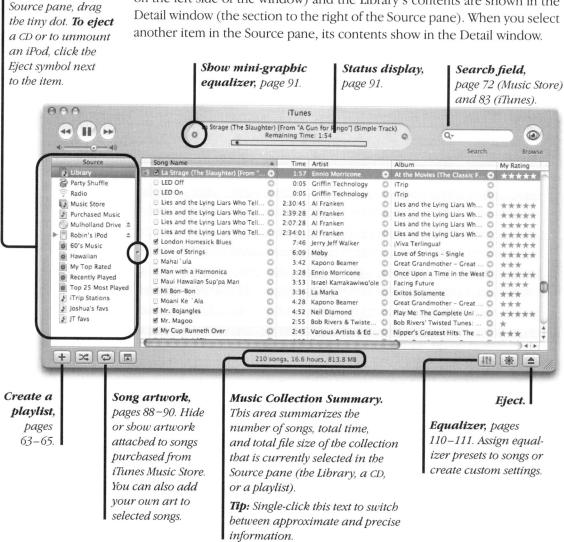

Create a playlist, pages 63–65.

Song artwork, *pages 88–90. Hide or show artwork attached to songs purchased from iTunes Music Store. You can also add your own art to selected songs.*

Music Collection Summary. *This area summarizes the number of songs, total time, and total file size of the collection that is currently selected in the Source pane (the Library, a CD, or a playlist).*

Tip: *Single-click this text to switch between approximate and precise information.*

Eject.

Equalizer, *pages 110–111. Assign equalizer presets to songs or create custom settings.*

In this example, an **iPod** is connected and chosen in the Source pane. For each item selected in the Source pane, you can customize the Detail window view to show the columns of information you want. See "View Options" on page 81.

This bar shows how much of the selected disk space is used and how much is still free, or available. In this example, because the iPod is selected in the Source pane, I see how much room I have left on my iPod.

Quick Links, *page 85.*
Click an arrow to link to a related album page at the iTunes Music Store.

Controller buttons, *page 82.*

Detail window, *pages 79–80.*

Multi-Function button, *pages 92–93.*

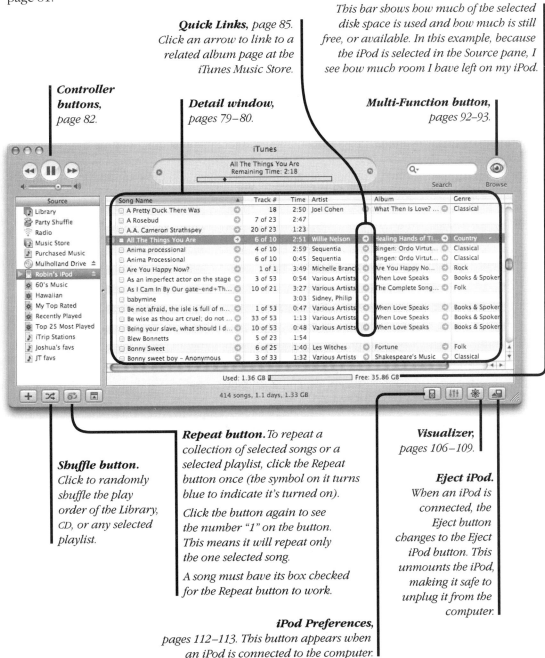

Repeat button. *To repeat a collection of selected songs or a selected playlist, click the Repeat button once (the symbol on it turns blue to indicate it's turned on).*

Click the button again to see the number "1" on the button. This means it will repeat only the one selected song.

A song must have its box checked for the Repeat button to work.

Shuffle button.
Click to randomly shuffle the play order of the Library, CD, or any selected playlist.

Visualizer, *pages 106–109.*

Eject iPod.
When an iPod is connected, the Eject button changes to the Eject iPod button. This unmounts the iPod, making it safe to unplug it from the computer.

iPod Preferences, *pages 112–113. This button appears when an iPod is connected to the computer.*

iTunes

Playing CDs

You can play any music CD in your Mac. Make sure your sound is on and turned up.

To play a music CD:

1. Insert a CD into the drive, label-side up.

2. Open iTunes, if it isn't already open:

    If the iTunes icon is in your Dock, click once on it.

    If there is no icon in the Dock, open the Applications folder, find the iTunes icon, then double-click it.

3. The CD icon appears in the Source pane, as shown below. Click the CD icon to see the song list and other information in the Detail window.

    If you're connected to the Internet, iTunes will automatically go to a CD database web site (Gracenote), retrieve the song titles and other data, and place the information in the appropriate columns.

    If you're NOT connected to the Internet when you insert a CD, song titles will appear as track numbers (as shown below). You can select the generic track names and type in real song names.

The "Song Name" column lists all the songs on the selected CD.

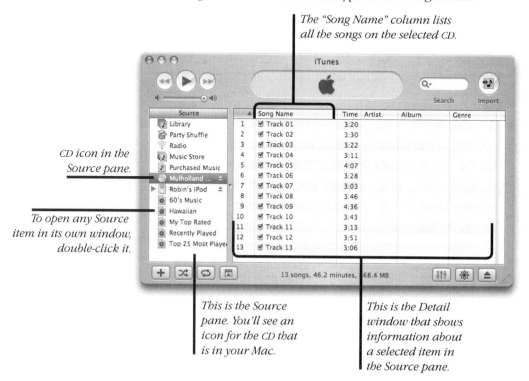

CD icon in the Source pane.

To open any Source item in its own window, double-click it.

This is the Source pane. You'll see an icon for the CD that is in your Mac.

This is the Detail window that shows information about a selected item in the Source pane.

To see the actual song titles, if they have not appeared:

1. Connect to the Internet (if you're not already).
2. From the Advanced menu, choose "Get CD Track Names."

If you want iTunes to do this automatically every time you put in a CD, see the information about iTunes preferences on page 99.

To choose the songs on the CD you want to play:

When you insert a CD, all of the songs have checkmarks next to them. If the box is checked, the song will play. To customize the list, check only the songs you want to hear. iTunes skips over songs that do not have a checkmark.

1. Click on the CD icon in the Source pane.
2. Click on a song in the "Song Name" column to select it.
3. Click the Play button (the middle controller button),
   or double-click the title in the "Song Name" column.

Click on the top line to toggle between album name and track name information.

Click on "Elapsed Time" to change it to "Remaining Time."

The Play/Stop/Pause button.

To check or uncheck all songs at once, Command-click on any box.

The Music Collection Summary gives information about selected items in the Source pane.

The iTunes Library

File formats: The MPEG-4 AAC format compresses song files to a smaller size than the MP3 format, without a noticeable quality difference. We encoded a 3-minute, 20-second song into both formats: the MP3 file encoded to 3.8 megabytes, the MPEG-4 file to 3.1 megabytes, a significant storage savings when you have a large library. If you have a highly refined ear for music, set the iTunes "Importing" preferences to encode songs in "Apple Lossless" format. This format encodes CD-quality music at half the size.

When you import (rip, encode) a music file from a CD, iTunes encodes it as an MPEG-4 AAC file (if you have QuickTime 6.2 or later installed) and places it in the iTunes Library. If you have an earlier version of QuickTime, iTunes encodes songs as MP3, or whatever format you last chose in the Importing preferences pane (see page 101). Once a song is in the Library's list, you can add it to a customized playlist for your personal enjoyment, as explained on the following page. *Simply playing songs from a CD does not add them to the Library.*

To add songs to the Library:

1. Insert a music CD into the drive, label-side up.

2. In the CD song list that appears, click to put a checkmark next to each song you want to add to the Library.

3. Click the "Import" button in the upper-right corner of the window.

You may already have music files somewhere on your computer that you want to add to the iTunes Library. There are two ways to do this:

▼ **Either** go to the File menu and choose "Add to Library…," then find and select your music files.

▼ **Or** drag a file from any location on your hard disk to the Library icon in the iTunes Source pane, as shown below.

Tip: Each song takes up at least 3 to 5 megabytes (depending on the file format specified in Preferences) of hard disk space, so make sure you have plenty of disk space available before you go crazy importing music files!

I selected the "Library" icon. This indicates the songs displayed in the Detail window are those stored in the Library.

For more about this Multi-Function button, see pages 92–93.

To import this AIFF file (.aif), I dragged it from a folder to the "Library" icon. The small round plus button tells you a song is being added to the Library.

This shows how much hard disk space is being used to store the music files in the Library.

Create Your Own Playlists

A **playlist** is your customized collection of audio files. You can create as many playlists as you like, and you can arrange the songs in any order you prefer by dragging selections up or down in the list. You create playlists so you can play custom collections of songs on your computer, download them to a portable MP3 player, or burn them onto CDs.

Create a new playlist and add songs to it

1. Type Command N, **or** click the "New Playlist" button (the **+**) at the bottom-left of the iTunes window. A new playlist icon will appear in the Source pane with a generic name of "untitled playlist."

2. Change the name of the new playlist to something appropriate by typing in the highlighted field.

   You can change a playlist name at any time: Click once on the title to highlight it, then click a second time to make the text editable. Type a new name in the highlighted field.

When you create a new playlist, iTunes assumes you'll want to change its name so it highlights the new name for you. Just type to replace the existing name.

To add selections to the playlist from a CD:

1. Insert a CD whose songs you want to add to a custom playlist.

2. Click the CD icon in the Source pane to open its song list.

3. Drag desired selections from the "Song Name" column and drop them on your new playlist in the Source pane, as shown below.

A mounted CD.

New playlist.

"New Playlist" button.

You can see I am dragging song #13 over to the new playlist in the Source pane.

When you drag a song directly from a CD to a playlist, the song is automatically **encoded (imported)** to the "AAC" format, or whatever format you last chose in the Importing preferences pane, then placed in the iTunes Library and added to the playlist.

5 🔄 ☑ So Much Trouble In ...

This icon to the left of a song name means encoding is in progress.

To add a song to a playlist from the Library:

Note: When you drag a song file from the Library to a playlist collection, as explained on these pages, the song remains in the Library. *You're not actually moving the digital file*—you're creating a *directory* that tells iTunes which songs are attached to different collections. You can put the same song in as many playlist collections as you want without bloating your computer with extra copies of large music files.

1. In the Source pane, single-click the "Library" icon to display your entire Library collection in the "Song Name" column.

2. Drag a selection from the "Song Name" column to a playlist icon in the Source pane.

There's **another method for creating a new playlist** that's even easier:

1. In the Source pane, single-click the "Library" icon to display your entire Library collection in the "Song Name" column.

2. Select the desired songs in the "Song Name" column (hold down the Command key and click each song).

    Note: The **checkmarks** *do not* indicate that a file is selected. The checkmarks indicate two things: songs that will *play* when you click the "Play" button (the right-facing triangle), and songs on a CD that will be *imported* when you click the "Import" button.

3. From the File menu, select "New Playlist From Selection...." iTunes will automatically create the playlist and add the selected items to it. To change the name of the playlist, click it twice and type a new name.

You can drag **multiple selections** all at once to the playlist:

▼ To make a *contiguous* selection of songs (songs that are next to each other in the list), Shift-click the song names. **Or** single-click on one song, then Shift-click on another song: all songs from the single-click to the Shift-click will be selected.

▼ To make a *non-contiguous* selection of songs (songs that are *not* next to each other in the list), Command-click song names.

This is a non-contiguous selection of songs.

Smart Playlists

Smart Playlists are collections of songs that are generated automatically when imported songs meet certain criteria that you define. iTunes put several Smart Playlists (indicated by the gear symbols) in the Source pane that make playlists based on '60s music, top ratings (see page 96), recently played songs, and your top 25 most-played songs. You can create new Smart Playlists that meet other criteria, such as your favorite Hawaiian songs.

🔆 '60s Music
🔆 My Top Rated
🔆 Recently Played
🔆 Top 25 Most Played

Smart Playlists display a gear symbol.

To create a new Smart Playlist:

1. From the File menu, choose "New Smart Playlist...." **Or** Option-click the "New Playlist" button—the "plus" symbol on the button changes to a "gear" symbol for Smart Playlist when you press the Option key.

2. In the Smart Playlist window that appears (below), use the menus and text fields to set conditions for a Smart Playlist.

3. Click OK.

Press the Option key to change the "New Play-list" button to a "New Smart Playlist" button.

Choose to match "any" or "all" conditions.

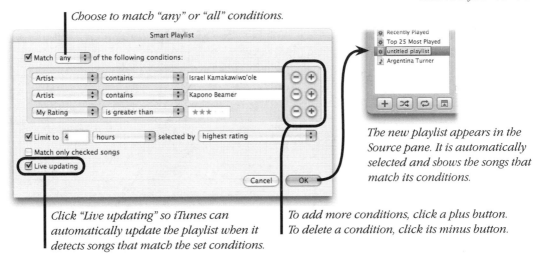

The new playlist appears in the Source pane. It is automatically selected and shows the songs that match its conditions.

Click "Live updating" so iTunes can automatically update the playlist when it detects songs that match the set conditions.

To add more conditions, click a plus button. To delete a condition, click its minus button.

A new Smart Playlist named "untitled playlist" appears in the Source pane (shown above-right). Any songs in your Library that meet the conditions you set are now listed in the "Song Name" column of the Detail window. Rename the playlist something descriptive.

Play the Radio

Click the "Radio" icon to open the **Radio Tuner** so you can tune into the **Internet radio stations** that are built into iTunes (or whose addresses you have entered). These stations play a wide variety of music, news, and talkshow programs (netcast in the "streaming MP3 format).

To play the radio in iTunes:

1. Click the "Radio" icon in the Source pane to see the radio options in the "Stream" column (the same column that is labeled "Song Name" when the selected Source is a CD or your Library).

2. Click the disclosure triangle of a radio category to see the various choices of streams (streaming Internet connections).

3. Double-click a stream to begin playing it. iTunes will open the designated URL (web address) and start playing the content.

Choose which columns to display in the Radio Tuner window: From the Edit menu, choose "View Options...."

iTunes uses technology called "Instant On Streaming" that allows content to start playing immediately. It continues to download data as the file plays. If you do not have a full-time Internet connection, connect to the Internet before you double-click your radio selection.

Some radio stations are available in several bit rates (kilobits per second), which affects the quality of the stream. Streams with higher bit rates sound better, but tend to break up over slow connections. If you have a dial-up Internet connection, choose streams with lower bit rates, such as 24 kbps.

To enter another radio address:

If you know the web address of a streaming MP3 radio station that's not in the iTunes Radio Tuner, you can manually enter it.

1. From the Advanced menu at the top of your screen, choose "Open Stream...."

2. Enter the web address in the text field in the "Open Stream" window. The address must be a complete URL, including the stream file name.

Music File Formats

iTunes works with six **audio file formats:** MPEG-4 AAC, MP3, CD-DA, AIFF, WAV, and Apple Lossless. Using the Import feature, iTunes can encode CD-DA files from a CD to MP3, AIFF, or WAV files. It can also encode MP3, AIFF, and WAV files to CD-DA format when burning a CD. Each file format is suited for a specific purpose.

To select an encoder when importing files, see page 101.

- ▾ **CD-DA** (Compact Disc Digital Audio) is the file format used on all music CDs. This format is also known as "Red Book" because the specifications were originally published in a book with a red cover, which started a tradition of naming CD specifications by color. When you burn a CD from a playlist, iTunes automatically encodes the files in the playlist as CD-DA formatted files so they'll play on CD players.

- ▾ **MP3** (MPEG 3) is a highly efficient compression system that reduces music files up to 90 percent, but maintains a very high quality. Highly compressed, MP3s are ideal for downloading from the Internet or for storing on your computer.

- ▾ **MPEG-4 AAC** (Advanced Audio Coding) format compresses files even smaller than MP3 without a noticeable loss of quality. When iTunes imports a song from a CD to your computer, by default it encodes the CD-DA formatted song to an AAC format. MP3s and AACs are ideal for storing music on your computer, requiring 80 to 90 percent less disk space than other formats.

If you have a version of QuickTime installed that's older than version 6.2, songs are by default imported in the MP3 format instead of the AAC format.

- ▾ **Apple Lossless** encodes CD-DA files (CD music files) into a size that's half the size of the original file, without any loss of quality. This format creates files that are larger than the MP3 and AAC formats, but if you have a discriminating ear for music, the Apple Lossless format provides the best quality possible.

- ▾ **AIFF** (Audio Interchange File Format) is sometimes referred to as Apple Interchange File Format. It is a music format used by the Macintosh operating system. Web designers use the AIFF format for sound files that can play in web pages on a Macintosh computer. The file size of the Beatles song "I Want To Hold Your Hand" is 24.3 MB as an AIFF file, compared to 2.7 MB as an MP3 file.

- ▾ **WAV** (Windows waveform format) is a music file format used by the Microsoft Windows operating system. Web designers use the WAV format for sound files that can play in web pages on a Windows computer. The file size of the Beatles song "I Want To Hold Your Hand" is 24.3 MB as a WAV file, compared to 2.7 MB as an MP3 file.

The iTunes Music Store

If you have a slow Internet connection, see page 104 to learn how to improve the quality of iTunes Music Store song previews.

The iTunes Music Store is really what makes iTunes such a cool app. More than 700,000 music tracks are available for you to preview, purchase, and download. And the collection is growing daily. The music represents all five major recording labels plus 200 independent labels. iTunes Music Store also lets you preview, purchase, and download thousands of audiobooks from Audible.com.

Browsing the iTunes Music Store is easy and fun. It just keeps getting bigger and better and (speaking from personal experience) more addictive.

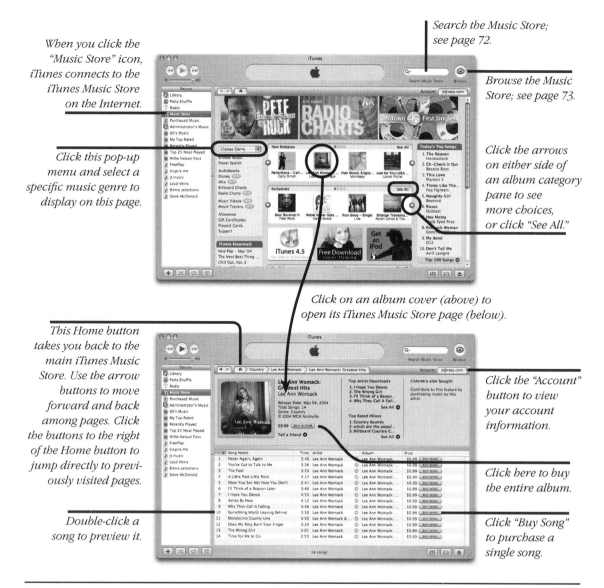

Search the Music Store; see page 72.

When you click the "Music Store" icon, iTunes connects to the iTunes Music Store on the Internet.

Browse the Music Store; see page 73.

Click this pop-up menu and select a specific music genre to display on this page.

Click the arrows on either side of an album category pane to see more choices, or click "See All."

Click on an album cover (above) to open its iTunes Music Store page (below).

This Home button takes you back to the main iTunes Music Store. Use the arrow buttons to move forward and back among pages. Click the buttons to the right of the Home button to jump directly to previously visited pages.

Click the "Account" button to view your account information.

Double-click a song to preview it.

Click here to buy the entire album.

Click "Buy Song" to purchase a single song.

Preview and buy songs and albums

iTunes Music Store provides a thirty-second preview of every song and book. Once you've selected an item, double-click it to play the preview.

You can copy a song preview *link* to your computer, in case you want to preview or purchase it later. Just drag the song from the iTunes Music Store to the Source pane on the left. A new playlist is automatically created, named after the song you just dragged from iTunes Music Store. You might consider creating a special playlist just for organizing preview links in one place, and naming it something like "Wish List," as we did in this example.

When you double-click a song in iTunes Music Store, its 30-second preview shows here.

When you drag a song preview to the Source pane, the music file is not really on your computer. It's a link to the preview on the Music Store. To play it, you must be connected to the Internet.

Later, when you're ready to listen to the preview links you copied, select the playlist in the Source pane to which you dragged a song preview ("Wish List" in this example). In the Detail window you can double-click a preview to play it, **or** you can click one of the *Quick Link* buttons (circled below) to link back to the iTunes Music Store page for that particular song's page. **Or** click a "Buy Song" or "Buy Album" button to purchase and download a song or album from this window. See pages 69–70 for details about buying songs.

Learn about Quick Links on page 85.

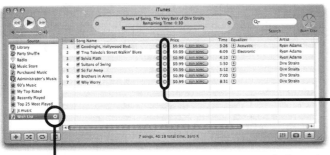

The Quick Link buttons next to the song previews take you to the iTunes Music Store page linked to that song.

The Quick Link button in the Source pane links to the iTunes Music Store.

Preview and buy audiobooks

The first time you try to buy music from the iTunes Music Store, you'll be asked to sign in to your existing account or to create a new account, as shown below. After you finish this quick and simple procedure, you can buy songs, albums, or audiobooks with the single click of a "Buy" button.

Enter your Apple ID and password, if you have one.

Click the Help button to learn more about creating a new account.

If necessary, click here to create a new account.

To buy audiobooks, click the "Audiobooks" link in the Music Store window. **Or** from the "Choose Genre" pop-up menu, select "Audiobooks." When the audiobooks page opens (below, top), select a book to show the preview/purchase page for that book (below, bottom).

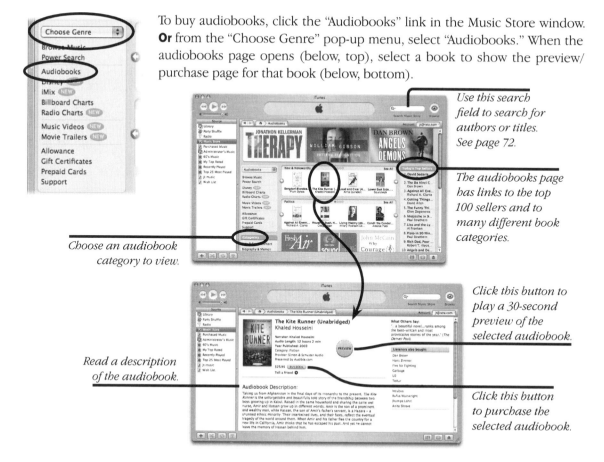

Choose an audiobook category to view.

Use this search field to search for authors or titles. See page 72.

The audiobooks page has links to the top 100 sellers and to many different book categories.

Read a description of the audiobook.

Click this button to play a 30-second preview of the selected audiobook.

Click this button to purchase the selected audiobook.

Copy iTunes Music Store links

Sometimes you want to tell someone about a great song or a good book you found. Or maybe you want to drop some hints for an upcoming gift occasion.

If you click on a song's "Tell a friend" link (shown on the right), an email message is sent to your friend (shown below) containing the associated album or book art, and a link to the song or book page in the iTunes Music Store.

iTunes creates a nice-looking email message for sharing your music discovery with a friend. The recipient clicks the "iTunes" button to go to the Music Store page for this song. Below this message is a link to download iTunes (Mac and Windows).

When you drag a link, song, or graphic from iTunes Music Store, it creates a URL file (a URL—Uniform Resource Locator—is a web address on the Internet) that links to a Music Store page. When you double-click a URL file that was created this way, iTunes opens the link and takes you to the related iTunes Music Store location. Drag a link, song, or graphic from the Music Store pages to your Desktop or to a folder so you can double-click the URL file later and go to the exact same page you were browsing earlier. You can drag the URL to an email message when you're ready to send it to a friend.

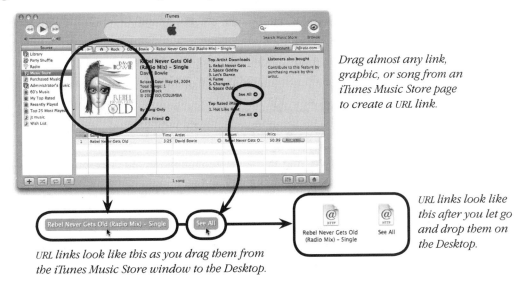

Drag almost any link, graphic, or song from an iTunes Music Store page to create a URL link.

URL links look like this after you let go and drop them on the Desktop.

URL links look like this as you drag them from the iTunes Music Store window to the Desktop.

Use Search, Power Search, or Browse to find music

Click on the magnifying glass in the Search field to show a menu from which you choose a search category: All, Artists, Albums, Composers, Songs, or Power Search.

After you choose a search category, the words under the text field change to show your selection. For instance, if you choose "Songs," the Search field is labeled "Search Songs."

To **search,** type a complete or partial name in the search field, then hit Return on the keyboard. The search results show in the bottom section of the iTunes window, as shown below.

Use the Search field menu to select the music category you want to search, or to select "Power Search...."

Type an album, artist, or song name.

The top section of the search results shows albums from which the found songs come. The bottom section shows the found songs.

To **Power Search,** choose "Power Search…" from the Search field menu. In the Power Search pane, shown below, enter as much information as possible, then click the "Search" button.

The Power Search pane.

Use the **Browse** button to search for *songs* by genre, artist, and album. Click the "Browse" button to show the Browser pane, circled below. Select a genre from the "Genre" column, then choose an artist from the "Artist" column, and then choose an album from the "Album" column. After you make your selections, the matching results show in the bottom section of the window.

To leave the Browser, click the "Browse" button again. You can also click the Back button (the left-facing arrow) or the Home button.

The "Browse" button.

The Browser pane.

The Browse results for "Poodle Hat."

You can also use the **Browse** button to search for audiobooks by genre, category, and author. Select "Audiobooks" in the "Genre" column. The next two columns change to the "Category" and "Author" columns. Make a selection in the "Category" column, then in the "Author" column. The results appear in the bottom section of the window.

Music charts

One way of finding great music is to select **Billboard Charts** or **Radio Charts** on the Music Store's main page. Choose "Radio Charts" to access the top playlists of more than 1,000 local radio stations in major U.S. markets. Choose "Billboard Charts" to browse Billboard's top pop, R&B, and country songs, categorized by year from 1946 to 2003.

This list of choices appears on the Music Store's home page.

Choose "Billboard Charts" (above-right) to browse through Billboard's top songs since 1946. The example on the left shows the top pop songs from 1963.

Watch music videos and movie trailers

The iTunes Music Store has evolved into an entertainment destination. Not only can you go there and listen to music previews for hours, you can watch music videos and movie trailers.

On the Music Store's Home page, choose "Music Videos" or "Movie Trailers" from the list of categories, shown to the left. When the movie trailer or music video page opens, click on the video you want to watch.

Most videos let you choose between large, medium, or small versions. *Large* is nice when you have a fast Internet connection, *medium* or *small* is much better for slower connections.

These buttons show what page you're on, and provide a trail back to the Home page.

The Movie Trailers page.

The Music Videos page.

Listening to song previews and watching video is much more enjoyable if you have a fast, broadband connection. If you have a slow dial-up modem connection (all dial-up connections are slow when you're trying to view video), the download time can be frustrating and the audio/video playback may skip or stop. You can set a couple of iTunes Preferences to help improve performance of the Music Store's streaming audio and video features (song previews, music videos, and movie trailers).

1. From the iTunes application menu, choose "Preferences...."
2. Click the "Store" button to show the Store preferences pane.
3. Select "Load complete preview before playing."

Also, you can increase the streaming buffer size. The buffer is the amount of streamed data that's stored in the computer's memory before the song or video starts to play.

1. Go to iTunes Preferences, then click the "Advanced" button.
2. From the "Streaming Buffer Size" menu, choose "Medium" or "Large."

If you have a fast Internet connection and you want streaming files to start playing sooner, set the streaming buffer size to "Small." Your computer will have to pre-load less data before it starts to play a streaming file.

Publish your own iMix playlist

Do you have a favorite mix of songs purchased from the iTunes Music Store that you'd like to share? If so, you can put them in a playlist and publish them as an **iMix**. iMix is an iTunes Music Store feature that publishes song mixes submitted by iTunes users. You must use music purchased from the Music Store. The published iMix plays just a 30-second preview of each song in the mix. But it's fun. And useful for sending song discoveries and recommendations to friends. Here's how to do it:

1. Create a playlist that contains only music purchased from the iTunes Music Store. A Quick Link button (a gray circle with a white arrow) automatically appears to the right of the playlist name in the Source pane, circled below. Click the Quick Link button.

2. The message shown below appears and says that you can publish your playlist. Click the "Publish" button in the message window.

To view an iMix collection submitted by an iTunes user, select "iMix" on the Music Store's Home page. When you go to any user's iMix page, you can rate the mix from one to five stars. The iMix main page shows the average rating for each published iMix.

Click here to publish your iMix.

Quick Link button.

3. Sign in with your Apple ID and password, shown on the right.
4. Click the "Publish" button to sign in. On the page that opens (shown below), type a title and description for your song mix.
5. Click the "Publish" button.

Click "Publish" to sign in. If you don't have an account, click the "Create Account" button to set one up.

After you click "Publish," iTunes sends you an email confirmation that includes a link to your iMix page.

Allowance, gift certificates, prepaid cards, and shopping carts

You've seen how easy it is to click the "Buy Song" button and download music through your Apple Account. But what if you'd like to buy music for family members or friends and let them download it to their own computer? iTunes Music Store provides several easy and convenient ways to do this.

Allowance: Set up an allowance when you want to let your kids buy a pre-set amount of music without a credit card. You can set a monthly amount between $10 and $200, in increments of $10.

1. Click the "Allowance" link on the Music Store's Home page.

2. In the setup window that opens, fill in the required information, then click "Continue" (the recipient of the allowance will need an Apple Account).

To cancel an allowance at any time, click the "Account" button in the iTunes Music Store.

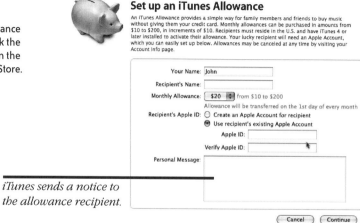

Set up an iTunes Allowance

An iTunes Allowance provides a simple way for family members and friends to buy music without giving them your credit card. Monthly allowances can be purchased in amounts from $10 to $200, in increments of $10. Recipients must reside in the U.S. and have iTunes 4 or later installed to activate their allowance. Your lucky recipient will need an Apple Account, which you can easily set up below. Allowances may be canceled at any time by visiting your Account Info page.

Your Name:	John
Recipient's Name:	
Monthly Allowance:	$20 ▼ from $10 to $200
	Allowance will be transferred on the 1st day of every month
Recipient's Apple ID:	○ Create an Apple Account for recipient
	● Use recipient's existing Apple Account
Apple ID:	
Verify Apple ID:	
Personal Message:	

iTunes sends a notice to the allowance recipient.

(Cancel)   (Continue)

3. A window opens asking you to confirm your purchase. Check the information, then click the "Buy" button. A message appears and tells you the allowance has been set up.

Gift certificates: What a great gift idea! Especially for last-minute gifts that don't have a chance of getting there on time.

1. Click the "Gift Certificates" link on the Music Store's Home page, then choose "Email" or "U.S. Mail" for delivering the gift certificate.

2. In the form that opens, fill in the required information. Use the "Amount" pop-up menu to set an amount from $10 to $200, in increments of $10. Click the "Continue" button.

3. A new window asks for your Apple Account password, then another window opens to confirm your information. Click the "Buy" button.

Prepaid cards: Here's another solution for gifts or for someone that doesn't have a credit card—purchase prepaid cards at Target stores. To redeem an iTunes Prepaid Card, the recipient clicks on the "Prepaid Cards" link on the Music Store's home page, then follows the instructions.

iTunes Prepaid Cards.

Shopping cart: Use a shopping cart if you want to store song selections and buy them later, or if you want to review the music that your children have chosen before it's purchased. To set up a Shopping Cart:

1. From the iTunes application menu, choose "Preferences…."

2. Click the "Store" button to open the Store preferences pane.

3. Select "Buy using a Shopping Cart." Music is added to your cart when you click an "Add" button. To purchase and download a *single song* in the shopping cart, click its "Buy Song" button. To purchase and download *all songs* in the shopping cart, click "Buy Now" at the bottom of the window.

When you enable an iTunes Shopping Cart, the "Buy Song" button in the Music Store changes to "Add Song."

A new "Shopping Cart" icon appears in the Source pane, as shown below.

iTunes and iTunes Music Store restrictions

In an effort to fight piracy, Apple has designed the iPod so that it's easy to transfer songs in one direction (from a computer to your iPod) and difficult to transfer music in the other direction (from the iPod to a computer). On the Internet you can find inexpensive or free third-party software products that let you see iPod's hidden music folder. You can then copy songs from the iPod to a computer. Go to **VersionTracker.com** and search for "iPod."

To remove songs from your iTunes Shopping Cart, select "Shopping Cart" in the Source pane, then select a song in the Shopping Cart and click the tiny Delete button that appears to the right of the "Buy Song" button.

Apple also puts some limitations on how many computers can play the music that you purchased from the iTunes Music Store. To play purchased music, you must "authorize" your computer using your iTunes Music Store account name and password. When you try to play a purchased song on an unauthorized computer, a dialog box opens asking if you want to authorize it. You can authorize up to five computers at a time. You can use someone else's computer to buy music from iTunes Music Store if you log in to your account and authorize the computer you're using, but remember to deauthorize it to prevent someone else from using your account. **To deauthorize a computer,** open iTunes, then from the Advanced menu choose "Deauthorize Computer…."

You're allowed to burn up to seven CDs of the same playlist, and you can burn unlimited CDs of single songs. You can copy your music collection to an unlimited number of iPods. Songs purchased from the iTunes Music Store belong to you. Use them in a movie, a presentation, or any other personal, non-commercial use.

The Source Pane

This is where you select the music collection that you want to display in the Detail window. Icons for the following types of sources can be found in the Source pane.

Library: This is your entire collection of iTunes music. Click the "Library" icon in the Source pane to view all the songs in iTunes. When you drag a song file from the Library to a playlist as explained on page 63 the song remains in the Library. You're not actually moving the digital file—you're creating a directory that tells iTunes which songs are attached to different collections. You can put the same song in as many playlists as you want without bloating your computer with extra copies of large music files.

Party Shuffle: This is an automated playlist that selects a designated number of songs and plays them for you, constantly refreshing the playlist with selections based on your Party Shuffle settings. See page 84 for details.

Radio: Listen to streaming Internet radio stations. Learn more on page 66.

Music Store: Click this icon to connect directly to the iTunes Music Store. This is where you find, preview, purchase, and download songs or audiobooks. It's packed with powerful features. Learn more starting on page 68.

Purchased Music: This playlist keeps track of the music you've purchased from iTunes Music Store.

CD icon: If you have a CD inserted in your CD drive, it shows here. Click it to see a list of songs on the CD.

iPod: If you connect an iPod, it's icon shows here. Click it to see the songs and playlists you've copied to it. See pages 112–116 for more information.

Shared playlists: If you've set iTunes to "Look for shared music," and if it finds a Shared Playlist on your local network, a new icon appears in the Source pane—a stack of documents with a music note on top. In the example shown above-left, "Quicksilver Music" is a shared music Library on a computer named Quicksilver. A click on the disclosure triangle will reveal all the playlists in that Library. Learn how to share your playlists with others on your network on page 86.

Smart playlists: These automated playlists have a gear symbol on them. Some were created by Apple for you, but you can create your own to automatically collect music in a playlist that meets your preset conditions. See page 65.

Playlists: Ordinary playlists have a note symbol on them. Learn more about playlists on pages 63–65.

If you want to **delete a playlist** in the Source pane, select it, then from the Edit menu choose "Clear."

Or Control-click on a playlist, then choose "Clear" from the menu that pops up.

Or select a playlist, then press the Delete key on your keyboard.

The Detail Window

The **Detail window** displays various columns of song information. The visible columns in the Detail window will vary depending on which type of collection you've selected in the Source pane and which options you've chosen in View Options (from the Edit menu). The columns typically displayed for the Library include Song Name, Time, Artist, and Album. We like to add "My Rating" and "Equalizer" settings; see page 81.

Select and play songs

To play any selection in the "Song Name" column, double-click its title. When that selection has finished, iTunes plays the next song in the list *that has a checkmark next to it.*

When you insert a CD, by default *all* the song titles have a checkmark next to them, which means they will all play in order when you click the "Play" button. The checkmark also determines which songs will be encoded and placed in the iTunes Library when you click the "Import" button.

- ▼ **To select (check) all songs at once,** Command-click on any *empty* checkbox.

- ▼ **To deselect (uncheck) all the songs at once,** Command-click on any checkbox that has a *check* in it.

- ▼ **To select a group of contiguous songs** in the song list, click on one song, then Shift-click another song. All titles between the two clicks will be automatically added to your selection.

- ▼ **To select a group of non-contiguous songs,** Command-click on the songs you want to select.

Resize or rearrange columns

If song titles are cut off by the narrow width of the "Song Name" column, or if one of the columns is too narrow or too wide, you can **resize the column.** Place your cursor over the thin, gray, dividing line that separates two columns. The cursor becomes a bi-directional arrow. Press-and-drag the line to the left or right as far as necessary to resize the column to your liking.

Drag the divider line left or right to resize columns.

To rearrange the columns, press on a column's title bar. When you start to drag, the arrow turns into a grabber hand as shown below. Drag the column left or right to a new position.

Above, you can see the grabber hand as it drags the Time column from its original position to the position between the Artist column and the Album column.

Organize the column information

The Detail window is always **organized** by the **selected** column. In the example above, the information is organized alphabetically by song name—you can see that the "Song Name" column heading is highlighted.

Click the small triangle to the right of a *selected* column name to **reverse the order** in which the information is displayed. For instance, if you select the column head "My Rating" and then click its triangle, the songs will be listed in order of how you rated them; click the triangle again to reverse the order of the ratings.

View Options

Set the Detail window to show just the information you want. Select a source in the Source pane, then from the Edit menu choose "View Options...." The top item in the "View Options" window is the name and icon of the selected source. As shown below, the options in this window change depending on the item you select in the Source pane. Check the columns you want to show in the Detail window, then click OK.

Most items in the Source pane have the same view options available as those for the Library, shown below-left. "Radio" and mounted CDs have fewer view options, as shown below. When "Music Store" is selected in the Source pane, no view options are available.

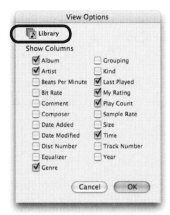

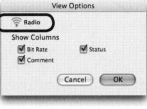

Select "Radio" in the Source pane, then choose which of these columns you want to show in the Detail window.

The items you choose here determine which columns are visible in the Detail window when you view a list of songs.

These are the View Options when showing a CD's contents in the Detail window. Select the "Disc Number" option if you want to identify multiple CDs that are part of a set. When a CD from a set of three is mounted, its disc number shows in the Detail window as "1 of 3," "2 of 3," or "3 of 3." When a single CD is mounted, its disc number shows in the Detail window as "1 of 1."

Controller Buttons

The three big round buttons are the controller buttons.

The **controller buttons** act like the controls on most any CD player.

- ▾ **To select the Next song,** single-click the Forward button (double arrows pointing to the right).

- ▾ **To Fast Forward** the current selection, press-and-hold the Forward button.

- ▾ **To select the Previous song,** single-click the Back button (double arrows pointing to the left).

- ▾ **To Rapid Rewind** the current selection, press-and-hold the Back button.

- ▾ The middle button toggles between **Play** and **Pause** when a CD or a song file on your computer is playing.

  The same button toggles between **Play** and **Stop** when the Radio Tuner is active.

Close, Minimize, and Zoom Buttons

As usual for every window in Mac OS X, you see the **three colored buttons** in the upper-left of the window, but they act a little differently in iTunes.

- ▾ Click the **red button** (the left button) to hide the iTunes window, even while music is playing. It won't affect the music.

  To show the player again, from the File menu choose "Show Current Song."

  Or use the keyboard shortcut Command 1 (one) to toggle between "Hide Player" and "Show Player" while iTunes is active.

- ▾ Click the center **yellow button** to minimize the player and send it to the Dock. To bring the player back to the Desktop, single-click it in the Dock.

- ▾ Click the **green button** (the zoom button to the right) to reduce the size of the player window to its smallest possible size, as shown below. Click the green button again to return to the full window size.

The Zoom button. ➡

This button collapses the entire iTunes window down to a compact, space-saving, cute little windoid.

iTunes Search

The **Search** field enables you to quickly find songs on your computer in the selected song list, songs from the Library, a CD, or a playlist. (To search for music to preview or buy in the Music Store, see pages 68–69.)

To search:

▼ In the Search field (circled, below), type one or more key letters or words that are in any part of the artist, song, or album name.

You don't need to hit the Return or Enter key—a list will appear instantly in the Detail window that includes only songs that contain your key words. As you type, the list will change constantly to reflect the matching results.

To focus a search, click the tiny triangle and choose a category.

For instance, in the example to the right I'm looking for a song by Bob Marley called "Crazy Baldhead." I start typing the word "crazy" into the Search field. The list instantly displays dozens of songs that match the letter "c" (the first letter typed). After typing the second letter ("r") the list changes to show the only two songs that have "cr" in either the song title, artist name, or album name; capital or lowercase letters don't matter. If I continue to type "crazy," the list will be narrowed down to a single choice.

Type your search in here.

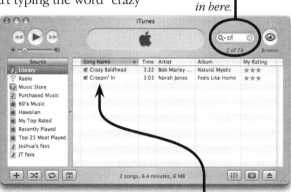

Search results.

Use the iTunes Browser to Search Large Playlists

When your Library contains a large collection of songs by many different artists, you can **browse** the Library contents by genre, artist, or album.

The "Browse" button.

1. With the Library selected in the Source pane, click the "Browse" button. **Or** from the Edit menu, choose "Show Browser." In the Browser pane that opens, select a genre, then an artist and album. The results display in the bottom pane.

2. To close the Browser pane, click the "Browse" button. **Or** from the Edit menu, choose "Hide Browser."

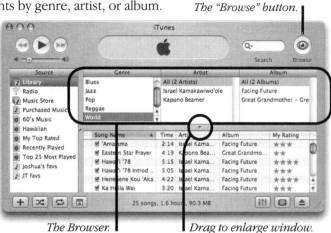

The Browser. | *Drag to enlarge window.*

You can choose whether or not to show "Party Shuffle" in the Source pane. Go to iTunes Preferences, click the "General" button, then check (or uncheck) "Party Shuffle."

Party Shuffle

The Party Shuffle automatically creates a **dynamic playlist** based on your settings (shown below). It constantly updates, adding a new song whenever the current song ends. You can add songs manually, delete songs, or rearrange the order of songs at any time. Songs that you add manually stay in the list.

To create a Party Shuffle playlist:

1. Select "Party Shuffle" in the Source pane. The informational (but not really useful) message shown below appears. Click "Do not show this message again," unless you want other users to see it. Click OK.

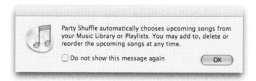

To create a new "Party Shuffle" playlist based on the same settings, click the "Refresh" button in the upper-right corner.

2. Party Shuffle instantly displays a playlist based on the default settings found at the bottom of the window, shown below.

Party Shuffle's automatic playlist.

Party Shuffle settings pane.

3. Use the "Source" pop-up menu to select the Library or any playlist as a source from which Party Shuffle can choose songs. Party Shuffle will see only songs that are checked. Unchecked songs in the source playlist will be ignored.

4. Click "Play higher rated songs more often" if you've *rated* your songs, as described on page 96.

5. Use the "Display" pop-up menus to set the number of *recently played* songs and *upcoming songs* (up to 100).

Quick Links

Quick Link buttons (an arrow inside a circle) can be seen in the "Song Name" column, the "Artist" column, and the "Album" column. They are literally quick links to pages in the iTunes Music Store. Different Quick Links for the same song may go to different Music Store pages, depending on the column the Quick Link is in. If you click on a Quick Link in the "Song Name" column, iTunes will search for that particular song.

All songs and albums have a Quick Link button, but it only works if the song is actually available in the iTunes Music Store.

Quick Link buttons also appear in the Source pane next to a *selected* playlist. These buttons are links to publish the playlist as an iMix (read about iMix on page 75). If you try to publish a playlist that contains some songs that were not purchased at the iTunes Music Store, iMix will ignore those songs and publish only the ones purchased there.

Click on a Quick Link in the "Song Name" column to search iTunes for that song. The window below shows the result of clicking the Quick Link circled on the left—the iTunes Music Store page highlights the song and shows all other songs from the same album.

The iTunes Music Store also provides links to the selected artist's top downloads, top-rated iMixes, and other suggested albums.

Share Music Over a Local Network

If you have two or more computers on a local network, users can **share their music collections** without copying any songs from one computer to another. iTunes can *stream* music files over a local area network (LAN) to a computer that has set iTunes Preferences to look for shared music. Streaming files play from one computer to another without being copied to it.

Set one (or more) of your computers to share its entire iTunes Library, or choose to share just certain playlists. **Here's how to do it:**

1. From the iTunes application menu choose "Preferences…," then click the "Sharing" button.

2. Select "Look for shared music" to make iTunes place an icon in the Source pane for any shared playlists it finds on the local network.

3. Select "Share my music" to make your iTunes music collection available on the local network to other computers that have been set to look for shared music (as in Step 2).

   If you select "Share my music," you must choose whether to "Share entire library" or "Share selected playlists." If you choose the latter, then you must select which playlists to share. Put a checkmark next to the playlists that you want to share.

4. Click "Require password" and type a password in the text field if you want to restrict access to your music.

5. Click OK.

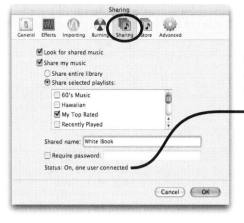

Check this "Status" line to see how many other computers are connected to your shared playlists.

iTunes automatically and instantly finds shared music on the local network and puts it in the Source pane, as shown here. Click one of the shared playlists to display its songs, or click the parent shared playlist ("White iBook" in this example) to see the contents of all the shared playlists.

Print CD Jewel Case Inserts, Song Listings, or Album Listings

Being able to burn a CD of your own customized playlists is really cool. Then you have to clumsily scrawl some kind of description on it with a felt tip pen so you'll know what's on it. Oh, wait . . . that was last century. Now you just select a design and let iTunes **print a beautiful CD case insert** that includes album art and a list of songs. You can also print song lists and album lists.

To print a CD jewel case insert, song listing, or album listing:

1. Select a playlist in the Source pane.

2. From the File menu, choose "Print...."

3. In the dialog box, choose one of the "Print" options: "CD jewel case insert," "Song listing," or "Album listing."

4. From the "Theme" pop-up menu, choose a layout style.

5. Click the "Print..." button to choose a printer.

The choices in the "Theme" pop-up menu change depending on the "Print" option you choose. CD jewel case themes are provided in both color and black and white.

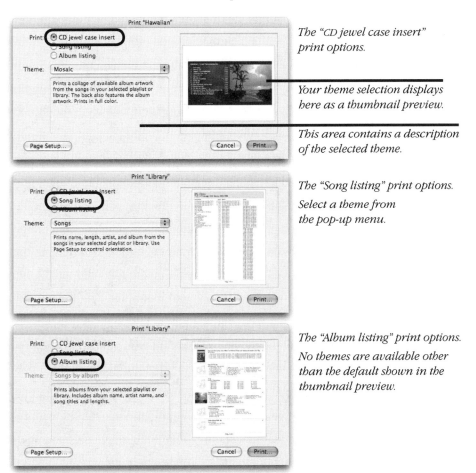

The "CD jewel case insert" print options.

Your theme selection displays here as a thumbnail preview.

This area contains a description of the selected theme.

The "Song listing" print options.

Select a theme from the pop-up menu.

The "Album listing" print options.

No themes are available other than the default shown in the thumbnail preview.

Song Information and Options

Get information about song tracks (shown below, left), add comments to songs, and adjust the volume control in the **Song Information** window.

To open the Song Information window:

1. Select one song track or multiple song tracks.

2. Type Command I to open the window.

If you made a single song selection, the Song Information window contains four tabs: "Summary," "Info," "Options," and "Artwork."

The **Summary** pane gives information about the selected song in your Library or playlist.

To get information about other songs in the selected playlist without leaving the Song Information window, click the "Previous" button or the "Next" button, shown circled below-left.

 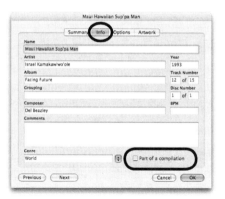

The **Info** pane, above-right, provides additional information, plus a Comments field in which you can add your own comments, such as "Use as theme for Amanda's wedding movie."

Mark songs or CDs as a "compilation" to store them together (above, right). When you mark a song as part of a compilation, a new folder is created in the iTunes Music folder named Compilations, and the song is placed in a sub-folder named for the album the song came from. When a CD is marked as a compilation CD, a new folder named for the CD is placed in the Compilations folder. This causes any song you import from the CD to be marked as "Part of a compilation."

Compilations can be copied to an iPod, shared with others by copying them to another computer, or burned onto a CD.

The settings in the **Options** pane allow you to set the Volume Adjustment for each individual song. This is helpful if you're a serious rocker and cranking up the other volume controls (the Sound settings in System Preferences, plus the iTunes window volume control) just isn't loud enough.

Use the "Equalizer Preset" pop-up menu to select one of the preset equalizer settings for the selected song. This setting can also be set in the main window if you have set View Options to show the Equalizer column.

Set "My Rating" for the selected song between one and five stars. This setting can also be set in the main window if you've set View Options to show the Rating column.

The Options tab also lets you set a "Start/Stop Time" for a song. In the event you want to **play or import just a section** of a long song, enter the "Start Time" and "Stop Time" times in a minutes:seconds format (00:00).

To determine which time settings you need, first play the whole song. Watch the Status display at the top of the iTunes window, and write down the beginning and ending "Elapsed Time" of your desired music segment. If you don't see the elapsed time in the Status display, click whatever time display is showing until "Elapsed Time" appears, as shown below-right.

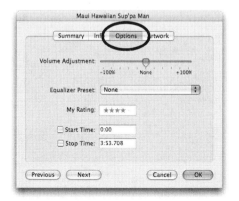

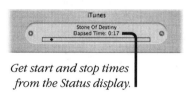

Get start and stop times from the Status display.

If you selected more than one song, the **Multiple Song Information** window, as shown to the right, combines all the previous information and options into one window. The Volume Adjustment affects all selected tracks.

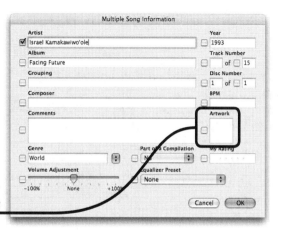

Double-click the "Artwork" box to open the "Choose a File" window, then select an image that's on your computer.

The **Artwork** pane displays the album artwork associated with the selected song. Songs you buy from the iTunes Music Store automatically include the album art and it appears in this window. This album art also appears in the Song Artwork pane of the main window (bottom of page). Click the Song Artwork button, circled below, to *show* the song artwork. Click the button again to *hide* the song artwork. To see a full-size version of the song artwork in its own window, double-click the song artwork.

To add other images to the Artwork pane so they'll be available, click the "Add…" button, then select an image stored on your computer. When there are multiple images in this window, only the *first* image will appear in the Song Artwork pane (bottom of page). To change artwork, drag the image you want to use in front of the other images in the Artwork pane, as shown below-right. Restart iTunes for your change to take effect.

Click "Add…" to add images to the Artwork pane.

Click these buttons to move to the previous or next song in the selected playlist.

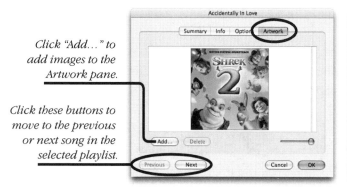

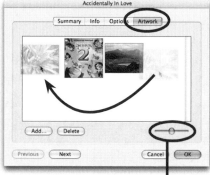

Use the slider to resize images.

Double-click the song artwork to open it full-size and in its own window.

You can also Control-click the artwork, choose "Copy" from the contextual menu, then paste the image into a document such as Mail, Photoshop, TextEdit, etc.

Click here to hide or show song artwork.

Status Display

When iTunes is playing a song selection from a CD, from the iTunes Library, or from a playlist, the **Status display** (at the top of the iTunes window) shows three lines of information: music identification, music track time, and an audio track bar.

The **music identification** (top line) in the Status display automatically scrolls through song name, album name, and artist name. Click on the top line to manually cycle through these three bits of song information.

The **time duration** of a song is shown in the middle line. Click on it to toggle between "Remaining Time," "Total Time," and "Elapsed Time."

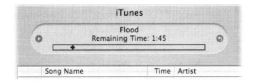

The **audio track bar** on the bottom line indicates the current location of playback in relation to the entire song. **To move to any point in a song,** drag the playhead (the small black diamond) left or right. **Or** just click anywhere along the length of the audio track bar to position the playhead.

When iTunes is playing the **Radio Tuner,** the Status display is similar.

Click the top line to manually toggle between the **URL** (Internet address) of the radio station and its **station name** or call letters. The middle line shows the **Elapsed Time** of the audio stream. The bottom line is a **blank audio track** line. You can't drag ahead or back in Radio streaming files.

No matter what you're listening to, you can turn the Status display into a mini **graphic equalizer:** Click the small round/triangle button on the left side of the window. This feature doesn't offer control of any kind, but it's fun. Click the equalizer button again to turn it off and return to the normal status information.

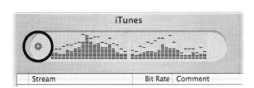

iTunes also includes a controllable equalizer; see pages 110–111.

The SnapBack button

The curved arrow on the right side of the Status display is a **SnapBack** button. The SnapBack button returns you to the song that's currently playing. For example, you play a song from a CD, then you switch to the Library, and then to the iTunes Music Store, and then to a shared playlist. You may not remember where the song that's playing is coming from, but when you click the SnapBack button, iTunes instantly shows the CD's contents and highlights the song that's playing.

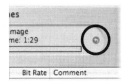

The Multi-Function Button

The button in the upper-right corner of the iTunes player changes appearance and functionality according to the type of source selected in the "Source" pane and if "Visuals" are turned on. That's why we call it the **Multi-Function button.** Following are its different states.

Browse: When you click on ***Library*** in the Source pane, the Multi-Function button becomes the "Browse" button. Click "Browse" and the top section of the iTunes window displays two new panes for browsing: Artist and Album. Click on any item (or multiple items) in these two panes and the display below will show only songs that match the selections above. When you've located the desired song or album, you can double-click it to play immediately, or drag the selection straight from the Browse results list to a playlist in the Source pane.

To add a Genre column to the Browse area: From the iTunes menu, choose "Preferences...." In the General pane, click the checkbox to "Show Genre When Browsing."

Import: When you click on a ***CD*** icon in the Source pane, the Multi-Function button becomes the "Import" button. "Import" copies selected songs into your iTunes Library. See more about importing on pages 94–95.

Refresh: When you click on ***Radio*** in the Source pane, the Multi-Function button becomes the "Refresh" button. Click the "Refresh" button to check the Internet for the latest radio listings available through iTunes.

You'll also see the "Refresh" button when you select the "Party Shuffle" playlist in the Source pane. Click the "Refresh" button to force iTunes to pick a new selection of upcoming songs to go in the "Party Shuffle" playlist.

Burn Disc: When you click on a ***playlist*** in the Source pane, the Multi-Function button becomes the "Burn Disc" button.

To burn a CD:

1. Select a playlist in the "Source" pane.
2. In the "Song Name" list, check any songs you want recorded on the new CD.
3. Click the "Burn Disc" button (shown top-right) and the button cover opens to reveal the actual "Burn Disc" icon (shown on the right).
4. The Status window will instruct you to insert a blank CD.
5. After you've inserted a disc, iTunes flashes a message in the Status window to click the "Burn Disc" button again.

6. When finished, a new CD icon representing your newly created music CD will appear on the Desktop.

Options: If you turn on ***Visual Effects*** (click the little icon that looks like an atomic isotope or flower on the bottom-right of the iTunes window), the Multi-Function button becomes the "Options" button. Click "Options" to present the "Visualizer Options" window, shown below. You can choose to display the animation frame rate, cap the animation frame rate at 30 frames per second, always display the song information, and set a faster display or a better quality display. See pages 106–109 for details about the visual effects.

OpenGL is the industry standard for visualizing 3D shapes and textures. This option is meant to improve the performance of the visualizer, but depending on your system, it may actually degrade performance. Try it and see what happens.

Import Music from a CD

To **rip** a file is to encode it (convert it) from one format to another. To copy a CD music track **to your computer,** you'll convert it (rip it) from the CD-DA format on the CD to the AAC format, or to whatever file format you choose in the Importing preferences pane.

To rip music files:

1. Insert a music CD; the CD tracks appear in the iTunes Detail window.

   If iTunes does not automatically go to the Internet and get the title names and other track information, go to the Advanced menu and choose "Get CD Track Names." (This will open your Internet connection if you're not already online.) After a few moments, the CD database will fill in the track titles, artist, album, and genre, if they're available online.

2. Select the tracks in the list you want to rip. By default all tracks in the list are checked when you first open a music CD. Uncheck any track that you don't want to rip and save on your computer.

3. Click the "Import" button in the upper-right corner of the iTunes window. The checked tracks will be ripped and added to the iTunes Library in the Source pane.

When a song has been imported, a green checkmark symbol appears next to the track.

An orange animated wave symbol appears next to a track that is in the process of being imported.

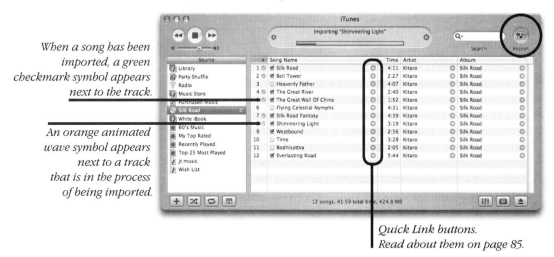

Quick Link buttons.
Read about them on page 85.

Rip multiple music files from a CD as one track

If you want to rip (import) two or more *adjacent* songs from a CD "Song Name" column so they will play as one track without a pause between the songs, use the "Join CD Tracks" command.

1. In the CD "Song Name" column, select the songs you want to join.

2. From the Advanced menu, choose "Join CD Tracks."

The CD "Song Name" column shows that two tracks have been joined for import.

3. Click "Import" in the top-right corner of the iTunes window.

Rip music files to other formats

When you import music from a CD, you may want to **encode a music file to some other file format,** especially if you plan to embed the file in a web page. You can change the Importing preferences so that imported files are encoded in the format you need.

1. From the iTunes menu, choose "Preferences…," then click the "Importing" button.

2. Change the "Import Using…" setting to one of the supported file formats in the pop-up menu.

3. In your Library list, put a checkmark next to the song (or songs) you want to encode. You can Command-click on any checkmark to clear all checkmarks, then make your new selection.

4. Click the "Importing" button in the Preferences window.

A copy of the song appears in the list of songs, identical to the original song listing. To determine which song is the newly formatted one, Control-click on one of the copies and choose "Get Info," then look for the "Kind" info. **Or** set "View Options" to show the "Kind" column (see page 81).

You can also **encode a copy** of a song that's already in your iTunes Library **into another file format.**

1. Set the "Importing" preference to the desired format, as explained above (AIFF, for example). Close the Preferences window.

2. Select a song (or songs) you want to encode to another format.

3. From the "Advanced" menu at the top of your screen, choose "Convert Selection to ____." iTunes changed the format option in this menu to whatever format you chose in Step 1.

If you have a CD with two tracks that have a cool transition between them, the transition might get lost if the songs import as two separate tracks. To keep the transition, use the "Join CD Tracks" command described here.

To convert all songs in a playlist or on a CD, hold down the Option key as you select "Convert selection to ____" from the Advanced menu.

Songs you bought from the iTunes Music Store use a "Protected AAC" format that prevents them from being converted to other formats.

Rate Your Songs

You can **rate songs** on a scale of one to five **stars.** The rating can be used to sort songs, create playlists, or as a criterion in creating Smart Playlists.

1. If the "My Rating" column isn't showing in the iTunes window, Control-click on one of the column heads, then choose "My Rating" from the pop-up menu that appears. **Or** from the Edit menu, choose "View Options…," then click the "My Rating" checkbox.

2. Click on a song you want to rate. Notice that five dots appear in the "My Rating" column.

3. Click on the first dot to add a single star. Click dots further to the right to add more stars to your rating. You can also drag across the dots to add stars.

To sort the current songs by your rating, click the "My Rating" column heading. The order of songs will be rearranged with the highest-rated songs at the top of the list. **To reverse** the order of the list, click the small triangle on the right side of the column heading.

You can also set a song's rating in the song information window (see pages 88–89). Select a song, then press Command I, or from the File menu choose "Get Info." Click the "Options" button, then set "My Rating" between one and five stars.

Export Playlists as Text Files or XML Files

iTunes lets you **export playlists** as text files (.txt) or as XML files (.xml).

Export playlists as text files if you want to archive the song information, or if you want to import the information into another program, such as a database application.

Export as XML if you want to use the playlist in iTunes on another computer. When you import the XML file into iTunes on another computer, iTunes looks in its Library for the songs listed in the imported playlist. Songs that are not in the Library will not show up in the "Song Name" column.

1. Select a playlist, then from the File menu, choose "Export Song List…" or "Export Library…."

2. In the "Save" window that opens, name the exported file, set the "Format" pop-up menu to "Plain Text" or "XML," then choose a location in which to save it.

The procedure above creates a file that includes information for every column in iTunes, even if some columns are not visible in your iTunes window.

To create a text file (.txt) of song information that includes only the columns you have made visible, select one or more songs in the "Song Name" column. Next, from the Edit menu, choose "Copy," then open *another* application such as TextEdit, and paste (from the Edit menu, choose "Paste").

iTunes Preferences

The **iTunes** preferences allow you to adjust a number of settings. From the iTunes application menu, choose "Preferences...."

General preferences

Click the **General** button to see the General preferences.

- ▼ **Source Text** and **Song Text:** Choose "Small" or "Large" text to display in the Source pane and in the "Song Name" column. The actual size difference between "Large" and "Small" is not dramatic, so most users will probably choose to leave these settings on the default choice of "Small."

- ▼ **Show: Party Shuffle** and **Radio:** Select these to make them appear in the Source pane.

- ▼ The **Show genre when browsing** option can be helpful when using the Browse feature (page 73) to search through a large collection of music files—it adds a "Genre" column to the "Artist" and "Album" columns that become visible when you click the "Browse" button.

- ▼ **Group compilations when browsing:** When you select this option it creates an item in the "Artist" column of the Browser (see page 73) named "Compilations" (see page 88). Click on "Compilations" to see a list of albums (in the "Album" column) that contain songs marked as compilations.

A compilation is a collection of songs that you choose to group together.

To make any song part of a compilation, select the song, then press Command-I to open the Song Information window. Click the "Info" button, then click "Part of a compilation."

In the Browser, the song will appear in "Compilations" under its album name.

- ▼ **Show links to Music Store:** This option determines if Quick Links will show in iTunes' Source pane and Detail window. A song's Quick Link provides a shortcut to that song's page on the iTunes Music Store site.

The **On CD Insert** pop-up menu offers options for what happens when you insert a CD. Choose one of these options:

▾ **Show Songs** displays the music titles, artist, and album information, but will not play music until you double-click a song. If you haven't retrieved the CD track names from the Internet, only the CD track numbers and times will show.

▾ **Begin Playing** automatically starts playing a CD when it's inserted.

▾ **Import Songs** automatically begins importing songs and placing them in iTunes' Library when a CD is inserted.

▾ **Import Songs and Eject** does the same thing as above, then automatically ejects the CD.

Connect to Internet when needed enables iTunes to connect to the Internet whenever you insert a CD so it can retrieve song titles and other information from CDDB, an Internet database of CD albums. iTunes will also connect to the Internet when you select "Radio" or "Music Store" in the Source pane. Also, whenever you click a Quick Link button (a white arrow in a gray circle), iTunes connects to the iTunes Music Store. If you have a modem connection instead of a full-time, broadband Internet connection, you may prefer to uncheck this item to avoid having your modem dial up at unwanted times.

If you choose not to check this option, you can manually retrieve CD titles whenever you choose: Connect to the Internet, then from the "Advanced" menu in the upper menu bar, choose "Get CD Track Names."

Check for iTunes updates automatically: This option checks Apple's web site to see if software updates are available for iTunes.

Use iTunes for Internet music playback sets iTunes as your default multi-media audio file player when you download an audio file or click an audio file link on the web.

Effects preferences

Click the **Effects** button to access several nice features.

▼ Check the **Crossfade playback** checkbox to fade music smoothly between songs without a long gap of silence. This effect is one of our favorites. The slider adjusts the amount of time it takes to fade out of one song and to fade in to the next song. Move the slider all the way to the right for the smoothest transition with the least silence between songs.

▼ Check the **Sound Enhancer** box to add depth and liven the quality of the music. The slider increases or decreases the effect, which is subtle but noticeable.

▼ Check the **Sound Check** box to make all songs play at the same volume level.

Leave this box unchecked if you want to vary the volume level of different songs using the volume control in the iTunes window.

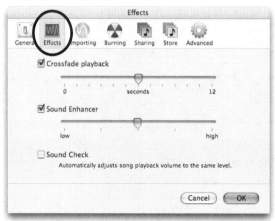

When you burn a CD, these effects do not carry over to the CD.

Importing preferences

Click the **Importing** button to set encoding and configuration preferences.

If you have a version of QuickTime installed that's older than version 6.2, songs are by default imported in the MP3 format instead of the AAC format.

▾ **Import Using** lets you choose which encoder will be used to import music files: AAC Encoder, AIFF Encoder, Apple Lossless Encoder, MP3 Encoder, or WAV Encoder (these file formats are described on page 67). The default setting of AAC is ideal for listening to and storing music on your computer because it combines maximum compression (smaller file sizes) and good sound quality.

▾ **Setting** is a quality setting.

For most users it's best to leave "Setting" on its default settings. If you want to learn all about customizing these configurations, see *The Little iTunes Book,* by Bob LeVitus, available from Peachpit Press.

▾ You can listen to a song as it's being ripped (encoded) by checking the **Play songs while importing** option. Encoding is very fast, usually four to ten times faster than the music plays if you have a newer system. The encoding of a song finishes well before the music has finished playing.

▾ Check **Create file names with track number** to force imported songs to be stored in your Music folder in the same order they appear on the CD.

▾ Check **Use error correction when reading Audio CDs** if you're having problems with CD audio quality. Error correction slows the importing process, but may be helpful.

Burning preferences

Click the **Burning** button to set the speed at which iTunes burns a CD, choose a format for the disc, and determine the amount of time between songs.

▼ **Preferred Speed:** From this menu, set the speed at which your CD burner will burn CDs. The default setting of "Maximum Possible" will let iTunes adjust to the speed of your hardware. If you have problems, try setting "Preferred Speed" to a low number.

▼ **Disc Format:** Choose a disc format for burning CDs.

Audio CD uses the standard CD-DA format common to all commercial CD players. You can store approximately 75 minutes of music on a CD using this format.

Gap Between Songs can be set to your own personal preference. Set the amount of pause you want between songs.

Use Sound Check creates a consistent volume for all songs.

MP3 CD format can store over 12 hours of music, but can only be played on computers and some special consumer CD players. If you want to store MP3 music files on CDs, choose "MP3 CD" for the most efficient storage solution.

Data CD formatted discs include all files in a playlist, but may not work in some players.

You can burn music CDs using either **CD-RW** discs or **CD-R** discs.

CD-RW (CD-ReWritable) discs will play in your computer, but most stereos and commercial CD players don't recognize them.

CD-R (CD-Recordable) discs can play on computers and most CD players.

Discs must be blank to record music on them. You can erase a CD-RW disc and then use it to burn a music CD. A CD-R disc cannot be erased, and it cannot be used if it already has files on it.

Sharing preferences

The **Sharing** pane is where you enable iTunes to share music with others on a local network. Instead of copying music from another computer on your network, you can have it *stream* to you (see page 80).

- ▼ **Look for shared music:** Check this box and your computer will look for other computers on the local network that have music sharing enabled (the next checkbox).

- ▼ **Share my music:** Select this option to make your iTunes Library or any playlist available to others on the network. With this option selected, choose to **Share entire library** or **Share selected playlists.**

  If you choose to share *selected playlists,* put a checkmark next to one or more of your playlists that are shown in the scrolling window pane.

- ▼ **Shared name:** Type a name to identify your shared music collection when it appears in another user's iTunes Source pane.

- ▼ **Require password:** If you want to limit access to your music collection, select this option. Type a password in the text field, then give the password to certain people. When anyone tries to access the shared playlist by clicking the shared playlist icon in their Source pane, they'll be asked for the password.

- ▼ **Status:** This line of text reports how many users on the local network are connected to your shared playlist.

Store preferences

The **Store** preferences pane lets you choose how you want to shop at the iTunes Music Store, along with several other options.

- ▼ **Show iTunes Music Store:** Put a checkmark in this box to show the "Music Store" icon in the Source pane.

  If you uncheck this box, the "Music Store" icon disappears from the Source pane, and all Quick Link buttons disappear from the Source pane and the Detail window.

- ▼ **Buy and download using 1-Click:** If you have an Apple Account, when you click a song's "Buy" button in the Music Store the song is purchased and downloaded immediately. Very easy and convenient.

- ▼ **Buy using a Shopping Cart:** This selection puts a "Shopping Cart" icon in the Source pane, under the "Music Store" icon. All "Buy Now" buttons in the Music Store change to "Add" buttons. When you click a song's "Add" button, the song is added to the shopping cart until you're ready to buy. Then you can click either a "Buy Song" button (to purchase a single song in the shopping cart) or click the "Buy Now" button to purchase all items in the shopping cart.

  A shopping cart is useful for collecting songs you want to consider buying or for reviewing songs that your children have selected.

- ▼ **Play songs after downloading:** If you want a song to automatically play as soon as it's downloaded, click this box.

- ▼ **Load complete preview before playing:** If a slow Internet connection causes the streaming previews in the Music Store to stutter and stop, click this box to ensure a full-quality song preview. iTunes will download the complete preview stream before playing it.

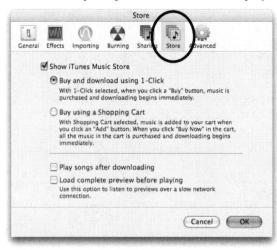

Advanced preferences

The **Advanced** button has settings to designate a location for storing your music files, as well as options for burning CDs.

- ▼ **iTunes Music folder location:** Music files created by iTunes are automatically stored on your startup hard disk. Specifically, they are stored in a folder called "iTunes Music," which is in a folder called "iTunes," which is in your "Music" folder. This folder contains all of the music files you've encoded. You can change this default location to any location you choose. Click the "Change…" button, then navigate to another folder on your hard disk and choose that other folder.

  Every individual user account will have an individual "iTunes" folder inside the home "Music" folder.

- ▼ **Streaming Buffer Size:** Refers to the Radio Tuner and the Music Store preview songs. The buffer size determines how much streaming data is cached (temporarily stored) on your hard disk when you listen to an Internet radio stream or play a preview. The buffer is like padding that compensates for connection problems that would affect the quality of a direct stream. If you've determined that your connection to the Internet is low-quality, change this setting from the default of "Medium" to the "Large" setting. A large buffer gives iTunes more downloaded streaming data to use for compensation as it deals with slow or faulty connections.

- ▼ **Shuffle by:** Shuffle the playing order of songs by *Song* or *Album*.

- ▼ **Keep iTunes Music folder organized:** This places song files into album and artist folders (in the iTunes Music folder), and names the files based on the disc number, track number, and song title.

- ▼ **Copy files to iTunes Music folder when adding to library:** Puts a *copy* of a song in the iTunes folder if you import songs from other locations on your computer. The song remains in its original location. This is similar to the "Consolidate Library" command in the Advanced menu, which puts a copy of all songs in your Library when the original is located somewhere else on your computer.

iTunes Visualizer

This is the "Visual Effects" button.

The **iTunes music visualizer** is mesmerizing. Just double-click a song to play it, click the "Visual Effects" button at the bottom-right corner of the iTunes window, and watch the show. Colors and patterns undulate and morph to the beat of the music that's playing. You can also turn Visuals on by pressing Command T, or by choosing "Turn Visuals On" in the Visuals menu.

Play iTunes' visuals within the iTunes window in three **sizes:** From the Visuals menu, choose Small, Medium, or Large (shown below).

You can also display iTunes' visuals in three different sizes while in **Full Screen** mode: From the Visuals menu, choose "Full Screen" to dedicate your entire screen to the visual effects.

Your previous choice of Small, Medium, or Large will still determine how large the actual visuals appear while in full-screen mode. The Small or Medium option will black out the extra screen space.

Toggle between "Full Screen" and "window view" of Visuals with the keyboard shortcut Command F. When in "Full Screen" mode, click the mouse anywhere on the screen to return to a song list without interrupting the music.

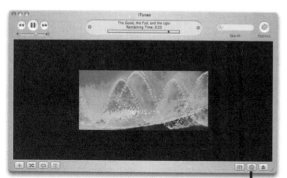

"Small" visual effects.

"Visual Effects" button.

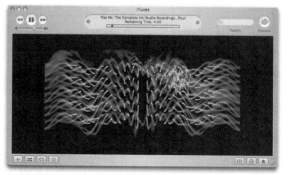

"Medium" visual effects.

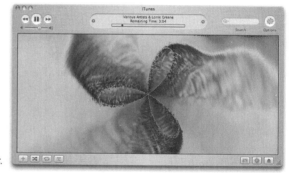

"Large" visual effects.

Visualizer configurations

The **iTunes Visualizer** can be even more fun if you know how to interact with it. The Visual Effects Generator uses three different **configurations** to create visuals. You can see these listed at the top-right of the screen if you press the C key while visual effects are playing. The three configurations listed change randomly and morph into one another as music plays. You can change any, or all, of these configurations while music is playing.

The first configuration in the list affects the **foreground** of the Visualizer, the primary lines and shapes that modulate and interact with the beat of the music more obviously than the other graphics on the screen. Cycle through all the built-in effects for this configuration by alternately pressing the Q and W keys (Q for the previous selection and W for next selection).

Press W to change the primary lines and shapes.

The second configuration in the list affects the **background** graphics, the shapes and patterns that stream from the primary shapes in the top configuration. Cycle through all the built-in effects for this configuration by alternately pressing the A and S keys (A for the previous selection and S for the next selection).

Press S to change the secondary shapes and patterns.

The third configuration in the list affects the **color scheme** applied to the visuals. Cycle through all the built-in effects for this configuration by using the Z and X keys (Z for the previous selection and X for the next selection).

Press X to change the color scheme.

To manually and randomly change configurations at any time, press the R key. Pressing the R key in beat with the music makes you the conductor of an amazing musical light show.

Press R to change everything randomly.

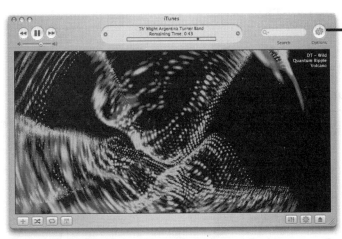

Click this button to set a few options. You can choose to display the animation frame rate, cap the animation frame rate at 30 frames per second, always display the song info, and set a faster display or a better quality display.

Press the C key while visuals are playing to see the current configuration of effects that are generating visuals for iTunes. They're displayed in the upper-right corner of the window, as shown above.

Visualizer modes

Cycle through three different visualizer modes by pressing the M key.

▾ **To play the random visual effects** generated by iTunes, press the M key to cycle to "Random slideshow mode."

▾ **To force iTunes to play the current configuration** until instructed otherwise, press the M key to cycle to "Freezing current config."

▾ **To play only the configurations that have been saved as presets** under the numeric keys, as described below, press the M key to cycle to the "User config slideshow mode."

Save a favorite configuration

When you change an individual configuration (by using the keys mentioned on the previous page), the new effect fades slowly in as the configuration description in the upper-right corner fades out. If you fall in love with an effect, you can save that particular configuration as a preset that can be activated at any time.

To save a favorite configuration as a preset:

1. Press the M key to cycle through the three different options: "Random slideshow mode," "User config slideshow mode," and "Freezing current config."

2. When you get to the "User config slideshow mode," stop. This mode plays configurations that you, the user, have saved as presets.

3. Wait until you see a visual effect you like, then hold the Shift key and tap one of the numeric keys (0 through 9) while the desired effect is playing. You can save up to ten different preset effects.

   Note: To get rid of an old preset, just save a new one over it, using the steps above.

   To play your preset, tap the number key that you assigned to your preset configuration. Try tapping different preset keys to the beat of the music for fantastic visual effects.

Visualizer Help

A separate **Help** file of keyboard shortcuts is available in the Visualizer feature of iTunes. While Visuals are turned on, press the **?** key (or the H key) to show "Basic Visualizer Help," a list of keyboard shortcuts that appears on the left side of the visual display.

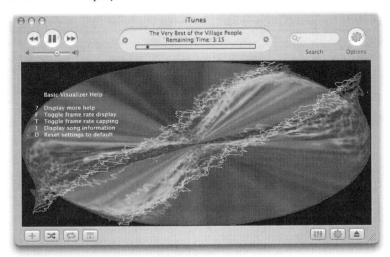

Press the **?** key again (or the H key) to toggle to another list of keyboard shortcuts, "Visualizer Config Help."

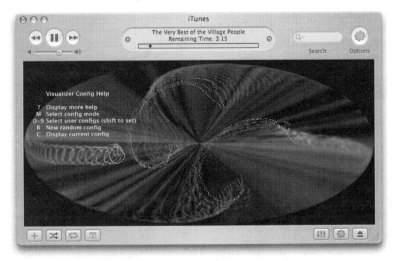

iTunes Equalizer

iTunes provides an **Equalizer** that enables you to make dramatic adjustments to the sound output of your music files. Make adjustments manually or select from over twenty presets. You can even save custom settings as a preset and add it to the preset pop-up menu, as explained below.

An equalizer represents the various frequencies of the sound spectrum, or more specifically, the spectrum of human hearing. The spectrum is expressed as a measurement known as *hertz* (hz).

The iTunes Equalizer represents the frequencies of the spectrum with vertical sliders, also known as **faders.** The faders are used to increase or decrease the volume of each frequency, expressed as *decibels* (dB).

> The lowest frequencies (bass): 32, 64, and 125 hz faders.
>
> The mid-range frequencies: 250 and 500 hz faders.
>
> The highest frequencies (treble): 1K through 16K (kilohertz) faders.

The Equalizer button.

To show the Equalizer, click the Equalizer button at the bottom-right corner of the iTunes window. Check the **On** box to activate the Equalizer.

Choose a preset from the pop-up **menu** to automatically adjust the faders.

The **Preamp** slider on the left side of the Equalizer is a secondary volume adjustment. If a music file was originally recorded too quietly or loudly, adjust the volume here. Or if you're looking for maximum room-booming sound, slide the Preamp up to the top.

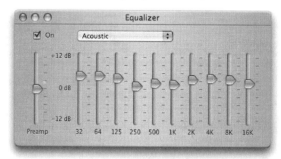

To save your custom settings as a preset:

1. Adjust the faders to your satisfaction.

2. From the pop-up menu (where it says "Acoustic" in the example above), choose "Make Preset...."

3. In the "Make Preset" dialog box, enter a name for your preset, then click OK.

   Your new, custom preset now appears in the pop-up menu.

If you choose, you can **rename equalizer presets** in the pop-up list, or **delete** the presets you don't use.

To edit the preset list:

1. From the pop-up menu in the Equalizer window, choose "Edit List...."

2. In the "Edit Presets" window (shown to the right), click on a preset to select it, then click the "Rename..." button or the "Delete" button.

To apply Equalizer settings to a song, use one of the following methods.

▾ **Either** select a song, then click the "Equalizer" button to open the Equalizer. Select a preset from the pop-up menu, or use the faders to create a custom setting.

▾ **Or** add an Equalizer column to the iTunes Detail window: From the Edit menu, choose "View Options...," check the "Equalizer" box, then click OK. An "Equalizer" column will appear in the Details window, from which you can choose a preset for each song in the list.

▾ **Or** Control-click on a column heading, then choose "Equalizer" from the pop-up menu that appears, as shown below. This adds the "Equalizer" column, from which you can select a preset for a song.

Control-click on a column heading to add an "Equalizer" column from this menu.

Click the pop-up button in the "Equalizer" column to see a contextual menu of equalizer presets.

Experiment with different sound settings by choosing various presets in the Equalizer column.

Robin's iPod

When you transfer your music collection to an iPod, a link is created between the iPod and your iTunes music library. If you connect the same iPod to someone else's computer, you'll get a message that asks if you want to delete everything on the iPod and replace it with the current music library. Probably not.

When you connect an iPod to your Mac, its icon appears in the Source pane.

Connect an iPod

The **iPod** and the **iPod mini** are portable digital music players and are designed to work with iTunes. For information about current models and prices, visit Apple's iPod web site at **www.apple.com/ipod/**.

In addition to storing up to 10,000 songs, the iPod can also act as a hard disk and store any computer files, including thousands of photos. With the proper accessories you can use it as a personal voice recorder. You can also import music that you create in GarageBand (Chapter 5).

iPod supports the most popular music formats: **MP3,** used by most digital music players; **AAC,** the file format used by iTunes and the iTunes Music Store; and **WAV,** a popular Windows format. iTunes encodes music to the AAC format because it creates smaller files while maintaining CD-quality audio.

Transfer songs to an iPod

1. Connect an iPod to your Mac using a FireWire or USB connection. The iPod appears in the iTunes Source pane (shown on the left).

2. Click the "iPod Preferences" button (shown on the opposite page, bottom-right of the iTunes window) to open the iPod Preferences window, shown below.

3. Select how you want to update the iPod—be careful!!

   Automatically update all songs and playlists: iTunes will *automatically* load all the audio files and playlists that you have in iTunes. Next time you connect the iPod, iTunes will **replace whatever is on the iPod with the current iTunes content without asking you.** This will delete songs from the iPod you may want to keep.

   Automatically update selected playlists only: iTunes will *automatically* update the playlists that are checked **and all other music on your iPod will be deleted!** (Also see Step 4.)

   Manually manage songs and playlists: This prevents any automatic actions. With this option selected you *manually* drag playlists or songs to the iPod icon (or its playlists) in the Source pane. **But you must eject the iPod before disconnecting it!**

unread books and unopened music from bn.com can be made for store credit. A gift receipt or exchange receipt serves as proof of purchase only.

Valid photo ID required for all returns, exchanges and to receive and redeem store credit. With a receipt, a full refund in the original form of payment will be issued for new and unread books and unopened music within 30 days from any Barnes & Noble store. Without an original receipt, a store credit will be issued at the lowest selling price. With a receipt, returns of new and unread books and unopened music from bn.com can be made for store credit. A gift receipt or exchange receipt serves as proof of purchase only.

Valid photo ID required for all returns, exchanges and to receive and redeem store credit. With a receipt, a full refund in the original form of payment will be issued for new and unread books and unopened music within 30 days from any Barnes & Noble store. Without an original receipt, a store credit will be issued at the lowest selling price. With a receipt, returns of new and unread books and unopened music from bn.com can be made for store credit. A gift receipt or exchange receipt serves as proof of purchase only.

Valid photo ID required for all returns, exchanges and to receive and redeem store credit. With a receipt, a full refund in the original form of payment will be issued for new and unread books and unopened music within 30 days from any Barnes & Noble store. Without an original receipt, a store credit will

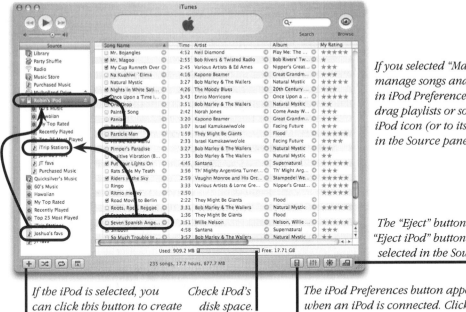

If you selected "Manually manage songs and playlists" in iPod Preferences, you can drag playlists or songs to the iPod icon (or to its playlists) in the Source pane.

The "Eject" button changes to the "Eject iPod" button when iPod is selected in the Source pane.

If the iPod is selected, you can click this button to create a new playlist on the iPod.

Check iPod's disk space.

The iPod Preferences button appears when an iPod is connected. Click it to open the "iPod Preferences" window.

4. Select any or all of these other options:

Open iTunes when attached: Automatically opens iTunes anytime you connect the iPod to your Mac.

Enable disk use: Use the iPod as an external hard disk; its icon will appear on the Desktop. The iPod is now a mounted volume like any other external hard disk *and you must unmount it before you disconnect it or take it out of the cradle!* See the next page for details.

Only update checked songs: This is only available if you have checked one of the automatic update options. Be careful—with this option checked, iTunes will ***instantly replace everything on your iPod*** with ***only*** the songs that are checked in iTunes.

Robin's iPod

An iPod disk icon appears on the Desktop when you choose "Enable disk use" in iPod Preferences.

Create new playlists on the iPod

You can create new playlists on the iPod without having to first create them in iTunes and drag them to the iPod.

1. Select the iPod icon in the Source pane.
2. Click the Plus button in the bottom-left corner of the Source pane.
3. Type a name for the new playlist.

Once you've created the new playlist, you can drag other songs or playlists from iTunes into it. You can even drag other playlists from the iPod into the new playlist.

When the iPod is connected to your Mac and used as a hard disk, its icon appears on the Desktop. The iPod screen blinks with the message "Do not disconnect."

This means you need to unmount the iPod before you disconnect the cable or take it out of its cradle: Control-click on the iPod icon, then choose "Eject iPod" from the contextual menu, as shown above. Or click the Eject button next to the iPod icon in the Source pane of iTunes or in a Finder window.

Use the iPod as an external hard disk

Even the smallest iPod provides a huge amount of storage. Instead of using iPod only for music storage, you can use it to store or transport any kind of computer files.

1. Connect the iPod to your Mac using the provided FireWire or USB cable. If an iPod icon does not appear on the Desktop, follow Steps 2 through 4. If the iPod icon does appear on the Desktop, skip to Step 5.

2. Open iTunes if it's not already open.

3. Select iPod in the Source pane, then double-click the iPod Preferences button on the bottom-right side of the iTunes window.

4. In the "iPod Preferences" window, select "Enable disk use" if it's not already selected.

5. Double-click the iPod icon that's on the Desktop. A Finder window opens that shows the iPod's contents (you will not be able to see your music files, which iPod has hidden from view).

6. Drag a file or folder located anywhere on your computer to the iPod window, as shown below, to copy it to your iPod.

To copy files from the iPod to a computer, drag the selected file or folder from the iPod window to the Desktop, or to any other location on the computer. You can store or transport huge folders of photos, applications, presentations, movies, or any digital files you have room for.

While the iPod is mounted as a hard disk, you can use it as a hard disk and listen to its songs through iTunes and the computer speakers, but you cannot use the iPod menu or hear music through iPod earphones.

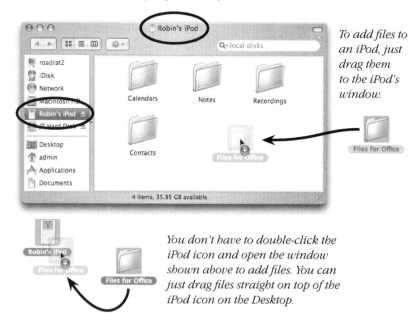

To add files to an iPod, just drag them to the iPod's window.

You don't have to double-click the iPod icon and open the window shown above to add files. You can just drag files straight on top of the iPod icon on the Desktop.

Create an On-The-Go playlist on the iPod

If you're away from your computer and want a new playlist with a different collection of songs, you can create a **temporary playlist directly on the iPod,** without access to your computer or iTunes.

iPod's menu screen.

1. Turn the iPod on. It does not need to be connected to a computer.

2. On the iPod's menu screen choose "Settings," then choose "Main Menu," then select "Playlists," and make sure it is set to "On."

3. Browse the iPod music collection and choose a song or playlist you want to add to the On-The-Go playlist. When the playlist or song shows on the iPod screen, select it. Press and hold the "Select" button (the round spot in the middle of the scroll pad) for two seconds. When you see the playlist or song title flash three times, the song has been added to the On-The-Go playlist.

4. Repeat Step 3 to add additional playlists or songs to the On-The-Go playlist.

To access the new playlist, choose "Playlists" from iPod's screen menu, then scroll to "On-The-Go" and press the Select button. This is an easy way to customize playlists while you're traveling.

The On-The-Go playlist can only contain songs that are already on the iPod. *The playlist is temporary*—the next time you connect the iPod to your computer, the playlist is deleted.

To remove all songs from the On-The-Go playlist, select the playlist on the iPod's screen, then scroll to the bottom of the list of songs and choose "Clear Playlist." Click the "Select" button (the round spot in the center of the scroll pad), then in the next screen confirm your choice (choose "Cancel" or "Clear Playlist").

You will only see the "Clear Playlist" option if you have iPod software 3.0.1 or later.

If you see a playlist called "On-The-Go 1," it probably doesn't have "Clear Playlist" at the bottom. Delete this playlist using iTunes.

Sync calendars and contacts from Mac to iPod

This isn't an iTunes feature, but since we're talking iPod, it's good to know. iPod can sync with the contact information in your Address Book application and with your appointments, events, and To Do list information in iCal. The easiest way to do this is if you have a Mac.com account (see Section 2). If you don't have a Mac.com account, you can sync your calendar and contact information manually, as shown on the next page.

To sync calendars and contacts using iSync (requires a .Mac account):

1. Open iSync. Mac.com members can download iSync from Apple's .Mac web site at **www.mac.com**.

2. From the Devices menu choose "Add Device...." Your iPod should appear in the "Add Device" window, shown below-left. Double-click the iPod icon to add it to iSync. The iPod icon now appears in the "iSync" window toolbar (below-right).

3. Click the iPod icon in the iSync toolbar to show the iPod pane, then choose which contacts and calendars you want to copy to the iPod.

4. Click the "Sync Now" button.

Double-click the iPod icon to add it to iSync's window, shown on the right.

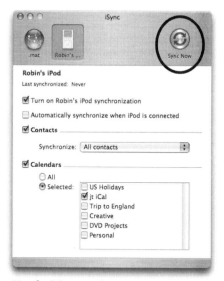

Use the "Contacts" pop-up menu to choose the contacts you want to copy to the iPod. Choose to copy "All" or "Selected" calendars to the iPod.

To manually copy calendars to iPod:

1. Open iCal and select a calendar. From the File menu choose "Export." The file will have a .ics extension.

2. Connect the iPod. Make sure "Enable disk use" is selected in iPod Preferences (click the iPod button at the bottom-right corner of the iTunes window), then double-click the iPod icon on the Desktop to open iPod in a Finder window (as shown below).

3. Drag the exported .ics file to iPod's "Calendars" folder.

4. Unmount the iPod.

To find your calendar on the iPod menu screen, select "Extras" from the screen menu, then scroll the menu to select "Calendars."

For an entire book's worth of detailed iPod information, get *Secrets of the iPod, Third Edition,* by Christopher Breen, published by Peachpit Press.

To keep up with all things iPod, visit *www.iPodLounge.com.*

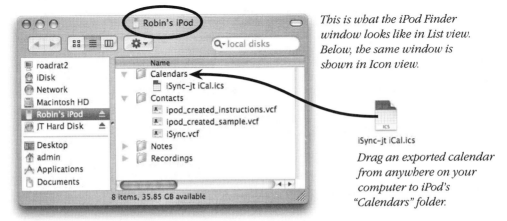

This is what the iPod Finder window looks like in List view. Below, the same window is shown in Icon view.

iSync-jt iCal.ics

Drag an exported calendar from anywhere on your computer to iPod's "Calendars" folder.

To manually copy contacts to iPod:

1. Connect the iPod. Make sure "Enable disk use" is selected in iPod Preferences (see page 114), then double-click the iPod icon on the Desktop to open iPod in a Finder window (as shown on the right).

2. Open Address Book.

3. Select a group from the "Group" pane of your Address Book and drag it to the "Contacts" folder in the iPod Finder window.

4. Unmount the iPod.

To find your contacts on the iPod, select "Extras" from the iPod screen menu, then scroll the menu to select "Contacts."

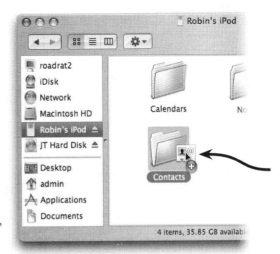

Drag "vcards" (contact information files) from Address Book to iPod's "Contacts" folder.

Menu Commands

The iTunes menu bar contains commands that are covered elsewhere in this chapter as we explain various features. It's usually easier to activate a command by clicking a button than it is to go to the menu bar and select a command. For instance, we never go to the File menu and choose "New Playlist" to create a new playlist. We just click the new playlist button (the plus sign) beneath the Source pane.

Most of the Menu commands have been explained in other parts of this chapter, but there are a few commands that only exist in one of the menu bar items. The following pages list the commands in each menu and give a brief description of each one.

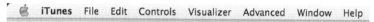

File menu

New Playlist creates a new playlist. See page 63.

New Playlist from Selection creates a new playlist based on the songs you have selected (highlighted) in iTunes.

New Smart Playlist creates a new Smart Playlist. See page 65.

Add to Library... opens a window from which you can choose songs that are stored on your computer, then add them to the iTunes Library. You can add an entire folder of songs all at once. The songs are just referenced by iTunes, not actually copied there, unless you also choose "Consolidate Library" in the Advanced menu.

Import... playlists that you've exported from another computer. An imported playlist will only show songs that are already on your computer or on a connected drive.

Export Song List... so you can have the same playlist on another computer. Select a playlist, then choose this command to make a copy. Copy the exported playlist to another computer, then go to the other computer and from the File menu choose "Import...." Choose "XML" from the "Format" menu. Exported playlists do not export the actual songs, just a list of the songs.

Export Library... saves a copy of all your playlists in XML format. Use the copy as a backup, or copy it to another computer to be imported.

Show Song File opens the folder in the iTunes Music folder that contains the song file whose name you selected in iTunes.

Show Current Song shows the current song (the one that's playing) in the iTunes window.

Burn Playlist to Disc burns a CD of the selected playlist. This is the same as clicking the "Burn Disc" button.

Publish Playlist to Music Store publishes a selected playlist as an iMix on the iTunes Music Store. Learn more about iMix on page 75.

Update Songs on iPod is available if you have an iPod connected and if you've selected one of the *automatic* updating options. See more about iPod on pages 112–117.

Page Setup... opens a normal Print dialog box in which you can choose settings, a printer, paper size, page orientation, and scale.

Print... gives you access to templates for printing CD jewel case inserts, song lists, and album lists.

Edit menu

Show Browser makes the iTunes Browser visible. Choosing this command is the same as clicking the "Browse" button. See more about the Browser on page 73.

Show Artwork makes the Song Artwork pane visible. This command is the same as clicking the Hide/Show Song Artwork button beneath the Source pane. There's more about song artwork on page 90.

View Options... lets you choose which columns of information will show in the Detail window.

Controls menu

Shuffle shuffles songs in a playlist or the Library. In Advanced Preferences, set to shuffle by song or album.

Repeat Off turns off the repeat feature. After a song plays, iTunes moves to the next song in the playlist that has a checkmark next to it.

Repeat On turns on the feature that repeats songs or playlists. When "Repeat On" is selected, the symbol on the Repeat button is blue.

Repeat One limits the repeat to just the song that's selected. When "Repeat One" is selected, the symbol on the Repeat button is blue and includes a small "1" symbol.

Mute turns the sound off. When "Mute" is selected, the little sound waves coming out of the speaker symbols that appear on either side of the volume slider disappear.

Visualizer menu

Turn Visualizer On starts the iTunes visual effects show in the iTunes window. When Visualizer is on, this command changes to "Turn Visualizer Off."

Small, Medium, Large are options for choosing how large the visual effects window will be. These settings affect the size of the display in the iTunes window and also in full-screen mode.

Full Screen displays visual effects full-screen, hiding the iTunes window.

Advanced menu

Open Stream... lets you enter the URL (web address) for an Internet radio station or other webcast. Type the URL in the "Open Stream" text field.

Convert Selection to AAC enables you to select a song and convert it to the file format shown in the menu command (AAC, in this example). The file format is determined by what you choose for "Import Using" in Importing Preferences. Read more about converting files on pages 67 and 101.

Consolidate Library... makes a copy of all songs that are stored in other places on your computer, and puts them in the iTunes Music folder.

Get CD Track Names connects to a CD database and enters the track names of a mounted CD into the iTunes window.

Submit CD Track Names lets you submit song information for a CD if the information is not available on the CD database that iTunes uses. Select a CD, then type Command I (Get Info). Enter the CD's artist, album, and genre information. Select each song on the CD, open Get Info, then enter the song name information. Finally, select the CD again, then from the Advanced menu, choose "Submit CD Track Names."

Join CD Tracks imports two adjacent CD tracks as one. See page 95.

Deauthorize Computer... disables the computer for buying music from the Music Store or for playing purchased music. To buy music from iTunes Music Store, you must authorize the computer you order from. You can deauthorize a computer to prevent others from using your Apple Account to buy music. Also, iTunes permits up to five computers to play purchased songs. If you want to use a particular computer to play purchased songs, but you've already authorized five computers, you can deauthorize one of them. Remember to deauthorize your computer before you sell it or give it away.

Check for Purchased Music checks to see if you have any purchased music that has not been downloaded yet.

Convert ID3 tags corrects the information in the Song Information window when it shows incorrectly. An ID3 tag is a song's information tag (the same information you find in a song's Get Info window). If a song's title and information are garbled, it was created by a program that stores information in a different way from iTunes. Select the problem songs, then choose this command. Songs play correctly even if the ID3 tags are wrong.

Window menu

Minimize sends the iTunes window to the Dock to get it out of the way, but does not interrupt the music.

Zoom replaces the large iTunes window with a tiny, space-saving window.

Bring All to Front brings all iTunes windows to the front. This could be useful if you have lots and lots of windows open.

Help menu

iTunes and Music Store Help contains lots of information and tips about iTunes and iTunes Music Store.

Music Store Customer Service connects to Apple's customer service site where there's lots of information about Music Store features.

iPod Help offers tips for iPods, plus a link to the iPod support web site.

Keyboard Shortcuts shows a complete list of keyboard shortcuts for iTunes.

Favorite Keyboard Shortcuts

These are the **iTunes keyboard shortcuts** that you'll have the most fun with:

Command 1	toggles between Show Player and Hide Player
Command T	toggles Visuals on and off
Command F	toggles full-screen mode on and off
DownArrow	turns the volume down
UpArrow	turns the volume up
LeftArrow	first tap selects the beginning of the current song; second tap selects the previous song
RightArrow	selects the next song
Option Command DownArrow	mutes the sound
Spacebar	toggles between Pause and Play
R	instantly changes Visualizer to a new random set of visual effects

Other keyboard shortcuts:

Command N	creates a new playlist
Shift Command N	creates a new playlist from the *highlighted* songs (*not* the songs that are checked)
Command A	selects all songs in the current song list
Shift Command A	deselects all songs in the current song list
Command R	shows current song file in the Finder
Command E	ejects a CD
Command M	minimizes Player window to the Dock
Command ?	launches iTunes Help
Command Q	quits iTunes
M	cycles through Visualizer modes
N	toggles between Normal and High Contrast colors
D	resets Visualizer to the default settings
I	displays song information
F	toggles Frame Rate Display on and off
B	displays the Apple logo briefly when Visuals are turned on

iMovie

3

Making movies is incredibly fun and easy with **iMovie.** Connect a digital video camera to your computer with a FireWire cable, launch iMovie, and you're ready to create home movies with soundtracks, transitions between scenes, special effects, and customized titles.

If you didn't get a **FireWire cable** with your camera, check the box your Mac came in—often there is a FireWire cable in it. If you don't have a cable, buy one at your local electronics store or order it from one of the many dealers online (searching for "firewire cables").

Digital video (DV) requires a lot of disk space—one minute of DV footage uses about 220 MB of hard disk space. A four-minute iMovie that contains soundtracks, transitions, and titles may use 4 to 6 *gigabytes* of disk space.

This is the icon that indicates a FireWire port.

If you're serious about making iMovies or if you just can't control yourself after making your first iMovie, buy an extra, very large hard disk to use when working with video. You'll be surprised how fast you can fill a dedicated 80 GB disk when you start making movies.

In this chapter

The Basic Steps

Making an iMovie consists of **five basic steps.** This chapter will walk you through each step.

1. Import video clips or still photos to the Clips pane (pages 125–127).

2. Edit the clips (pages 128–132).

3. Place edited clips into the movie Timeline (pages 133–135).

4. Add transitions, titles, effects, audio, and chapter markers (pages 137–150).

5. Export the iMovie (pages 152–159).

As you shoot video, keep in mind that every time you start and stop the camera, iMovie will interpret that as a "clip." Each clip will appear in its own little slot in the "Clips pane." You can then rearrange the order, edit each scene individually, and much more. Clips can be short or long. You can split a clip, cut a segment out of one clip and make it a separate clip, etc. iMovie makes every step of the process easy and fun.

Import Video Clips

Before you can **import,** you must connect the camera to the Mac.

To connect your camera:

1. With the camera **turned off,** plug one end of the FireWire cable into the camera and the other end into the Mac's FireWire port.

2. Switch your camera to "VTR" (Video Tape Recorder) or "Play," *not* "Record."

3. Open iMovie, if it's not already open.

4. **Turn on** the camera. In a couple of seconds, the Monitor area of iMovie will display the words "Camera Connected," as shown below.

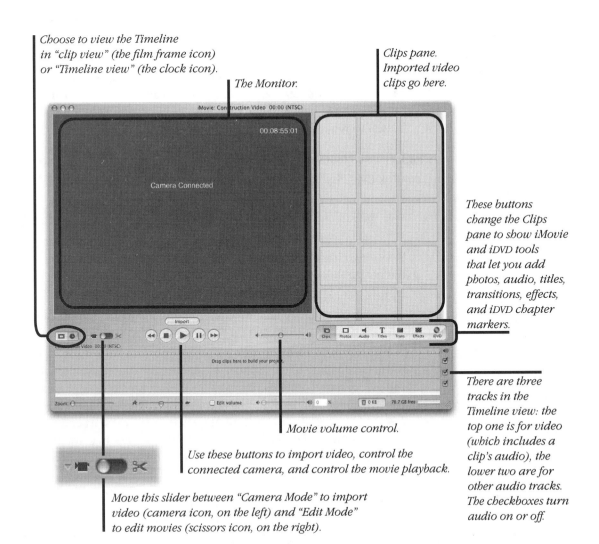

Choose to view the Timeline in "clip view" (the film frame icon) or "Timeline view" (the clock icon).

The Monitor.

Clips pane. Imported video clips go here.

These buttons change the Clips pane to show iMovie and iDVD tools that let you add photos, audio, titles, transitions, effects, and iDVD chapter markers.

There are three tracks in the Timeline view: the top one is for video (which includes a clip's audio), the lower two are for other audio tracks. The checkboxes turn audio on or off.

Movie volume control.

Use these buttons to import video, control the connected camera, and control the movie playback.

Move this slider between "Camera Mode" to import video (camera icon, on the left) and "Edit Mode" to edit movies (scissors icon, on the right).

To create a new iMovie project:

1. From the File menu in iMovie, choose "New Project…."

2. In the "Save As" dialog box that opens, name your project.

3. Choose the location where you want it saved. Be sure to pick a drive or partition that has plenty of unused disk space! We have several external FireWire drives that we use just for our movie projects.

4. Click the "Save" button.

To preview the raw footage:

Tip: Don't forget to rewind the tape in your camera before you try to preview it. If the iMovie Monitor shows only a blue screen, you're probably looking at unrecorded tape that comes after your last recorded scene.

1. In the iMovie interface, click the "Camera Mode" button, as shown up close on the previous page.

2. Then click the "Play" button (the big triangle) to play the video in the iMovie Monitor.

    At this point you are just *previewing* the video. iMovie does not digitize and import any video until you click the "Import" button. **To economize disk space,** preview your footage, then rewind and import just the best footage. Use the controls below the "Import" button to rewind, pause, play, stop, and fast-forward.

To import video footage into iMovie:

1. Click the "Play" button to view the raw footage.

2. When you see footage you want to import, click the "Import" button (see the call-out on the opposite page). The "Import" button is blue when it is selected and importing files.

    You can go backwards while in Play mode (click the Reverse arrows), but not while importing.

3. To stop importing, click the "Import" button again. Each time you start and stop importing, iMovie will place that segment, called a "clip," into a separate slot in the Clips pane at the upper-right corner of the iMovie window.

    If you have plenty of disk space, you can let the camera run. iMovie will detect scene changes (by analyzing differences in color and contrast), import the individual scenes as separate clips, and place each one in the Clips pane. Typically, every time you start and stop the camera while filming creates enough differences in color and contrast that iMovie can recognize these shifts as scene changes and will create separate clips.

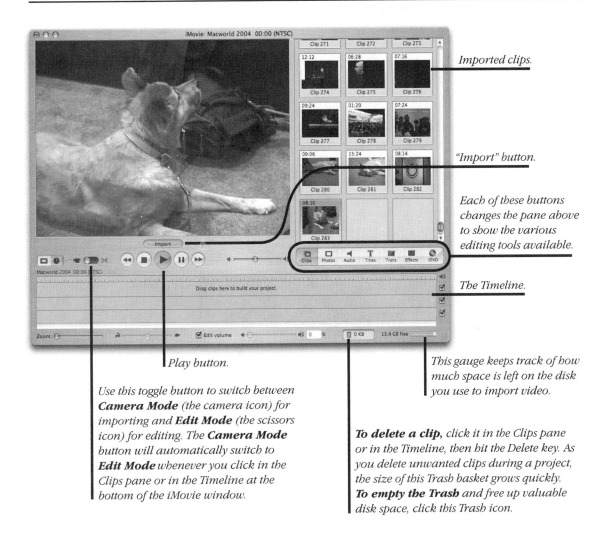

Imported clips.

"Import" button.

Each of these buttons changes the pane above to show the various editing tools available.

The Timeline.

Play button.

Use this toggle button to switch between **Camera Mode** *(the camera icon) for importing and* **Edit Mode** *(the scissors icon) for editing. The* **Camera Mode** *button will automatically switch to* **Edit Mode** *whenever you click in the Clips pane or in the Timeline at the bottom of the iMovie window.*

This gauge keeps track of how much space is left on the disk you use to import video.

To delete a clip, click it in the Clips pane or in the Timeline, then hit the Delete key. As you delete unwanted clips during a project, the size of this Trash basket grows quickly. *To empty the Trash and free up valuable disk space, click this Trash icon.*

To capture live video with a video camera:

You can import live video (without first recording it to tape) into iMovie with any compatible digital video camera, even an iSight camera.

1. Plug the **camera's** FireWire cable into your computer.
2. **Set the video camera** to "Camera" or "Record" (not "VTR" or "Play").
3. **Set iMovie** to Camera Mode" (shown to the right).
4. Click the "Import" button in **iMovie.**

If you're using an iSight camera, first go to iChat's "Video" preferences, disable the option to "Automatically open iChat when camera is turned on," then turn iChat off. The "Import" button changes to "Record with iSight."

In iMovie, move the button to the left for Camera Mode. Click the camera icon to choose from a list of recently connected cameras.

Edit the Video Clips

Clips often contain more footage than you want to use in your movie. You can preview a clip and select just the portion of it that you want to keep.

To display and preview a clip:

1. Single-click a clip in the Clips pane to select it. The clip is displayed in the Monitor area. A blue "scrubber bar" appears, as shown below on the left side. The scrubber bar represents the time length of the clip.

2. Preview the entire clip by dragging the playhead (the large white triangle, circled below) across the scrubber bar, **or** click the Play button.

Click on a clip to display it in the Monitor.

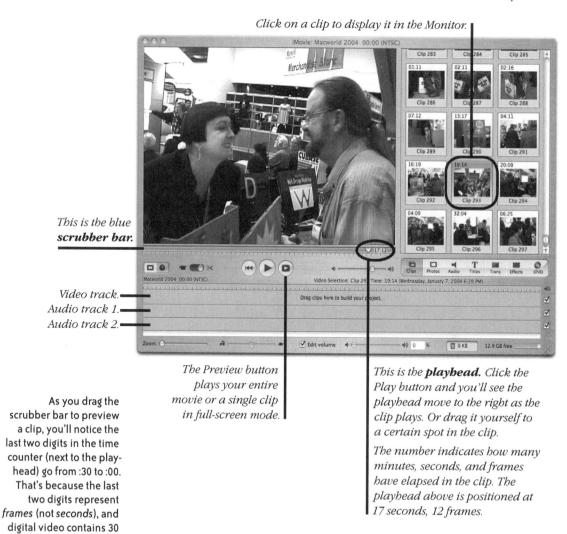

This is the blue scrubber bar.

Video track.
Audio track 1.
Audio track 2.

As you drag the scrubber bar to preview a clip, you'll notice the last two digits in the time counter (next to the playhead) go from :30 to :00. That's because the last two digits represent *frames* (not *seconds*), and digital video contains 30 frames per second.

The Preview button plays your entire movie or a single clip in full-screen mode.

*This is the **playhead.** Click the Play button and you'll see the playhead move to the right as the clip plays. Or drag it yourself to a certain spot in the clip.*

The number indicates how many minutes, seconds, and frames have elapsed in the clip. The playhead above is positioned at 17 seconds, 12 frames.

Many **clips** are longer than necessary and should be **trimmed** or **cropped.**

▼ **Trim:** Select and delete *unwanted* video frames either at the beginning or the end of a clip.

▼ **Crop:** Delete all frames in a clip *other than* the selected frames.

To trim a clip:

1. Beneath the scrubber bar, locate the "crop markers," two small triangles (they appear when your mouse gets close to the bottom of the scrubber bar). Drag the crop markers (shown below) to select the segment of a clip that you *want to delete.*

2. From the Edit menu, choose "Clear" to delete all of the selected frames, **or** press the Delete key.

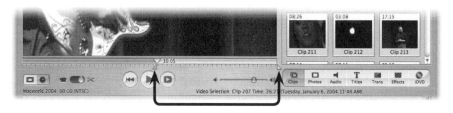

To crop a clip:

1. Drag the crop markers to select a range of frames in the clip that you *want to keep.* The selected frames are highlighted in yellow.

2. From the Edit menu, choose "Crop" to delete all of the frames that were *not* selected.

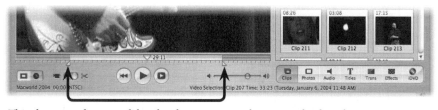

This shows a selection of the clip that is going to be cropped. After choosing "Crop" from the Edit menu, this section is all that will remain of the clip.

After you edit a clip, you're going to drag the clip from the Clips pane to the **Timeline** at the bottom of the iMovie window (as explained on the following pages and on page 134) so you can put your movie together.

Tip: When you crop or trim a clip in the Clips pane, the deleted data goes in the Trash, located just below the pane. Once a clip is in the Trash, you can't take it out.

Because even a moderate amount of editing results in a huge amount of Trash, you can preserve disk space if you click on the Trash icon occasionally to empty it.

Tip: When you crop and trim clips as described above, *you eliminate the possibility of ever going back later to use segments of clips that you deleted.* You might want to keep the original, unedited footage available and accessible. In that case, **copy and paste** a clip segment, as explained on the following page.

Editing is very much a trial-and-error activity. For that reason, we like to keep the original imported clips in the Clips pane, then **copy** segments of clips (in the Monitor) and **paste** them into the Timeline (instead of dragging the clips straight from the Clips pane to the Timeline). This makes it possible to go back to the original, unaltered clips in the Clips pane at any time to access any footage that was deleted.

To copy and paste a clip:

1. Use the crop markers to select a range of frames that you want to add to your movie's Timeline.
2. Press Command C to copy the selection.
3. Click in the Timeline at the bottom of the iMovie window.
4. Press Command V to paste the selection into the Timeline. It will be pasted wherever the playhead is positioned.

   If there are already other clips in the movie track, you can place the copied selection wherever you want: Click on an existing clip in the movie track to select it. Press Command V (Paste) and your selection will be pasted *to the right* of the clip you clicked on.

To use the Monitor to trim or crop a clip that's already in the Timeline:

After you've made a "rough cut" of your movie, you often want to fine-tune the duration of clips that are in the Timeline to sync with the beat of an imported soundtrack, or just to change the pacing of the movie.

1. Click on a single clip in the Timeline to show it in the Monitor.
2. Use the crop markers beneath the Monitor's scrubber bar to select a range of frames in the clip.
3. If you want to *crop* the clip (delete everything in the clip *except* the selected frames), go to the Edit menu and choose "Crop." The clip in the Timeline shortens to show the new selection.
4. If you want to *trim* the clip (delete the *selected* frames), use the crop markers beneath the scrubber bar to make a selection of frames, then press Delete.

   If at any time you want to recover parts of the original clip, it is still in the Clips pane, unharmed. This is called non-destructive editing.

Select a clip in the Timeline, then use the Monitor's crop markers to select a range of video frames in that clip. The selection is highlighted in the scrubber bar and in the Timeline.

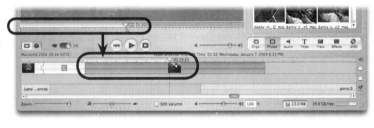

To trim clips directly in the Timeline:

Another *easy* way to trim (shorten) a clip is to do it directly in the Timeline by dragging an edge of the clip.

When you position your pointer over the *right edge* of a clip, the pointer turns into an arrow that indicates which direction you can drag the edge. If the arrow points left, it means you can drag left to shorten the video clip. If the arrow points left *and* right, it means the video clip was previously trimmed and you can recover the trimmed frames by dragging right.

When you position your pointer over the *left edge* of a clip, the pointer turns into an arrow pointing right, meaning you can shorten the clip by dragging the edge to the right. If the arrow also points *left,* there are hidden frames of video to the left that you can recover by dragging the clip's edge to the left.

As you hover over a clip in the Timeline Viewer, a small information tag appears to identify the clip. It disappears after about 10 seconds, or as soon as you move the pointer away from the clip.

You can shorten this clip by dragging its right edge.

*You can shorten **or** lengthen this clip, as indicated by the double-facing arrow.*

Notice that complete clips (clips that haven't been trimmed or cropped) have **rounded edges** in the Timeline. When you trim frames from one or both edges, the clip corners become **square** instead of rounded.

This is a close-up of clips in the Timeline. The shapes of the corners tell you if there are trimmed frames available in case you want to lengthen a clip.

Recover footage from a cropped or trimmed clip

Depending on how you placed a clip in the Timeline and whether or not you've emptied the Trash, you may be able to recover footage that has been trimmed.

- ▼ When you drag a video clip straight from the Clips pane to the Timeline, then click on the clip in the Timeline, the clip is displayed in the Monitor. If you trim or crop the clip in the Monitor, the trimmed/cropped data is put in the Trash. Before you empty the Trash, you can recover the data by dragging the edge of the trimmed clip in the Timeline to reveal the trimmed footage. Once you've emptied the Trash (by clicking the Trash icon), that data cannot be recovered.

- ▼ When you click a video clip in the Clips pane, the clip is displayed in the Monitor. If you trim or crop the clip in the Monitor, the trimmed/cropped data is put in the Trash. You can recover the data by dragging an edge of the trimmed clip in the Timeline *if* you haven't emptied the Trash.

- ▼ If you select a clip in the Timeline, you can use the crop markers under the scrubber bar to *select* (highlight in yellow) a section of the video clip, then *copy* the selection and *paste* it into the Timeline. This method makes all footage recoverable because the original clip is left unaltered in the Clips pane. This method of placing video in the Timeline also allows you to drag the edge of a clip to recover trimmed or cropped frames.

- ▼ You can also recover trimmed or cropped frames from a video clip in the Clips pane or in the Timeline if you Control-click on the clip, then from the pop-up contextual menu choose "Restore Clip."

Notice the edges of the clips: Complete clips (untrimmed and uncropped) in the Timeline have round-cornered edges. When frames have been trimmed or cropped from one or both sides of a clip, the trimmed/cropped edge of that clip has square corners. See the illustration on the previous page.

Keep track of your trash

The Trash icon at the bottom of the iMovie window tells you how much data you've deleted from your project. You may want to leave the data there in case you need to recover some of it later. Empty the Trash to make more disk space available for your project.

Place Clips in a Movie

There are two editing views available for the Timeline: the **Clip Viewer** (click the film frame icon, shown below) and the **Timeline Viewer** (click the clock icon, shown below). If you place a clip in either the Timeline Viewer or the Clip Viewer, it automatically appears in the other area. To switch between the two views, click one of the two icons.

Click this icon to show the Clip Viewer.

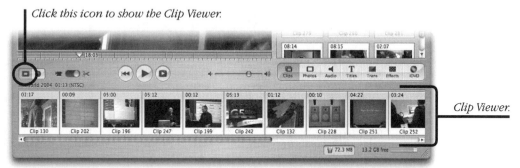

Clip Viewer.

This Timeline view (Clip Viewer) gives a large view of clips, lets you rearrange the order of clips by dragging them, and also allows you to drag clips from the Timeline back to the Clips pane.

Click this icon to show the Timeline Viewer.

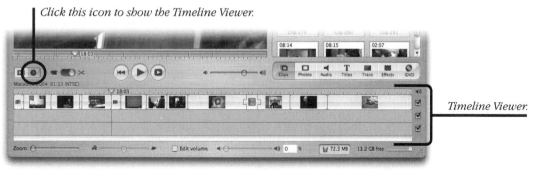

Timeline Viewer.

This Timeline view (Timeline Viewer) shows the video and audio tracks. In this view you can add audio tracks, edit the duration of audio and video clips, adjust the volume of clips, or use the checkboxes on the right side of the Timeline to mute the audio of an entire track.

—continued

The Timeline

Use the **Timeline** to arrange the order of clips, add transitions between clips, add effects, create titles, and add audio to your movie.

To add clips to the Timeline:

- ▼ **Either** drag the clips you imported from the Clips pane to the Timeline.

- ▼ **Or** as explained on the previous pages, copy segments of clips and paste them into the Timeline.

To rearrange clips in the Timeline:

1. Click on a clip in the Timeline to select it.

2. Press Command X to delete it from its current position in the Timeline.

3. Select a clip (click on it) in the Timeline immediately to the left of where you want the new clip.

4. Press Command V to paste the clip to the right of the selected clip. **Or** place the playhead where you want to paste the clip, then press Command V.

   If the playhead is in the middle of an existing clip, the new clip will split the existing clip. If the playhead is in a blank space between two clips, the clip to the right will be nudged over as much as necessary to accommodate the pasted clip.

*The **Zoom** slider shows the Timeline at different levels of magnification.*

A low zoom level makes more clips visible in the Timeline.

A higher zoom level makes it easier to precisely place the playhead or to drag a soundtrack to a certain position. When you use clips of very short duration, you need a higher zoom level to see them clearly.

The Clip Viewer

You can also use the **Clip Viewer,** shown below, to place and rearrange clips, add transitions and effects, and create titles. You cannot work with soundtracks while using the Clip Viewer, but unlike in the Timeline, you *can* drag clips out of the movie and back to the Clips pane.

To show the Clip Viewer, click the film frame icon.

To place clips in a movie using the Clip Viewer, either drag clips from the Clips pane to the Clip Viewer, **or** use the copy-and-paste technique explained on page 130.

To rearrange clips in the Clip Viewer, simply drag a clip to a new location.

This clip is 15 seconds, 24 frames long. The duration of each clip is shown at the top of the clip in a 00:00:00 format— minutes:seconds:frames.

This is the Clip Viewer.

To rename clips here in the Clip Viewer, or in the Clips pane, just click on the clip number to highlight the text, then type the name.

Render clips

When you add titles or transitions to a movie or add effects to clips, iMovie automatically "renders" or builds them so you can preview your additions. The progress of the rendering shows as a red render bar moving across the bottom edge of a clip or transition.

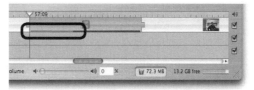

In the Clip Viewer: *The red progress bar shows an effect being rendered.*

The checkerboard symbol at the top of the clip indicates that an effect is applied to the clip.

In the Timeline: *The red progress bar shows a transition's render progress.*

Tip: **To stop a render in progress,** press Command Period.

Other effects, such as slow motion and reverse direction clips, also need to be rendered, but that rendering is delayed until you export the movie.

Preview the Assembled Clips

To preview your movie, move the playhead (the white triangle, circled below) in the Timeline to the beginning of the movie or wherever you choose, then click the Play button.

Notice that if you click on a specific *clip* in the Timeline, only that clip shows and plays in the Monitor. **To load the entire movie** into the Monitor, click anywhere in the Timeline *except* on a clip (click in the Timeline above the clips or in one of the audio tracks).

*When the Monitor displays the entire movie, the **scrubber bar** is divided into segments. Each segment is a separate clip in the movie.*

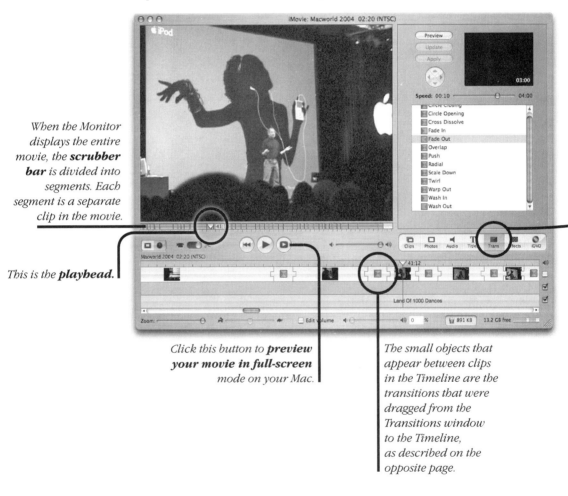

*This is the **playhead**.*

*Click this button to **preview your movie in full-screen** mode on your Mac.*

The small objects that appear between clips in the Timeline are the transitions that were dragged from the Transitions window to the Timeline, as described on the opposite page.

Add Transitions, Titles, Effects, and Audio

If your movie requires precise synchronization between music tracks and video footage, it's best to assemble all your clips in the Timeline before adding transitions because some transitions can alter clip lengths. For some movies, this may not be an issue.

Transitions

A **transition** is a visual effect that creates a bridge from one scene to the next scene. It might be a cross-dissolve, a fade-out, a spinning image, or any of a wide variety of other effects.

To add a transition effect between two clips:

1. Click the "Trans" button to reveal the Transitions pane, shown below.

2. To preview the effect in the small preview window, click on a transition. To play the effect full-size in the Monitor, click the "Preview" button.

3. Use the "Speed" slider to determine the time duration of the transition in seconds and frames (00:00).

4. Drag the selected transition to the Timeline or Clip Viewer and drop it between two clips of your choosing.

   To delete a transition at any time: Click on the transition icon in the Timeline, then hit the Delete key.

Tip: A limited number of transitions come with iMovie, but you can download others from the Apple web site at **www.apple.com/imovie,** or buy collections of transitions and effects from third-party vendors that are listed on the Apple website.

To change a placed transition:
Select it in the Timeline, make changes in the Transitions pane, then click "Update."

Cross Dissolve vs. Overlap:
The Cross Dissolve transition smoothly dissolves from one scene to another, retaining full motion of the first scene until it dissolves away.

The Overlap effect freezes on the last frame in a scene as it dissolves into the next scene.

Use the direction control to set the direction of some transitions, such as "Push."

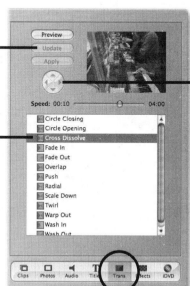

Add titles to your movie

A **title** is text that you place in its own frame or on top of a clip. A title can show credits, act as a caption, or add comments. There are many styles of titles to choose from and you can use different typefaces, sizes, and colors.

To add titles to your movie:

1. Select a clip in the Timeline (click once on it). The clip you select will show in the thumbnail window when you click on a title style.

2. Click the "Titles" button to reveal the Titles pane, then select a title style.

3. Type your title text into the text fields at the bottom of the window.

4. Use the font pop-up menu to select a font.

5. Use the font slider to enlarge or reduce the type.

6. Click the "Color" box to choose a font color from a palette.

To modify an existing title, change any of the settings, then click the "Update" button.

Show a large preview in the Monitor.

Some title styles let you set a direction.

Set the speed of the title effect and how long the title will pause on the screen. These setting options vary according to the title style chosen.

Click a triangle to show multiple variations of a title style.

Font menu.

Font size slider.

Type your title here. Different title styles give you different amounts of space for text.

Click a title style in the list to show a small preview here. This preview uses the currently selected clip in the Timeline.

Choose your title style here. When finished with your title, drag this same line down to the Timeline.

Font color.

Uncheck "Over black" to superimpose the title over a clip.

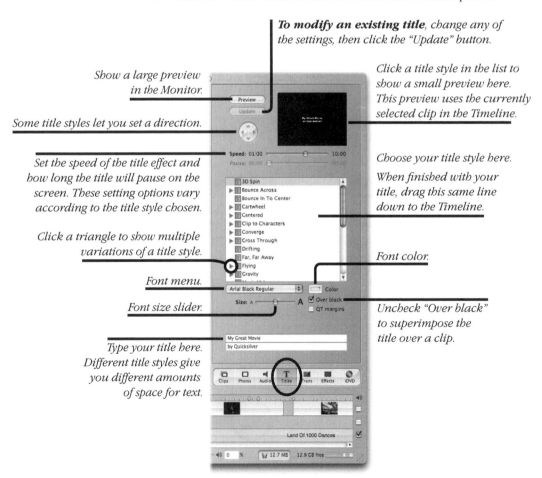

7. By default, a title is superimposed over a video clip. If you want to superimpose a title over a black background instead of a clip, check the "Over black" box in the Titles pane. This option creates new frames for the title sequence and does not affect other clips. It does, however, add to the length of your movie.

8. If you plan to export the movie as a QuickTime file, check the "QT margins" box to allow the title to expand within the limitations of the QuickTime margins.

If you plan to burn a DVD and show it on a television, make sure this button is *not* selected or your type may be cut off on the edges, or leave it unchecked all the time to play it safe for any media.

9. Drag your selected title style from the list of styles to the desired position in the Timeline: on top of a clip if you want to superimpose the title over video; adjacent to a clip if you want the title to be against a black background.

To delete or update a title:

▼ If the title is a separate clip "over black," select the title clip, then press Delete.

▼ If the title is superimposed over another clip, select the clip (created when you dragged the title effect to the Timeline), then press Delete.

▼ You can select a title in the Timeline, then change its settings in the Titles pane. After you adjust the settings, click the "Update" button.

Use bookmarks to mark key frames

Place **bookmarks** to mark key frames in the Timeline where you want to sync an audio track with a video clip, or where you want to trim or place a clip. Press Command B to place a Bookmark at the playhead position, **or** from the Bookmarks menu, choose "Add Bookmark."

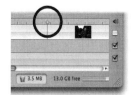

Bookmarks appear as green diamonds in the Timeline.

Try this: Place an audio track in the Timeline, then play the track. As the music plays, press Command B at the downbeat of the music. Then edit the length of video clips so they start and stop at Bookmarks. Preview the movie and watch the scenes change to the beat of the music. Music video!

To delete one Bookmark, position the playhead on top of it. From the Bookmarks menu, choose "Delete Bookmark."

To delete all bookmarks, go to the Bookmarks menu and choose "Delete all Bookmarks."

Place Still Photos in the Timeline

There are several ways to place photos in iMovie. The easiest and most convenient method is to **click the "Photos" button.** The Photos pane replaces the current pane to the right of the Monitor and shows the tools you'll use for selecting photos, setting a duration, and adding motion to photos.

The Photos pane is divided into the "Ken Burns Effect" section (see the next page) and the "Photo Library" section. The Photo Library section contains all the photos that are currently stored in iPhoto. From the pop-up menu you can select any iPhoto album you've created, and the scrolling pane will display only the photos in that album.

1. Click on a photo to select it, or Command-click on multiple photos.
2. Turn the Ken Burns Effect on (or off).
3. Click the "Apply" button. The photo is placed in the Timeline to the right of existing clips.

You can also **drag photos from the Photos pane** to the Timeline. The current Ken Burns Effect settings (such as duration) will be applied to the photo.

Another method for placing photos in the Timeline is to simply **drag a photo from any location** on your computer straight to the Timeline. The current Ken Burns Effect settings will be applied to the photo.

You can also **import photos into iMovie,** as explained on the next page.

Tip: **To change the duration** of a photo in the Timeline:

Drag the photo's edge left or right in the Timeline.

Or double-click a photo to open the "Clip Info" window, then type a duration in the "Duration" field, using a format of "seconds:frames."

(If you applied the Ken Burns Effect to the photo, you must use the Ken Burns Effect settings to alter the photo duration.)

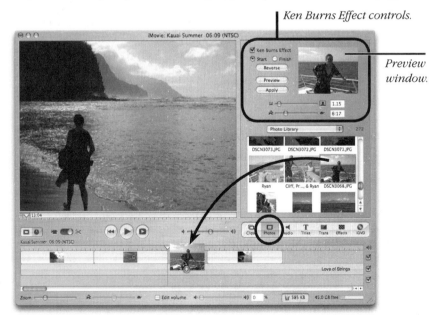

Ken Burns Effect controls.

Preview window.

One way to place a photo in a movie is to drag it to the Timeline from the Photos pane.

Import still photos

You may want to use photos in your movie that are not in iPhoto. Perhaps you have a collection of scans in some other folder, or a CD of photos from someone else. You *could* import those photos into iPhoto to make them accessible from the iMovie Photos pane, but you don't have to. You can, instead, import them from wherever they're stored.

To import from a CD or from any location on your computer:

1. From the File menu, choose "Import…."

2. In the sheet that drops down from the iMovie title bar, locate a photo or a folder of photos that you want to import. Select a single photo, or multiple photos, then click the "Open" button.

The imported photo is placed in the Clips pane (not the Photos pane). The photo's duration is automatically set to the duration setting in the Ken Burns Effect pane. If the Ken Burns Effect was turned on *before* you imported the photo, the *effect* will also be applied to the imported photo.

Pan and Zoom Still Photos

Click the "Photos" button in the button bar to show the "Ken Burns Effect" pane. Ken Burns is a documentary filmmaker who popularized the technique of slowly panning across still photos and zooming in or out to achieve visually interesting and dramatic effects.

To apply a Ken Burns effect to a still photo:

1. From the pop-up menu in the Photos pane, choose your iPhoto Library or any iPhoto album to display.

2. Click a photo in the Photos pane to show it in the small Preview window above.

3. Click the "Start" button, then set a time length for the effect with the Duration slider (the bottom slider).

4. In the Preview window, drag the photo to any position you like, then adjust the Zoom slider (the top slider) to set the zoom level for the start of the effect.

5. Click the "Finish" button, then adjust the Zoom slider to set the zoom level for the effect's finish. To reposition the final position of the image, drag the image in the Preview window.

6. Click "Preview" to see the effect full-size in the Monitor, **or** click the thumbnail image in the Photos pane to it in the small Preview pane.

7. Click the "Apply" button to apply the effect to the photo and automatically place it in the Timeline at the current playhead position.

Tip: After you set the "Start" settings for a Ken Burns effect, you can Option-click the "Finish" button to automatically apply the same settings to the end of the effect.

With the "Finish" button still selected, Shift-drag the thumbnail image left or right, up or down. This makes it easy to create a perfectly aligned and smooth horizontal or vertical pan.

Effects

An **effect** is a visual distortion or alteration that is applied to a clip. The effect may be used for aesthetic reasons or for visual impact. A limited number of effects come with iMovie, but many more are available from third-party vendors.

To add effects to a clip in your movie:

1. Single-click a clip in the Timeline to select it.

2. Click the "Effects" button to show the Effects pane.

3. Select an effect from the Effects list.

4. Use the "Effect In" and "Effect Out" sliders to set the amount of time it takes for the effect to fade in and to fade out.

5. If there are other settings sliders below the Effects list, set those as well. Some effects have more adjustment options available than others.

6. When you're satisfied with the effect, click the "Apply" button.

Click the "Preview" button to preview the effect full-size in the Monitor. Click the effect name in the Effects pane to see a preview in the small Preview pane. Click the "Apply" button to apply the effect to the selected clip.

Tip: If you want to apply an effect to just part of a clip, split the clip into sections, then apply an effect to just one section. Position the playhead where you want to split the clip, then from the Edit menu, choose "Split Video Clip at Playhead." See page 162.

To remove an effect after it has been applied to a clip, select the clip in the Timeline and hit the Delete key.

Show a large preview in the Monitor.

Click an Effects style in the list to show a small preview here. This preview uses the currently selected clip in the Timeline.

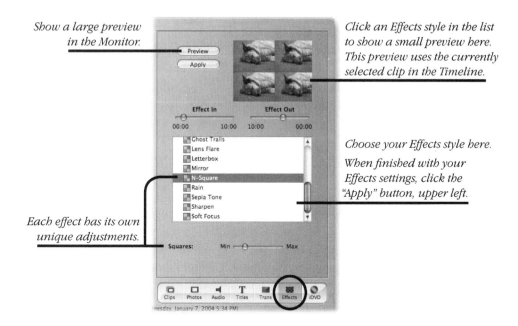

Choose your Effects style here.

When finished with your Effects settings, click the "Apply" button, upper left.

Each effect has its own unique adjustments.

Some effects, such as Electricity (shown below) and Fairy Dust, let you grab the effect in the thumbnail preview window and drag it to a new position.

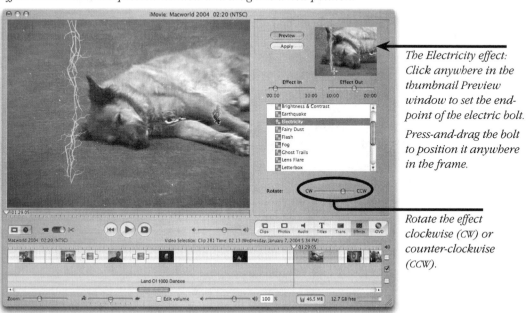

The Electricity effect: Click anywhere in the thumbnail Preview window to set the end-point of the electric bolt.

Press-and-drag the bolt to position it anywhere in the frame.

Rotate the effect clockwise (CW) or counter-clockwise (CCW).

Audio

Audio *editing* is critically important to the perceived professionalism of your movie. When you video a scene, the background noise often is distracting or even unbearable. Editing enables you to lower or mute the volume of problem clips and add a background music track or a narrative voice-over. Even if the existing audio is fine, you can enhance the aesthetic and emotional impact of your movie just by having fun with additional soundtracks and narration clips. If you're making an instructional video, narrative voice-overs can add clarity and comprehension to your project.

Place as many **audio clips** in iMovie's two soundtracks as you need. You can drag imported audio clips to any position on the current audio track in the Timeline. You can also drag audio clips from track 1 to the second audio track, track 2. Audio clips can overlap on the same track or in separate tracks. When two audio clips in two different audio tracks overlap, both are audible. The advanced audio-editing features of iMovie allow you to adjust and control the volume in overlapping tracks.

For instance, you can lower the volume of a background music clip while someone in a video clip is talking. Or you can fade-out the audio of a video clip as you raise the volume of a background soundtrack. The volume of each individual audio and video clip is editable. In fact, you can make multiple volume adjustments to a single clip. See "Advanced audio editing" on pages 148–149 to learn more about adjusting the volume of audio and video clips.

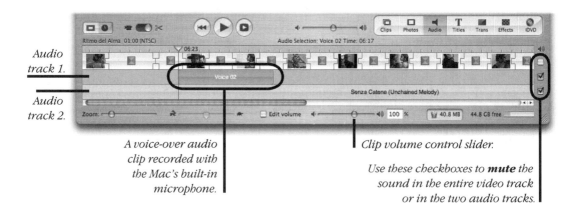

Audio track 1.

Audio track 2.

A voice-over audio clip recorded with the Mac's built-in microphone.

Clip volume control slider.

Use these checkboxes to **mute** the sound in the entire video track or in the two audio tracks.

To add audio files to your movie:

1. Click the "Audio" button to reveal the Audio pane.

2. Position the playhead (the white triangle) in the Timeline where you want the audio clip to start.

3. The Audio pane's pop-up menu lets you choose a source location from which to select an audio file: Choose the iTunes Library (or any iTunes playlist), iMovie Sound Effects, or a CD that is inserted in your CD drive (shown below). The source you select is displayed in the scrolling Audio pane.

4. Click on an audio clip in the Audio pane list to highlight it.

5. Click the "Place at Playhead" button to place the audio clip in the Timeline. **Or** drag a clip from the list of audio files to any position in the Timeline.

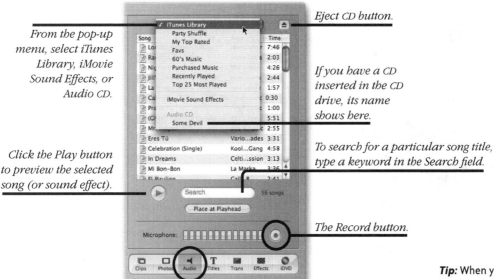

From the pop-up menu, select iTunes Library, iMovie Sound Effects, or Audio CD.

Eject CD button.

If you have a CD inserted in the CD drive, its name shows here.

Click the Play button to preview the selected song (or sound effect).

To search for a particular song title, type a keyword in the Search field.

The Record button.

To record a narration clip:

Narrative voice-overs are a great way to add interest to your movie. If your computer has a built-in microphone or if you've connected an external mic, click the Record button to begin recording your voice; the button's outer ring is red when recording. Click the button again to stop recording. (If the Record button is grey, you don't have a microphone.)

The voice clip automatically appears in the Timeline when you start talking, starting at the current playhead position. After you finish recording, you can move the audio clip to any position in the Timeline.

Tip: When you use the computer's built-in microphone to record a narrative voice-over, the sound quality may not be acceptable to you. Try recording the narrative with your video camera, speaking straight into the video camera microphone. Then import that video clip into iMovie, place it in the Timeline, extract the audio (as explained on page 149), and delete the video clip.

To import an audio track from your computer:

You can import MP3, AIFF, AAC, or WAV sound files.

You may have audio files in various formats that are stored on your computer but not in iTunes, therefore not accessible from the Audio pane. You can import audio files from anywhere on your computer straight into a Timeline audio track.

1. From the File menu, choose "Import File…."

2. In the Finder sheet that drops down from iMovie's title bar, locate an audio file that is stored on your computer, select it, then click "Open." The entire audio file is placed in one of the audio tracks in the Timeline.

    If some of your MP3 file names are gray, it means you can't use them in the movie because iMovie can only import MP3s that support the QuickTime format.

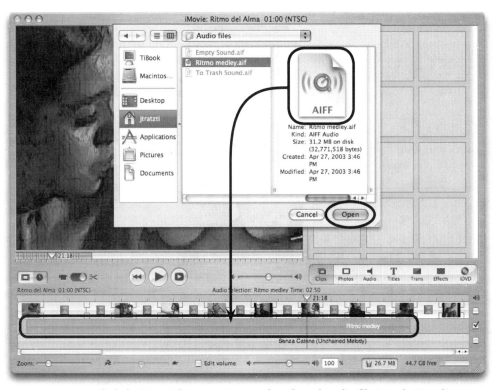

Click the "Open" button to import the selected audio file into the Timeline.

To review and import a CD soundtrack:

You can drag a song from the list to any position in the Timeline, **or** follow these steps:

1. Insert a CD into your CD drive.

2. Select the CD from the pop-up menu at the top of the Audio Track pane. The CD's title is listed under the "Audio CD" heading, shown to the right. The CD songs display in the Audio pane.

3. **To review** CD tracks *without* importing them, click on a song, then click the Play button (circled on the right).

4. **To import** a song, select a song from the list (click on it once).

5. In the Timeline, move the playhead (the white triangle) to the point you want the song to start.

6. Click the "Place at Playhead" button.

The CD title appears in the Audio pane's pop-up menu, above.

Adjust and edit the audio clips

To adjust the position of an imported audio file in the Timeline, drag the entire clip left or right.

To crop the start and stop points of an audio clip, drag either edge of the audio clip toward the center of the clip. When you hover your pointer over a clip edge, it turns into a double-arrow icon, as shown below. **To fine-tune the cropping** of an audio clip, select it, then use the left and right arrow keys on your keyboard. Single-click an arrow key to crop the audio clip one frame at a time. Shift-click an arrow key to crop ten frames at a time. **To recover cropped audio,** just drag (or arrow-click) the clip edge outward (away from the center).

You can **drag** an audio clip from one audio track to another. This helps keep clips organized and accessible when you need to overlap audio files, such as a music track and a sound effect (as shown on the next page).

As with video clips, cropped audio clips have square corners on an edge that has been cropped. Audio clips have round corners on uncropped edges.

Shorten an audio clip's duration by dragging one or both clip edges towards the center of the clip.

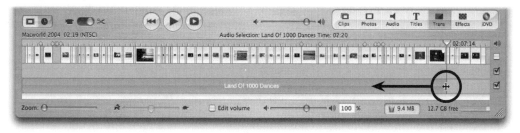

Advanced audio editing

iMovie 4's **advanced audio-editing features** are similar to those used in Final Cut Pro and other professional-level editing software. This feature gives you control over the placement and the duration of audio fade-ins and fade-outs. It enables you to easily create professional effects, such as lowering the volume of a background music track while a voice-over narrates the video, then lowering the video clip volume so the background music is emphasized. Very cool stuff. And easy.

1. Click the "Edit Volume" checkbox (circled below). A volume-level line appears in every audio and video clip.

2. **To adjust the volume of an entire clip** (audio or video), select the clip, then move the clip volume control slider left or right. In the example below, the audio clip in the bottom track is selected and the volume control slider is set to 40% of the original volume. The volume slider will only affect clips (audio or video) that are *selected* (highlighted).

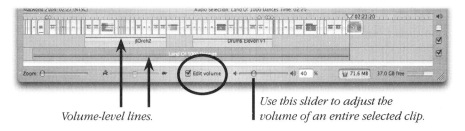

Volume-level lines.

Use this slider to adjust the volume of an entire selected clip.

3. **To adjust the volume of multiple clips,** select two or more clips, then move the clip volume control slider left or right to adjust the volume of all selected clips at once.

4. **To set various volumes in a single clip,** or to create gradual changes of volume in a clip, click on the volume-level line.

   A *volume marker* appears on the volume-level line. When the marker is *selected,* it is slightly larger and *yellow.* When it's *not selected,* it's *purple.* **Drag markers up or down** to raise or lower the volume. The percentage number next to the clip volume control slider changes as you drag. Create as many markers on the volume-level line as necessary to create the changes in volume you want.

When you manually drag the playhead through a clip in the Monitor or through the Timeline, it's called "scrubbing."

5. **To hear audio as you scrub through your movie,** hold down the Option key as you drag the playhead in the Timeline. The faster (or slower) you drag, the more distorted the sound is. This can be useful for locating a specific section of music or dialog.

When you click or drag a volume marker, a purple square appears to the left, marking the start point of volume change. The yellow marker marks the end point of volume change. Grab the purple square and move it *away* from the yellow marker to increase the duration of the volume change, making it more gradual. **Or** move it *closer* to the yellow marker to make the volume transition happen faster. In the example below, the volume of the video clip on the left is lowered as the volume of the soundtrack is increased.

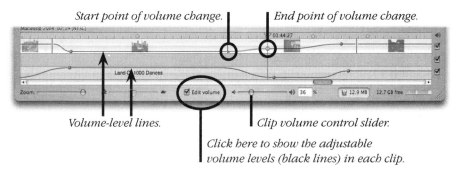

Start point of volume change. ‖ ‖ *End point of volume change.*

Volume-level lines. *Clip volume control slider.*

Click here to show the adjustable volume levels (black lines) in each clip.

In the example below, two audio clips are sharing the same track. The short volume line represents a short clip of music ("Ritmo medley") underneath a longer audio clip ("Unchained Melody"). Since they are both audible, we adjusted the volume of the "Unchained Melody" clip to zero and left the other clip to play. We usually would drag the shorter clip to the upper audio track to avoid confusion, but it works this way too.

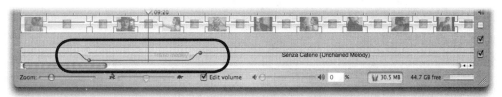

When you drag an audio clip on top of another audio clip, both clips are audible.

To extract audio from a video clip: You might want to use the audio from a video clip—*without* the video. Select a clip in the Clip Viewer or in the Timeline Viewer. From the "Advanced" menu, choose "Extract Audio." The extracted audio is automatically placed in audio track 1 (the top audio track in the Timeline). The audio remains in the source clip but is muted. You can delete the video clip and use just the audio clip.

To restore the clip's audio, select the clip, click "Edit Volume," then adjust the volume control slider to the desired volume. A volume setting of 100% restores the volume to its original state.

Create Chapter Markers in a Movie

One of the best ways to share movies is to burn them onto a DVD. And one of the biggest advantages of DVD is the ability to jump to predesignated markers in a movie, called "chapters."

Chapter markers you create in iMovie are automatically exported with your movie when you create an iDVD project (see the next page). See Chapter 4 to learn about the amazing iDVD application.

To add chapter markers:

Tip: To avoid the possibility of losing chapter markers, apply effects to video clips *before* you add chapter markers to your movie.

1. Open an iMovie project that is completed.

2. Click the "iDVD" button in the iMovie toolbar to show the iDVD Chapter Markers pane.

3. Move the playhead in the Timeline to a position where you want to place a chapter marker.

4. Click the "Add Chapter" button in the Chapter Markers panel. A thumbnail image for the chapter appears in the iDVD pane.

5. Replace the clip name with a meaningful chapter name.

   Later you can choose to let iDVD use these chapter names when automatically creating menus and submenus for imported movies.

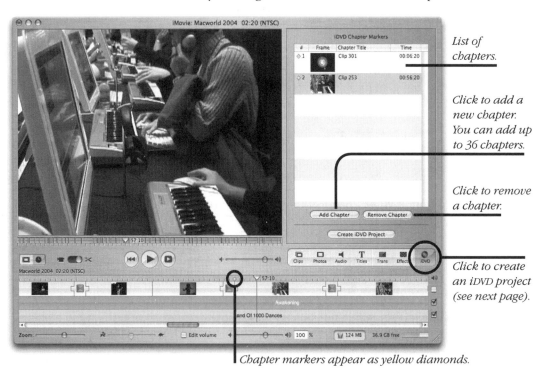

List of chapters.

Click to add a new chapter. You can add up to 36 chapters.

Click to remove a chapter.

Click to create an iDVD project (see next page).

Chapter markers appear as yellow diamonds.

Create an iDVD Project

After you edit a movie, iDVD can immediately transform it into an iDVD project in which menus and submenus are created automatically. An iDVD window opens, ready for you to customize the DVD design and burn the movie (or several movies) onto a blank DVD.

This is a really quick way to create a DVD project. You can add additional content to the DVD project after it opens, such as other movies, slideshows, and DVD-ROM content. **See Chapter 4 for details.**

To create an iDVD Project:

1. Open an iMovie project that is finished.

2. Click the "iDVD" button in the pane area to open the iDVD pane.

3. Click the "Create iDVD Project" button.

   You may get a message asking if you want to render certain clips. Click "Render and Proceed." After iMovie renders the necessary clips, iDVD launches.

4. In the iDVD window that opens, choose a design theme and customize the design if you choose. iDVD automatically creates a main menu with two links: **Play Movie** plays the movie from the start and recognizes chapter markers; **Scene Selection** links to a submenu in which each chapter marker is a link.

iDVD automatically builds a main menu ("Macworld 2004," below-left), and a submenu ("Scenes 1-7," below-right) that contains links to the chapters you created in iMovie (previous page). You can change themes, add additional movies or slideshows, and do all sorts of other customization to your iDVD project.

iDVD named each scene by the chapter name we assigned in iMovie. We forgot to rename clip 301 in iMovie, but all of this text is editable and can be changed at any time.

Tip: If you aren't ready to create a DVD project, but you want to **prepare your movie for iDVD,** export the movie as "Full Quality DV." See pages 152 and 159.

Later, when you open a DVD project, you can import the DV file into iDVD.

Share a Movie

Once you've finished creating your movie, you can store it on your hard drive, but that uses a lot of disk space, and the only place you can show it is on your computer. Since iMovies are usually large, from several gigabytes on up, you can't pass them around on a Zip disk or even on a CD. To **share** your movie with others, you need to export the movie in a format that *can* be shared. iMovie is able to export movies in a variety of formats, depending on its final intended use.

To share your movie:

1. From the File menu, choose "Share…."

2. A sheet drops down from iMovie's title bar to provide six ways to share a movie: Email, HomePage, Videocamera, iDVD, QuickTime, and Bluetooth. Click one of the icons at the top of the sheet to show the options available for that category. The sheet for each category you choose provides options for that category and a description of the file that will be exported.

The sharing options shown below change according to which icon you select at the top of this drop-down sheet.

Email: Send a small movie to someone through email. iMovie will compress the movie to 10 frames per second (digital video is usually 30 frames per second) and 160 x 120 pixels with monaural sound (not stereo). Even a short and highly compressed movie makes a large file, so don't send long movies through email unless absolutely necessary.

1. In iMovie, from the File menu, choose "Share...."

2. From the "Send email using" pop-up menu, choose the email program you use: America Online, Eudora, Mail, or Microsoft Entourage. If one or more of these options is grayed-out, it means iMovie cannot find them on your computer.

3. Type a name for the exported movie in the "Name of saved movie" text field.

4. Click the "Share" button. The chosen email application opens with the exported movie attached to a new message form.

5. Type a message, address the email, then click "Send."

Instead of emailing an entire movie to someone, select just a few clips in the iMovie Timeline, then in the Email sharing sheet click "Share selected clips only." iMovie will export a movie from only the selected clips.

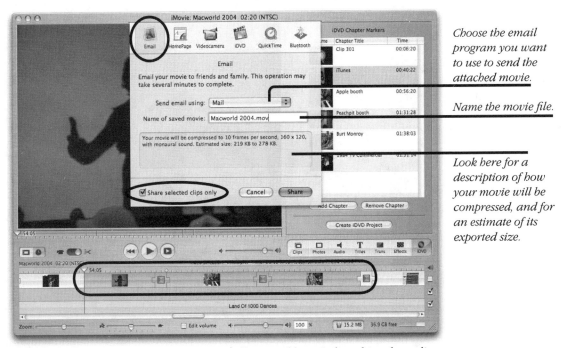

Choose the email program you want to use to send the attached movie.

Name the movie file.

Look here for a description of how your movie will be compressed, and for an estimate of its exported size.

To make the exported movie's file size as small as possible, we selected just three clips in the Timeline, then checked the "Share selected clips only" checkbox in the Email Sharing sheet.

HomePage: If you have a .Mac account, you can share your movie by uploading it to your iDisk and publishing it on the Internet through HomePage. See Chapter 8 to learn all about HomePage.

iMovie automatically compresses the movie into a format necessary to play on a QuickTime Streaming Server, the type of server that's used with your .Mac account and HomePage. After compression, iMovie moves the exported movie file to the "Movie" folder on your iDisk.

1. In iMovie, from the File menu, choose "Share…."

2. Type the name you want to use for your exported movie. Don't change the extension (.mov).

3. If you want to conserve storage space on your iDisk, select several clips in the Timeline, then choose "Share selected clips only." Instead of exporting the entire movie to your iDisk, iMovie will export only the selected clips.

4. If your iDisk is almost full, click the "Buy More Space" button to log in to your .Mac account and purchase more iDisk storage space.

5. Click the "Share" button.

This is a description of how the file will be compressed, plus an estimate of the exported file size.

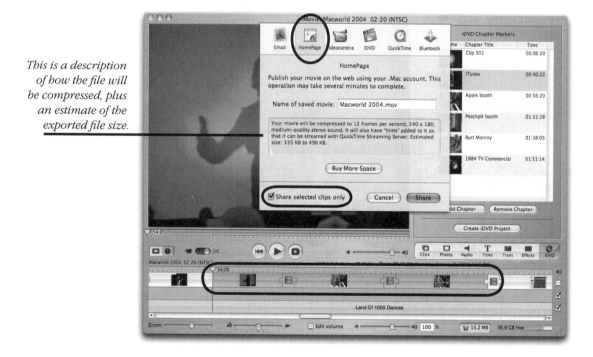

6. Next, the .Mac login page opens in your web browser. Enter your name and password.

7. A .Mac HomePage window opens as shown below. Choose one of the movie page themes from the templates provided to open an *editable* HomePage movie page (below, bottom-right).

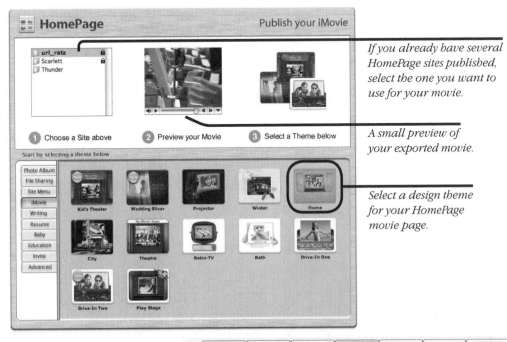

If you already have several HomePage sites published, select the one you want to use for your movie.

A small preview of your exported movie.

Select a design theme for your HomePage movie page.

8. Edit the movie page (shown on the right) by customizing the text in the text fields, then click the "Preview" button to preview the page. If you're satisfied with how the page looks, click the "Publish" button.

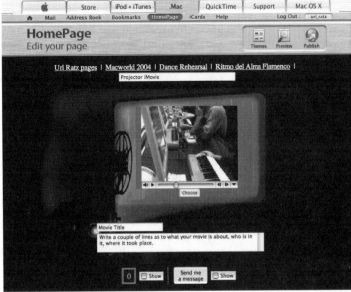

Video camera: An easy way to share a movie with others is to copy the edited movie onto a tape in your video camera. You can then connect the camera to a TV or digital projector to show it. Or you can send the tape to a friend, relative, or associate.

1. Put a *blank* video tape in the camera. (Or make sure the tape is positioned at a point where you will not record over other footage.)

2. Connect the camera to your computer with a FireWire cable.

3. Put the camera in VTR or Play mode.

4. In iMovie, from the File menu, choose "Share...."

5. In the "Video camera" sheet (shown below), set how many seconds for the camera to get ready, how many seconds of black appear before the movie, and how many seconds of black appear at the end of the movie.

6. Click the "Share" button.

You can choose to export only selected scenes to a video camera.

Your edited movie is copied to the digital video tape in your camera. The tape in your camera can usually store from 60 to 90 minutes of movies. You can not only attach your camera to a TV or projector to show your edited movies, you can also copy movies from your camera to a VHS tape. If your movie contains scenes that are in slow motion or reversed, iMovie will tell you that it needs to render those scenes before it can export the movie.

iDVD: This sharing option opens your movie in iDVD, ready for any customization you may want to add (see Chapter 4). iDVD is amazing software for putting a collection of movies, slideshows, and DVD-ROM content onto a DVD disc that will play on your computer (if you have a supported DVD drive) and will also play on most commercial DVD players.

Sharing through iDVD opens iDVD and automatically creates a main DVD menu and submenus based on chapter markers that you placed in the movie. If some scenes in your movie need to be rendered because they use a motion effect such as slow motion, iMovie alerts you that it needs to render those scenes before you can open the movie.

Click the "Share" button to open your edited movie in iDVD. Your movie is now part of an iDVD project and is saved in your Documents folder as "your-project-name.dvdproj."

Tip: This export option immediately starts a DVD project by opening your movie in iDVD.

If you want to import your movie into a DVD project later, export the movie as "Full Quality DV," as explained on pages 158–159, then import the full-quality DV file into an iDVD project when you're ready.

Learn more about iDVD on page 151 and in Chapter 4.

QuickTime: QuickTime format is a popular standard for multimedia files. QuickTime compresses movies so that their sizes are manageable for transport and delivery, either on the web or other media.

QuickTime provides several compression options, depending on how the movie is to be shared. From the "Compress movie for" pop-up menu, select one of these compression options:

▼ **Email:** This compression option is suitable for sending a small movie to someone through email. It compresses your movie to 10 frames per second, sized to 160 x 120 pixels, with monaural sound (one channel, not stereo). If your movie is very long, even this highly compressed format will produce a file that's too large for email. A 10-second QuickTime movie with the above setting is around 200 kilobytes. To keep movie size as small as possible, you can select several clips from the Timeline, then choose "Share selected clips only" in the drop-down sheet (circled below).

▼ **Web:** This option creates a QuickTime movie file that is a typical web page size—12 frames per second, 240 x 180 pixels, with medium-quality stereo sound.

▼ **Web Streaming:** Choose this compression setting to create a QuickTime file that uses the same settings as the "Web" option, but also includes "hints" to the file that enable web streaming.

Web streaming movies do not have to wait for the entire movie to download to your computer before they can play. In fact, streaming movies don't download to your computer at all. Instead, the movie starts playing after a buffer of data is received by your computer, and continues to play until the stream of data ends.

Streaming movies can be streamed with QuickTime Streaming Servers, such as .Mac's HomePage.

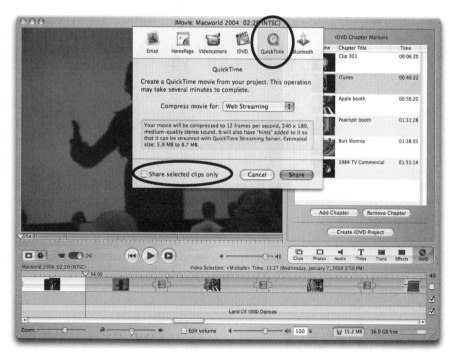

▼ **CD-ROM:** This option compresses your movie to half of full quality—15 frames per second, 320 x 240 pixels, and full-quality stereo sound—ideal for copying to another computer or to a CD. The final file size is approximately twice that created by "Web" or "Web Streaming" compression.

▼ **Full Quality DV:** Choose this compression option to save a QuickTime movie that is full quality—30 frames per second, 640 x 480 pixels, and full-quality stereo. This is the format used by iDVD to make a DVD. The final file size is many times larger than the files created with the other compression schemes listed here. A *10-second* test file compressed as "Web" weighed in at 500 kilobytes—and 32.4 megabytes when compressed as "Full Quality DV."

▼ **Expert Settings:** If you've upgraded your QuickTime software to QuickTime Pro, you can use *custom* export settings that you've set in QuickTime. QuickTime Pro enables you to edit, save, import, and export multimedia files using a large selection of file formats. You can upgrade at **www.apple.com/quicktime/upgrade** for $29.99.

Bluetooth: If you want to send a QuickTime movie to a Bluetooth-enabled device, such as a PDA or cell phone, choose this option to create a file that is low-quality but very small in file size, making it suitable to copy across the very limited bandwidth provided by Bluetooth devices.

When you export a movie using the Share options of "Email," "HomePage," or "iDVD," a copy of the file is put in a "Shared Movies" folder that iMovie creates in your movie project folder.

If you use the Share option of "Video camera," a copy is made to a tape in the camera, not to a folder on your computer.

If you use the Share option of "QuickTime," you choose a location in which to save the file.

iMovie Preferences

Check the iMovie Preferences to see if there are any options you want to change. From the iMovie application menu, choose "Preferences…" to open the "Preferences" window.

General

Display:

Display short time codes: Abbreviates the time code of 00:00:00:00 (hours:minutes:seconds:frames) to show only the necessary data (for example, 32:12 instead of 00:00:32:12).

Play sound when export completed: A sound alerts you that your movie has finished the export procedure.

Automatically start new clip at scene break: During the import process, iMovie interprets major changes of color and contrast as scene breaks. Since these noticeable changes of color and contrast usually happen when you start recording, a separate clip is automatically created during import for every time you started and stopped the video camera. Uncheck this option if you want video from your camera to import as one continuous clip (until you click the "Import" button to manually stop the import).

Show locked audio only when selected: Choose to always show locked audio clips in the Timeline (as explained on page 165), or just when a locked audio clip is selected.

Timeline:

Show audio track waveforms: Show a graphic representation of the audio in audio tracks, as shown on page 164. Waveforms can help visually align audio accents or spikes with key frames in video clips.

Keep playhead centered during playback: This option is meant to keep the playhead stationary and centered in the Timeline during playback, as movie clips scroll by. This option is disabled unless you're using a G5 computer.

Enable Timeline snapping: As you move the playhead, Timeline snapping makes the playhead snap to the edges of video and audio clips, chapter markers, bookmarks, silent areas in audio tracks, and the previous position of the playhead. A yellow snap line appears under the playhead when it snaps to an item in the Timeline. Snapping helps to precisely align audio and video.

Play snap sounds: This option adds a sound effect when the playhead snaps to an item.

Advanced

New clips go to:
Choose to place new imported clips in the **Clips Pane** or directly in the **Movie Timeline.**

New projects are:
Select a video format for your project. **NTSC** is the standard format for North America, **PAL** is the standard in Europe.

Playback quality:
These quality settings affect only the computer playback quality, *not* the quality of the final exported movie.

Choose **High quality** for a better image. Macs with a G4 or G5 processor use this setting as a default. If your playback is jumpy or uneven, try the "Standard quality" setting.

Standard quality is the default setting for Macs with a G3 processor.

Enhanced video playback greatly improves playback quality on a computer screen by reducing interlacing artifacts (the jagged edges that are visible in interlaced video).

Other settings:

Extract audio in paste over:
Extracts the audio in a new video clip that you use to "paste over" an existing video clip. See page 164.

Filter audio from camera: Filters out *some* noises that may happen during the import process. If you hear beeps or strange noises while importing video, make sure this option is selected.

Play video through to camera:
Allows you to play a movie simultaneously in iMovie and in your camera. Connect your camera to a TV Monitor to see how your movie will look on a TV as compared to your computer screen.

Advanced Tips

Here are a few more tips that you can use to make your movies even more fun and professional.

Split video clips at the playhead position

If you want to apply an effect to just part of a video clip, *split* the video into segments, then apply the effect to one of the segments.

1. Position the playhead over a video clip where you want to start the effect, then from the Edit menu choose "Split Video Clip at Playhead." **Or** use the keyboard shortcut Command T. A vertical dividing line appears on the clip under the playhead.

2. Move the playhead to the position in the clip where you want the effect to end, then press Command T again. Another vertical line appears in this position, dividing the clip into three segments.

3. Select the center segment, then apply any effect you want.

You can also create interesting effects by splitting video clips into multiple segments, then adding transitions between the segments.

Create a still frame

You can make a still frame (a static image) from any single frame of video in your movie. Use the still frame as a background for a title, just for visual effect, or to simulate a slideshow effect. One of our favorite techniques is to create a still frame of the last frame of a clip, then place the still frame after the clip, creating a freeze frame effect for the end of the clip. You can set the duration of the still frame to whatever length you want.

1. Select a clip in the Clips pane or in the Timeline.

2. Position the playhead so the frame you want is showing in the Monitor.

3. From the Edit menu, choose "Create Still Frame." The still image is placed in the Clips pane.

4. Drag the new still frame to a position in the Timeline.

The default duration for a still frame is five seconds. **To change the duration,** double-click the still frame clip. In the "Clip Info" window that opens, type in a new duration.

Save a single frame in another format

Occasionally you'll find that you need a copy of a single frame that you can email to someone or use as a photo in any number of ways.

1. Select a clip in the Clips pane or in the Timeline.

2. Position the playhead so the frame you want is showing in the Monitor.

3. From the File menu, choose "Save Frame As...."

4. In the Finder sheet that drops down from iMovie's title bar, name the file, select a file format from the pop-up menu (JPEG or PICT), and choose a location to save the file.

5. Click "Save."

Reverse a clip's direction

To reverse a clip's direction, select the clip, then from the Advanced menu choose "Reverse Clip Direction." **Or** Control-click on a clip, then from the contextual menu choose "Reverse Clip Direction."

Create a color clip

Create color clips to use as transitions between scenes, as backgrounds for titles or captions, as an artistic element, or to replace a black color space between two clips.

When there's an *existing* blank space between two clips (in the Timeline), iMovie creates a black color clip to fill the space. The color clip is visible in the Clip Viewer. To replace the black with another color, double-click the black color clip to open the "Clip Info" window, click the color box to choose another color, then click "Set."

To create a *new* color clip: In the Timeline, drag two clips apart to create a blank space between them. Position the playhead over the blank space, then from the Advanced menu choose "Create Color Clip." **Or** after dragging the clips apart, switch to the Clip Viewer and double-click on the black color clip to open the "Clip Info" window.

You can use color clips as placeholders in the Timeline until you get the video footage you want for a particular scene. For instance, if you're making a music video, you may have an idea for one section of music that's 15 seconds long. You can place a 15-second color clip at the spot you need video, then edit the rest of the movie. When you've had time to video the missing scene, you can paste the new video in place of the color clip.

When you use color clips for a transition, add "Cross Dissolve" or a "Fade In" and "Fade Out" transition to either side of the color clip to soften it.

Extract audio in paste over

You may eventually be in an editing situation where you want to **replace existing video** in the Timeline, but **keep the audio** of the original clip. For example, the original video clip may have narration you want to use, but you want to replace the video with new shots of whatever the narrator is talking about. You can replace the original video but retain its audio with a "paste over."

1. Make sure that "Extract audio in paste over" is selected in iMovie preferences.

2. Select a video clip *you want to insert*. Use the crop markers under the Monitor to select the specific video frames that you want to paste, then press Command C to copy the selection.

3. Position the playhead at the first frame of video *to be replaced*. If you're replacing just part of an existing video clip, use the crop markers to select the specific frames to be replaced.

4. From the Advanced menu, choose "Paste Over at Playhead." The audio of the *pasted* video is muted (set to zero), and the *original clip's audio* is placed in audio track 1, below the pasted video.

To do a paste over of a replacement video clip *including* the audio, *uncheck* "Extract audio in paste over" in iMovie Preferences.

The pasted video clip with its audio muted (the black volume line is moved to the bottom of the clip) replaces the original video clip.

The original clip's audio is extracted and placed in audio track 1.

Music in track 2.

With "Edit volume" selected, the volume of each audio track can be adjusted so the narration in track 1 fades in as the music in track 2 fades out. See pages 147–149 for more audio-editing information.

▼ The newly pasted video replaces an equal amount of existing video.

▼ Any excess video longer than the selected frame range of existing video is not pasted.

▼ If the pasted video is shorter than the selected frame range of video to replace, the additional frames are filled with a color clip.

▼ Pasted-over still images expand to fill the selected frame range.

Lock an audio clip to a video clip

You may have an audio clip in one of the audio tracks that you want to start playing at a certain point in a video clip. But you want to experiment by moving the video clip around in the Timeline. You can lock the audio clip to the video clip so they move together.

1. Place the playhead at the point in a movie where you want the audio to start playing.

2. Place an audio clip in the Timeline so that it lines up with the playhead.

3. With the audio clip selected, from the Advanced menu, choose "Lock Audio Clip at Playhead."

To unlock the clip, select it, then from the "Advanced" menu, choose "Unlock Audio Clip." **Or** Control-click the audio clip and choose "Unlock Audio Clip," as shown at the bottom of the page.

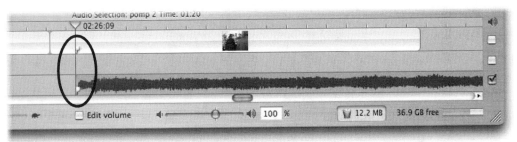

Yellow pins in the audio and video clips indicate the point at which the two clips are locked together. When you drag one of the clips, the other one will move with it.

Use iMovie's contextual menus

Many of the menu commands are available through pop-up contextual menus. Control-click on clips in the Clips pane, on clips or transitions in the Timeline, on audio clips, on the Monitor, or on a blank spot in the Timeline to see what commands are available at your finger tips.

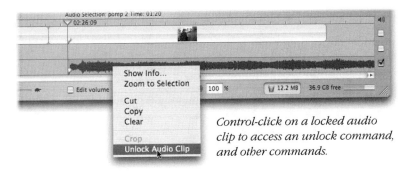

Control-click on a locked audio clip to access an unlock command, and other commands.

Extract audio from a clip

To extract audio from a clip, select one or more video clips in the Timeline, then go to the Advanced menu and choose "Extract Audio." The extracted audio file is placed in the Timeline below the corresponding video clip. Yellow pins are automatically placed in the audio and video clips (on the left edges) to lock the extracted audio in sync with the video. You can also Control-click on a video clip, then choose "Extract Audio" from the contextual menu.

The extracted audio appears as an audio clip directly beneath the video clip it came from. The audio is actually still in the video clip, but muted. If you click the "Edit volume" box, you'll see the audio level (a black line) in the video clip set at zero.

Keep track of free disk space

Located below the Clips pane, next to the Trash, the **Free Space status bar** alerts you to how much free space is left on the disk or partition being used for your movie. The bar indicator is color-coded to indicate the amount of free disk space.

> **Green:** More than 400 megabytes available
> (about 2 minutes of imported DV footage).
>
> **Yellow:** Less than 400 megabytes available
> (just under 2 minutes of imported DV footage).
>
> **Red:** Less than 200 megabytes available
> (about 1 minute of imported DV footage).

If you have less than 100 megabytes of free disk space available, you cannot import more video until you remove clips from the Clips pane or empty the iMovie Trash.

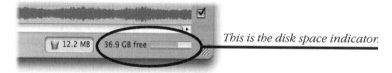

This is the disk space indicator.

 iDVD

iDVD can't help you *make* movies or photos, but it can help you *assemble* finished movies and photos into a beautiful presentation in the robust, interactive, and convenient DVD medium.

iDVD also lets you put any kind of digital content on the DVD in folders. That is, the same disc that plays your movies can also deliver any kind of other files to your audience: PDF files, applications, high-resolution photos, archived files, websites, or almost anything else you want to make accessible on a disc.

DVD technology has changed our capabilities and our expectations, both in our creative pursuits and in our approach to business, training, and marketing solutions. Not to mention it's just too much fun, especially when the software is this powerful and easy.

In this chapter

What Do You Need to Make DVDs?

If your computer has a SuperDrive, Apple's special drive that reads and writes DVDs, you can use the iDVD software to quickly create professional-looking DVDs that will play on almost any current DVD player, whether it's a DVD-capable computer or a home player.

You also need blank discs to burn your content onto. iDVD uses a type of "general media" disc called DVD-R. You can order them from the Apple store online or buy them from stores that sell Apple products. You can find very low prices on the Internet for bundles of generic-brand DVD-R discs, but you'll have better luck (a lower failure rate) with name-brand DVD-R discs that do not fall into the dirt-cheap category.

A DVD disc officially claims to hold 4.7 GB (gigabytes), but due to various factors ranging from marketing hype to variances in techniques for translating bits to gigabytes, you really have approximately 4.3 GB of space to work with, or about 90 minutes of video (including video used in motion menus). But that's a lot, especially compared to the 650 MB (megabytes) of storage space you get with a CD-R disc.

iDVD allows up to a total of 99 movies and slideshows (in any combination) on a single DVD disc. Of course, the length of your movies, the number of images in your slideshows, and how much DVD-ROM content you want to include on the disc will affect exactly how many movies and slideshows will actually fit on your DVD.

If you don't have a SuperDrive

At the moment if you do not have a SuperDrive, **you cannot burn** DVD projects created in iDVD using an external DVD burner.

You can build an iDVD project on a Mac that doesn't have a SuperDrive, then "archive" the project and copy it to a Mac that has a SuperDrive to burn it onto a DVD. See page 197 to learn about archiving iDVD projects.

What iDVD does NOT do

You do not use iDVD to *create* content, but to *organize and present* content that you've already created in another application. Before you open iDVD, you need to have some content available, such as iMovies that have been prepared for iDVD (as explained on page 151) or still photos in iPhoto.

DVD menus

Throughout this chapter we refer to the DVD **menu.** In the world of DVD design and authoring, the term "menu" means the DVD interface that the user clicks on to view the contents.

We also use "menu" to refer to iDVD's main window in which you create your project's appearance and navigation, as shown below.

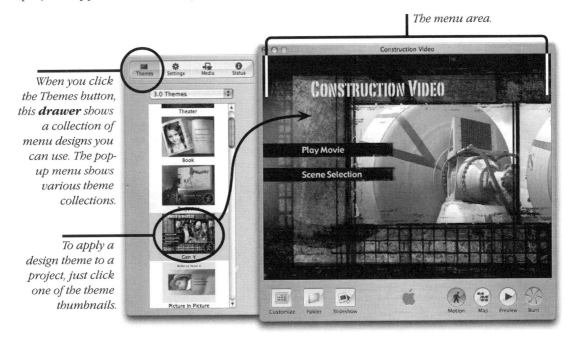

The menu area.

*When you click the Themes button, this **drawer** shows a collection of menu designs you can use. The pop-up menu shows various theme collections.*

To apply a design theme to a project, just click one of the theme thumbnails.

Start by Selecting a Theme

DVDs use "menus" to provide navigation to the content on the disc. iDVD provides various **menu themes** for you to choose from. Many of them contain motion and are called "motion menus." If you have a lot of content to squeeze onto a disc, you can economize disc space by using static menus instead of motion menus.

A single iDVD menu can contain a maximum of 12 buttons which link to movies and slideshows, or to other submenus, which can also contain up to 12 buttons. One DVD project can contain a maximum of 99 menus.

Double-click the iDVD icon (in your Applications folder) to open the program.

To select a theme:

Tip: If you don't have any movie content yet, follow the tutorial that came with iDVD and use the content included in the iDVD "Tutorial" folder.

1. Open iDVD, then from the File menu choose "New Project."

2. In the "Save As" dialog box, name your project and choose the location where you want to save it.

3. Click the "Customize" button in the bottom-left corner of the iDVD window to open the Customize drawer.

4. Click the "Themes" button at the top of the drawer to display the possible options.

5. Choose a menu design style from the scrolling list of thumbnails.

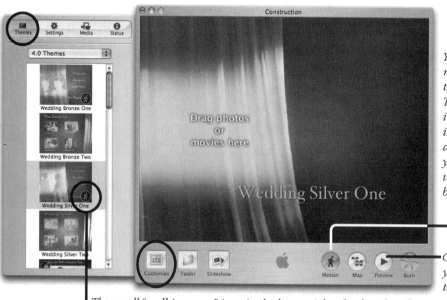

You can turn menu motion on or off with the "Motion" button. Turn it off while editing your DVD to make iDVD more efficient, and turn it on when you're ready to preview your project or burn the final DVD.

Click this to preview your project at any time.

The small "walking man" icon in the lower-right of a thumbnail means that theme contains motion. A CD icon appears in the upper-left corner means the menu includes an audio track.

Drop Zones

Some of the menu themes have **Drop Zones** into which you can drag a movie, a slideshow, or a still image. Drop Zones hold single images, movies, or slideshows, but do not link to anything.

To remove an image or movie from a Drop Zone, just drag the image *out* of the Drop Zone.

As you drag a movie from the Customize drawer to the Drop Zone, the Drop Zone highlights with a striped border. You can also drag an image or a movie from any Finder window to the Drop Zone.

Click the "Customize" button to open the Customize drawer on the left.

To customize the background of a menu and retain the Drop Zone, Option-drag a movie or an image on top of the background (but not into the Drop Zone). A blue highlight will appear around the window to indicate you are replacing the existing **background** image.

The Settings Pane of the Customize Drawer

You can customize several aspects of your DVD menu. If the drawer shown below is not visible, click the "Customize" button at the bottom of the window. Click the "Settings" button at the top of the Customize drawer.

Click the "Settings" button to show the Settings pane of the Customize drawer. All of these settings are explained on the following pages.

Duration setting

The "Duration" slider shown below sets how long a motion menu plays before it loops (repeats). The maximum loop duration allowed is 15 minutes (if your media is that long). Most DVD designers will create motion loops that are much shorter than that, usually around 30 seconds in duration. Long loops are really unnecessary because most people will make a selection and leave the current menu before a 30-second loop starts repeating. If you hope to get a lot of content into your DVD project, you should be aware that *longer* loops take up more storage space on the final DVD.

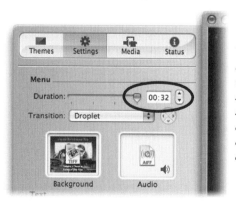

When you drag a movie into a menu Drop Zone or onto a menu background, you can set its duration. Either drag the slider, use the Up and Down arrows, or type a duration amount in the text field using a format of minutes:seconds.

Transition setting

Ordinarily when a button on a menu is clicked, the visual on the screen jumps abruptly to the next menu, to a movie, or to a slideshow. The "Transition" pop-up menu lets you select a transition effect that softens the jump to the next menu or to the selected content. Transitions add visual interest and a touch of professional sophistication.

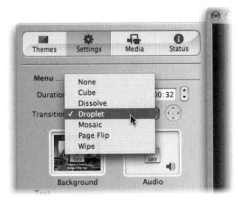

Experiment with various transitions to see which one you want to use. Or choose "None" if you want to keep it simple and economize on disc space when you burn your project to a DVD.

The "Transition" pop-up menu is disabled until you add links (buttons) to other menus or to some other content (movies or slideshows).

Customize a menu's background and audio settings

There are a couple of ways to **customize a menu background.** You can drag a photo or a movie into the "Background" well (circled to the left), **or** you can drag a photo or movie into the background area of the existing menu. When you drag a movie file into the "Background" well, any Drop Zone that may have been included in the selected theme is *removed.* If you want to *keep* the Drop Zone as part of the menu design, *Option*-drag the movie you want to use as a menu *background* to the menu area, but *not* into the *Drop Zone* area. You can then drag a different movie into the Drop Zone. iDVD composites the two movies into one amazing menu visual.

In the example below we started with the wedding theme template shown on page 170. From a Finder window we Option-dragged a movie ("pool cleaner.mov") to the menu background. Holding down the *Option* key preserves the Drop Zone. We then dragged another movie ("bug.mov") from a Finder window to the template's Drop Zone (the area with a striped border). As explained on the next page, we changed the default title ("Wedding Silver One") to "Costa Rica." Finally, we dragged three different movies from Finder windows to the menu background to automatically create the text buttons that play each movie ("Jungles," "Monkeys," and "Resorts") when selected. On the next page we explain how to customize the text buttons that are automatically created when you drag movie files to a menu background.

To create a custom background, we Option-dragged the "pool cleaner" movie into the menu's background area.

For added effect, we dragged the "bug" movie file into the Drop Zone.

Some themes include a soundtrack. You can **customize a menu's soundtrack** by dragging an audio file from any Finder window into the "Audio" well (shown below).

To mute a menu's soundtrack, click the tiny speaker icon in the "Audio" well.

Text and Button settings

Each theme includes placeholder text for a title. **To customize the title text,** click on the default text in the menu to select it, then type a new title. **To remove the title,** choose "No Title" from the "Position" menu.

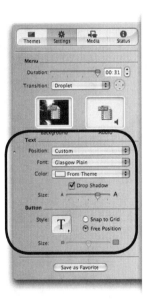

To customize the title position, select the title, then choose an alignment option from the "Position" pop-up menu (Left, Center, Right, Custom). **To position a title anywhere,** select the title, choose "Custom" from the "Position" pop-up menu, then drag the title anywhere in the menu.

To customize the position of text buttons, select a button, click the "Snap to Grid" button in the "Button" section, then choose an alignment option from the "Position" pop-up menu (Left, Center, or Right).

To customize the position of picture buttons, select the "Free Position" button in the "Button" section, then drag the button to any position.

To customize the position of button captions *in relation to a button's picture,* select a button, then from the "Position" pop-up menu select one of the options (Top, Center, Bottom, Left, or Right). **To remove button captions,** choose "No Text" from the "Position" pop-up menu.

To customize the caption size of buttons, select a button, then use the "Size" slider in the "Text" section to change the font size.

To customize the size of picture buttons, select a button, then use the "Size" slider in the "Button" section to change the button size.

To customize the font and color of buttons, select a button, then choose any font from the "Font" pop-up menu. Choose a font color from the "Color" pop-up menu.

Button settings

To create a button that links to a movie or slideshow, drag a movie file or a folder of photos from any Finder window to the iDVD menu, as shown in the example below. You can also drag files from the Media pane, as described on pages 180–181.

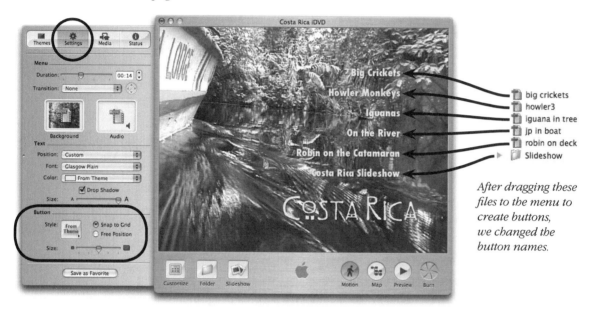

After dragging these files to the menu to create buttons, we changed the button names.

When you drag movie files (or a folder of photos) to the menu, iDVD automatically creates text buttons that link to the corresponding file or folder. The button names are the same as the file or folder from which they were created. You can edit button names after you've added them to the menu.

The large **"From Theme"** pop-up button (shown above in the Settings pane of the Customize drawer) lets you customize the **style** of existing buttons. Click on the pop-up button to see a graphical menu of button choices.

If you customize a menu by changing the button style to something other than the default theme style, you may need to reposition or resize buttons in the menu to correct the alignment or to prevent buttons from overlapping.

▾ To show buttons as they were designed for the selected theme, choose the default, "From Theme."

▾ To convert picture buttons (buttons containing a movie or photo) to text buttons, choose the "T" option.

Or choose one of the other custom shapes in the pop-up to change text buttons to picture buttons, or to change the appearance of a picture button.

▾ To customize the placement of buttons, select "Snap to Grid" or "Free Position." When "Snap to Grid" is selected, choose an alignment option from the "Position" pop-up menu.

Save a customized menu as a favorite

When you've created a custom menu that you want to use again for other menus, or for other iDVD projects, click the "Save as Favorite" button at the bottom of the Settings pane (circled below).

In the dialog sheet that drops down, name the menu design and select the checkbox options you want. If you want the favorite to be accessible to other users who have user accounts on this computer, check the box "Shared for all users." To make the favorite available to the current user only, deselect this checkbox.

To *replace* an existing favorite, name the current favorite the same as the favorite you want to replace, then select the "Replace existing" checkbox. Click OK.

Depending on the speed of the computer you're using, it may take a few seconds to save your settings as a favorite.

To use a favorite, click the "Themes" button at the top of the Customize drawer, then from the pop-up menu in the Themes pane choose "Favorites." Your customized menu design now appears as a thumbnail image in the Themes list (shown below). Click on a favorite in the Favorites list to apply its settings to the current menu. You can also see favorites, identified by a ribbon icon, when you select "All" from the pop-up menu.

The Favorites list.

The ribbon icon indicates a favorite.

Delete a favorite

If you decide to **delete a favorite** that you've created, you must go to the Favorites folder in which favorites are stored and manually throw it away.

1. Quit iDVD.

2. Find the Favorites folder where the favorite is located.

Costa Rica menu.favorite

This is what a favorite file looks like in the Favorites folder.

   If you selected "Shared for all users" in the "Save as Favorite" dialog sheet (shown on the previous page), the favorite is saved in a "Favorites" folder located deep within the Library folder on your *startup disk*. Look inside the Library folder for the iDVD folder. Next, locate the Favorites folder. The favorites you've saved are located there. The folder path looks like this: YourStartupDisk/Library/iDVD/Favorites.

   If you did not select either of the checkboxes, **or** if you selected the "Replace existing" checkbox, the favorite is saved in a Favorites folder located deep within your *Home folder.* The folder path looks like this: YourHomeFolder/Library/iDVD/Favorites.

3. Drag the favorite from the Favorites folder to the Trash.

Customize a motion button

A **motion button** is a small window that contains either a movie or a slide-show, and links to a movie, slideshow, or another menu. You can set the duration of a motion button movie loop up to 15 minutes, and you can also set the point at which the button movie starts playing.

1. Click on a motion button in a menu.

   If there's not a motion button in the menu, you can create one by dragging a movie icon from the Movies panel to a menu.

   When you click a motion button, a "Movie" checkbox and slider appear above the button (shown below).

2. Check the "Movie" checkbox if you want the button to contain motion (play a movie or slideshow). Move the slider left or right to scrub through the movie or slideshow to the point you want the motion to start playing.

3. Uncheck the box if you want the button to contain a static image. If you uncheck the "Movie" checkbox, you can use the slider position to set a poster frame, or preview image — a static image that displays in the button to represent the movie or slideshow.

You can add motion buttons to a menu by dragging movie files (or a folder of photos) from any Finder window to the menu. You can also drag movies or photos from the Media pane of the Customize drawer. See the following pages for more information about the Media pane.

You can change text buttons into motion buttons by selecting a motion button style from the "Style" pop-up menu located in the Settings pane.

You cannot have motion buttons and text buttons in the same menu.

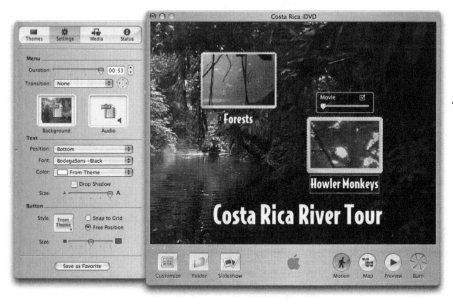

To change a motion button into a static button, uncheck the "Movie" checkbox, then use the slider to select a preview image that represents the movie. Or, drag a still photo into the motion button window.

When you use the "Duration" slider in the Settings pane to set the duration of a button, it also affects the duration of the background movie and background audio. The maximum loop duration shown on the slider is determined by the longest media clip used in the current menu.

If you lower the separator bar, you'll see a list of playlists instead of a second pop-up menu.

The Media Pane of the Customize Drawer

Select the "Media" button at the top of the Customize drawer to show the Media pane. This pane shows movie files, photos, and audio files that are on your computer. Click the pop-up menu at the top of the Media pane (shown on the left) to choose the kind of media files you want to access—audio, photos, or movies.

Audio media

When you choose "Audio" from the Media pop-up menu (shown above-left), a list displays the iTunes Library and all iTunes playlists. Select a playlist to show all the music files in that playlist in the lower section of the pane. Use any song you see as menu background music or slideshow music.

▼ **To preview a song,** select it in the list and click the Play button in the bottom-left corner of the drawer. Click the Play button again to stop. You can also double-click a song to preview it.

▼ **To change a menu's background music,** drag a song's icon from the Audio panel into the menu window. When a blue border highlights the menu window, let go of the icon. **Or** select a song name in the list, then click the "Apply" button in the bottom-right corner of the drawer.

▼ **To add a song to a slideshow,** open the Slideshow editor by double-clicking a slideshow button in a DVD menu. Then drag a song's icon from the Audio panel to the "Audio" well in the Slideshow editor. Learn more about slideshows on page 188.

You can alter the Media pane to allow more space for browsing its contents: drag the dimpled separator bar up until the top panel becomes a pop-up menu, as shown above.

The Play button.

Photos media

Choose "Photos" from the Media pop-up menu to access all the photos you've put into iPhoto. You can select any image from this pane to use as a menu background or a button image. You can even drag an iPhoto album to the menu background to create a slideshow.

- ▼ **To use a still image** for a menu background, drag the image from the Photos panel into the menu window. When you see a blue border highlight the edges of the menu window, let go of the image.

- ▼ **To replace the image** on a menu button (if the menu uses picture buttons), drag an image from the Photos pane and drop it on top of the button.

- ▼ **To replace an existing image or a movie in a Drop Zone,** drag a photo from the Photos pane on top of the Drop Zone. When you see a striped-border highlight appear around the Drop Zone, let go.

- ▼ **To add one or more images to a slideshow,** open the Slideshow editor by double-clicking a slideshow button in the menu window (see details on pages 189–191). Then drag the image (or images) from the Photos pane to the Slideshow editor.

- ▼ **To add an entire slideshow,** create an album in iPhoto that includes the photos you want to use, then drag the iPhoto album from the Photos pane to the menu. You can also drag a folder of photos from the Finder to the menu.

Use the Search field to find media files in a selected album, playlist, or movie folder. The lower pane changes to show only files whose name matches the letters or words you've typed in the text field.

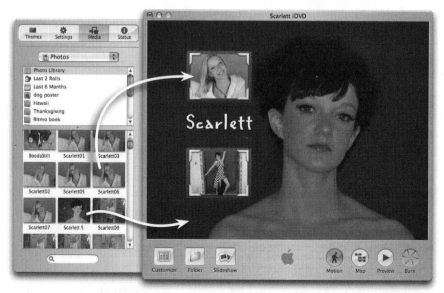

You can drag still photos on top of existing motion buttons. And you can drag a still photo onto the background area to create a photo menu background.

If you drag the Media pane's dimpled separator bar up, the contents of the upper pane—iPhoto images—are moved to a pop-up menu (shown above). To show the pop-up menu's contents in a pane again, drag the bar down.

Movies media

The Movies pane shows movie files that you can drag to menu backgrounds, buttons, or menu Drop Zones. iDVD automatically shows the Movies folder that's in your Home folder, but you might have other movies located in other folders or perhaps on other drives.

To make other folders that contain movies visible in the Movies pane list shown below: Go to the iDVD application menu, choose "Preferences," then click the "Movies" icon at the top of the Preferences window. Click the "Add..." button, then choose a folder containing movie files from the "Open" dialog box that appears. **Or** you can simply drag a folder of movie clips from any Finder window to the Movies pane list.

Select a folder in this list to show its contents in the pane below. You can add other movie folders to this Movies pane list.

The lower pane shows the contents of the selected folder above.

To preview a movie clip in the Media pane, select it, then click the Play button. Or double-click the movie thumbnail.

To add a movie or a slideshow to a Drop Zone, drag a movie file or a folder of photos on top of a Drop Zone. When the Drop Zone border highlights with a striped border, let go. If part of the image area is cut off, use your mouse to drag the movie or photo around inside the Drop Zone.

Three ways to drag a movie from the drawer (or the Finder) to a menu:

- ▼ *Drag* a movie from the drawer to the menu background: The movie will become a button that links to that movie.
- ▼ *Option-drag* a movie to the menu background: The current background will be replaced, but the Drop Zone will remain.
- ▼ *Command-Option-drag* a movie to the menu background: The current background will be replaced, and the Drop Zone will disappear.

The Status Pane of the Customize Drawer

The meters in the Status pane give information about the size of your project and the progress of background file encoding.

- ▼ **DVD Capacity:** Shows how much space your project currently requires and the maximum space available. A DVD-R can usually hold approximately 4.3 gigabytes, or around 90 minutes of video. Click on the text to the right of the meter to show how many minutes your project currently takes.

- ▼ **Motion Menus:** Shows how many minutes your motion menus take, out of an allowed maximum of 15 minutes (one gigabyte). The duration total shown includes motion menus, still menus (each still menu uses one second), transitions, and autoplay movies.

- ▼ **Tracks:** Counts how many video tracks and slideshows are used in the project. The maximum number of tracks in a project is 99.

- ▼ **Menus:** Counts how many still menus and motion menus are used in the project. A maximum number of 99 menus is allowed.

- ▼ **Background Encoding:** Show the progress of iDVD's background file encoding that happens invisibly while you design and build your project (if you enabled background encoding in iDVD's Preferences).

The Encoder settings you choose in iDVD Preferences will affect how many minutes of video will fit on a disc. See the following page.

Movies that you place in an iDVD project must be encoded to a certain format that meets official DVD specifications.

If your computer's performance is slowed down by so much intense processing, you can choose to turn off background encoding in iDVD Preferences. When you finish your project, iDVD will encode the files before burning the project to a disc.

Preferences

iDVD's preferences let you customize some of the settings for making DVDs. From the iDVD application menu, choose "Preferences." Click on one of the three icons at the top of the Preferences window to see the options for that category.

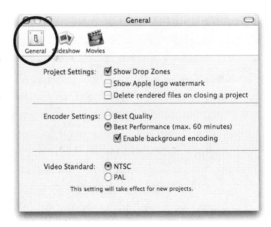

General settings

Project Settings

▼ Check "Show Drop Zones" to show the Drop Zone areas in the Theme menus.

▼ Uncheck "Show Apple logo watermark" if you want to remove the Apple logo from the DVD menu design.

▼ Check "Delete rendered files on closing a project" to preserve hard disk space. If you plan to burn other DVDs of the same project, uncheck this option to avoid having to encode and render the project again.

Encoder Settings

▼ **Best Quality:** Choose this if you want the best quality possible, **or** if you have more than 60 minutes of video. iDVD will evaluate how much video you have and produce the best quality possible for the number of minutes in the project.

▼ **Best Performance:** Choose this if you have less than 60 minutes of video in your project; it will burn faster, but perhaps with less quality.

    ▼ **Enable background encoding:** If you chose "Best Performance," this option allows iDVD to begin encoding the movies you've placed in the DVD menu into the MPEG-2 format required by the official DVD specifications. If background encoding slows down your computer, uncheck this box, and iDVD will postpone the encoding until you're ready to burn the project onto a DVD.

Video Standard

NTSC uses 29.97 frames per second, and PAL uses 25 frames per second.

Choose "NTSC" if your DVD will be played on a consumer DVD player in the USA. The USA, Japan, and some non-European countries use the NTSC format, while most European and other countries use the PAL format.

Slideshow settings

When iDVD optimizes photos for a DVD slideshow, it converts them to a low resolution of 72 ppi (pixels per inch). If you check **Always add original slideshow photos to DVD-ROM,** a folder of all the original high-resolution photos is *also* placed in a folder on the DVD disc, which lets anyone drag the photos from the disc to their own hard drive. Uncheck this option if you want to conserve space on the DVD, or if the viewer doesn't need access to the original images. You can also set this option in the Slideshow editor.

To ensure that the entire image displays on a television, select **Always scale slides to TV Safe area.** To see the TV safe area a DVD menu design, go to the Advanced menu in the menu bar and choose "Show TV Safe Area." What you see inside the gray border is the area that will display accurately on a TV screen.

Movies settings

These settings let you choose whether iDVD will create chapter marker submenus and where iDVD should look for movie files.

Automatically create chapter marker submenu

Chapter markers allow you to jump to different sections of a DVD movie while it is playing. If this option is chosen, when you drag a movie with chapter markers to a menu, iDVD creates two menu buttons: one that plays the movie, and one named "Scene Selection" that links to a new submenu containing buttons that link to the chapter markers in the movie. If there are more than 12 chapter markers in the movie, iDVD creates another submenu containing buttons that link to the other chapter markers. iDVD can have a maximum of 12 buttons per menu.

Look for my movies in these folders

iDVD automatically looks for movies in the Movies folder that's located in your Home folder. Because movies take up so much disk space, it probably won't take you long to realize you need an additional location (or two) in which to store movies, such as an external FireWire drive. If so, you can add those other locations for iDVD to search. Just click the "Add…" button to show the "Open" window, then select any folder on any drive. Your selection will appear as shown on the right.

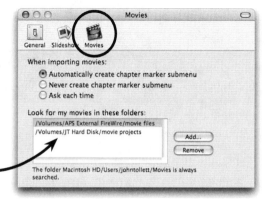

Create Additional Menus

A single iDVD menu can technically contain up to 12 buttons, but the design theme you choose may not be suitable for that many buttons. Or you may want to organize your content so that additional menus help to create a more effective presentation. In either case, additional menus, or **submenus,** are often an essential element in DVD design.

Create submenus

Open or create a project that has one main menu, then click the "Folder" button at the bottom of the menu window to create a button named "My Folder." Double-click this new button to open its new menu, into which you can drag more movies or create more slideshows. A submenu automatically contains a navigation arrow that lets viewers return to the previous menu.

If you've already placed a number of buttons on a menu and decide you need a submenu, you can select multiple buttons (Shift-click on the buttons), then from the Project menu choose "New Menu from Selection." iDVD replaces the selected buttons with a new button called "My Folder," which links to a new submenu containing the buttons that you selected.

The main menu.   *A submenu.*

We created the three buttons in the menu above by clicking the "Folder" button at the bottom of the window. The top button's name has been changed from "My Folder" to "Nepal." Each button links to a new submenu, like the one shown to the right.

This submenu contains buttons that link to four different movies. We created the buttons by dragging movies from the Customize drawer to this submenu background. iDVD takes care of all the design work. Notice the "back" arrow in the lower-left corner that iDVD created.

Create a scene menu

Video-editing software, such as iMovie, lets you place **chapter markers** in a movie to mark specific sections of it. If you did that, then iDVD can automatically create **scene menus** that link to those chapter markers. iDVD can import up to 99 chapter markers for one movie.

To create scene menus (if you made chapter markers in iMovie):

1. Drag a movie containing chapter markers into the iDVD window.

   iDVD automatically creates two buttons: a "Play Movie" button that plays the movie and a "Scene Selection" button that links to a new submenu. If the menu already contains one or more buttons, iDVD creates a submenu that includes the "Play Movie" and "Scene Selection" buttons.

2. Click the "Scene Selection" button (below, left) to go to that submenu. iDVD automatically creates a menu that lists the chapter markers (scenes) as buttons (below, right). iDVD allows a maximum of 12 buttons per menu, and some themes allow less than 12. If there are more scenes in a movie than a menu allows, a right-facing arrow links to another menu containing more scene selection buttons.

iDVD creates as many submenus as necessary until all chapter markers in a movie have been accommodated, up to the maximum of 99 markers.

The title and text buttons were created automatically by dragging a movie containing chapter markers to the menu window. Double-click the "Scene Selection" button to open the linked submenu that iDVD also creates (as shown to the right).

The submenu, its title, and the text buttons that link to the movie's chapter markers were all created automatically. The button names are picked up from the chapter marker names that were set in the video-editing software, iMovie. You can select any button and rename it.

Create a Slideshow

A DVD slideshow is a quick and easy way to present your photos.

1. Click the "Media" button in the Customize drawer, then select "Photos" from the pop-up menu.

2. Select an album (folder) from the list of iPhoto albums and drag it to the menu. iDVD automatically creates a button named for the album.

   Or drag a folder of photos from the Finder to the menu to create a slideshow button that is named the same as the folder of photos.

   Or click the "Slideshow" button on the bottom edge of the menu to create an *empty* slideshow button called "My Slideshow." If you use this technique, you must use the *Slideshow editor* to add photos to the slideshow.

3. To open the **Slideshow editor** (shown on the next page), double-click the new slideshow button that appears in the menu.

4. Use the Slideshow editor to customize your slideshow, as explained on the next page.

Drag a photo album to the menu.

The "Slideshow" button creates a new and empty slideshow button in the menu.

Using Slideshow Editor

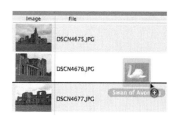

To add additional photos to a slideshow, drag an entire iPhoto album, multiple photos, or a single photo from the Photos pane (or from the Finder) to the Slideshow editor window. As you drag items to the editor window, a black line indicates where the item will be placed when you drop it (shown on the right).

To rearrange the order of photos in a slideshow, drag one or more photos up or down the list of images in the editor.

To delete photos in a slideshow, select one or more photos, then press the Delete key.

To make a slideshow repeat, click the "Loop slideshow" checkbox.

To display Back and Next arrows for a slideshow, click the "Display ◄► during slideshow" checkbox. If the "Slide Duration" pop-up menu is set to "Manual," the Back and Next arrows can serve as a reminder to use the DVD remote control to change images.

To add original photos on DVD-ROM: Click this checkbox to add the original, full-resolution photos to the final DVD. When you burn your project to a DVD, a folder containing the original photos will be on the disc, accessible for anyone who has a computer with a DVD drive. This option is also in iDVD Preferences.

iDVD compresses the photos in a slideshow, converting them to the low resolution of 72 ppi that is required by DVD specifications.

Click here to switch between List view and Icon view.

Use the Search field to search iPhoto for specific photos.

More slideshow settings

From the **Slide Duration** pop-up menu choose how many seconds each slide will show. Choose "Fit to audio" if you've added audio and want the slideshow to fit the duration of the selected audio track. If the audio track is shorter than the slideshow, the track will repeat until the slideshow finishes.

Choose "Manual" if you want the user to advance each slide. You cannot include audio when you choose "Manual."

From the **Transition** pop-up menu choose a style of transition from one photo to the next. If the transition you select is *directional,* click one of the directional arrows on the small toggle icon (circled below) to choose which direction the transition moves.

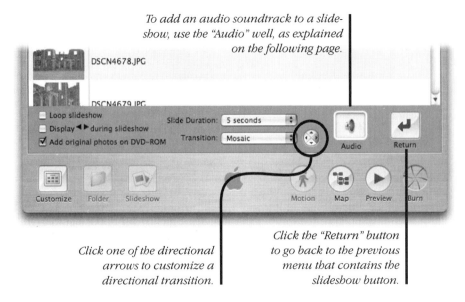

To add an audio soundtrack to a slide-show, use the "Audio" well, as explained on the following page.

Click one of the directional arrows to customize a directional transition.

Click the "Return" button to go back to the previous menu that contains the slideshow button.

iDVD image file formats

iDVD slideshows can use any file format supported by QuickTime, such as JPEG, PICT, and TIFF. When iDVD creates a slideshow it scales photos to 640 x 480 pixels, the standard DVD size and proportion. Photos that are not 640 x 480 will be scaled down, but will retain their original aspect ratio (proportions). So a vertical photo will be resized to 480 pixels tall, with black bands on either side to fill out the 640-pixel width.

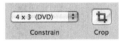

If you want your photos to fill the DVD window, use an image-editing program to crop them to 640 x 480 pixels. You can use iPhoto to crop photos to fit a DVD window: From iPhoto's "Constrain" pop-up menu, choose "4 x 3 (DVD)" as shown on the left.

Add music to a slideshow

It's easy to add a soundtrack to a slideshow:

1. Click the "Customize" button at the bottom of iDVD's window to show the Customize drawer.

2. Click the "Media" button at the top of the drawer.

3. Choose "Audio" from the pop-up menu.

   The iTunes Library and all of your iTunes playlists appear in the upper pane of the drawer, and the lower pane shows the songs in the selected playlist.

4. Select any song and drag it from the Audio pane to the "Audio" well, as shown below.

   Or drag an audio file from anywhere on your computer to the "Audio" well (also shown below).

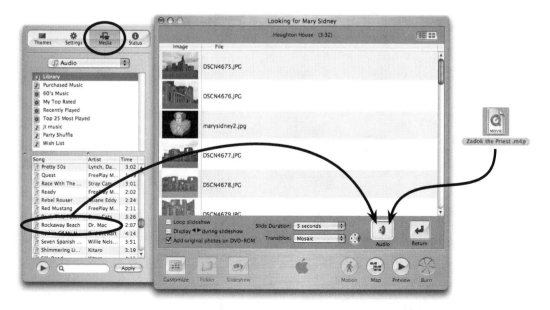

To delete an audio soundtrack from a slideshow, drag the audio file's icon *out* of the "Audio" well.

iDVD will accept audio file formats that are compatible with QuickTime and iTunes, including AIFF, WAV, MP3, M4P, and AAC.

Using Map View

Map view shows a graphic representation of your iDVD project. Menus, sub-menus, movies, and slideshows appear as icons, with navigation lines that show the connection path between items.

Map view is where you can add an **autoplay** movie or slideshow. An autoplay movie automatically plays when a DVD is inserted in a player, then moves on to the main menu. This is similar to the FBI warning screen you've seen on commercial DVDs. Although you probably don't need an FBI warning for your project, it might be fun to add a fake one. Or you can find other creative ways to use the autoplay feature.

To create an autoplay movie, drag a movie or slideshow from the Media pane or the Finder onto the project icon (the first item in the map view diagram). **To delete an autoplay movie,** drag it out of the project icon.

In the example below, I dragged a movie with chapter markers to the main menu, creating two primary links—"Play Movie" (which is the entire movie) and "Scenes 1-8" (which links to the movie's scenes, identified by chapter markers). The "Scenes 1-8" menu links to the "Scenes 9-10" menu, and they both are linked to the movie scenes that have been identified by chapter markers that were placed in the movie.

Some of iDVD's themes include autoplay movies. These short movies act as intros to the main menu.

Themes that include autoplay movies display an autoplay symbol on them in the Themes pane, as shown above.

To add an autoplay movie or slideshow, drag a movie or slideshow to the project icon.

Project icon.　Main menu.　The entire movie.

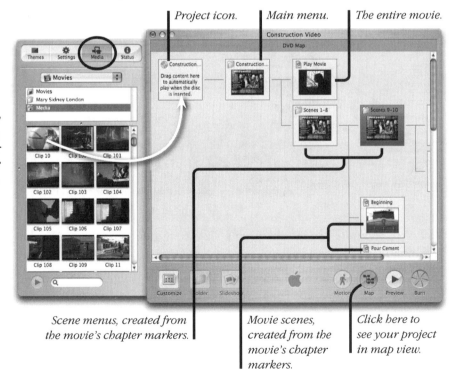

Scene menus, created from the movie's chapter markers.

Movie scenes, created from the movie's chapter markers.

Click here to see your project in map view.

Map view makes it easy to find specific elements of a project and navigate to them, especially when the project is large and complex. From within map view you can:

- ▼ Open a menu for editing: Double-click the menu icon.
- ▼ Open a slideshow in the Slideshow editor: Double-click the slide-show icon.
- ▼ Preview the entire project: Select the project icon, then click the "Preview" button.
- ▼ Preview a menu, movie, or slideshow: Select the item, then click the "Preview" button.
- ▼ Loop an autoplay movie, a movie, or a slideshow: Select the item's icon, then from the Advanced menu choose "Loop Movie" or "Loop Slideshow."

In map view, when a movie or slideshow is set to loop, it is marked with this looping icon.

If your project isn't completely visible in the map view window, use the scroll bars to move the project diagram. Or if you place the pointer in an empty area of the window, it turns into a little hand icon, which you can use to drag the diagram around the window.

Create a Music DVD

How about creating a music DVD with visuals for a party or special event? Or just to impress your friends.

1. Click the "Customize" button to open the Customize drawer, then click the "Themes" button.

2. Select a theme, click the "Slideshow" button, then double-click the new button to open the Slideshow editor.

3. In the Customize drawer, click the "Media" button, then choose "Audio" from the pop-up menu.

4. Drag an iTunes playlist from the Media pane to the Slideshow editor's "Audio" well. Set "Slide Duration" to "Fit to Audio" and click the "Loop slideshow" checkbox.

If you want to display photos or graphic images of any kind while the music plays, drag images (or a folder of images) from the Media pane or the Finder into the Slideshow editor.

Or you can display just one image, such as a list of the songs playing. Create a graphic of the song list in a graphics application. Make it 640 x 480 pixels, 72 ppi, and save it as a JPEG. Drag the graphic into the Slideshow editor. The graphic will be displayed as the playlist plays.

A DVD can hold a lot of music files, but check the Status pane to make sure you have enough room for all the songs and pictures you've dragged to the Slideshow editor.

iDVD Specifications, Formats, and Limitations

Most of these items are mentioned in various other places in this chapter, but it may be helpful to summarize them here, in one place.

▾ iDVD can use any format that QuickTime recognizes, such as JPEG, PICT, PNG, TIFF, or Photoshop.

▾ Image sizes of 640 x 480 pixels work well, but larger sizes can be used and will be resized by iDVD to 640 x 480.

▾ A resolution of 72 ppi is ideal, although you can use higher-resolution images and iDVD will convert them to 72 ppi.

▾ Images smaller than 640 x 480 pixels will be enlarged by iDVD, usually adversely affecting the image quality. If you use a large quantity of high-resolution images in a slideshow, you may notice iDVD acts sluggish, but the final DVD will be okay.

▾ Each slideshow you create can have up to 99 photos.

▾ In the Slideshow editor, if you set the "Slide Duration" pop-up menu to "Manual," you cannot include music with the slideshow.

▾ MPEG-1 files, QuickTime VR movies, and movies with sprite or Flash tracks cannot be added to an iDVD project.

▾ iDVD accepts audio files that are supported by QuickTime, such as AAC, MP3, M4P, AIFF, and WAV.

▾ Each iDVD menu is allowed a maximum of 12 buttons.

▾ A slideshow in a Drop Zone can have a maximum of 30 photos.

▾ iDVD projects can have a combined total of 99 tracks (movies and slideshows). Of course, that depends on the duration of the content. You're still limited to 4.3 gigabytes of storage space.

▾ iDVD projects can contain up to 99 menus.

▾ iDVD will recognize up to 99 chapter markers in a movie.

▾ NTSC is the video standard for North America and Japan.
PAL is the video standard for most of Europe and elsewhere.

Create DVD-ROM Content

In addition to menus, movies, and slideshows, DVDs can store and deliver any files from your computer, making them accessible for anyone with a DVD drive. This data storage feature is called DVD-ROM (DVD–Read Only Memory). A small business may want to include PDFs, forms, documents, maps, or other data on a disc. Or when you create a DVD slideshow, you may want to include the original, high-resolution photos on the disc for someone to use in a brochure or family album. Remember that files you add to the DVD-ROM section of a disc adds to the total space used for the rest of the project. Be sure to check the Status pane as you add files to ensure that everything will fit on a disc.

To put DVD-ROM content in your DVD project:

1. From the Advanced menu, choose "Edit DVD-ROM Contents…."

2. In the "DVD–ROM Contents" window that appears, click the "Add Files…" button. Browse and select the files you want, then click the "Open" button.

   Or drag files from the Finder directly into the "DVD-ROM Contents" window.

You can create new folders to help organize files, you can change the order of folders and files, and you can delete items from the DVD-ROM section of the disc.

- ▼ **To create a new folder,** click the "New Folder" button at the bottom of the window. Double-click the new folder to rename it.

- ▼ **To reorganize** the DVD-ROM contents, drag the folders up or down in the list, or drag files and folders in or out of other folders.

- ▼ **To delete** an item from the DVD-ROM content, select the item, then press the Delete key on your keyboard.

To access the DVD-ROM content that's on a DVD disc:

1. Insert the disc in a DVD drive.

2. Double-click the DVD disc icon on the Desktop.

3. In the window that opens, double-click the folder named "DVD-ROM Contents."

   The folder may also have the same name as your project.

4. Drag any of the folder's content to your computer's hard disk to copy it to your computer.

Add Text to a Menu

A menu usually has a text title and the buttons in a menu often have a word or two of descriptive text associated with them. But you may want more extensive text included in a menu that provides comments, a description of the content, or any other creative use of text.

1. From the Project menu, choose "Add Text." Default text, also known as a text object, appears on the menu that says "Click to edit."

2. Double-click the text to select it, then type the text you want to use.

3. Click the "Customize" button to open the Customize drawer, then click the "Settings" button.

4. Use the pop-up menus in the "Text" section of the Settings pane to customize the text position, font, and color.

You can add as many text blocks as you want. In the example below, we added a second text block so we could make "ROBIN" larger than the rest of the text.

When you add a text object to a menu, by default the text style is based on the menu's *title* style.

Instead of typing, you can copy text from another application, select the default text in a text object, and then paste the new text into the text object.

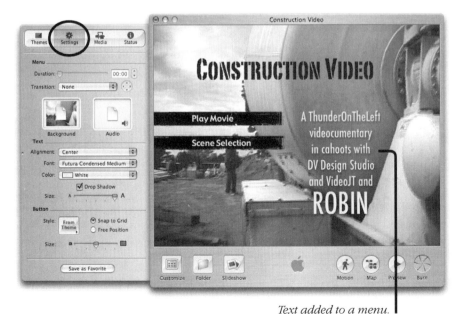

Text added to a menu.

Change the Name of a DVD

The final DVD that you burn will be named the same as your iDVD project.

To change the disc name:

1. From the Project menu, choose "Project Info…."

2. Type a new name in the "Disc Name" box.

   Do not use spaces—a space in the name will be replaced with an underscore. You can use numbers, upper- and lowercase characters from A to Z, and the underscore.

Archive Your Project

Archiving a project keeps all the assets together and linked, making it easy and convenient to store complete projects. Or you may need to move a project to another computer that has a SuperDrive, or so someone else can work on the project.

To archive an iDVD project:

1. From the File menu, choose "Archive Project."

2. In the Archive Project dialog sheet that drops down, type a name for the project and choose a location to save the archived files.

3. Click the "Include themes" checkbox to archive the themes with the project. This is important if you've used custom themes or want to use your theme in future versions of iDVD. You can uncheck this checkbox if you've used standard iDVD themes.

4. Click the "Include encoded files" checkbox to avoid having to re-encode project files after they're moved to another location. If you're more interested in archiving speed and economizing hard disk space, uncheck this option.

5. Click the "Save" button. iDVD adds "Archived" to the file name.

The Advanced Menu

The Advanced menu contains items that can be very helpful in the creation of your DVD project. The items in the Advanced menu are:

Show TV Safe Area

Some TVs do not show the entire image area of a menu or image. The outer edges of DVD menus and movies may be distorted or clipped completely. iDVD provides guide lines that you can turn on or off that give an approximation of a "TV Safe area." When you design menus you should make sure that important elements, such as text and buttons, fall within the TV Safe area.

To show the TV Safe area:

From the Advanced menu, choose "Show TV Safe Area." After you check the placement of menu elements, you can turn off the TV Safe area display. From the Advanced menu, choose "Hide TV Safe Area."

Inside the gray border is the TV Safe area.

Motion

When you use this menu command to start or stop the motion of a motion menu, it's the same as clicking the "Motion" button on the bottom edge of the menu window. To be efficient, turn motion *off* while working on a project and designing menus. Be sure to turn motion *on* when previewing a project or burning a disc.

Apply Theme To Project

Choose this option to apply a selected theme to every menu in a project.

Apply Theme To Folders

Choose this option to apply a selected theme to a *specific menu and its submenus.* If you look at a project's diagram in map view, you can see that menu icons in the diagram have a *folder icon* in the upper-left corner.

1. Open a menu whose theme you want to change. An easy way to navigate to any menu is to click the "Map" button (page 192), find the icon for the menu you want to modify, then double-click it to open it in the iDVD window.

2. Open the Customize drawer, click the "Themes" button, then click on the theme you want to use.

The selected theme will be applied to that menu and any of its submenus. Click the "Map" button again to verify that the new theme has been applied where you expected. The icon of the selected menu, and its submenus, will show the new theme.

Loop

With a movie or slideshow selected in a menu, or selected in the map view of a project, select "Loop" to make the movie or slideshow repeat endlessly.

Delete Encoded Assets

iDVD projects take an extraordinary amount of disk storage space. Choose this option when a project is finished to reclaim a lot of disk space taken up by the special DVD-encoded files that iDVD had to create for the final disc.

Edit DVD-ROM Contents...

Select this option to add computer files of any kind to the final DVD. Any files you add to the DVD-ROM section of a DVD can be copied to any computer with a DVD drive. See page 195 for details.

Preview Your DVD

The iDVD remote control.

As you edit your DVD project, you should preview it often. First, click the "Motion" button to turn on motion menus, then click the "Preview" button to see how your final project will look.

While in **Preview mode,** a remote control appears on the screen that lets you test the DVD as if you were using a real remote control on a consumer DVD player. **To return to DVD-editing mode,** click "Preview" again. For better efficiency, when you return to editing *disable* motion menus by clicking the "Motion" button at the bottom of the iDVD window.

Burn Your Project to a DVD

When you're satisfied with your menus and you've added all the movies, slide-shows, and DVD-ROM content, it's time to encode, render, and "multiplex" all those files into the official DVD format and burn them onto a DVD. Happily, all those complex operations happen with a click of the "Burn" button.

***Multiplexing**, also known as "muxing," refers to the process of assembling DVD assets into an official format that DVD players can use.*

1. **Preparation:** Make sure your Energy Saver preferences are NOT set to make the Mac go to sleep.

   Make sure your hard disk has as least twice as much free space available as the project takes up. Check the "DVD Capacity" meter (see page 183) to see the size of the project.

   Click the "Motion" button at the bottom-right of the iDVD window.

2. Place a blank DVD-R disc in your SuperDrive.

3. Click the "Burn" button in the bottom-right corner of the iDVD window to open the aperture and reveal the Burn icon.

4. Click once again on the "Burn" icon which is now pulsating. iDVD starts rendering, encoding, multiplexing, and burning all the files and menus that are part of the DVD project.

The "Motion" and "Burn" buttons are down here.

GarageBand

Think of GarageBand as your own private recording studio. Even if you're not a musician and didn't even play in the high school band or sing in the church choir, you'll soon be composing and arranging music soundtracks that will amaze everyone. If you do happen to have musical talent on any level, GarageBand provides the studio of your dreams.

If you don't play a musical instrument, use the provided musical loops to compose original arrangements, then enjoy playing them in iTunes. And with the help of iDVD, iMovie, and iPhoto, you can use your musical compositions for DVD menu audio tracks and movie or slideshow soundtracks.

GarageBand is capable of much more than we can cover in this short chapter, but we'll get you started with the basics and enough information to make GarageBand one of your favorite, mind-blowing, creative pastimes.

A rapidly growing collection of GarageBand web sites provides training, tech support, forums, soundtrack loops, and other music-community offerings.

One popular GarageBand site is MacJams (www.MacJams.com). Be sure to check out their Buyer's Guide for great advice on accessories (keyboards, microphones, and other stuff).

Create a New Song File

Double-click the **GarageBand** icon in your Applications folder to open it. If this is the first time you've opened GarageBand, the window shown below appears. Click "Create New Song."

In the "New Project" window that appears (shown below), type a name for your project and choose a location to store it. The default location is the GarageBand folder inside the Music folder that's located in your Home folder, but you can choose any location you prefer.

The bottom pane of the window contains the song's Tempo, Time, and Key settings.

Tempo is the speed of the song measured in beats per minute (bpm). You can set the tempo anywhere between 60 bpm (slow) and 240 bpm (fast).

Time, such as 4/4, defines *how many* beats (the number before the slash) will be in a single measure, and what *length* of note will have a value of *one* beat (the number after the slash). In 4/4, the 4 after the slash indicates that quarter notes will equal one beat.

You can change these settings at any time in the "Track Info" window (see pages 223–225).

Key is the central note that determines the pitch of all other notes.

Click the "Create" button to open the GarageBand window, shown below.

Grand Piano track.

When GarageBand opens, it automatically includes a Grand Piano track, and an onscreen keyboard floats on top of the window, as shown here. For now, drag the keyboard out of the way, or click the red button in its top-left corner to close it.

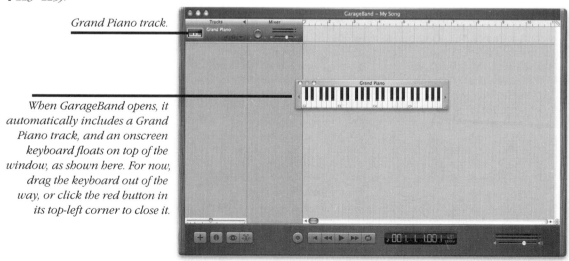

The GarageBand Interface

As an easy way to get started, take a quick look at the components that make up the the GarageBand window. The next several pages provide an overview and description of the tools contained within this main window.

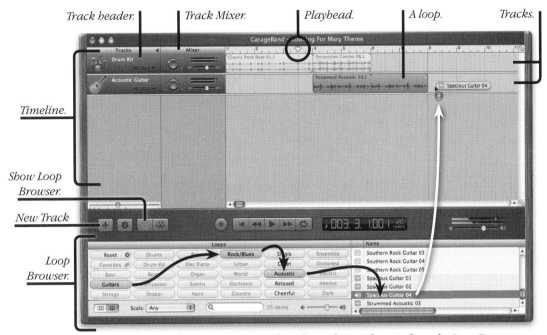

The GarageBand concept is simple—choose loops of music from the Loop Browser, then drag the loops to the Timeline, and arrange them in a limitless variety of ways to create original compositions.

The **Playhead** indicates the current position in a track. Move to any point in a track by dragging the Playhead to the position where you want to start playing a song.

The **Timeline** holds the various tracks that you create and provides the space for you to edit and arrange loops of music into a masterful composition.

Create **Tracks** by dragging *loops* (prerecorded clips of music) from the Loop Browser into the Timeline. Each track usually contains loops from a single instrument, but you can drag loops from different instruments into a single track. You can also click the "New" Track button (see page 212). If you've connected a musical instrument or a microphone to your computer, you can record original music or vocals to a track (see page 231).

—continued

Each track includes a set of controls for the loops in that track:

In the **Track header,** the *track name and icon* identify the track. By default the track is named for the instrument loop you dragged to the track. **To change a track name,** Command-click it and type in a new name.

The small row of buttons in the Track header are **Mute, Solo,** and **Volume Curve.**

▾ **Mute:** Click the speaker icon to turn a track on or off.

▾ **Solo:** Click the headphones icon to mute all tracks but that one (click again to *unsolo* the track).

▾ **Volume Curve:** Click the disclosure triangle to reveal the volume curve track (shown below). Click on the volume curve (the straight line) to add points to the line. Drag the points up or down to adjust the volume, left or right to affect the duration of a volume change.

The **Track Mixer** includes a *pan control* to adjust the balance of sound between left and right speakers and a *track volume control* to adjust the entire track's volume. This slider doesn't affect the volume of a track if you've edited the volume of individual loops by adding points to the volume curve, as shown below.

Audio level meters.

Track volume control.

Above the volume control are two audio level meters, one each for left and right speakers. If the volume exceeds acceptable levels, the meter shows the clipped or distorted area as orange and red in the meter. The small round warning lights (*clipping indicators*) to the right of the meters turn red when the audio volume is high enough to cause audio distortion known as *clipping*. Click on the *clipping indicator* lights to turn them off.

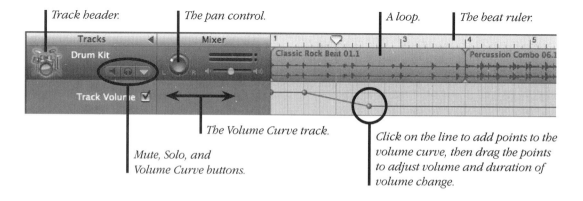

Track header.   *The pan control.*   *A loop.*   *The beat ruler.*

The Volume Curve track.

Mute, Solo, and Volume Curve buttons.

Click on the line to add points to the volume curve, then drag the points to adjust volume and duration of volume change.

Drag the **Zoom slider** left or right to zoom in or out of the Timeline. Drag left to show more loops in the window, or drag right to show fewer loops in greater detail.

The **Track Info** button (the letter "i") opens the selected track's "Track Info" window where you can change instrument settings and add effects to a track. See pages 223–225 for more information.

Click the **Loop Browser** button to reveal the Loop Browser, a collection of music loops from which you can choose to build a song. Click the **Browser View** buttons in the lower-left corner of the browser to view the loops in *Button View* or *Column View.*

▾ **Button View** (shown below) contains a collection of keyword buttons representing different instruments and music styles. When you select a button, other buttons that don't relate to that selection are dimmed. Loops that fit the criteria of all *selected* buttons will appear in the Results pane on the right side of the Loop Browser.

▾ **Column View** (shown on the next page) contains a "Loops" column from which you choose "By Genres," "By Instruments," "By Moods," or "Favorites." Choose one of the loop keywords, then make keyword selections from the next two columns to narrow the selection of loops that appears in the Results pane on the right.

To turn off a keyword button selection in Button View, click it again.

To turn off all keyword button selections, click the "Reset" button in the upper-left corner of the Loop Browser.

—continued

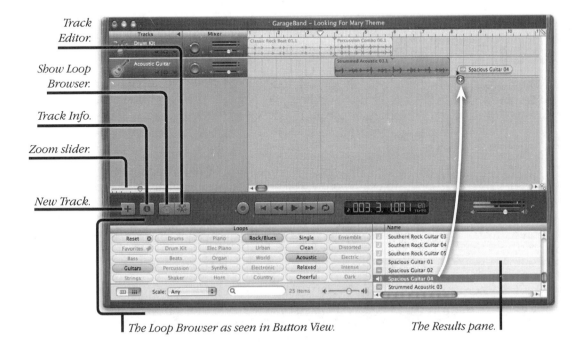

Track Editor.

Show Loop Browser.

Track Info.

Zoom slider.

New Track.

The Loop Browser as seen in Button View.   The Results pane.

The Loop Browser as seen in Column View.

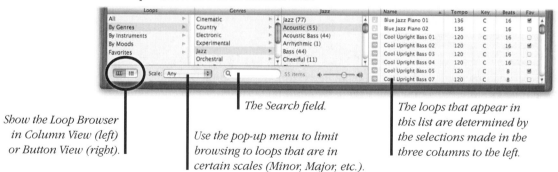

Show the Loop Browser in Column View (left) or Button View (right).

The Search field.

Use the pop-up menu to limit browsing to loops that are in certain scales (Minor, Major, etc.).

The loops that appear in this list are determined by the selections made in the three columns to the left.

Use the **Search field** (shown above) to find certain loops quickly. Select a loop category in the first column, then type a keyword in the Search field that might appear in a loop name. Press the Return key to show any matches in the right-hand pane.

Click the **Track Editor** button (circled below) to open the Track Editor pane in place of the Loop Browser pane. In the example below, a Grand Piano track (a *Software Instrument*) is selected in the Timeline. The notes, represented by gray and black horizontal bars, were created by clicking on the keys of the software keyboard.

Velocity refers to how hard you press the keys on a MIDI keyboard. Different levels of pressure produce different sounds. The Desktop piano keyboard simulates velocity by detecting a click's location. Click the top of a key for low velocity notes; click on the bottom of keys for high velocity notes.

- ▼ A black bar indicates a *high velocity* note with a louder volume. Gray bars indicate *low velocity,* softer notes.
- ▼ Drag notes up or down in the Track Editor to change their pitch. Drag notes left or right to change their position in the music.
- ▼ To change a note's duration, drag its right edge to the left or right.
- ▼ In the "Region" column, click the "Fix Timing" button to accurately align notes in the grid so they match the music beat perfectly.
- ▼ Drag the "Transpose" slider to change the key + or − 36 semitones.

Transpose.

Click here to show the Track Editor.

To extend a note's duration, hover over the right edge of the note to change the cursor to an arrow, then drag to the right.

To create a note directly in the Track Editor, Option-drag an existing note to a new position. The copied note will have the same duration as the original, but the pitch will depend on where you position the copied note.

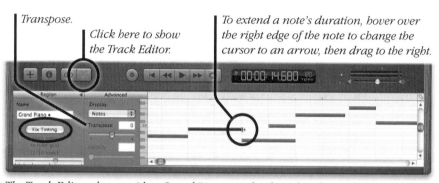

The Track Editor, shown with a Grand Piano track selected in the Timeline.

Real Instruments are colored blue in the Timeline and in the Track Editor. **Software Instruments** are colored green. See page 226–227 for more information about **Real vs. Software Instruments.**

Drag the "Transpose" slider to change a loop's key.

The Track Editor with a Guitar track selected in the Timeline.

If a *Real Instrument* is selected in the Timeline when you open the Track Editor, the content in the Editor pane looks different, as shown above.

▼ **To change a loop's *key*** in increments of a single semitone (up to 36 semitones), drag the "Transpose" slider left or right. Drag the slider to the left to lower the key, or to the right to make the key higher. In the example above, I copied a Guitar loop in the Timeline to make four identical loops. Then I selected each loop and transposed a different number of semitones. You can see above that the key of the selected loop (the darker one) has been adjusted to +2 semitones.

▼ From the Track Editor you can select and delete an entire loop or sections of a loop. *Single-click* in the *center* third of a loop to select the entire loop (shown below, left).

Press-and-drag in the *bottom* third of a loop to select a fragment of the loop (shown below, center).

▼ *Drag* the *top* third of a loop to move it around in the Track Editor pane (shown below, right).

▼ You can drag a loop to *overlap* another loop. The overlapped section of the bottom loop will be replaced by the overlapping section of the top loop. If you decide later to recover the overlapped section of a loop, drag the bottom-left or bottom-right edge of the shortened loop. An overlapped loop adopts the key of the overlapping loop.

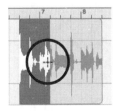
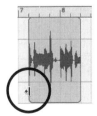
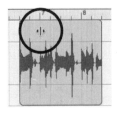

In the Track Editor, the pointer changes appearance when it hovers over a different area of a loop.

—continued

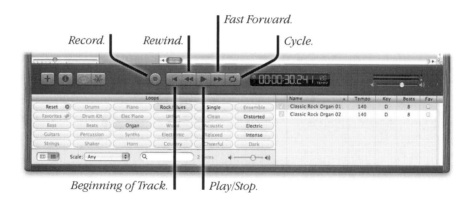

Record.   *Rewind.*   *Fast Forward.*   *Cycle.*

Beginning of Track.   *Play/Stop.*

The **Transport Control** buttons include *Record, Beginning of Track, Rewind, Play/Stop, Fast Forward,* and *Cycle* (loop).

- ▼ **Record:** Click this when you've connected a MIDI-compatible keyboard, a guitar, or a microphone and you're ready to record an original track, or if you want to record a track using the Desktop keyboard. Click the Record button again to stop recording.

- ▼ **Beginning of Track:** Click to jump the Playhead to the beginning of the track.

- ▼ **Rewind:** Click to move the Playhead back in the track one measure. Press and hold the Rewind button to move the Playhead back continuously.

- ▼ **Play:** Click to start playback of a song or cycle region. Click the Play button again to **stop** playback. You can also use the Spacebar on your keyboard to start and stop playback.

- ▼ **Fast Forward:** Click to move the Playhead forward in the track one measure. Press-and-hold the Fast Forward button to move the Playhead forward continuously.

- ▼ **Cycle:** Click to turn looping on and off. To designate a *cycle region* (a segment of the Timeline you want to loop), click the Cycle button. A *cycle region bar,* a yellow-orange area, appears at the top of the window to indicate the segment of the Timeline that will loop. Drag either edge of the bar to change the cycle region.

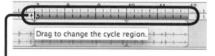

The cycle region is indicated by a yellow-orange shade.

The pointer turns into a double-arrow icon when hovering over the edge of the cycle region.

The Time and Tempo display.

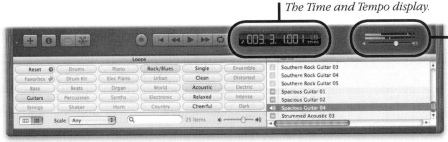

The Master volume slider and level meters.

The time in this example is shown as musical time, indicated by the music note icon.

Time display: Shows the position of the Playhead in *musical time* or *absolute time*. Musical time is shown as measures, beats, and ticks; absolute time is shown as hours, minutes, seconds, and fractions of a second. *Click on the left side* of the time display to change to absolute time as shown on the right. The absolute time display shows a small clock icon in the top-left corner.

The tiny clock in the upper-left corner indicates absolute time. When showing musical time, this becomes a tiny music note.

To change the Playhead position from within the Time display, click on one of the numerals, then drag *vertically* up or down. You can also double-click one of the numerals in the Time display, type a value, then double-click the numeral again to set it.

Tempo display: Shows the current tempo. **To change the tempo,** click on the Tempo area of the display, then drag the Tempo slider that opens to a new tempo. If the Time display is set to show absolute time, the Time display changes as you adjust the tempo.

Master volume slider and level meters: Control and monitor the output volume of the entire song.

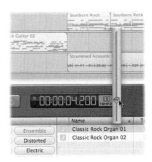

- ▼ Drag the *Master volume slider* left or right to adjust the song's final output volume.

- ▼ The two *level meters* located above the volume slider show the activity of the left and right audio channels, which are left and right speakers. Volume levels that are too high can't be accurately reproduced and will cause sound *distortion,* also referred to as *clipping.* If clipping occurs, the small round lights to the right of the meters (called *clipping indicators*) turn red. Monitor the volume levels as you create a composition to make sure the volume stays within a safe range. If the clipping indicators turn red, lower the volume, then click the clipping indicator lights to reset them.

The Tempo slider pops up when you click the Tempo area of the Time display.

The clipping indicators glow red when volume settings are causing audio distortion problems.

Compose Your First Song

Yes, it's possible to go from musically challenged to brilliant composer in one day or less. Possibly *much* less. Just locate some prerecorded **loops** in the Loop Browser that you like, then drag them around in the Timeline in any order that sounds pleasing. If you want to juice it up some more, experiment with adding more tracks with other instruments, fade the volume in and out at key points, then add some effects or adjust existing effects.

If you haven't already created a new song file, see page 202. The following pages explain the basic steps of finding loops, adding tracks, placing loops in tracks, arranging and mixing your song, then exporting it to an iTunes playlist.

Find loops for your song

The Loop Browser button.

To deselect a button, click it again.
To deselect all buttons, click the "Reset" button in the top-left corner of the browser.

Drag buttons to rearrange them in the Loop Browser.

To reset the buttons to the default layout, open the Preferences window, then click the "Reset" button (see "Keyword Layout" on page 228).

Unless you're recording your own original music (as explained on page 231), you'll create original compositions by placing loops of music in the Timeline. To locate the loops you want to use, use the Loop Browser.

1. Click the Loop Browser button (the eye icon) to open the Loop Browser. If the browser is already open, you can click this button again to close it.

2. Choose the *view* in which you prefer to browse for loops: *Column View* or *Button View* (see pages 205–206 for more details).

3. **If you browse in Button View,** click the browser's keyword buttons to narrow your search. When you click a keyword button, other buttons that don't relate to that category are dimmed. The loops that appear in the Results pane change as you click different buttons.

   If you browse in Column View, the idea is the same. Select a keyword in each column to narrow your search for different types of loops.

4. Loops that match the criteria of your search, determined by keyword selections, appear in a list in the Results pane.

Click here to show the Loop Browser.

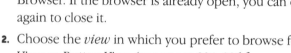

The Loop Browser.

Button View is selected.

The Results pane.

Preview loops

As you browse the loop selections, you really have no idea what they really sound like unless you listen to them.

▼ Click a loop name or icon in the Results pane to preview it.
   A speaker icon appears next to the loop while it plays.

▼ To stop the preview, click the speaker icon.

▼ To adjust the preview's volume, drag the volume slider located at the bottom of the browser.

▼ As you browse and preview loops, you can mark your Favorites for easy access later. Click a loop's "Fav" checkbox in the Results pane (circled below) to mark it as a favorite.

   To show Favorites in Button View, click the "Favorites" button in the top-left corner of the browser.

   To show Favorites in Column View, click "Favorites" in the "Loops" column.

A selected keyword button.

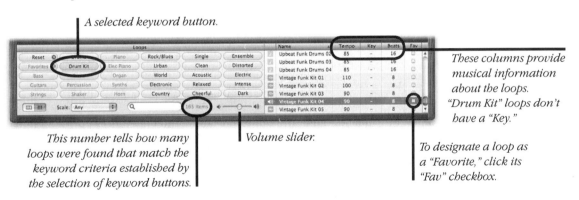

These columns provide musical information about the loops. "Drum Kit" loops don't have a "Key."

This number tells how many loops were found that match the keyword criteria established by the selection of keyword buttons.

Volume slider.

To designate a loop as a "Favorite," click its "Fav" checkbox.

At this point you may notice that some loops shown in the Loop Browser are green and have a music note icon, while others are blue with a waveform icon. GarageBand includes loops of two kinds: *Software Instruments* and *Real Instruments.* See pages 214–215 for more information about using Software Instrument loops vs. Real Instrument loops.

Software Instrument loops are green and have music note icons.

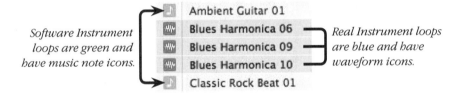

Real Instrument loops are blue and have waveform icons.

Building a song with tracks

Tracks, along with loops, are GarageBand's main building blocks. As you add tracks, they're stacked on top of each other in the Timeline. This makes it possible to overlap the sound of many different instruments. You can reorganize the tracks by dragging them up and down in the list of tracks, but the order of tracks won't affect the sound.

Each track you add can hold one or more loops. A track may contain more than one kind of instrument loop (a drum loop and a guitar loop, for example), but every loop in a track must be either a *Software Instrument* loop or a *Real Instrument* loop; Software and Real loops cannot be in the same track. There are two basic ways to add a track to GarageBand—go through the "New Track" window (shown below), or drag loops from the Loop Browser to the Timeline (shown on the following page).

Use the "New Track" window to add a new track:

1. From the Track menu, choose "New Track," **or** click the "New Track" button (the plus sign icon) beneath the Timeline.

2. In the "New Track" window that opens, click the "Real Instrument" button or the "Software Instrument" button (Software Instruments require a lot more processing power).

3. From the left column, choose an instrument category, then choose an instrument from the right column. If you plan to *record* a track, you can choose a "Basic Track" in the "Real Instrument" pane. A "Basic Track" has no effects applied to it, but you can add them later.

4. Click OK. A new track is added to the Timeline.

The number of tracks you can add to a song depends on how much memory your computer has installed. A maximum of 255 Real Instrument tracks or 64 Software Instrument tracks are allowed.

GarageBand automatically sets the maximum number of tracks your computer can support without affecting performance. You can change this setting in preferences (see page 230).

When you first open GarageBand, a Grand Piano track is automatically added to the Timeline. If you want to delete this default track (or any other track), select it, then press Command-Delete.

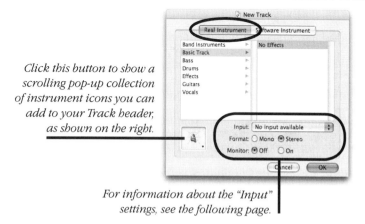

Click this button to show a scrolling pop-up collection of instrument icons you can add to your Track header, as shown on the right.

For information about the "Input" settings, see the following page.

To change the icon that appears in the header of a track, scroll through this collection of icons.

"Input" settings in the "New Track" window:

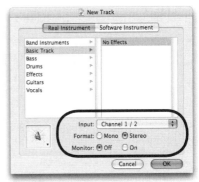

- ▼ If you have a musical instrument or microphone connected to your Mac, the "Input" pop-up menu shows the *instrument input source*. The example on the right shows a MIDI-compatible keyboard connected to the computer. If you have multiple devices connected, choose one of them here.

- ▼ From the "Format" menu, choose "Mono" or "Stereo." By default, Real Instrument loops have a "Stereo" format.

The "Input" settings.

- ▼ To hear your recorded music or vocals through the speakers as you record, set "Monitor" to "On." If you have a problem with feedback, choose "Off."

Drag loops from the Loop Browser to the Timeline:

1. Use the Loop Browser to select a loop you want to use in your song.
2. Drag the loop from the Results pane of the Loop Browser and drop it into the Timeline area of the GarageBand window.

As shown below, GarageBand automatically creates a track and places the loop in the track.

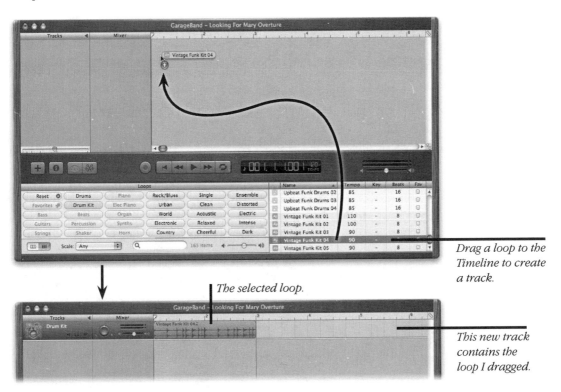

Drag a loop to the Timeline to create a track.

The selected loop.

This new track contains the loop I dragged.

Add loops to a track

Drag multiple loops to a track to compose your song. Experiment with different loops to see how they sound next to an existing loop. Drag some loops to other tracks to see how certain instruments sound when playing at the same time. For instance, you can place a drum loop in one track, a southern rock piano in a second track, and a horn section in a third track, all playing at the same time. The example below shows what such an arrangement could look like.

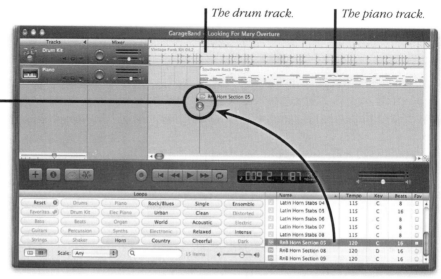

The drum track.   The piano track.

As you drag a loop to the Timeline, a black vertical line appears under the loop icon to show the position of the loop's start point. Let go of the loop when the vertical line is positioned at the point you want the loop to start playing.

A graphic display of notes in a Software Instrument loop.

Notice above how the top track ("Drum Kit") looks different from the second track ("Piano"). The loop in the top track, "Vintage Funk Kit," is a *Real Instrument* loop and it contains an audio waveform. The loop in the second track, Southern Rock Piano, is a *Software Instrument* loop and it contains a graphic representation of the notes. Software Instrument loops require more computer processing power than Real Instrument loops, so you may want to convert some Software Instrument loops to Real Instrument loops as you add them to the Timeline (see pages 226–227 to learn more about Real Instruments and Software Instruments).

Convert loops and regions

A loop or a collection of loops adjacent to each other in a track is called a **region** (learn more about regions starting on page 217). You can convert a *Software Instrument* loop or region to a *Real Instrument* loop or region. You might want to do this to reduce processing demands on your computer, since Software Instruments require more processing, or perhaps you prefer working with Real Instrument loops and waveforms in the Track Editor instead of Software Instruments and individual notes (see page 218).

To convert a Software Instrument loop to a Real Instrument loop:

▼ Drag a loop from the Loop Browser to an existing Real Instrument track (Real Instrument tracks and Real Instrument loops are *blue*).

Or Option-drag a Software Instrument loop from the Loop Browser to an empty area in the Timeline to convert the loop and create a new Real Instrument track for it.

To convert a Software Instrument region to a Real Instrument region:

1. "Solo" a track (mute all other tracks) that contains only the region you want to convert. **To solo a track,** click the small headphones icon in the Track header; all other tracks will be turned off.

2. From the File menu, choose "Export to iTunes."

3. Go to the location on your computer in which the exported song file is stored: Open your Home folder, open the Music folder, open the iTunes folder, open the iTunes Music folder, then look for a folder whose name is the same as the "Album Name" set in the "Export" pane in the GarageBand preferences (see page 230).

4. Drag the exported file into an existing Real Instrument track in the GarageBand Timeline.

   Or drag the file to the Timeline in an empty area beneath existing tracks to create a new Real Instrument track.

You can also **drag audio files from the Finder** to the Timeline. Drag an audio file (AIFF, WAV, MP3, or AAC) from anywhere on your computer to the Timeline. The "protected AAC" format is not supported. Songs purchased from the iTunes Music Store are in the protected AAC format. MP3 and AAC files that you drag to the Timeline are converted to the AIFF format.

Control your Timeline view

If you **lock** the Timeline and editor Playheads, the Timeline and the Track Editor display the same part of a song. When you click the *Play* button, both Playheads move to the right until they reach the middle of the Timeline, then they stop and remain stationary as the Timeline scrolls by beneath them.

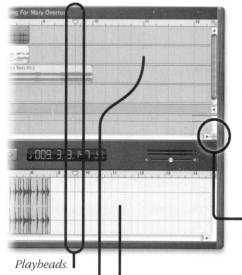

If you **unlock** the Playheads, the Timeline remains stationary and the Playheads move to the right until they are out of sight. With the Playheads unlocked, you can work with one part of the song visible in the Timeline and another part of the song visible in the Track Editor.

To lock the Timeline and editor Playheads, click the pair of small white triangles (circled, to the left). When the two triangles are aligned, they are locked (click again to unlock them).

The two aligned triangles (above) indicate locked Playheads. Unaligned triangles indicate unlocked Playheads.

Playheads.

Timeline.

Track Editor.

Monitor GarageBand's processing

Click the Play button and watch the Playheads as they move across the Timeline. The top triangular part of the Playhead changes color to show how much of the computer's processing power GarageBand is using. A white Playhead means your computer is handling the task without a problem. If the Playhead turns orange, the computer is starting to struggle to process all the digital information in real time. A red Playhead means GarageBand is over-taxed and may not be able to finish playing the song.

You may be able to improve GarageBand's performance by deleting some tracks, especially Software Instrument tracks. You can also set a lower number of maximum tracks and notes in GarageBand preferences as shown on pages 228–230. GarageBand demands a lot of processing power and works best with newer computers (as in the G5) that have lots of memory installed.

Arrange and modify regions in your song

A loop placed in a track is considered a **region.** You can make as many changes as you want to a region's position, duration, pitch, or sound effects without affecting the original loop. As you work on your song, "loop" refers to the original, unchanged audio clip, and "region" refers to the version of the audio clip that's in the Timeline, modified or not.

Ways to modify a region:

▼ **To delete a region** (loop) from a track, select it, then press Delete.

 Or select a region in a track, then press Command X.

 Or from the Edit menu choose "Cut."

▼ **To copy a region and place it somewhere else,** select it, then press Command C (or from the Edit menu, choose "Copy"). Select a track into which you want to paste the copied region, position the Playhead where you want the beginning of the region to be placed, then press Command V (or from the Edit menu, choose "Paste").

 Or Option-drag a region to a different position in the track or to another track. The original region stays in its position and a copy of the region is dragged to the new position.

▼ **Resize** a region to change its duration.

 To lengthen a region's duration, place the pointer over the top half of the region's right edge. The pointer changes to a *loop pointer.* Drag the edge to the right to lengthen the region. A duplicate waveform of the original loop shows in the new lengthened area (shown below). This is known as "looping." The region will loop (repeat) seamlessly and smoothly. You can stretch the region out as far as you need to make the loop repeat as many times as necessary.

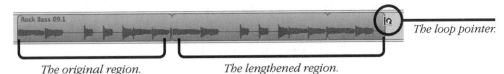

The loop pointer.

The original region.   *The lengthened region.*

 To shorten a region's duration, place the pointer over the bottom half of the region's right edge. The pointer changes to a *resize pointer.* Drag the edge to the left to shorten the region.

The resize pointer.

—continued

Try this technique to add interest to a track: Paste multiple copies of the same loop next to each other, then transpose each of the loops a different amount (+1, −1, +2, etc.).

▼ You can **Transpose** most regions to a different key, up or down, in semitone increments. There are 12 semitones in an octave.

Regions created with Real Instrument loops (blue regions) can be transposed up or down a maximum of 12 semitones.

Regions created with Software Instrument loops (green regions) can be transposed up or down 36 semitones, or three octaves.

Regions created from Real Instrument *recordings* (purple regions) cannot be transposed.

To transpose a region:

1. Click a region to select it.

2. Click the *Track Editor* button (the scissors icon) to open the Track Editor. The selected track is displayed in the Editor pane.

3. In the "Advanced" column of the Track Editor, drag the "Transpose" slider left or right to lower or raise the region's key.

The selected region.

The Track Editor button.

Click this small triangle to hide or show the "Advanced" column.

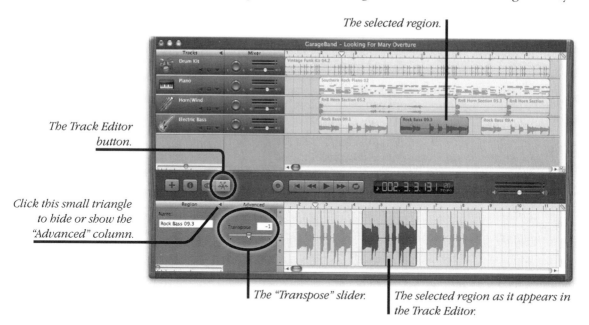

The "Transpose" slider.

The selected region as it appears in the Track Editor.

Transposing sometimes moves an instrument out of its natural range and then it doesn't sound right. If this happens, try transposing the region up or down an entire octave (12 semitones).

▼ **Split a region** to divide it into separated sections that can be moved, modified, copied or deleted. If you want a region to start playing somewhere in the middle, split it and delete the first section. **Or** split a region, then drag the two pieces apart in the Timeline to create a short pause between sections of the music.

Select the region you want to split, then from the Edit menu choose "Split."

▼ **Join two or more** Software Instrument regions (green regions) to make it easy to rearrange entire sections of music. To join regions they must be adjacent to each other in the same track.

You can also join a *recorded* Real Instrument region with another Real Instrument region, but two Real Instrument regions created from loops cannot be joined.

1. Select the regions you want to join. To make a multiple selection, hold down the Shift key as you select regions.

2. From the Edit menu choose "Join Selected."

When you join a *recorded* Real Instrument region (a purple region) to another Real Instrument region (a blue region), a dialog opens to ask if you want to create a new audio file. Click "Create" to join the regions and place them in a new Real Instrument region.

Two selected regions that are to be joined.

The two regions joined as one.

▼ To **Rename** a region, select the region in the Timeline, then click the Track Editor button. In the "Region" column of the Track Editor, type a new name into the "Name" field.

The Track Editor button.

—continued

▼ **To move regions** anywhere in the Timeline, even to other tracks, drag them. If you move a region so it overlaps another region, the overlapped section of the other region will be clipped. **To recover the clipped content,** drag the bottom-right or bottom-left edge of the clip with the resize pointer (page 217).

▼ **To edit the individual notes** of Software Instrument regions (green regions): Select a Software Instrument region, as shown below, then click the Track Editor button (the scissors icon). Each note of the region is represented in the Track Editor Timeline as a rectangle. **To change the pitch of a note,** drag it up or down in the grid. **To change a note's position** in the music, drag it left or right. **To change a note's duration,** grab its right edge and drag left or right.

Software Instrument regions are green and contain graphic representations of music notes.

Real Instrument regions are blue and contain audio waveforms.

The Timeline grid button.

The selected Software Instrument track.

The Timeline Zoom slider.

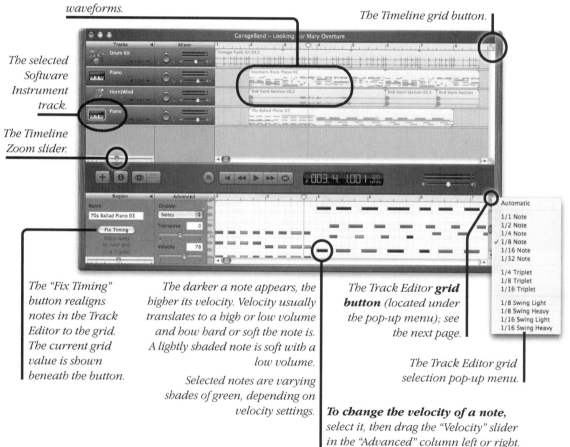

The "Fix Timing" button realigns notes in the Track Editor to the grid. The current grid value is shown beneath the button.

The darker a note appears, the higher its velocity. Velocity usually translates to a high or low volume and how hard or soft the note is. A lightly shaded note is soft with a low volume.

Selected notes are varying shades of green, depending on velocity settings.

*The Track Editor **grid button** (located under the pop-up menu); see the next page.*

The Track Editor grid selection pop-up menu.

To change the velocity of a note, select it, then drag the "Velocity" slider in the "Advanced" column left or right. (If the Advanced column isn't showing, click the tiny triangle in the Region column heading.)

▼ Set a **cycle region** (a region that repeats, or loops) when you want to preview a specific section of a song as you work on its arrangement or if you want to record over a specific part of a song. **To set a cycle region,** click the Cycle button (the looping arrows). A yellow cycle region ruler appears just below the beat ruler. Drag this yellow ruler to the section you want to cycle. Drag either end of the yellow ruler to adjust the region selection.

If you don't see the yellow ruler, just press-and-drag in an empty section of the cycle ruler to set the cycle region to a new position.

*Drag the edges of the **yellow** ruler to designate the region you want to loop.*

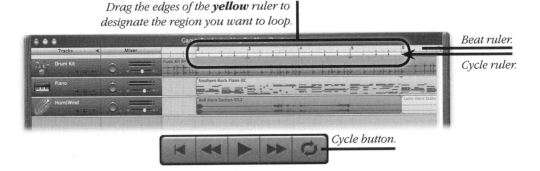

Beat ruler.

Cycle ruler.

Cycle button.

Change the grid

There are two **grid buttons** that look like tiny ruler icons; see the opposite page. These let you set the Timeline grid and the Track Editor grid to any of the note values shown in their pop-up menus, also shown on the opposite page. When the grid value is set to "Automatic," the grid value changes automatically as you zoom in or out of the Timeline or Track Editor. The Triplet and Swing settings can completely change the rhythm and feel of a region. **To test the effect,** try this grid-setting experiment:

1. Place a Software Instrument loop, such as "70s Ballad Piano" in the Timeline. Select it, click the Play button, and listen to it.

2. Click the Track Editor button (scissors icon) to open the Track Editor.

3. Click the Track Editor's grid button and choose "1/8 Swing Heavy" from the pop-up menu.

4. Select a note in the Track Editor, then press Command A to select all the notes in the region.

5. Click the "Fix Timing" button in the "Region" pane (shown on the opposite page). The notes realign themselves to the Swing grid you selected.

Listen to the region again and notice the difference in rhythm and beat emphasis. A different grid selection won't make any difference unless you make sure to do Steps 4 and 5.

Mix Your Song

After you've placed and arranged the loops, tracks, and regions (the main building blocks of your song), you're ready to **mix** your song. Mixing a song is the process of fine-tuning the individual parts so they work together as a pleasing, cohesive whole. This usually includes adjusting the volume of tracks and regions to emphasize or downplay certain instruments or themes, changing the pan position (the balance of left and right speakers) of certain regions, and adding effects to tracks or regions to enhance sound or to give it a special character.

Adjust track volume

Multiple tracks playing at the same volume level sound okay, but you can add richness and interest by setting individual volume levels for different tracks. You can also independently modify the volume of any region, or any portion of a region, and control how fast the volume fades in or out.

To adjust the volume of an entire track: In the "Mixer" column of the Track header, drag the volume slider left or right.

To make multiple volume adjustments to a track: Click the small disclosure triangle in the "Tracks" column to show the *Volume Curve* track. The horizontal colored line (the "curve") represents the track's volume. Click anywhere on the volume line to create control points (small colored spheres). Drag control points up or down to raise or lower the volume. Drag control points left or right to change the duration of a volume change.

Click to show a Volume Curve track below this track.

A selected control point's dark outline makes it look slightly larger.

Volume Curve track.

To enable the Volume Curve settings, check this box.

To disable the Volume Curve settings and return volume control to the Volume slider in the "Mixer" column, uncheck this box.

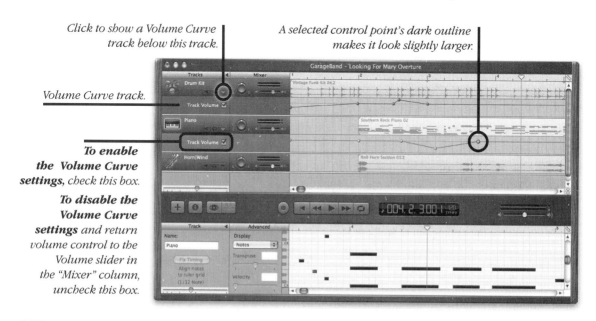

Add pan position

Pan position refers to the balance of sound between the left and right speakers and is also known as *stereo placement*.

To adjust track pan position, press-and-drag the white marker on the pan control to the left or right. You can also click anywhere around the dial and the white marker will jump to that position.

If a track is playing while you adjust the pan control, you can hear the sound moving from one speaker to another (if you have stereo speakers connected to your computer).

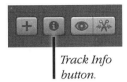

Pan control.

You can't fully appreciate and enjoy some aspects of GarageBand (like pan control) unless you have stereo headphones or stereo speakers connected to your Mac.

Add effects

To further enhance the sound of specific instruments and your entire composition, you can add adjustable, high-quality sound effects such as compression, echo, reverb, equalizer settings, and more.

You can apply effects to a single track or to the entire song (referred to as the Master Track in the "Track Info" window).

Track Info button.

To add effects to a track:

1. Select a track in the Timeline.

2. Click the Track Info button (the letter "i") to open the "Track Info" window.

   Or double-click a Track header.

The top section of the window contains an Instrument button (Real Instrument or Software Instrument, depending on the type of track selected) and a Master Track button.

Click the Instrument button to show categories in the left pane. Choose a category, then choose an instrument or effect from that category in the Master Track pane on the right. Experiment with different settings. Some combinations make a dramatic change in how the track sounds and others make subtle changes, depending on the instruments in the selected track.

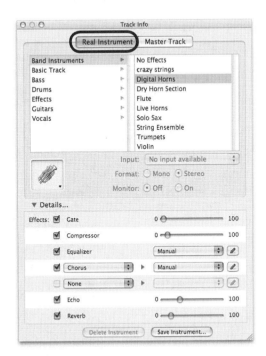

—*continued*

The "Details" pane on the bottom half of the "Track Info" window is a collection of effects you can choose to use or turn off. If you don't see the Details pane, click the disclosure triangle next to "Details…" to open the pane.

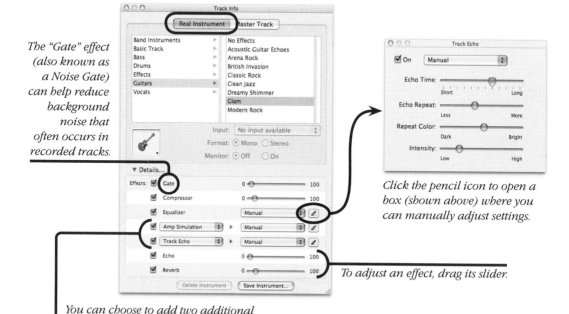

The "Gate" effect (also known as a Noise Gate) can help reduce background noise that often occurs in recorded tracks.

Click the pencil icon to open a box (shown above) where you can manually adjust settings.

To adjust an effect, drag its slider.

You can choose to add two additional effects to the set of effects included in the "Details" pane. From these pop-up menus, choose an effect, then choose a preset for that effect from the adjacent pop-up menu.

Or choose "Manual" from the adjacent pop-up menu, then click the pencil icon to open a window of manual adjustments for the chosen effect.

As you experiment and change settings, a dialog box will ask if you want to save the current settings. Choose "Save" to name the settings and add them as a preset to the Track Info list (see the next page). Choose "Don't Save" if you just want to preview instruments and effects. Or check the "Never ask again" checkbox.

Software Instrument "Track Info" windows look similar to Real Instrument "Track Info" windows (above-left).

Click the **Master Track** button to work with settings that affect the sound of the entire song rather than just a single track. In addition to choosing instruments and effects, you can also change the **tempo, time,** and **key** in the "Master Track" pane. If the song is playing as you change settings, you can hear the effect immediately.

To change instrument and effect settings, select a *category* in the upper-left pane, then select an *instrument or effect* in the upper-right pane. Click the Play button in the main window so you can hear the changes as you try different settings.

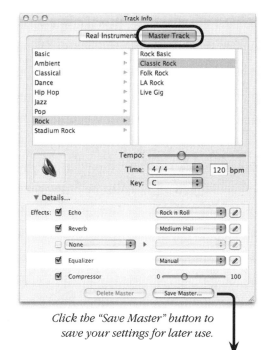

The lower "Details" pane provides a standard set of effects, plus a menu from which you can choose one additional effect. As shown on the previous page, when an effect is modified by choosing "Manual" from its adjacent pop-up menu, you can click the pencil icon to open a separate window in which you can make manual adjustments to the effect.

Click the "Save Master" button to save your settings for later use.

When you make customized changes to the sound of the Master Track, you can **save the settings** to use later.

1. Choose the settings and effects you want.
2. Click the "Save Master" button.
3. In the "Save Master" dialog, type a name for the settings.
4. Click "Save." The new name appears in the upper-right pane of the "Track Info" window, as shown to the right.

If you turn off "Echo" and "Reverb" effects in the Master Track settings, they will be disabled in the Instrument pane settings.

Unless you're a musician, the effects names are unfamiliar and strange. The best way to learn what the various effects are about is to listen to them, but here are definitions of a few:

The saved settings are added to the effects list in the "Master Track" pane.

Compressor: Adjusts the difference between the loudest and softest parts of a song or track.

Chorus: A delay effect in which copies of the sound are played back slightly out of tune to simulate several voices or instruments.

Flanger: Similar to Chorus, but played back more out of tune.

Phaser: Adds a whooshing sound.

Real Instruments and Software Instruments

Real Instrument loops are created by recording real instruments in a studio (or at home with GarageBand).

Software Instrument loops are MIDI (Musical Instrument Digital Interface) voices. They are created digitally and are actually mathmatical descriptions of musical sounds, which requires intensive computer processing to play.

GarageBand uses two different instrument formats—Real Instruments and Software Instruments. Throughout this chapter we've scattered explanations of the differences and pointed out instances where one or the other format was used. In case you didn't start at the beginning of this chapter and read straight through, this brief summary of Real and Software Instruments will help you understand and identify them in GarageBand.

The GarageBand Timeline can contain both Real Instrument tracks and Software Instrument tracks.

Real Instruments

Real Instruments appear as both *tracks* and *loops.* Real Instrument tracks and loops are always *blue.* And the Volume Curve that's located beneath a Real Instrument track is blue. Blue equals Real Instrument format.

Blue loops.

Blue headers.

A Real Instrument track in the Timeline. Blue Volume Curve.

Real Instrument loops in the Loop Browser are blue and have blue waveform icons. When you drag a blue loop (a Real Instrument loop) from the Loop Browser to the Timeline, it automatically creates a Real Instrument track.

Blue shading and blue icons.

Real Instrument loops as seen in the Loop Browser.

Only Real Instrument loops can be placed in Real Instrument tracks. You can place different kinds of musical instruments (drums, guitars, harmonica, etc.) in a single Real Instrument track, as long as they're all in the Real Instrument format (blue).

Since Real Instruments require less processing power during playback than Software Instruments, you may have fewer performance problems if you use mostly Real Instrument loops.

A Real Instrument loop in the Track Editor.

A Real Instrument loop in the Track Editor appears as a blue waveform. In the Track Editor you can transform (change the pitch) a Real Instrument loop, or select and transform just part of a loop.

Software Instruments

Software Instruments appear as both *tracks* and *loops*. Software Instrument tracks and loops are always *green*. Software Instrument loops in the Timeline are green and the Volume Curve beneath a Software Instrument track is green. Software Instrument loops in the Loop Browser have green music note icons and green backgrounds.

Green headers.

Green loop.

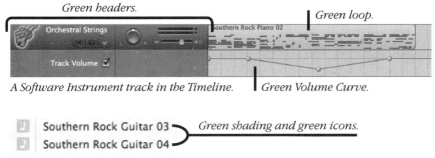

A Software Instrument track in the Timeline. Green Volume Curve.

Southern Rock Guitar 03 — *Green shading and green icons.*
Southern Rock Guitar 04 —

Software Instrument loops as seen in the Loop Browser.

Only Software Instrument loops can be placed in Software Instrument tracks. Various musical instruments can be placed in a single Software Instrument track, as long as they're all in the Software Instrument format (green).

A Software Instrument loop in the Track Editor is green and shows each individual note as a rectangle. In the Track Editor you can fix the timing of notes, alter the rhythm by changing the grid value, transpose any note or change its velocity, and from the "Display" pop-up menu you can choose to show graphic representations of notes, modulation, pitchbend, or sustain effects.

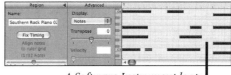

A Software Instrument loop in the Track Editor.

Software Instruments require more processing power during playback than Real Instruments. You may be able to avoid some performance problems, such as audio stuttering or a Playhead that has trouble keeping up with audio, if you convert Software Instrument loops to Real Instrument loops when you add them to the Timeline.

To convert a Software Instrument loop to a Real Instrument loop:

Also see page 215 about converting.

▼ Drag a Software Instrument loop to an existing Real Instrument track in the Timeline.

▼ **Or** Option-drag a Software Instrument loop to an empty space in the Timeline, below existing tracks. A new Real Instrument track that contains the loop is automatically created.

GarageBand Preferences

The GarageBand preferences window lets you choose certain behaviors and lets you set options that suit your hardware and your preferred way of working with music files.

To open the preferences window, go to the GarageBand application menu and choose "Preferences…." The top of the window contains four category buttons. Click each one to see the options available for that category.

General preferences

Metronome: A metronome is a device that clicks at regular, preset intervals so musicians can keep an accurate beat as they play music. Choose to have GarageBand's metronome play just during a live recording session, or during playback and live recording.

Keyword Browsing: Uncheck "Filter for more relevant results" to increase the number of loops found by a keyword search in the Loop Browser.

Keyword Layout: If you rearranged the keyword buttons in the Loop Browser, you can return them to the default layout. Just click the "Reset" button.

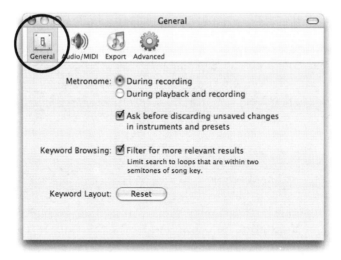

Audio/MIDI preferences

Audio Output: Choose the speakers you want to use for playback as you compose your song. Choose "Built-in Audio" to use your built-in computer speaker or headphones. If you have external speakers connected, you can choose them from this menu.

This setting overrides the existing audio output settings in the Sound preferences pane of System Preferences.

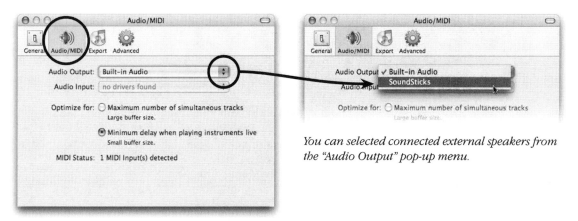

You can selected connected external speakers from the "Audio Output" pop-up menu.

Audio Input: If you have an input device connected to your computer, such as an audio interface for MIDI keyboards or some other instrument, you can select the device from this menu. This setting overrides the existing audio input settings in the Sound preferences pane of System Preferences.

Optimize for: These settings attempt to help optimize the performance of GarageBand when recording live instruments. Choose **Maximum number of simultaneous tracks** if you don't have *latency* issues or if you have a slower computer (slower than a G5). Also try this setting when your song contains a lot of tracks.

In audio recording, *latency* is the delay you may hear between playing a sound and recording it on the computer. It is caused by the amount of time it takes for a real instrument sound to reach the input port and be digitally processed by the computer.

If you have *latency* problems while playing/recording your musical instrument, choose **Minimum delay when playing instruments live** to set a small buffer size and reduce latency. This setting uses more of the computer's processing power to speed up the processing of audio input signals and may affect overall performance on slower computers.

MIDI Status: Shows how many MIDI devices are connected to the computer.

Export preferences

Enter the information that you want to appear in iTunes when you finish your song and export it (as explained on page 232).

iTunes Playlist: iTunes creates a new playlist in which to organize your exported songs. Type a name for the playlist if you want to change the default name assigned.

Composer Name: Type your name or any name you want to appear in the iTunes "Composer" column.

Album Name: Type in the name you want to appear in the iTunes "Album" column. This will also be the name of the folder that stores your exported GarageBand songs. The folder is located in the iTunes Music folder that's located in your Home folder (Home/Music/iTunes/iTunes Music Folder/ Your Album Name).

Advanced preferences

From the **Maximum Number of Tracks** pop-up menus, select how many Real Instrument tracks and Software Instrument tracks are allowed in a song. Select "Automatic" to let GarageBand choose the best number based on your computer's speed and how much RAM is installed.

From the **Voices per instrument** pop-up menu, select how many notes a Software Instrument can play at one time. If you select "Automatic," GarageBand

will choose the best number based on your computer's speed and the amount of RAM installed.

Adding Loops to Timeline: Check **Convert to Real Instrument** if you want Software Instrument loops to automatically convert to Real Instrument loops when dragged to the Timeline. If you don't select this checkbox, you can still convert a Software Instrument loop to a Real Instrument loop if you Option-drag it to an empty area in the Timeline, beneath existing tracks. **Or** drag it to an existing Real Instrument track.

Record Live Instruments or Vocals

You can create totally original music by recording your own instruments or vocals. Connect a musical instrument, such as a guitar, a MIDI keyboard, or a microphone, then record into a Real Instrument track.

Some MIDI keyboards and other instruments can plug directly into your computer. Some instruments and microphones may need to connect to an audio interface device that connects to the computer.

To connect an electric guitar, you can buy an adapter for about $20 that lets you plug directly into the computer. To connect several input devices at a time, such as a mic, a guitar, and a keyboard, consider buying a FireWire or USB audio adapter. You'll find excellent advice about these and other recording products at MacJams.com. Go to **www.MacJams.com** and click the "Buyer's Guide" link.

To record in a Real Instrument track:

1. Connect an instrument or a microphone to your computer.

2. Select an *existing* Real Instrument track in the Timeline and place the Playhead where you want to start recording.

   Or create a *new* track: Click the New Track button (the plus sign), then click the "Real Instrument" button in the "New Track" window (page 212). Choose an instrument or effect from the left and right panes, then click OK.

3. Click the Record button, then play the instrument or sing into the microphone. As you record, a region that contains your music is created in the track.

4. To stop recording, click the Record button again.

To record in a Software Instrument track:

1. Connect a MIDI-compatible keyboard to your computer.

   Or open the onscreen music keyboard, shown here. From the Window menu, choose "Keyboard."

2. Select an *existing* Software track in the Timeline and place the Playhead where you want to start recording.

   Or create a *new* track as described in Step 2 above.

3. Click the "Record" button, then play the connected keyboard or click the keys of the onscreen music keyboard. As you record, a region that contains your music is created in the track.

4. To stop recording, click the Record button again.

To scroll the visible keys and show other keys, click the triangle on the left or right side of the keyboard.

To stretch the keyboard and show more keys at a time, drag the bottom-right corner to the right.

Click the top of a key for a soft note. Click the bottom of a key for a hard, louder note.

The Master Track

In addition to Real and Software Instrument tracks, GarageBand includes a **Master Track.** To show the Master Track in the Timeline, from the Track menu choose "Show Master Track."

The Master Track contains a Volume Curve that lets you to edit the volume of the entire song (all tracks). As explained on page 222, click on the Volume Curve (the straight line) to add control points, then drag the control points up or down to adjust the volume. Drag control points left or right to shorten or lengthen the duration of the volume change. Click the "Master Volume" checkbox to enable or disable the Master Track volume edits.

The Master Track.   *Click on the line to create control points, then drag control points up or down to change the song's volume.*

Export Your Song to iTunes

When your song is finished, export it to iTunes so you can share it with others in a variety of ways. Once it's in iTunes, you can burn it to CD, use it in an iPhoto slideshow, or use it as a soundtrack in iMovie, then put the movie on the Internet using .Mac Homepage. You can use it as a background audio track in an iDVD menu, or just play it along with other songs in your iTunes collection.

Tip: When you're ready to add more music loops to your collection, you can buy GarageBand Jam Pack, a selection of more than 2,000 prerecorded loops, including more than 100 additional realistic instruments and effect settings. You can find Jam Pack at www.apple.com/garageband.

To export your song to iTunes:

1. Open GarageBand preferences, then click the "Export" button.

2. Type names in the text fields that you want iTunes to use for a new playlist containing your song, a composer name (your name will do), and an album name. See page 230 for more information about Export preferences.

3. From the File menu, choose "Export to iTunes." Your song now appears in the iTunes Library, named the same as your GarageBand song file. It also appears in the automatically created playlist that you just named.

   If you skip Steps 1 and 2, GarageBand will fill in the information for you, based on your computer's name, as shown on page 230.

Exported song files are saved as AIFF files (a standard Mac audio format).

Section *two*
.Mac apps

.Mac (pronounced "dot Mac") is a collection of tools and services that are available if you subscribe to a one-year .Mac membership for $99.95. For most people, the value of a .Mac membership far exceeds the price tag.

Each .Mac membership includes the software and services explained in this section: An **email account** with 15 megabytes of email storage space; **WebMail** for access to your email account and Address Book from any Mac or PC in the world; **iDisk** storage, 100 megabytes of personal storage space on Apple's servers; **HomePage,** web-based software for creating and publishing web pages; **iSync** to synchronize Address Book and iCal calendar information between multiple computers; **Backup** software to archive important files to your computer, to removable discs, or to your iDisk; **Virex** software for virus protection; **Slides Publisher** to publish your own slideshows over the Internet; and personalized **iCards** (electronic greeting cards) using your own photos. Membership also gives you access to a members-only technical support service, free software, and other perks.

Go to **www.mac.com** and click "Join Now." Or sign up for a sixty-day free trial, complete with an email address, to help you decide if you should join.

iDisk

When you become a .Mac member, you have instant access to your **iDisk**—100 megabytes of personal storage on Apple's servers. You can upgrade your iDisk storage capacity at any time (for a fee), up to 1,000 megabytes.

Your .Mac account relies on iDisk to make its best features a reality: creating web pages, backup protection of important files, synchronization of address books with your Mac, customized iCards, online calendars, slideshow screensavers, and whatever else Apple may offer in the near future.

You may want to use your iDisk to store files in a safe, remote location as personal backups or to store important files so you can retrieve them from any other location. Any files stored on your iDisk are accessible by you or (if you choose) a guest at any time, from almost any computer (Mac or PC).

Sharing files with others is effortless using iDisk Utility, which is a free download from Mac.com. Just set permissions and give someone your .Mac name and password to allow them to upload or download files to your Public folder. The iDisk Utility also makes it easy to monitor your iDisk space, access other .Mac members' Public folders, or purchase additional storage space.

iDisk is a wonderful asset that you'll use more and more as you become familiar with all the ways it can enhance your ever-expanding iLife.

Put iDisk on Your Desktop

When you sign up for a .Mac account, you automatically get 100 megabytes of hard disk space on a large computer at Apple, which his called your **iDisk.** You can "mount" your iDisk so it appears on your Desktop just like any other hard disk, then copy files between your Mac and the iDisk—you are really copying files from your Mac to Apple's computer (or vice versa). Once files are on your iDisk (at Apple), you can access them anywhere in the world.

To open your iDisk:

If you don't see the Go menu, you are not at the Finder—just click on any blank space you see of the Desktop and that will take you to the Finder.

1. If you haven't already connected to the Internet, do so now.

2. From the Go menu in the Finder, choose "iDisk," and then choose "My iDisk" from the submenu, as shown below.

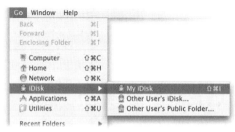

If you've *never* logged in to your .Mac account before: The Mac will probably ask you to enter your member name and password before you can mount your iDisk.

After the first time you log in to your .Mac account: When you choose "My iDisk" from the Go menu, a window opens that displays your iDisk, as shown below. Amazing. Don't get confused with these folders *that are named exactly the same as the folders in the Home folder* on your computer. The icon in the title bar (the iDisk crystal ball) indicates you're looking at folders on Apple's servers.

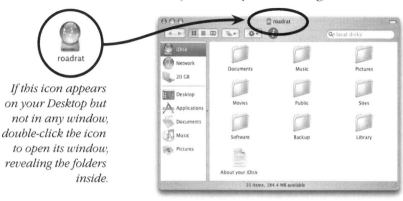

If this icon appears on your Desktop but not in any window, double-click the icon to open its window, revealing the folders inside.

How does your Mac know which iDisk to open?

How does your Mac know which iDisk is yours? Once you have set up an account, your member name and password appear in the .Mac System Preferences: Click the "System Preferences" icon in your Dock, then click the ".Mac" icon. You can see below the member name and password.

This is the System Preferences icon in the Dock.

If you have more than one .Mac account, you can go to a different account: First change the member name and password in this .Mac preference pane. Choosing "My iDisk" in the Go menu opens the account that is entered here, so change the account name and password and "My iDisk" will change.

An even quicker way to access a different iDisk without having to change your .Mac preferences is to choose "iDisk" from the Go menu on your Desktop and then "Other User's iDisk..." in the submenu.

You can set or change your .Mac account information in the .Mac preference pane.

Other ways to open your iDisk

▼ **Click the iDisk icon in the window Sidebar** (as shown to the right). An iDisk icon appears in the Sidebar of all Finder windows, giving you quick access to your iDisk at all times.

If the iDisk icon does not appear in the Sidebar: From the Finder menu, choose Preferences...." Click the "Sidebar" icon. Make sure that "iDisk" has a check next to it.

▼ **Use iDisk Utility,** as explained on page 241–242.

iDisk Contents

When you double-click the **iDisk** icon on your Desktop to open its **window,** you're actually looking at files and folders that are on Apple's server. This explains why the window is a bit slow to open (especially if you're using a telephone modem to connect instead of broadband).

This example shows an iDisk whose storage space has been upgraded (increased; see page 242), so the status bar shows more space available (184.4 MB) than your iDisk window may show.

This is an iDisk window. The folders you see here are actually on one of Apple's servers (computers)!

The icon in the title bar is your only clue that you are not in your own Home folder on your Mac.

All of your iDisk folders are **private** and accessible only to you (or someone who knows your password), except the folder called Public.

Documents folder: Drag into this folder any kind of document that you want to store and make available to yourself over the Internet. This folder is private and only you have access to it.

Music folder: Drag music files and playlists to this private iDisk folder so you can have access to them from anywhere in the world.

Pictures folder: Drag individual photos (or a folder of photos) that you plan to use in a HomePage website into this iDisk Pictures folder so you'll have access to them when you're building the web page.

Movies folder: Drag movies that you might use in a HomePage web site into this iDisk Movies folder so you'll have access to them when you're building the web page.

Public folder: Put files and folders here that you want to make accessible for other people. Unless you set up password protection (see page 242), *other people who have your .Mac member name can access files that you drag to your iDisk Public folder.* You can open any other Public folder that doesn't use password protection if you have that person's .Mac member name.

Sites folder: The Sites folder stores any web pages that you've created using HomePage. You can also store sites that were created with any other web authoring software.

Software folder: The Software folder contains software provided to you by Apple, as well as other Mac OS X software that you can download by dragging files to your computer. There's also a folder named "Extras" that contains royalty-free music files you can use in your iMovies. If you see anything you want in these folders, drag it to your Desktop.

The contents of this folder do not count against your iDisk storage space allotment.

Backup folder: When you use **Backup,** Apple's software for .Mac members (see Chapter 10), this is where the archived files are put.

Library folder: This folder contains application support files. Anything that needs to be in this folder will automatically be placed there.

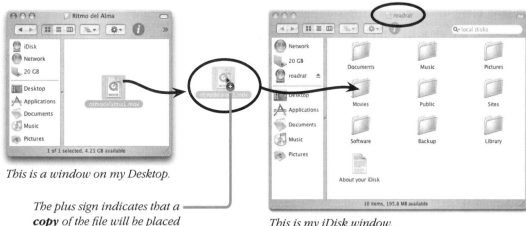

This is a window on my Desktop.

*The plus sign indicates that a **copy** of the file will be placed on the iDisk.*

This is my iDisk window.

To copy files TO your iDisk, *drag files or folders from your computer to one of the folders in the iDisk window.*

To copy files FROM your iDisk, *drag them from the iDisk window to your Desktop.*

It's Easy to Get Confused!

When you open your iDisk, you may notice that it looks almost exactly like your Home window. You can tell it's your iDisk, though, because of the name of the window and the icon in the title bar, as shown on the previous pages.

But as soon as you open any folder on your iDisk, the iDisk icon in the title bar disappears, and you can no longer tell if the Movies folder you opened is the Movies folder on Apple's server or your own folder on your hard disk!

This is the Path menu. If you don't see it in your Toolbar, you can add it: Go to the View menu and choose "Customize Toolbar...."

This is how you can check: Hold down the Command key and click on the title bar of any window—it will drop down a menu that tells you where that folder/window is stored. Or use the Path menu, if it's in your title bar.

Is this folder (window) on my hard disk or the iDisk at Apple?

Command-click on the title bar to see where this open folder (window) is actually located.

Save Directly to Your iDisk

You can save any document or photo in any application directly to your iDisk: From the File menu, choose "Save As...," then from the "Where" menu, choose your iDisk and the folder you want to save into, as shown below.

Keep in mind that if you continue to work on a file that you saved to your iDisk, *you are actually working directly on Apple's computers.* It's best to save to the iDisk when you're finished with a file.

Working at your Mac on a document that is stored on Apple's server means your Mac has to send every tiny little thing you do across the country to Apple. If you try it, you'll notice your actions on the screen get twitchy, slow, and cumbersome!

Manage Your iDisk with iDisk Utility

The **iDisk Utility** software is the easiest way possible to manage your iDisk—and the software is free if you have a .Mac account. With iDisk Utility you can open your other accounts without changing your .Mac settings, set access privileges for your iDisk, set password protection for your Public folder, monitor your iDisk storage capacity, add extra storage to your iDisk, and open other .Mac members' Public folders.

iDisk Utility

To download iDisk Utility from the .Mac web site:

1. Go to www.Mac.com.

2. Click the "iDisk" icon in the website sidebar, then log in to your .Mac account with your member name and password.

3. Click the "iDisk Utility" button to open the download page.

4. Click the "Download iDisk Utility" button to download the software.

5. Follow the instructions in the installer window that opens. iDisk Utility is installed in the "Utilities" folder, which is located in the "Applications" folder.

6. Double-click the "iDisk Utility" icon. Its window opens, as shown below.

Tip: For convenience and easy access, keep the iDisk Utility in the Dock: While the iDisk Utility is open, Control-click (or press and hold) its icon in the Dock to show the contextual menu, then choose "Keep in Dock."

To open a Public Folder, either yours or another member's:

1. Open iDisk Utility (see above for downloading and installing).

2. Click "Open Public folder," then enter your .Mac member name (or another member's name) in the "Member Name" field. Click "Open."

3. An icon representing your other account or another member's Public folder appears on your Desktop, as shown to the right. Double-click this icon to open that **Public folder** into a window from which you can access the folders and files you find there.

dearrobin

This only gets you into your or someone else's Public folder. If you want to access all of the folders in your account, use the other pane, "Open iDisk," as explained on the following page.

Tip: If you or anyone you know needs to access an iDisk from a machine running **Windows XP,** download the free **iDisk Utility for Windows XP.** Installation instructions are included with the download.

You'll find it in the iDisk section of Mac.com.

To open another iDisk:

In the iDisk Utility, click the "Open iDisk" icon to access an entire iDisk for which you have a member name and password. This might be another account of yours, or it might be someone else's.

To set access privileges or password protection:

Use iDisk Utility's "Public Folder Access" pane to set access privileges or password protection for your Public folder. Now, this does not mean that people going to your Public folder *on the web* will need to enter a password—this password only applies to .Mac users using the iDisk Utility to open your Public folder. You might want to allow your students or co-workers to post files for you, for instance—check the box to "Read-Write," then check the box to "Use a Password...."

If you want other .Mac users to be able to put files in your Public folder, check the "Read-Write" box. If you do that, it's a good idea to then add a password—otherwise anyone with iDisk Utility can put stuff in your folder!

To add more iDisk Storage:

In iDisk Utility, click "iDisk Storage" to see how much space you're using and how much you have left. If you need more, click the "Buy More" button to see available options and prices, as well as to purchase more storage.

iCards

7

If you've never had the urge to send an email postcard to friends, **iCards** could change your attitude. This ever-changing collection of beautiful, eye-catching images is a notch or three above what you usually get from other online greeting card services. A great-looking card with a postmark captures attention more effectively than a plain old email message. You can even use one of your own photos that you've copied to your iDisk, instead of a photo from the iCard Image Library. Because iCards are such a great way to announce events, HomePage uses it to announce newly created web sites. You can also use your .Mac Address Book for quick-click iCard addressing. So start uploading your favorite photos to the Pictures folder in your iDisk. If you haven't signed up for a .Mac account yet, you're missing a powerful lot of *fun*. And a lot of *powerful* fun.

In this chapter

Mail

Address Book

Bookmarks

HomePage

iDisk

iCards

Send an iCard

Anyone can send **iCards** to friends and family, even without a .Mac account, but to send an iCard *using your own photo,* you do need a .Mac account. An iCard is simply an electronic postcard you can send to anyone on any computer. iCard is far better than most Internet postcards for two reasons: The quality of the graphics is superior, and iCards are sent straight to the recipient instead of requiring a visit to a web page to "pick up" a card.

To send an iCard from the iCard Image Library:

1. Go to **www.mac.com** and click the "iCards" button in the sidebar.

2. On the iCards welcome page, shown below, click on a specific iCard thumbnail or one of the many iCard categories to display more card options. Once you click a card thumbnail, it opens a full-sized, editable version of the card (next page).

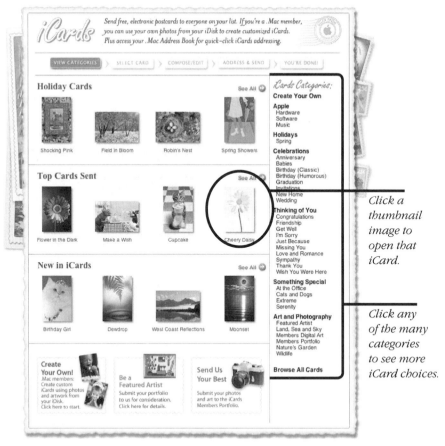

Click a thumbnail image to open that iCard.

Click any of the many categories to see more iCard choices.

3. On the editable iCard version that appears (shown right), select a type style and write a message, then click the "Continue" button.

4. The next page previews your card and lets you address the card to as many recipients as you like.

If you're logged into your .Mac account already, your name and email address will automatically be placed in the name and email fields. You can also override these and type in a different name and return address.

If you want to receive a copy of the email, check the box to "Send myself a copy."

To protect the privacy of multiple recipients, hide their email addresses: Check the box to "Hide distribution list." This will make sure the address field of the email says "Apple iCards Recipients" instead of recipients' email addresses.

Enter a recipient's email address in the address field. To add multiple addresses, separate each address with a comma.

Or choose a recipient from the "Choose a Quick Address" pop-up menu.

Or click the "Address Book" button (circled on the right) to access your .Mac Address Book list, shown on the next page. Put a checkmark next to the addresses you want placed in iCard's address field. See Chapter 9 to learn more about the .Mac Address Book and Quick Addresses.

—continued

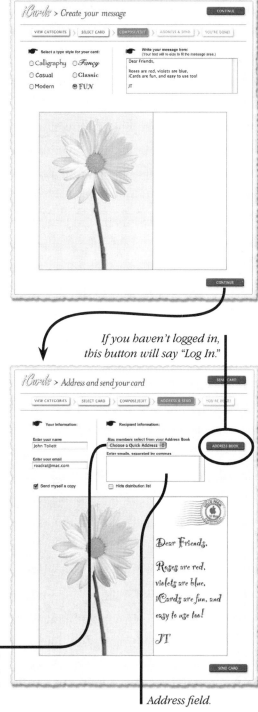

If you haven't logged in, this button will say "Log In."

This pop-up menu contains addresses that you've set as Quick Addresses in .Mac's Address Book. You can set up to ten contacts as Quick Addresses.

Address field.

To select recipients from your Address Book, place a check in the box next to the name of the recipient(s) you want to add. Use the scroll buttons to scroll up or down the list, or use the search field to find a specific name or address. Click the "Return to Card" button when you have selected all the recipients you want added.

These buttons scroll up or down the address list.

Put checkmarks next to addresses you want placed in iCard's address field.

*Enter names or addresses in this **search field**, then click the magnifying glass to do the search.*

Checked addresses from Address Book are automatically placed into iCard's address field.

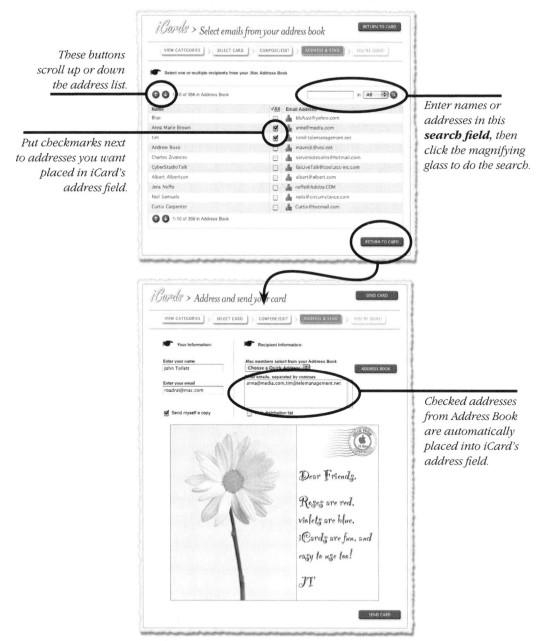

5. Click the "Send Card" button in the top-right or bottom-right corner.

6. A "Congratulations" page opens (shown at the bottom of the page), with the option "Send Same Card" to someone else, "Return to Category" to choose another photo or "Return to iCards Main" to go to the main iCards menu. Once you see the "Congratulations" page, it means your iCard has been successfully sent.

Create Your Own iCard

Apple's iCard images are beautiful, but you probably have photos of your own that you'd like to use. It's easy—**first copy some photos to the Pictures folder on your iDisk** (see Chapter 6 to learn how to do that).

To create your own iCard:

1. On the iCards welcome page, click "Create Your Own" (shown below) to open the "Select an image" window.

.Mac members can upload photos to the iCard collection for others to use.

2. Choose a photo or folder name by selecting it from the pop-up menu. This pop-up menu shows the contents of the Pictures folder on your iDisk.

Select a folder from this pop-up menu. The folder's contents are listed in the pane below.

*To see a **preview** in the preview pane to the right, single-click an image name in the list.*

Tip: If you can't see the contents of your Pictures folder, click the "Update Folder" button.

Or try using a different browser.

Click to choose the image shown.

This pop-up menu lets you navigate back to the Pictures folder after you've drilled down to sub-folder levels looking for an image.

3. When you see the picture you want, click "Select This Image."

4. In the "Create your message" window (below), select a type style.

5. Type your message in the text box (circled below).

6. Click "Resize your image to fit card" to trim your photo to fit iCard's proportions. If you don't like the results, uncheck the box and compare the two settings.

7. Click the "Continue" button.

Type your message here.

—continued

8. The next page previews your card and lets you address the card to as many recipients as you like.

> **Enter your name and email address** in the name and email fields if they're not automatically placed there.
>
> If you want to receive a copy of the email, check "Send myself a copy."
>
> **Enter a recipient's email address** in the text box. **Or** select an address from the "Choose a Quick Address" pop-up menu.
>
> **Or** click the "Address Book" button to access addresses contained in your .Mac Address Book.
>
> **To add multiple addresses,** separate each address with a comma.

9. Click the "Send Card" button in the bottom-right corner.

> In the "Congratulations" page that opens, choose to "Send Same Card" to someone else, "Return to Category" to create another card, or "Return to iCards Main" to start over.

Click here to go back and make changes to your card.

When you send an iCard to multiple recipients, you can protect their privacy by hiding their email addresses. If you click the "Hide distribution list" checkbox, the iCard's address field will say "Apple iCards Recipients" instead of listing all the email addresses.

Click here to send your card.

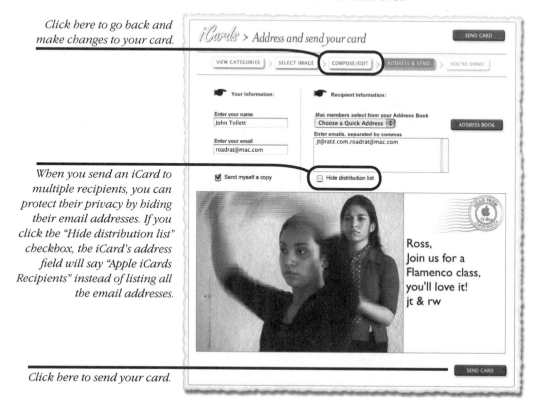

HomePage

8

While some people complain that a .Mac account costs $99 a year, this one feature called **HomePage** alone would be worth many times more than the price tag. The templates that come with HomePage are the best-looking template-based web page authoring solutions you'll find anywhere. Being able to publish a collection of photos or streaming QuickTime movies on a great-looking page within minutes is not just convenient, it's amazing. And fun. The flexibility to easily update and rearrange pages makes website management enjoyable rather than a time-consuming headache.

The ability to publish photos, text, and movies in a professionally designed environment will inspire your creative thinking. If you're a creative professional, the simplicity and elegance of HomePage will inspire ideas for more efficient communication with your clients and associates.

In this chapter

Add Photos, QuickTime Movies, and HTML files to iDisk

HomePage gets all the photos, movies, and HTML files from three folders *on your iDisk:* the Pictures folder, the Movies folder, and the Sites folder. That means, of course, that before you start a project in HomePage, you must first copy the photos, movies, and files you need to your iDisk folders.

So log in to your iDisk (see Chapter 6), and drag individual photos or an entire folder of photos from your hard disk to the **Pictures** folder on your iDisk.

Drag QuickTime movies to the **Movies** folder on your iDisk.

If you plan to use external HTML files (created in an HTML editing program) on your HomePage, drag those HTML files to the **Sites** folder on your iDisk.

Use images from Apple's Image Library

Many HomePage Themes offer access to Apple's Image Library in case you don't have pictures of your own to use. You can select from those that Apple provides in iDisk's **Image Library** folder. When you see a photo box in a template with the "Choose" button, click the button and select the "Image Library" folder to choose an image.

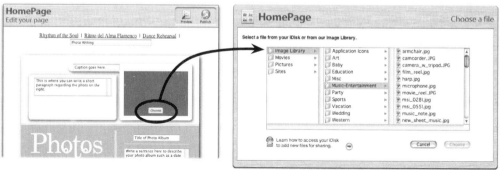

Click a template photo's "Choose" button to get to the "Image Library" folder.

A file-size reminder

When you drag photos to the Pictures folder on your iDisk, you can use those photos on web pages. But make sure the images you place in the Pictures folder are reasonable file sizes—the smaller an image is, the faster it will download. HomePage automatically creates small thumbnail versions of photos for most pages, but those thumbnails link to the original full-sized photo that you put in the Pictures folder. If the original photos are unnecessarily large, some of your web pages will be painfully slow to download, plus you'll fill up your allotted server storage space very quickly.

Ideally, photos destined for a web page should be saved in the JPEG format with a resolution of 72 ppi and a maximum size of 640 x 480 pixels.

Build a Website with HomePage

With **HomePage** you can easily create and publish a single web page, an entire website, or several sites. Choose from a variety of beautiful themes that are designed to display photo albums, QuickTime movies, résumés, invitations, external HTML files, and more.

1. From the .Mac web page (**www.mac.com**), click the "HomePage" icon (shown left).

2. If you're not already logged in, enter your member name and password in the .Mac login window to access the HomePage opening page (shown below), from which you can build a single web page or a collection of pages.

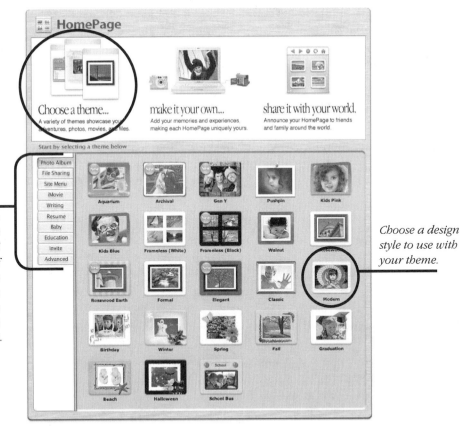

Click one of the theme tabs that seems to be a good fit with the type of website you want to create. Each theme provides multiple design styles for you to choose from.

Choose a design style to use with your theme.

—continued

3. If you choose a design style from the "Photo Album" theme selections, the "Choose a folder" window opens and shows the photos in the Pictures folder *of your iDisk.* Choose a folder of photos to place in your new HomePage Photo Album, then click "Choose."

If no folders of photos are showing, it means you have not yet copied any from your computer to the Pictures folder on your iDisk. See Chapter 6, or click the small button in the bottom-left corner to "Learn how to access your iDisk."

This folder is automatically on my iDisk.

The middle column shows the folder I copied to my iDisk.

The far-right column shows the contents of the folder.

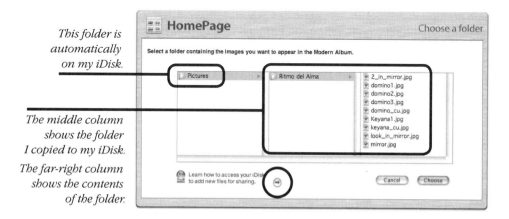

4. An editable page based on your theme choice opens (below). Click the "Preview" icon to see how the page will look on the web. **To toggle back and forth between Preview and Edit modes,** click this button.

This page is currently in Edit mode. Click the "Preview" button to preview the page.

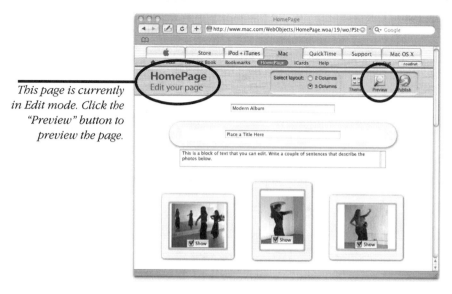

5. In Edit mode, edit the headline, text, or captions. You can also choose between a two- or three-column layout, change the theme, or preview the page. When you're satisfied with the results, click the "Publish" button.

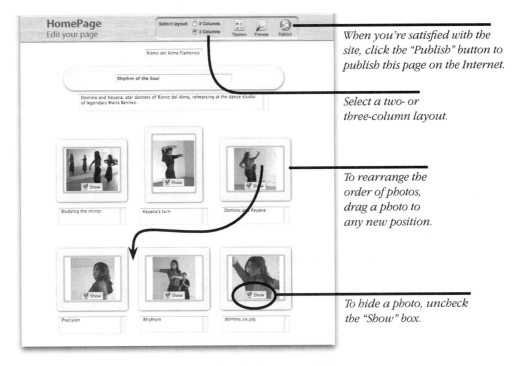

When you're satisfied with the site, click the "Publish" button to publish this page on the Internet.

Select a two- or three-column layout.

To rearrange the order of photos, drag a photo to any new position.

To hide a photo, uncheck the "Show" box.

After you click "Publish," the window shown below opens to give you the web address of your new site. Click the iCard button to send announcements to friends if you like.

6. Click "Return to HomePage" to add more pages or sites (next page).

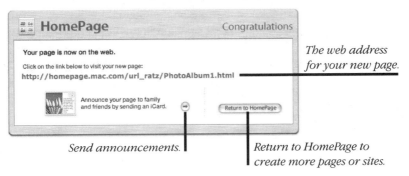

The web address for your new page.

Send announcements.

Return to HomePage to create more pages or sites.

—continued

7. Return to HomePage and you'll see it looks different now. The Photo Album we just created is listed in the "Pages" pane.

You'll certainly want to add more pages to your site. To add another page, click the "Add" button beneath the "Pages" pane.

Click this button to add a password to your site.

The Pages page.

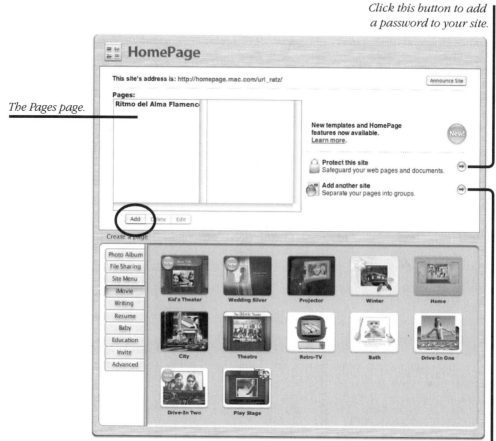

Click this button to add another site, instead of adding pages to the existing site. See page 264.

Add another page

For this example, the next page we add will contain a QuickTime movie. If you haven't copied a QuickTime movie to the Movies folder on your iDisk, do so now. (See Chapter 3 for information on editing movies and exporting as QuickTime for the Internet.)

1. Click the "iMovie" tab in the Theme pane of the window (circled below), then select a theme. When you click the theme icon, the new page template opens (shown below).

Click on a design style.

2. Type the default text in the text boxes with your own messages, then click the "Choose" button (below) in the QuickTime window to select a QuickTime movie.

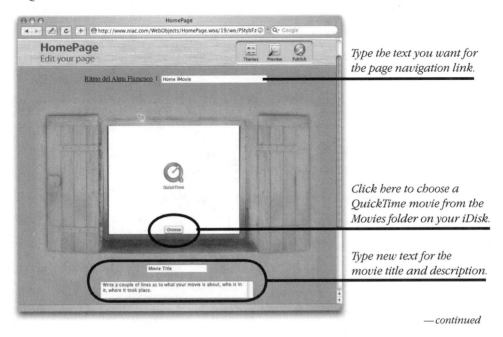

Type the text you want for the page navigation link.

Click here to choose a QuickTime movie from the Movies folder on your iDisk.

Type new text for the movie title and description.

—continued

3. From the "Choose a file" window, choose a QuickTime movie that has been copied to the Movies folder on your iDisk. Click "Choose" to place the selected movie on the iMovie page.

A preview of the selected QuickTime movie.

No movies in the Movies folder means you have not yet copied any from your computer to the Movies folder on your iDisk.

Click the small button in the bottom-left corner to "Learn how to access your iDisk," or see Chapter 6.

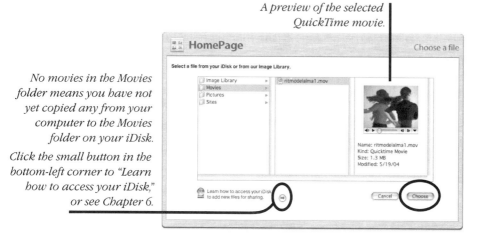

4. After the QuickTime movie is selected, a window opens (below). You can make additional changes here, or click the "Publish" icon to publish the page on the Internet.

Click "Preview" to preview any changes you make.

Click "Publish" to publish to the web.

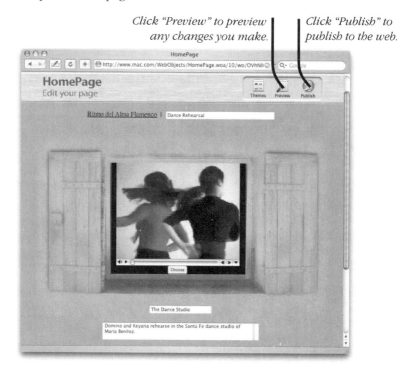

5. After you click "Publish," a dialog box will open asking you whether you want to visit the new page or return to HomePage.

6. Return to HomePage and notice the "Pages" pane has added the new page to the list (below). **To determine which page is the first page of the site,** drag a page name to the top of the list. Bold text indicates the first page a visitor will see.

Add password protection to a site

You can enable password protection to restrict who can visit your site.

1. Select a site in the "Pages" list of HomePage, as shown above and on page 256.

2. Click the small arrow button next to the padlock icon, shown below.

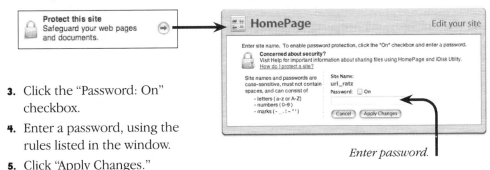

3. Click the "Password: On" checkbox.

4. Enter a password, using the rules listed in the window.

5. Click "Apply Changes."

Enter password.

Create a Site Menu for Your Existing Pages

After you've made a couple of individual pages, you can create a **Site Menu** page. The Site Menu page contains a link for each page you've created (photo albums, movie pages, invitations, etc.). It provides an overview of the entire site's content. Sounds complex? No, it's incredibly easy.

1. In the main HomePage window, click the "Site Menu" tab (shown below).

2. Click one of the design style icons (circled below) to open "Edit your page," a window that contains an image link for each page of the selected site.

    In this example, the two pages we've created are considered a "site." Later we'll explain how to create new sites (see page 264).

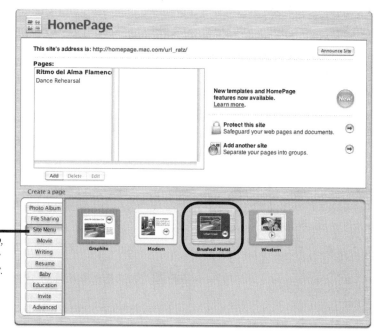

Click the "Site Menu" tab, then select a design theme to the right.

3. To customize the text, add more items, or delete items from this Site Menu page, make the changes directly on the page that comes up (shown at the top of the next page).

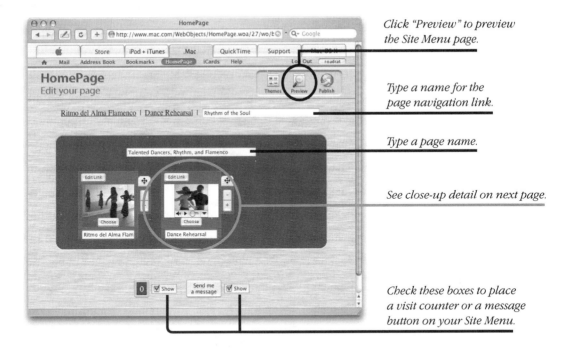

Click "Preview" to preview the Site Menu page.

Type a name for the page navigation link.

Type a page name.

See close-up detail on next page.

Check these boxes to place a visit counter or a message button on your Site Menu.

4. After making your edits, click the "Preview" icon (above) to see the final page design. This example has just two image links, but you can add as many as necessary. Keep in mind that too many images on the Site Menu page creates a slow-loading, long-scrolling page.

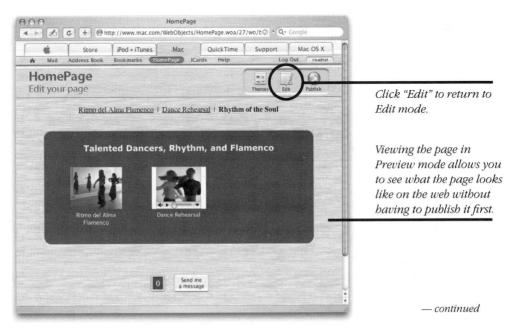

Click "Edit" to return to Edit mode.

Viewing the page in Preview mode allows you to see what the page looks like on the web without having to publish it first.

— continued

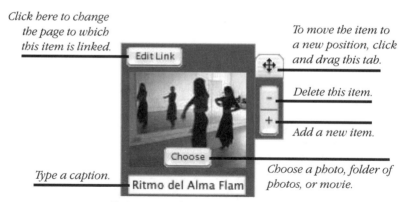

Click here to change the page to which this item is linked.

Edit Link

To move the item to a new position, click and drag this tab.

Delete this item.

Add a new item.

Choose

Type a caption.

Ritmo del Alma Flam

Choose a photo, folder of photos, or movie.

Close-up view from previous page.

5. Before you click the "Publish" icon, you need to set this as the first page. It has links to all the pages of the site, so it makes sense that it should be the first page you see.

Click the "HomePage" link in the top-left corner to open the main HomePage window (shown below).

The "HomePage" link.

Click here to return to the main HomePage window, as shown on the next page.

6. Locate the name of the site menu page in the "Pages" pane, then drag the name to the top of the list. The name will change to bold type, indicating it is now the first page.

7. To publish the page, click the "Edit" button beneath the Pages pane, then click the "Publish" icon on the "Edit" page that opens.

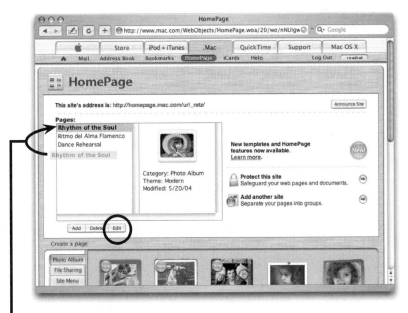

Drag the site menu page just created to the top of the list to make it the first page.

Create Another Site

You can add a variety of unrelated pages to your site, but it's much better to organize your pages into related groups, called sites. When you create a new site, HomePage changes to show both a "Sites" pane and a "Pages" pane, as shown below.

To create a new site:

1. Go to HomePage.

2. Click the small arrow button next to "Add another site."

3. Enter a site name in the "Create a site" window. To include password protection, click the "Password: On" box.

4. Click "Create Site."

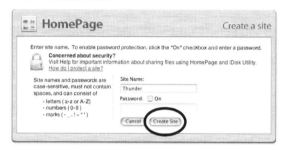

5. The top section of HomePage now includes a "Sites" pane in addition to the "Pages" pane, as shown below.

6. To add pages to the new site, select the site name, then click the "Add" button under the "Pages" pane.

Select a site.

Click "Add" to add a page to the site.

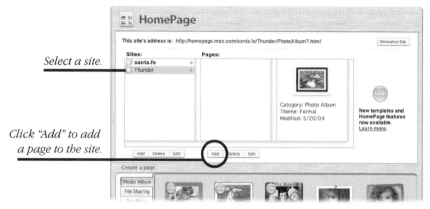

Site management

HomePage makes it easy to manage your sites. Use the buttons beneath the "Sites" pane and the "Pages" pane to add, delete, and edit pages or sites. Change themes or page designs whenever you want. Rearrange the order of pages in a site, or move pages from one site to another site.

- ▼ **To add pages** to the new site, select the site name, then click the "Add" button under the "Pages" pane and create new pages. As you add to the new site, the page names are added to the "Pages" pane.

- ▼ **To delete pages** from a site, select the page name, then click the "Delete" button beneath the "Pages" pane.

- ▼ **To move pages** from one site to another, select a page in the "Pages" list and drag it to a site folder in the "Sites" list.

- ▼ **To add new sites,** click the "Add" button beneath the "Sites" pane, as explained on the opposite page.

- ▼ **To delete a site,** select its name and click the "Delete" button beneath the "Sites" pane.

- ▼ **To add, change, or remove a password** for a site in the "Sites" pane, click the "Edit" button beneath the "Sites" pane.

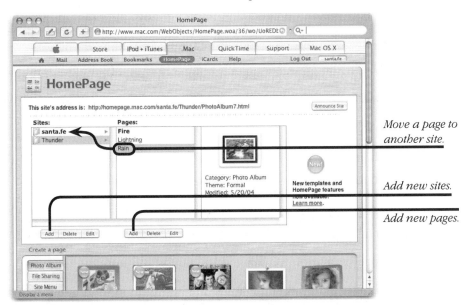

Move a page to another site.

Add new sites.

Add new pages.

When the "Thunder" site (above) is selected in the "Sites" pane, all the pages associated with that site are shown in the "Pages" pane. This example shows how a page can be dragged from its current location (in the "Thunder" site) to another site (the "santa.fe" site).

— continued

This is a final page published on the Internet as described on the previous pages. To add more content later, log in to HomePage, select the page in the "Pages" pane, then click the "Edit" button.

Adding External HTML Pages with HomePage

HTML (HyperText Markup Language) is a code that's used to create web pages.

Up until now, HomePage has been writing all the HTML code for you. But you can also utilize external HTML files (HTML files that you have created in an HTML editing program such as Dreamweaver, GoLive, BBEdit, etc.). To add external HTML files for use in HomePage, first drag the HTML files and their subfolders into your iDisk's **Sites** folder (for full details on iDisk, see Chapter 6).

1. In the main HomePage window, click the "Advanced" tab (shown below).

2. Click the "External HTML" icon to browse the HTML files that you have copied to the "Sites" folder on your iDisk.

Click "External HTML" to add previously created HTML pages to the site.

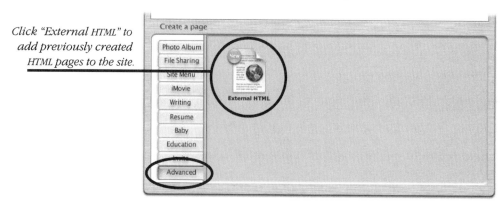

3. When you click the "External HTML" icon, a window opens to display HTML files located in your iDisk's Sites folder (below). Select a file in the middle column and then click "Choose."

   If no files are showing, it means you have not yet copied any HTML files from your computer to the Sites folder on your iDisk.

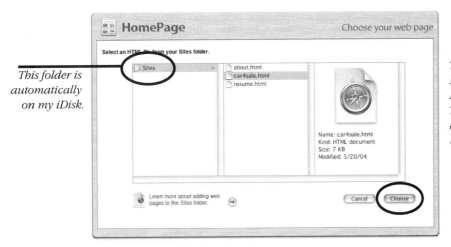

This folder is automatically on my iDisk.

The middle column shows the HTML files I copied to my iDisk. The far-right column displays details about the selected file.

4. A page displaying the HTML file opens (below). Notice that any embedded graphics you link in subfolders copied to the iDisk Sites folder also display on the web page. Click the "Publish" icon to publish the page when you are done. A "Congratulations" window appears, telling you the URL of the page you just published.

Only the Site Menu link name is editable.

To edit the rest of the page, you need to use an HTML editor and recopy the altered HTML file(s) to your Sites folder. HomePage can display external HTML pages, but cannot edit their content.

- Mail
- Address Book
- Bookmarks
- HomePage
- iDisk
- iCards
- Backup
- iSync
- Virex
- iCal
- Support
- Account

At the moment, extra storage costs are:

300 MB: $100/year

500 MB: $180/year

1000 MB: $350/year

Buy More iDisk Space

You can create multiple sites with HomePage, limited only by the amount of your iDisk storage space on Apple's servers. You can **purchase** up to a thousand megabytes (almost one gigabyte) of **iDisk storage** in addition to the 100 megabytes provided with your .Mac membership.

To upgrade your iDisk storage, go to the .Mac web page and click the "Account" icon at the bottom of the sidebar (left). Enter your account name and password in the login window when prompted. The "Account Settings" window then comes up (below). Click the "Buy More" button in the lower-right corner to buy more iDisk storage space.

Click here to purchase extra space.

iDisk Utility

You can also use a very handy utility called **iDisk Utility.** If it's not on your computer you can download it from the .Mac website at **www.mac.com**.

For full details on iDisk and iDisk Utility, see Chapter 6.

1. Open iDisk Utility, then click the "iDisk Storage" icon in the toolbar.

2. Click the "Buy More" button in the bottom-right corner to open a page from which you can buy more iDisk storage space.

.Mac Webmail

Your .Mac account includes a **webmail** feature that lets you check your mail or send mail from any computer with an Internet connection anywhere in the world. You can check your .Mac email account, or set up .Mac webmail to check any other email accounts you have.

The .Mac webmail Address Book gives you online access to all your contacts when you use iSync to synchronize the Address Book on your computer.

Apple's documentation sometimes refers to webmail as Mac.com Mail, and at other times as .Mac (dot Mac) Mail. We use the term ".Mac webmail" because webmail is a common term for a mail service that you access through a web browser. Call it what you will, .Mac webmail is another good reason your .Mac account is such a great value.

Mail
Address Book
Bookmarks
HomePage
iDisk
iCards

.Mac Webmail

When you sign up for a .Mac account, you get a .Mac **email** account with 15 megabytes of storage space for your email messages (which is a lot of email). See the Mail chapter (Chapter 16) for details about your .Mac account and how to set it up to send and receive email—it's great. **The advantage of webmail** is that you can check all your mail in all of your accounts (except AOL) from any web browser on any computer anywhere in the world.

It's easy to start using .Mac webmail:

1. Go to the Mac.com web site, then click the "Mail" icon in the sidebar (shown to the left).

2. Log in to your .Mac account with your member name and password.

3. Your personal .Mac webmail page opens, as shown below.

   From this web page and other linked pages you can perform all your email tasks just like at home, even if you happen to be in Ankara.

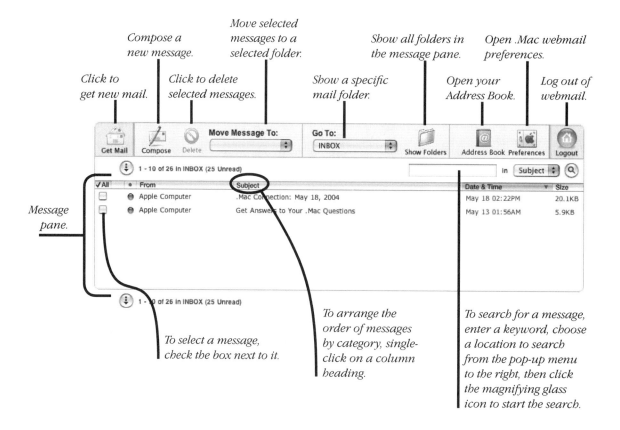

Compose a new message.

Move selected messages to a selected folder.

Show all folders in the message pane.

Open .Mac webmail preferences.

Click to get new mail.

Click to delete selected messages.

Show a specific mail folder.

Open your Address Book.

Log out of webmail.

Message pane.

To select a message, check the box next to it.

To arrange the order of messages by category, single-click on a column heading.

To search for a message, enter a keyword, choose a location to search from the pop-up menu to the right, then click the magnifying glass icon to start the search.

Get your Mail and Read It

1. Click "Get Mail" to collect any new messages and show them in the "Inbox" message pane, along with any other existing messages.

2. Single-click on a message in the list to open it in its own page.

Compose and Send a Message

1. Click the "Compose" icon to open a new message page.

2. Type an email address in the "To" field.

    To send the same message to more than one person, type their addresses in the same field with a comma after each email address. Or put one or more addresses in the Cc (carbon copy) field.

3. Type a subject that will not be confused for junk mail! For instance, don't use "Hi!" or "No embarrassment" or just the person's name. Type a subject that will make it clear to the recipient what your message is about, that it pertains specifically to that person, or that it is clearly from you to someone who knows you.

See the following pages for creating your Address Book and some quick tips for entering email addresses.

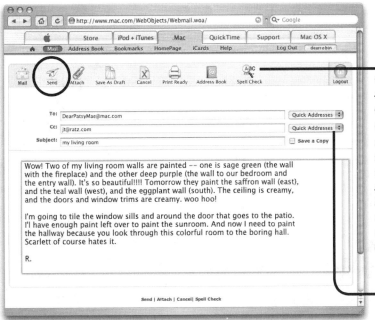

Click this to check the spelling of your entire email message; see Step 4.

Or *Control-click on any word whose spelling you're not sure of and a little menu will pop up with spelling options. You won't leave this message window in the process, as you will with the "Spell Check" option.*

See the following page for directions on how to add up to ten names in this "Quick Addresses" menu. Once a name is in this menu, just choose it to address your message.

4. If you want to check the spelling, click the "Spell Check" icon in the toolbar. It will find misspelled words and provide you with alternative spellings in multiple languages. When finished, click the "Edit" button to return to your message window.

5. When finished with your message, click the "Send" icon in the toolbar.

Use the Address Book

The **Address Book** in the .Mac webmail is similar to the Address Book on your hard disk (as explained in Chapter 16). You can synchronize the one on your hard disk with the one in .Mac webmail; see the following pages for details. Just as on your hard disk, there are two different ways of viewing the Address Book, and each version provides different options. Just for clarity's sake on these two pages, we'll call one the Main Address Book in webmail and the other the Compose Address Book in webmail.

The Main Address Book in webmail

If you look carefully, you'll notice there are two links to the Address Book on the main .Mac Mail page, circled below. Click on either one and it will open the same thing—your Main Address Book, as shown far below.

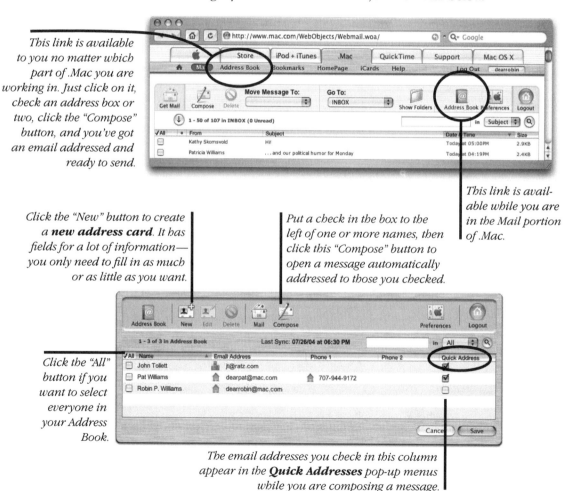

This link is available to you no matter which part of .Mac you are working in. Just click on it, check an address box or two, click the "Compose" button, and you've got an email addressed and ready to send.

This link is available while you are in the Mail portion of .Mac.

*Click the "New" button to create a **new address card**. It has fields for a lot of information—you only need to fill in as much or as little as you want.*

Put a check in the box to the left of one or more names, then click this "Compose" button to open a message automatically addressed to those you checked.

Click the "All" button if you want to select everyone in your Address Book.

*The email addresses you check in this column appear in the **Quick Addresses** pop-up menus while you are composing a message.*

The Compose Address Book in webmail

In .Mac webmail, after you click on the "Compose" icon and get a page with the email message, you have what looks like the exact same Address Book icon in the toolbar. Click on it and the **Compose Address Book** opens.

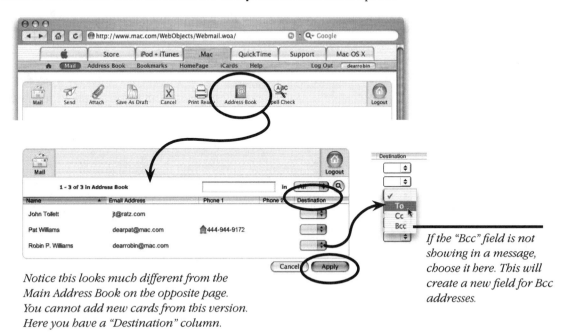

Notice this looks much different from the Main Address Book on the opposite page. You cannot add new cards from this version. Here you have a "Destination" column.

If the "Bcc" field is not showing in a message, choose it here. This will create a new field for Bcc addresses.

In the **Destination** column, choose in which field you want a person's address to appear. You can choose any number of people to send the same message to. When you go back to the email composition page (after you click the "Apply" button), your selections are shown in the various address fields of the email form.

Cc stands for Carbon Copy or Courtesy Copy.

*Bcc stands for Blind Carbon Copy. Addresses you put in the Bcc field **are not visible** to anyone else receiving the message.*

A little whining

This Address Book is actually rather lame at the moment. If you have a lot of contacts in your list, there is no way to go straight to someone with a name like "Tollett"—you have to just keep redrawing the web page with the next collection of names. On a slow connection, this can be deadly. Also, there is no way to make a Group mailing list, nor do existing Groups import when you synchronize this Address Book with the one on your hard disk (shown on the next page). Hopefully, this will change.

Synchronize your Address Books

Using **iSync,** another feature of a .Mac account, you can synchronize the Address Book on your hard disk to the .Mac webmail Address Book so you always have access to current contact information, no matter where you are. (See Chapter 11 for details about iSync.) You need to do this before you leave home, of course, because you must do it at your own computer.

To set up synchronization (part 1):

If you have never used iSync before, you must download the iSync software and then "register" your Mac to the .Mac synchronization server (if you need more details than what is provided below, see Chapter 11).

1. Download iSync from the Mac.com site, if you haven't already.

2. Make sure you are connected to the Internet. Open iSync.

3. Click the ".mac" icon on the iSync panel to expand the window and show the available options.

4. If you have not yet registered your Mac, click the "Register" button in the pane that opens (shown to the left). In the next pane that opens, name your computer. After a few seconds, .Mac registers your computer and you'll see the window shown below.

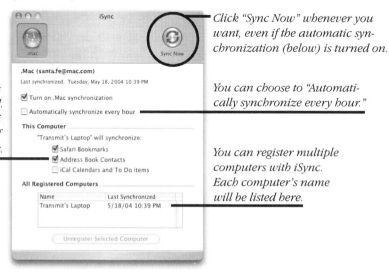

Click "Sync Now" whenever you want, even if the automatic synchronization (below) is turned on.

Make sure that "Address Book Contacts" is checked. You can also sync Safari bookmarks and iCal items if you check those boxes.

You can choose to "Automatically synchronize every hour."

You can register multiple computers with iSync. Each computer's name will be listed here.

5. Check "Turn on .Mac synchronization" if it's not already checked.

6. Click the "Sync Now" button, located in the top-right corner.

   The synchronization takes a few moments, depending on the size of Address Book and other data on your Mac.

To sync your Address Book (part 2):

7. Click the "Address Book" icon in the toolbar of the .Mac webmail page (shown on the previous page). The Main Address Book in webmail opens, shown below.

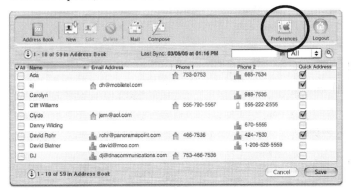

8. Click the "Preferences" icon on the Address Book page, circled above, to open the Address Book Preferences page, shown below.

9. Click the checkbox to "Turn on .Mac Address Book Synchronization."

10. Click the "Save" button. You may be asked if you want to "Sync" (synchronize both Address Books) or "Reset" (replace the webmail Address Book with the contents of your hard disk Address Book).

Besides synchronizing your Address Book, you can also use the pop-up menus shown here to set various options for your Main Address Book in webmail.

To turn on synchronization, *check this box. Use the iSync application to set how often to synchronize your Address Book (see Chapter 11).*

Also check this out.

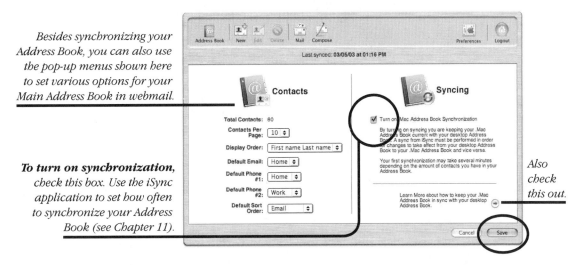

Attach a File to a Message

You can attach a file that's on the computer you're working on.

1. Click the "Attach" icon in the toolbar to open the attach page.

2. Click the "Choose File" button. From the drop-down sheet, locate a file you want to attach, then click the "Choose" button.

When you click this button, a sheet drops down from the browser's title bar.

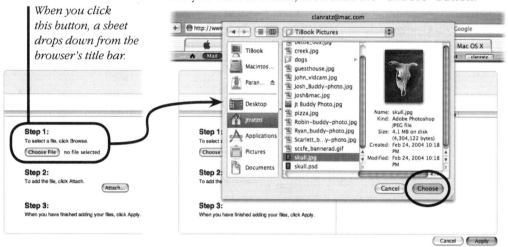

3. Click the "Attach" button to add the selected file to the "Attached Files" column (below-right). Repeat Steps 1 and 2 to add additional files. When you're finished adding attachments to the list, click the "Apply" button to return to the composition page.

To remove an attached file, click the "Remove" button.

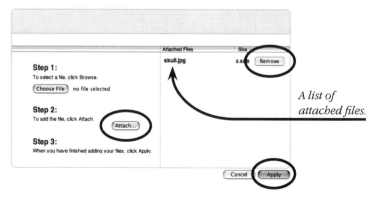

A list of attached files.

4. Your email header now shows a list of attached files. Address the email, type your email message, then click "Send."

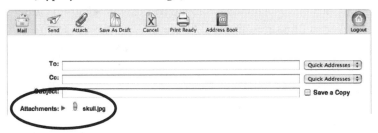

5. When the recipient gets your message, attachments are listed in the email header. If the attachment is an image or a one-page PDF, it will be displayed in the body of the message.

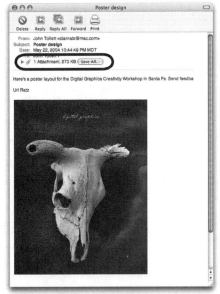

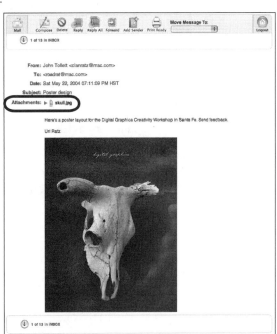

The email with its attachment, as seen in Mail (above) and .Mac webmail (right).

The "Go To" Menu

The "Go To" pop-up menu in the .Mac webmail toolbar lets you choose which folder's content to show in the message pane, such as INBOX, Deleted Messages, or Sent Messages. If you've set the option in Preferences to "Check Other POP Mail" (as explained on page 282), you can open your other POP email accounts from this menu.

Make New Folders for Organizing Mail

If you get a lot of mail, it's good to create **extra folders** so you can organize your messages. As shown below, you can check the boxes to select
any number of messages, then go to the "Move Message To" menu and tell
them where to go. Use the "Go To" menu to choose to see the messages in
a particular folder.

*You can see that I
selected three messages.
Now when I choose
to "Move Message
To" the folder named
"Pilgrimage," those three
messages will disappear
from the Inbox and go
to the other folder.*

To make new folders, simply click the "Show Folders" icon in the toolbar,
circled above. This opens the page you see below.

Notice in the new toolbar there are icons to make new folders, empty
selected folders, or rename or delete folders.To get back to the main Mail
window, click the "Mail" icon.

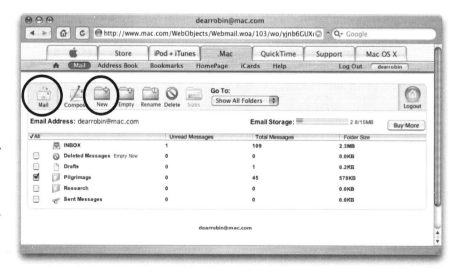

Non-Tip: Unfortunately,
there is no feature yet for
filters or rules where you
can have certain email
automatically go to
certain folders.

Set Webmail Preferences

On the .Mac webmail page, click the "Preferences" icon to open the Preferences page, as shown below. The various customizable options are categorized by the three buttons at the top of the page—the "Viewing," "Composing," and "Account" buttons.

Viewing preferences

Time Zone: Select a time zone from the pop-up menu. This setting affects the information that appears in the "Date & Time" column of the main Mail window. You can choose to see email arrival times based on your local time or another time zone.

Messages Per Page: Choose how many messages appear at a time on a Mail page. If you get a lot of junk mail, choose a higher number so you can delete more messages at once.

Show "All Headers" Option: Check this to put a "Show All Headers" button in the top-right corner of the Mail window (circled below). Then you can click the button to show additional email header information for a selected message, which is a lot of technical information most of us don't need or want to know. To return to the usual abbreviated header information, click the button again, which has changed to say "Hide All Headers."

After you complete your settings, click the **Save** button.

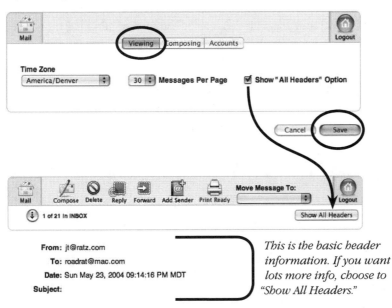

This is the basic header information. If you want lots more info, choose to "Show All Headers."

Composing preferences

Include Original Message in Reply: When you reply to an email message by clicking the "Reply" button, this option makes a copy of the original message and places it in your reply. This can help remind the recipient what the previous correspondence was about.

Add Bcc Header: This adds a blind carbon copy (Bcc) field to the address section of a new message. The identity of those in a Bcc field is hidden from all recipients.

Save Sent Messages To: Choose a folder in which messages you *send* will be saved automatically.

Move Deleted Messages To: Choose a folder in which *deleted* messages will be stored automatically.

From (Your Name): Type the name you want automatically placed in the "From" field of emails that you send.

Photo: This automatically puts an image of your choice in every message you send. If the photo area is blank, the button beneath it says "Choose"; click that button to add a photo. A window similar to the Attach File window opens (as shown on page 276) in which you can choose a file. Not everyone who gets your email will see the photo; it depends on what software they use to check mail.

Signature: An email "signature" is whatever you type into the edit box shown below. This will automatically appear at the end of all email messages you send from this account. It might be your contact information, a favorite quote, a message to the world, or anything you like.

After you complete your settings, click the **Save** button.

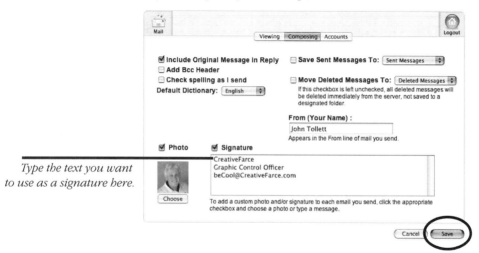

Type the text you want to use as a signature here.

Account preferences

Email Aliases: This is a really neat feature. You can create almost any number of aliases, or pretend email addresses, and messages to those addresses will arrive in your main .Mac account—color-coded, even—but your actual address is still private. For instance, let's say you want to buy some diet pills online but you know as soon as you do that, they will sell your email list to every drug company on the face of the planet and you'll get hundreds of pieces of junk mail a day. Well, use an alias address instead, then after your order arrives, deactivate (don't delete) the alias until next time you need it. While it's deactivated, you won't receive any mail at that address.

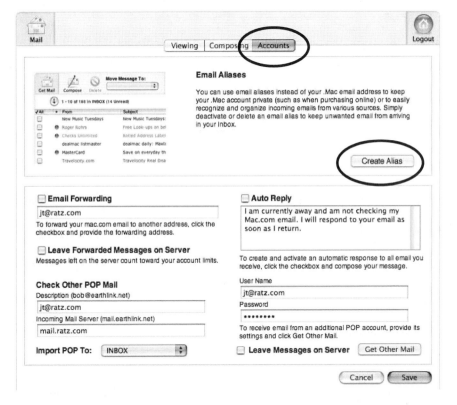

To make a new alias,
click "Create Alias."
After you make the
first one, you won't see
this screen anymore—
you'll see the one
shown below, where
you can add, delete,
or edit aliases.

*The **color-coding***
will only appear in
webmail, not in the
Mail program on your
hard disk.

To deactivate an alias,
click the round radio button to select
it. Then click the "Edit" button, which
will give you a page with a button to
make the alias "Inactive."

*If you **delete** an alias, you can never*
make another alias with that name
again (nor can anyone else).

Email Forwarding: Designate an email address to which your mail for this account is automatically forwarded.

Leave Forwarded Messages on Server: Any messages you have forwarded will be stored on the .Mac server so you can access them later from this account. These messages count toward your 15 MB email storage limit.

Auto Reply: If you can't check your email for a period of time, say while you're on vacation, check this option and type the response you want people to get when they send you email. "I'll be back on April 1."

Check Other POP Mail: Lets you check one other POP email account from your .Mac Mail account (see page 396 for a description of a POP account; .Mac email is IMAP, as is AOL).

Enter the email address you want to access through .Mac webmail, its corresponding incoming mail server address, the account user name, and the account password. You can get this information from your email provider if you don't know it. Or if this is an email address you use regularly, you probably have this information already in the account preferences settings of the email program you normally use (such as Mail).

Import POP to: This is very important! If you are going to bring in mail from another account, first make yourself a new folder with the name of that account (see page 278). Then **before you import,** choose that folder name from this menu. All of the mail from your other account will then be separate from your .Mac account.

To access your POP mail from the main Mail window, select the account name from the "Go To" pop-up menu in the toolbar.

Leave Messages on Server: Check this if you want the POP mail server to store messages for access later; otherwise once you check the mail, messages you have read on this computer will not be available on another one.

Get Other Mail: Click this to get messages from your POP email account immediately.

Backup 10

Sooner or later, every computer user learns (usually the hard way) the wisdom of regularly backing up important files. It's a simple concept, but most of us suffer from a human operating system bug called "optimism." We think our data is safe. Instead, we should assume the worst is going to happen—corrupted files, theft, fire, lost files, accidentally trashed files, mistakenly overwritten files—and prepare accordingly.

A Mac.com membership includes **Backup,** your personal software for effortlessly backing up the files you can't afford to lose. You can back up to removable media, such as CDs and DVDs, to your iDisk, to a FireWire or USB disk drive, or to all of these for extra security and peace of mind.

Some files are too large to fit on iDisk, a CD, or even a DVD. Backup can break large files apart and use multiple discs to create a backup copy. When you need to restore such files, Backup rejoins them on your hard disk.

Important Note about Backups

If you have very important files, **don't rely on one backup.** Make at least two, and store them in different locations. People have had their offices broken into and all of the computers stolen, plus all the backup disks. A fire has the same result. So make at least two backups and send one to your mother or your bank vault or your east-coast office.

Download and Install Backup

Before you can start using Backup, you must first **download** it from Apple's Mac.com web site.

1. Go to the Mac.com web site (**www.mac.com**) and click the "Backup" icon (the red umbrella) in the web page's sidebar.

2. You'll be asked to log in using your Mac.com membership name and password.

Backup 2 is the latest version of Backup as of this writing.

3. From the "Backup" page that opens, click the "Download Backup 2" icon (shown below) to open the "Download Backup" page.

4. Click the Download *link* for the version of Backup that is compatible with your version of Mac OS X, circled below.

Note: Turn off Energy Saver before you use Backup, or Sleep might interrupt the process.

5. After downloading is finished, install the software as usual (double-click the .dmg or .pkg file and follow the directions).

6. Find the "Backup" icon in the Applications folder, then double-click it to open the "Backup" window, as shown on the next page.

The Backup Window

The main **Backup window** puts a lot of information and functionality into a compact space.

- ▼ From the **pop-up menu,** choose the location to which you want to save backed-up files. **Or** choose to "Restore" backed-up files and copy them to your hard disk.

- ▼ The **QuickPick** items in the "Items" column (package icons) are *groups* of files that are all backed up at once.

- ▼ When you choose "Back up to iDisk" in the pop-up menu, the **status bar** shows how much space on your iDisk is used and how much space is available.

- ▼ Items that are *checked* in the **Back Up** column will be copied when you click the "Backup Now" button, or when a backup is scheduled.

Tip: The pop-up menu allows you to choose to save files to your iDisk, an external drive or a removable CD or DVD (DVD option only available on Macs with a DVD-writeable drive built in or attached).

When **Back up to iDisk** is selected, the *iTunes QuickPick package* includes only *playlists,* due to the limited storage space that is available with iDisk storage.

When **Back up to CD/DVD** or **Back up to Drive** is selected, the *iTunes Quick-Pick package* includes the entire *Library* of song files.

The *disc spanning* technology that Backup uses to copy large files to multiple discs means virtually unlimited storage.

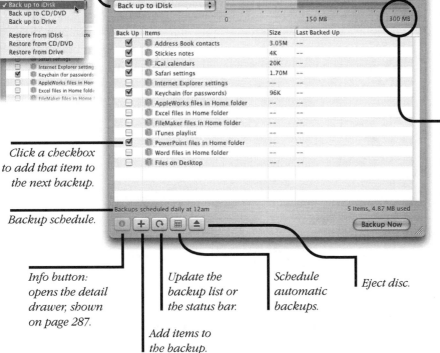

Pop-up menu.

Status bar.

Click a checkbox to add that item to the next backup.

This iDisk has been upgraded to 300 megabytes of storage instead of the usual 100 megabytes.

Backup schedule.

Info button: opens the detail drawer, shown on page 287.

Update the backup list or the status bar.

Schedule automatic backups.

Eject disc.

Add items to the backup.

Add Items to the List

Tip: To add items to the backup list from remote locations such as CDs, DVDs, or your local network, copy the items to your hard disk first.

The easiest way to **add files or folders** to the backup list is to *drag* them to the "Backup" window. You're not actually copying the files yet, just creating a list of the files you want to back up.

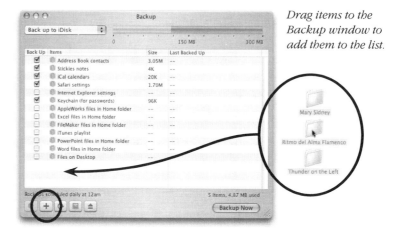

Drag items to the Backup window to add them to the list.

Tip: When an alert symbol appears next to an item in the backup list, Backup cannot find the original item. You may have renamed, moved, or deleted it.

Or click the "Add items" button (the plus sign, circled above) to make a Finder sheet slide down from the top of the window (shown below). Find a file or folder you want to add to the list, then click "Choose."

Note: Applications cannot be added to the backup list.

Delete items from the backup list

To remove an item from the backup list, select a file, then press the Delete key. QuickPick items (the package icons) cannot be removed.

The Details Drawer

To open the **Details drawer,** select a file or folder in the backup list, then click the "Info" button (the icon with the letter "**i**"). The Details drawer slides open to show information about your selection. If you selected a **folder,** the drawer shows the contents of the folder and any subfolders that may be present. If you selected a *QuickPick* item (one with an icon that looks like a little package), the drawer shows the contents of the QuickPick package.

Exclude individual items from the backup

To exclude items *in a folder* from being backed up:

1. Select a folder in the "Items" column, as shown to the right.

2. Click the "Info" button to open the Details drawer.

3. In the Details drawer is a list of items in the selected folder. Uncheck the items you don't want to back up.

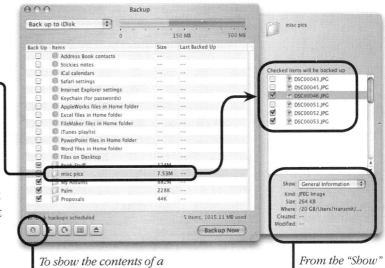

To show the contents of a selected (highlighted) item in the list, click this "Info" button.

From the "Show" pop-up menu, choose "General Information" or "Backup Information."

A dash indicates one or more items stored in that folder are not checked and will not be included in the backup.

Back Up to Your iDisk

When you're ready to back up files, you can choose your **iDisk** location to save files into, depending on how much space is available. If there's not enough room on your iDisk, the empty area of the status bar is colored red. If you need more storage, from the Backup application menu choose "Buy Storage." Your browser will open to a .Mac upgrade page where you can log in and order up to 1,000 megabytes of storage.

The best reason to back up files to your iDisk is so you can access them from anywhere in the world. Everything will go into a folder called "Backup."

1. From the pop-up menu, choose **Back up to iDisk** to save your files to the Backup folder on your iDisk.

2. Select the items in the backup list you want to back up.

To select all items in the backup list, from the Edit menu choose "Select All."

To check all checkboxes in the backup list, from the Edit menu choose "Check All."

To uncheck all items in the backup list, from the Edit menu choose "Uncheck All."

Available iDisk space. This iDisk has been upgraded to 300 megabytes.

3. Click "Backup Now."

4. A window tracks the progress of items as they upload to your iDisk.

Back Up to a Disk Drive

Backup allows you to back up your files to any internal or external hard disk drive connected to your Mac, including USB and FireWire devices. Backing up to a hard disk is the fastest way to back up large amounts of data and your storage capacity is only limited by the size of the drive you back up to.

1. From the pop-up menu, choose **Back up to Drive.**

2. Select the items in the backup list that you want to back up.

3. Click the "Set" button (above) to specify a backup location. A sheet slides down (below, right) prompting you to *create* or *open* a backup location.

If this is your first time backing up to a drive, click the "Create" button to create a new backup. **If this is not your first time,** click "Open" to open an earlier saved backup so you can update it with your most recent data; skip to Step 5.

4. If you click the "Create" button, a drop-down sheet prompts you to choose a location (a hard disk) for your backup data (below-left). Once you've chosen a hard disk, give your backup a clear name in the "Save As" field. Click the "Create" button to continue.

5. Click "Backup Now" to start the process.

Available disks appear in the sidebar of the drop-down sheet.

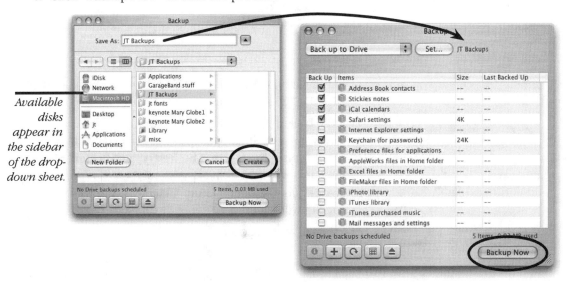

Tip: It's a good idea to back up your data to a different drive than the one it's on because many data-loss disasters happen to an entire drive at one time. However, you can also back up data to the same drive by saving it to a different folder. This creates a duplicate of the data on the same drive—not as good as having a backup on a separate drive, but better than no backup at all.

Back Up to a CD or DVD

Tip: From Backup you can order blank CDs or DVDs and have them delivered to your door: From the Backup application menu, choose "Buy Media." A .Mac web page will open in which you can log in to your .Mac account and order CD and DVD media.

See the previous two pages for backing up to your iDisk or to a disk drive.

You must have an internal CD-RW drive or a SuperDrive to use this option.

Backing up files to an optical disc (CD or DVD) instead of to your iDisk or hard drive makes sense if you need additional backups or you don't have an extra disk drive. You might not have access to an Internet connection and your iDisk, or your iDisk may not have enough space to hold all your backups. CDs offer a good alternative backup and DVDs an even better one since they hold much more data than a CD.

1. From the pop-up menu, choose **Back up to CD/DVD.**
2. Select the items in the list that you want to archive.

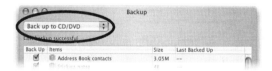

3. Check the "Est. Required Discs" in the bottom-left corner of the Backup window, circled below, to see how many CDs or DVDs are required to back up the selected items.
4. Click "Backup Now."

This estimate of how many discs you'll need is just an estimate. **Make sure you have extra discs available,** *just in case!*

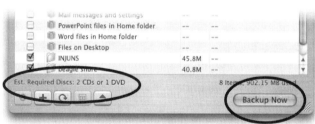

5. Insert a blank CD or DVD into the drive.
6. In the window that opens (left), name your backup, then click the "Begin Backup" button.
7. If the backup requires more than one disc, the current disc ejects when finished and a prompt notifies you to insert another disc. **The last disc burned is the "master" disc of the backup set.** Label the last disc of the set as the master disc. When you want to restore the data at a later date, Backup will ask for the master disc to start the restore.
8. Click OK when Backup is finished.

Schedule Your Backups

You can schedule **automatic backups** of files to your iDisk or attached disk drive. Of course, your disk drive must be powered on and you must be connected to the Internet for an automatic backup to your iDisk.

1. From the pop-up menu, choose **Back up to iDisk** or **Back up to Drive,** depending on which device you want to schedule your backup to.

2. Click the "Schedule" button in the bottom-left corner of the window. The schedule sheet slides down into view.

3. **Schedule iDisk/Drive Backups:** Choose "Daily" or "Weekly."

4. **Frequency Options:** Choose when to perform the backup. If you chose "Weekly," you'll get an option to choose the day of the week. Click OK.

The Schedule button.

Remove Items or Clear Your iDisk

You cannot go to your iDisk and remove files directly, but you can go through Backup to remove selected items. For your other disks, however, you cannot throw away individual items.

To remove a backed-up item from your iDisk:

1. Open Backup.

2. From the pop-up menu in the upper-left corner of the "Backup" window, choose "Restore from iDisk."

3. In the window, select the item you want to remove.

4. Go to the Edit menu and choose "Remove from List."

To clear the iDisk Backup folder of its entire contents, from the pop-up menu choose "Restore from iDisk." Then go to the Edit menu and choose "Clear iDisk Backup Folder."

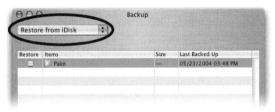

Restore Files from an iDisk

To copy backed-up files from your iDisk back to your computer:

1. From the pop-up menu, select "Restore from iDisk."

2. In the "Restore" window, choose items in the list to restore.

3. Click "Restore Now."

From any computer that can log in to your iDisk (use the iDisk Utility, if necessary; see Chapter 6), you can drag files from the Backup folder in your iDisk to your hard disk. This will never remove the original file from the iDisk—it just makes a copy. (You cannot drag files *into* the Backup folder.)

Restore Files from a Disk Drive

To copy backed-up files from a backup drive to your computer:

1. From the pop-up menu, select "Restore from Drive."

2. Click the "Set" button to locate the backup you want to restore from and the drive that it's located on.

3. In the "Restore" window, choose items in the list to restore.

4. Click "Restore Now."

Restore Files from a CD or DVD

To copy backed-up files from a CD or DVD back to your hard disk:

1. From the pop-up menu, select "Restore from CD/DVD."

2. Backup will ask for the master disc of the backup set. Insert it. (If you don't know which one is the master disc, see page 290.)

3. In the "Restore" window, choose items in the list to restore.

4. Click "Restore Now."

⊚ *iSync*

iSync is an easy and convenient way to keep your iCal calendars and your Address Book information synchronized between multiple Macs. You can also synchronize your iCal and Address Book information between your computer and your Mac.com account.

iSync can even synchronize iCal calendars and contact information with iPods, Palm OS devices, and some Bluetooth-enabled wireless phones.

A Palm OS device is any PDA (Personal Digital Assistant) that uses the Palm operating system. To use iSync with one of these devices, the device must have Palm Desktop 4.0 or later and iSync Palm Conduit 1.2 or later installed.

In addition to a .Mac account, iSync requires a newer computer running Mac OS X version 10.2.5 or later.

If you hate the idea of manually re-entering all your calendar and contact information into another computer or in your .Mac account's Address Book, download this free application to make synchronization a quick and easy task.

The "iSync" window shows any devices you have added to iSync.

Download, Install, and Register

To start using iSync, you must download and install it.

1. Go to Apple's iSync web site at **www.apple.com/isync**.

2. Click the "Download iSync" icon.

3. From the "Get iSync" web page, fill out the short registration form for iSync (name and email address), then click the "Download iSync" button.

4. After the download is complete, follow the instructions in the installation window that opens.

5. In the Applications folder, locate iSync and double-click its icon to open it.

6. Register your computer to the Mac.com synchronization server: Click the "Register" button (circled below). In the next pane that appears, type a name (something clear enough that you will recognize later) to identify this computer to the .Mac synchronization server, then click "Continue" (shown below-right).

7. When registration is finished, select "Turn on .Mac synchronization," as shown on the next page.

After iSync installation is finished, you can throw the install folder in the Trash.

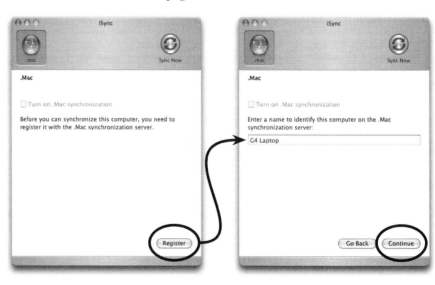

To register more than one computer to a Mac.com account, you must perform the registration process from each individual computer. All computers registered to a specific Mac.com account will be listed in the "All Registered Computers" pane.

When you first open iSync, all you see is a toolbar that contains a couple of buttons—the ".mac" button and the "Sync Now" button. Click the ".mac" icon in the iSync toolbar to open the .Mac synchronization drawer shown below. If another device icon appears in the toolbar, such as the iPod icon shown below, it means you've *added a device* to be synced with iSync. Click the device icon to open a synchronization drawer that is specific to that device. Learn how to add a device on pages 299–302.

After selecting iSync options, click the "Sync Now" button. The items you selected for synchronization (Safari bookmarks, Address Book contacts, and iCal calendars and To Do items) will be copied to your .Mac account iDisk.

The "iSync" window as it appears with its drawer closed.

Click the ".mac" button to open a drawer that shows your .Mac account synchronization options.

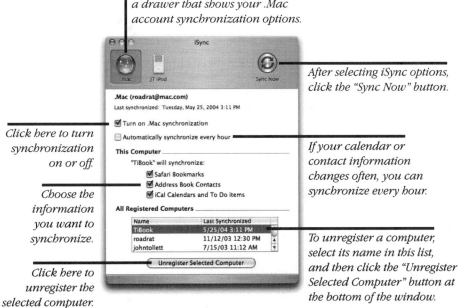

After selecting iSync options, click the "Sync Now" button.

Click here to turn synchronization on or off.

Choose the information you want to synchronize.

If your calendar or contact information changes often, you can synchronize every hour.

Click here to unregister the selected computer.

To unregister a computer, select its name in this list, and then click the "Unregister Selected Computer" button at the bottom of the window.

Mac-to-.Mac Synchronization

Syncing your Mac to your .Mac account creates a duplicate copy of your local data on the Apple server and helps you keep both versions current by comparing and synchronizing the latest changes between them.

Add a check next to the items you want to synchronize.

1. Open iSync if it's not already open and click the ".mac" button in the toolbar to reveal the .Mac synchronization options (left).

2. Place a checkmark next to the items you want to sync.

3. Click the "Sync Now" button.

   iSync compares the items you checked in the window with the latest data on Apple's synchronization server. If it's your first time syncing, iSync copies the data from the computer you're sitting at to Apple's server.

During a sync, the "Sync Now" button changes to the "Cancel Sync" button.

4. If you see the "Data Change Alert" window (below), it means there's a difference between the data on the .Mac server and the data on your local computer. The alert tells you how many items will be added to, deleted from, or modified on your computer. Click "Cancel" if you want to avoid making any changes to your computer.

If iSync needs to change any data on your computer when it syncs, you'll see this "Data Change Alert" message, warning you that data on your computer will be changed.

Data Change Alert			
More than 5% of your bookmarks will be changed by this synchronization.			
The following changes will be made if you proceed:			
	Add	Delete	Modify
This computer	70	–	–
(?) ☐ Do not show this dialog again		Cancel	Proceed

You can change how often you see this alert message in the iSync Preferences (see page 298).

Mac-to-Mac Synchronization

Many people work on two or more computers—perhaps one at the office and one at home, or there may be multiple computers in one office or home. To synchronize all the computers so they have the same Address Book, Safari bookmarks, and/or iCal calendar information, perform a **Mac-to-Mac synchronization.**

1. Open iSync if it's not already open.

2. Click the "Sync Now" button.

   The first time you sync, iSync copies the items you checked in the .Mac synchronization window (Address Book, Safari bookmarks, and/or iCal data) from the computer you're sitting at to Apple's synchronization server.

3. Go to another Mac that you've registered (as described on the previous pages), open iSync on that computer, then click "Sync Now." The information on the .Mac synchronization server is copied to the current computer.

   If you already have existing data on the current computer, iSync will ask if you want to **merge** the data with .Mac, or **replace** it with the .Mac data (below). Click the "Replace with .Mac" button to have the .Mac server use its version of files to overwrite the files on the computer you're sitting at.

The items you've chosen to sync are listed here.

Synchronization Tips

Below are a few tips and techniques that can be helpful when using iSync.

▼ **If you change your mind** after performing a synchronization, you can **revert** to the previous version of files: From the Devices menu, choose "Revert To Last Sync...." In the alert window that opens, click the "Revert to Last Sync" button.

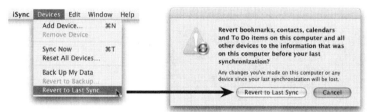

▼ If you want to **replace** the iCal and Address Book information on *all* computers and devices with the information on a *specific* computer or device, you can perform a **one-way synchronization:** From the Devices menu, choose "Reset All Devices...." Then from the pop-up menu, choose the source from which to transfer data to all other computers and devices that you've added to iSync.

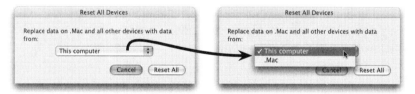

iSync Preferences

The iSync icon in the menu bar.

To set your iSync preferences, from the iSync application menu, choose "Preferences...."

▼ "Show iSync in menu bar" places an iSync icon in the upper-right corner of the menu bar, giving easy access to the "Open iSync" and "Sync Now" commands.

▼ From the "Show Data Change Alert when" pop-up menu, choose how much data to be synced requires changes before the "Data Change Alert" window appears. From the pop-up menu, choose "any," "more than 1%," "more than 5%," or "more than 10%."

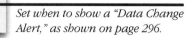

Set when to show a "Data Change Alert," as shown on page 296.

Add Other Devices and Synchronize

iSync can also synchronize Address Book and iCal information to several other devices:

▼ **Palm OS devices** such as Palm Tungsten and Zire, the Handspring Treo, the palmOne Visor, or the Sony Clié models.

▼ **iPod,** Apple's wildly popular MP3 player.

▼ **Bluetooth-enabled and other wireless phones,** such as the models offered by Sony Ericsson, Nokia, Motorola, and Siemens. Motorola also makes USB phones that are compatible with iSync.

For a current list of iSync device compatibility, visit **www.apple.com/isync/devices.html.**

To add other devices to iSync:

1. From the Devices menu, choose "Add Device...."

2. Double-click any device that is *discovered* and shown in the pane below to add it to the "iSync" window toolbar.

3. If a device doesn't show up in the window, click the "Scan" button to search again for any available devices.

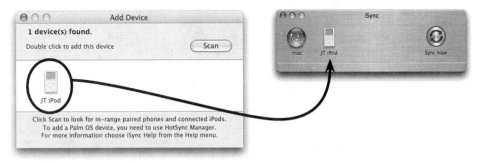

iPod and iSync

Tip: To sync iPod, you must have iPod software version 1.2 or later installed.

Download the most current iPod software at **www.apple.com/ipod.**

If you previously set up your iPod to act as a FireWire disk and dragged your contact list or calendars to the hard disk, *delete those files before you go through the iSync process*—iSync can only do this correctly if it originally put the files it needs on your iPod.

1. Connect your iPod to your computer using the FireWire cable that came with your iPod.

2. Open iSync.

3. If iPod doesn't automatically appear in the "iSync" window, do this: From the Devices menu, choose "Add Device…," then double-click the iPod icon in the "Add Device" window.

4. In the "iSync" window toolbar (shown below), click the "iPod" button to slide open the iPod drawer. Click the top checkbox to turn on iPod synchronization.

5. Choose the items you want to synchronize:
   Check the **Contacts** box to sync Address Book information.
   Check the **Calendars** box to sync iCal calendar information.

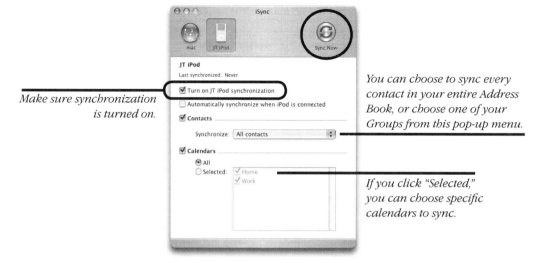

Make sure synchronization is turned on.

You can choose to sync every contact in your entire Address Book, or choose one of your Groups from this pop-up menu.

If you click "Selected," you can choose specific calendars to sync.

6. Click "Sync Now." The drawer closes so that only the toolbar is visible. iSync grabs the requested information and transfers it to the iPod.

The synchronization bar shows the sync in progress.

7. If you reopen the iPod drawer after synchronization, as shown below, the iSync window now shows a "Last synchronized" date.

   To perform future syncs to iPod, open iSync, click the "iPod" button, then click "Sync Now."

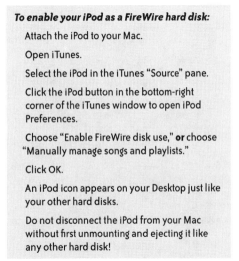

To enable your iPod as a FireWire hard disk:

Attach the iPod to your Mac.

Open iTunes.

Select the iPod in the iTunes "Source" pane.

Click the iPod button in the bottom-right corner of the iTunes window to open iPod Preferences.

Choose "Enable FireWire disk use," **or** choose "Manually manage songs and playlists."

Click OK.

An iPod icon appears on your Desktop just like your other hard disks.

Do not disconnect the iPod from your Mac without first unmounting and ejecting it like any other hard disk!

8. **If you did NOT enable your iPod to act as a FireWire hard disk,** the iPod screen should display a big checkmark and a message that it's okay to disconnect. Just disconnect it from the FireWire cable or the cradle.

   If your iPod IS enabled as a hard disk (you can see its icon either on your Desktop or in your Computer window), first **select and eject** the iPod icon, *then* disconnect it from the cable. When in hard disk mode, the iPod's screen will display a warning symbol and a message that it is *not* okay to disconnect, which means you must unmount and *eject* the iPod before disconnecting it.

Palm OS devices and iSync

To sync a Palm OS device with a computer, make sure Palm Desktop 4.0 or later is installed, along with iSync Palm Conduit 1.2 or later, which is available for download at **www.palmsource.com.**

Tip: Sync your Palm OS device with only one computer. If you add your Palm device to iSync on more than one computer, the information may not sync correctly.

1. Open the Palm HotSync Manager software.
2. From the HotSync menu, choose "Conduit Settings."
3. In the "Conduit Settings" window, double-click "iSync Conduit," then select "Enable iSync for this Palm device."
4. Click OK. Quit HotSync Manager.
5. Open iSync.
6. Click the Palm OS device icon in the "iSync" window.
7. Click "Sync Now."

Bluetooth

Bluetooth-enabled wireless phones and iSync

To sync a Bluetooth-enabled wireless phone, it must be in "discoverable" mode; the computer you want to sync the phone with must be Bluetooth-enabled or have a Bluetooth adapter connected.

Tip: You can sync your phone with only one computer. If you add your phone to more than one computer, the information may not sync correctly.

1. Open System Preferences, then click the "Bluetooth" icon. If you have Bluetooth installed, the icon automatically shows in the System Preferences window.
2. In the "Devices" pane, select your phone in the list, then click "Pair New Device" to pair your computer with the phone.

   A dialog box appears to let you choose which services to use with your phone: Select the checkbox to "Synchronize your Contacts and Calendar."

Tip: More information about Bluetooth and Bluetooth adapters can be found at **www.apple. com/bluetooth.**

3. Open iSync.
4. If you don't see your phone icon in the "iSync" window, from the Devices menu, choose "Add Device...."
5. Double-click the phone in the "Add Device" window to add it to iSync.
6. Click "Sync Now."

.Mac Slides Publisher **12**

If you are a .Mac member, you can download a piece of software from www.mac.com called **.Mac Slides Publisher.** This software copies selected photos from your computer to your iDisk and publishes them as a screen-saver slideshow, complete with slow zooms and cross-dissolve transitions. Friends can *subscribe* to your slideshow and use it on their own computers as a screensaver.

Users running Mac OS X version 10.2 or later on their Macs—even if they're *not* .Mac members—can subscribe to any .Mac member's slideshow. And they don't have to download any software to do it. It's just another brilliant feature the Mac provides so you can share your iLife with friends, family, and associates.

Download .Mac Slides Publisher

To create a slideshow that friends can subscribe to as a screensaver, first download the .Mac Slides Publisher software from the Mac.com web site.

To download the software so you can publish a slideshow for others to use (you must be a .Mac member):

1. Go to **www.mac.com**.

2. Log in with your screen name and password.

3. Click the link called ".Mac Downloads."

.Mac Downloads
Get the latest
software, utilities,
and member specials
all in one place.

4. This takes you to a web page of downloadable software links. Click the "Mac_Slides_Publisher.dmg" link to download the software.

 .Mac Slides Publisher | Learn More | System Requirements
Mac_Slides_Publisher.dmg (English Only) ◄

Or click the "Learn More" link (shown in the link above) and visit the page shown below. From this page, click the "Download .Mac Slides" button to open the "Download .Mac Slides Publisher" page, as shown on the next page.

As time goes by, the software might be moved to another part of the web site or its name might change! If you don't find it here, poke around the .Mac site.

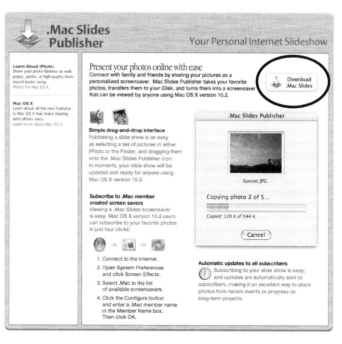

Click on the "Download" link (circled below) to start the download.

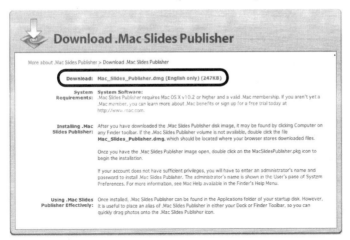

If you aren't using Safari to download .Mac Slides Publisher, you might not see the window in Step 5 automatically. If this is the case, look on your Desktop and double click the .dmg icon shown below. After the file uncompresses, you should see the window shown in Step 5.

Mac_Slides_Publisher.dmg

5. After the download is complete, a window will open (shown below). Double-click the "package" called "MacSlidesPublisher.pkg."

Mac Slides Publisher

Ta da! This is the application that will let you publish slideshows, as explained on the following pages.

6. Follow the on-screen instructions in the Installer to install the software. You will be asked for your Administrator name and password.

7. When the Installer is finished, look in your Applications folder for the application named "Mac Slides Publisher." You can throw away the .dmg file and eject the "Mac Slides Publisher" hard disk icon, if they are still on your Desktop, by dragging them to the Trash.

Publish a Slideshow

You must be a Mac.com member to publish a slideshow.

To publish a slideshow for others to use:

1. Follow the directions on the previous pages to download and install the .Mac Slides Publisher software.

2. Connect to the Internet, if you're not already.

Tip: If you dragged the "Mac Slides Publisher" icon (or any icon) to a Finder window toolbar, you can Command-drag it to the Desktop to remove it.

If you dragged the icon to the Sidebar, you can drag it to the Desktop to remove it.

3. Position the icon for the "Mac Slides Publisher" where you will be able to see it when you have pictures accessible or iPhoto open. You can drag the application icon to the Dock, into a Finder window Toolbar or Sidebar, or make an alias on your Desktop (to make an alias, hold down Command and Option while you drag the application icon to the Desktop).

Mac Slides Publisher

This is the application icon. It's in your Applications folder after you download and install it.

Note: Every time you drop photos on the "Mac Slides Publisher" icon, you replace the existing slideshow with the new photos!

4. **To publish a slideshow,** simply drag photographs to the "Mac Slides Publisher" icon and drop them on top of it.

   ▼ The only files that will work are .jpg or .jpeg files (same things). This is the format a digital camera most often uses.

   ▼ You can drag .jpg files from a Finder window (shown below) or from the iPhoto window (shown on the following page).

   ▼ You must drag over all the files you want in the slideshow at once—that is, you cannot drop two photos on the icon, then go get three more, etc. You must select every photo you want in the slideshow and drag them all at once to the icon. You cannot drop a folder on top of the publisher icon.

To select more than one photo, hold down the Command key and click on the images you want to use. Then *let go* of the Command key and *drag one* of the selected files—they will all follow along.

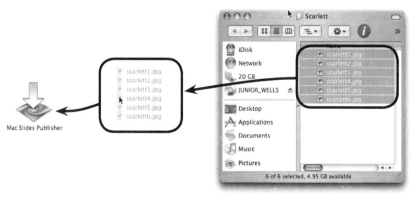

You can drag photos directly from an iPhoto window and drop them on the Publisher icon, as shown here. Notice only 9 of the 39 photos have been selected. You can't drag the photo album icon (or a folder) onto the "Mac Slides Publisher" icon; *you must select individual pictures.*

This may look like it's dragging only one image, but the number "9" in the shadow image tells you it's really dragging the nine selected images.

Mac Slides Publisher

As soon as you "drop" (let go of) the images on the "Mac Slides Publisher" icon, a window opens to display the progress of the photos being uploaded to your iDisk.

When the process of copying the photos to your iDisk is complete, you'll get an opportunity to **announce your slideshow,** shown below.

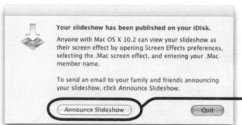

Click the "Announce Slideshow" button to send an automatic email to selected contacts that contains complete directions for subscribing to your new .Mac Slideshow.

Subscribe to a Published Slideshow

You do not need to be a .Mac member to subscribe to anyone's slideshow, but you do need to be connected to the Internet.

Tips: When you subscribe to a .Mac slideshow, your Mac will go online to the .Mac member's slideshow every time you connect to the Internet. If it finds new photos, they will be automatically downloaded to your Mac. If you connect with a dial-up modem, you might not want your computer downloading files without you knowing it!

To prevent automatic downloading, uncheck the "Selected" box in the Subscriptions pane of "Desktop & Screen Saver" preferences.

To see what a slideshow looks like on your screen, click the "Test" button in the "Desktop & Screen Saver" preferences window.

1. Open System Preferences, then click on "Desktop & Screen Saver."

2. Click the "Screen Saver" tab to show the Screen Saver options.

3. In the list of available screensaver effects on the left side of the pane, single-click ".Mac."

4. To the right, click "Options." A "Subscriptions" sheet (as shown below) slides down from the window's title bar.

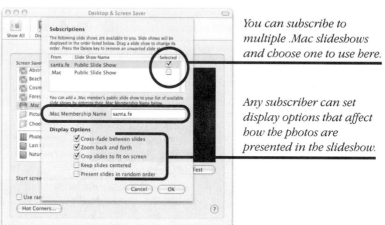

You can subscribe to multiple .Mac slideshows and choose one to use here.

Any subscriber can set display options that affect how the photos are presented in the slideshow.

5. In the center of this sheet, type the screen name of the .Mac member who has published a slideshow to which you want to subscribe.

6. Choose the "Display Options" you'd like, check the slideshow you want to display, then click OK.

7. It will take several minutes for the slideshow to download to your Mac. Once it has, you do not have to be online to view the slideshow.

Virex

13

Your Mac.com membership not only gets you a lot of things that are useful, it can also prevent you from getting lots of things that are harmful—like *viruses* and other nasty, disgusting stuff that lurks on the Internet and on seemingly nice people's media that you may need to put in your computer. Traditionally, Macs have had significantly fewer problems with viruses than PCs, but why take chances? Especially when your .Mac account includes a free download of **Virex,** anti-virus software from the top-ranked anti-virus research center in the world that employs researchers in sixteen different countries.

Virex automatically checks for updates regularly, providing maximum protection against viruses and other types of code that can harm your computer or your files. Virex can scan individual files, folders, or your entire computer. When a virus or harmful code is detected, Virex can repair or delete the infected file.

It doesn't get any safer or easier than this. Download Virex and breathe easy.

Download Virex from Mac.com

Virex's outward simplicity and ease of use disguises the complex and sophisticated technology behind it.

To download and install Virex:

1. Go to the Mac.com web site (**www.mac.com**) and log in with your member name and password.

2. Click the Virex link in the sidebar (circled on the left).

3. On the page that appears, click the "Download Virex" icon.

4. On the "Download Virex" page that opens, click the English Virex link (shown below).

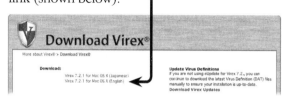

5. Once the download to your Desktop is complete, double-click the .pkg file (left) in the Finder window that opens to launch the Virex installer.

6. Follow the Installer instructions that appear. The installation places Virex in the Applications folder.

Virex 7.2.pkg

The .pkg file (above) should appear in a Finder window after downloading is complete. If it doesn't, look for the .dmg file (below) on your Desktop; double-click it to open a window with the .pkg file in it.

Virex_7.2.1.dmg

Run Virex

1. Double-click the Virex icon in the Applications folder.

2. In the sheet that slides down, enter your administrator password so Virex can perform an automatic "eUpdate" in which it connects to the Internet and checks for the latest virus definition files (DAT files).

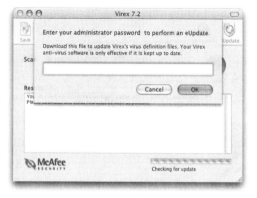

Scan for infected files on your Mac

Virex can scan items on your computer and check them for virus infections. You can select which files, folders, or volumes (partitions or other disks) you want to scan. Scanning an entire disk can take a while, so some scans are better to schedule while you're away or asleep.

See the following page about the "Scan & Clean" button.

1. From the "Scan" pop-up menu, choose one of the items to scan.

   Or click "Choose" in the pop-up menu to open a Finder window in which you can select any folder, file, or volume.

2. Click the "Scan" button, shown right.

Or use this **quick scan method:** Select one or more items on your computer, then drag them onto the "Scan" button or onto the Virex icon in the Dock.

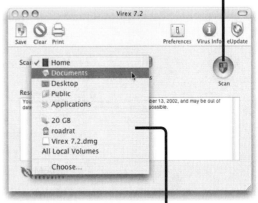

Update the Virus Definitions

An estimated 62,000 viruses have been identified, but we'd estimate that 99 percent of them are for Windows machines. Although the Mac rarely gets a virus, they do keep changing so it's recommended that you update Virex's **virus definition files** (DAT files) at least once a month. Virex calls this *electronic* procedure "eUpdate."

The "Scan" pop-up menu lets you choose specific places for Virex to scan.

▼ **To automatically check** for DAT updates, open Virex. Each time Virex opens it connects to Apple's DAT update web site and checks for new virus definitions.

   To prevent Virex from automatically checking for updates, change the setting in the "Virus Update" section of the preferences (see page 313).

▼ **To manually check** for DAT updates at any time, click the "eUpdate" button in the toolbar.

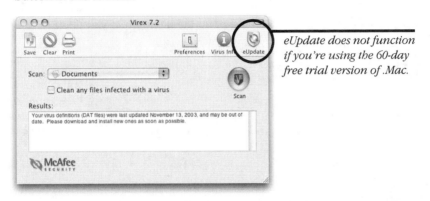

eUpdate does not function if you're using the 60-day free trial version of .Mac.

The Virex Window and Toolbar

The Virex window provides everything you need to keep your computer free from viruses.

Save: Click to save the results of a scan or eUpdate (shown in the "Results" pane) as a text file.

Clear: Click to clear the "Results" pane.

Print: Click to print the contents of the "Results" pane.

Preferences: Click to open the preferences window, shown on the next page.

Virus Info: Click to connect to the *NAI Virus Information Library* (http://vil.nai.com). This web site provides detailed information about viruses, where they come from, how they work, and how to remove them. It also provides information about virus hoaxes, so you can check to see if a virus warning you receive from someone is real or not.

eUpdate: Click to connect to Apple's DAT update web site and check for the latest virus definition files.

Scan: From this pop-up menu choose the files, folders, or volumes you want to scan for viruses.

Clean any files infected with a virus *checkbox:* Check this box if you want Virex to attempt to clean an infected file. When you select this box, the "Scan" button changes to a "Scan & Clean" button. If Virex can't clean an infected file, it *removes* the file from your computer.

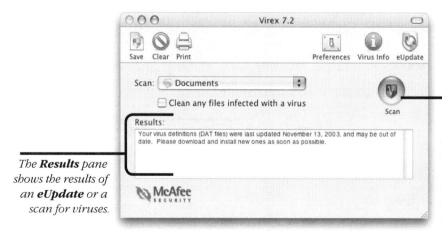

*The **Results** pane shows the results of an **eUpdate** or a scan for viruses.*

*When this box is selected, the **Scan** button changes to **Scan & Clean.***

*Click the **Scan** button to scan items you selected in the pop-up menu.*

Or drag and drop items from anywhere on your computer on top of this button.

Virex Preferences

Click the "Preferences" button in the toolbar to make the preferences sheet slide down, as shown below. The options offered are:

Scan inside compressed (.gz) and archived (.tar) files: Scanning inside compressed files slows scan times, but is much safer than uncompressing files before scanning them. When you uncompress a file that contains an executable malicious virus file, it runs its harmful code immediately upon being uncompressed. You should scan *inside* compressed files.

Archived files are safer, because when you extract them, executable files do not run immediately. To speed up scans of archived files, you can safely *extract* them before scanning.

Automatically scan at login: Scans your *Home* folder each time you log in. This can seem slow, especially if you're in a hurry.

Show detailed results information: Provides additional scan information in the "Results" pane during the scanning procedure.

Remove macros from potentially infected files: Attempts to remove infected macros from *Microsoft Office* files (the most common source of viruses for the Mac).

Robin is very proud to have a Microsoft-free environment.

Automatically delete infected files: Automatically deletes infected files if cleaning attempts fail.

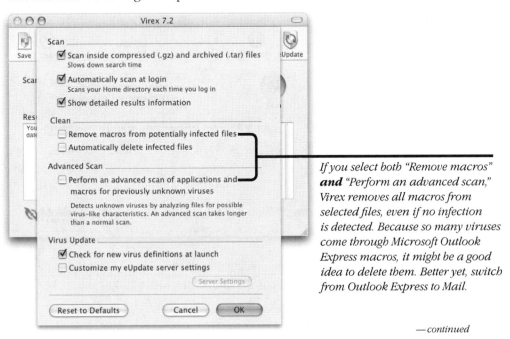

*If you select both "Remove macros" **and** "Perform an advanced scan," Virex removes all macros from selected files, even if no infection is detected. Because so many viruses come through Microsoft Outlook Express macros, it might be a good idea to delete them. Better yet, switch from Outlook Express to Mail.*

—continued

Perform an advanced scan of applications and macros for previously unknown viruses: Analyzes files for unknown viruses. Advanced scans are slower than normal scans.

Check for new virus definitions at launch: Automatically performs an "eUpdate" each time Virex opens.

Customize my eUpdate server settings: When this option is selected, you can click the "Server Settings" button to open the "eUpdate Server Settings" window, shown below.

▼ The "Type" pop-up menu provides two options: "HTTP" and "FTP."

▼ The default setting is "HTTP" and connects to the Apple DAT update web site. You should not change this setting or the URL (web address) that shows in the "Server URL" text box.

▼ Type your Mac.com account user name and password in the text fields shown.

▼ The "FTP" option is for users who know an FTP server where they can download virus definitions. Some users may have access to virus definition files on their local network and can enter the network address and other necessary information in the "FTP" pane.

Reset to Defaults: Click this button to reset all options to their default settings.

Section three

Mac OS X apps

The applications in this section are productivity applications that were designed specifically to run on the latest version of the computer world's state-of-the-art operating system, Mac OS X. The following chapters explore the applications that let you efficiently organize, create, and manage email, contact information, calendars, and to-do lists: **Mail, Address Book,** and **iCal.**

Mac OS X includes communication applications that make it convenient, efficient, and fun to be productive: **iChat AV** provides instant messaging in text, audio, and video formats for keeping communication lines open with family, friends, and associates. **Rendezvous** makes file-sharing and communication on a local network effortless. **Safari,** Mac's custom-built web browser, offers top browsing speed and cutting-edge features for viewing and organizing World Wide Web content.

While other Mac applications inspire creativity, these Mac OS X apps enhance the efficiency and productivity of your ever-expanding digital lifestyle.

iCal

14

iCal is a personal calendar, an organizer, and a scheduler built around the idea that you need more than one calendar to manage the different aspects of your life. You can create as many specialized calendars as you want: one for work, one for family, another for school, etc. You can choose to display just one calendar at a time or any selection of calendars.

Use iCal's **To Do list** to prioritize and manage your busy day, week, or month. Add an **event,** such as a party, to iCal and let iCal email invitations to selected people in your Address Book. iCal can **notify** you of upcoming events and appointments with an alarm sound, email alert, or display message on your screen. And iCal's **search** feature let you easily find any event or To Do item that you've added to your calendar.

You can even **publish** your own calendar online so you (or friends, family, or coworkers) can check it from any computer, anywhere in the world. The number of calendars you create is limited only by the amount of free disk space on your computer. All sorts of iCal calendars are available online that you can subscribe to—many organizations, bands, and entertainment companies are posting iCalendars on their web sites.

iCal requires Mac OS X 10.2 or later.

In this chapter

The iCal Window

iCal's customizable window provides access to all calendars, views, events, and lists. Color-coding makes it easy to view multiple calendars in one window and instantly know whether there are any overlapping events. For instance, you can easily tell if Mom's meetings might make her miss a Proust reading or if your afternoon meeting might coincide with Junior's soccer game.

Your list of calendars

The upper-left pane of the iCal window shows the **list of calendars** that you have created or to which you have subscribed. You can select any calendar in the list to show just that calendar's information (check its box) in the View pane, or you can select multiple calendars so they show simultaneously in iCal (check any or all of the boxes).

To change the number of days that display in the weekly calendar view, press Command Option any number from 1 through 7 (e.g., Command Option 3 displays three days instead of seven).

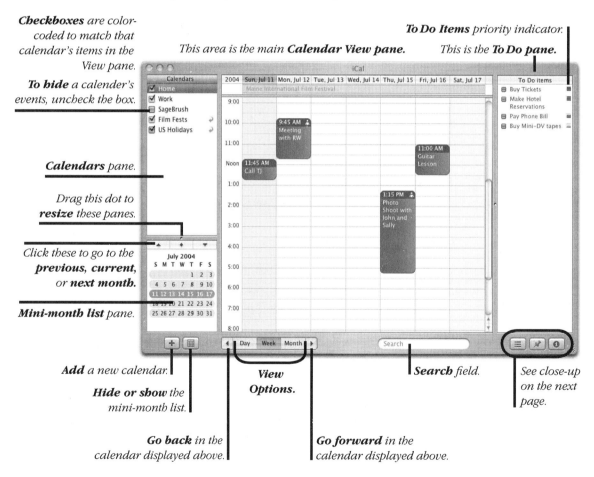

Checkboxes are color-coded to match that calendar's items in the View pane.

To hide a calender's events, uncheck the box.

*This area is the main **Calendar View pane.***

To Do Items priority indicator.

*This is the **To Do pane.***

Calendars pane.

Drag this dot to **resize** these panes.

Click these to go to the **previous, current,** or **next month.**

Mini-month list pane.

Add a new calendar.

Hide or show the mini-month list.

View Options.

Search field.

See close-up on the next page.

Go back in the calendar displayed above.

Go forward in the calendar displayed above.

This is a closeup of the **hide-and-show buttons** located in the bottom-right corner of iCal's window.

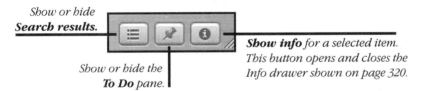

Show or hide
Search results.

Show or hide the
To Do *pane.*

Show info *for a selected item. This button opens and closes the Info drawer shown on page 320.*

Choose a calendar view

The appearance of the main Calendar View pane changes according to which view option you choose: Day, Week, or Month.

Next.

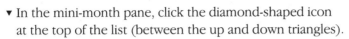

Previous.

▼ **To choose a view preference,** click one of the View Option buttons at the bottom of the iCal window (shown on the right).

▼ **To go to the *previous* or *next* day, week, or month** in any view, click the triangles on either side of the View Option buttons.

The mini-month pane

The mini-month pane lets you jump to any day, week, or month of any year.

▼ **To display a particular month** in iCal's main Viewing pane, click the month you want to see in the mini-month list.

▼ **To scroll forward or backward in time through the mini-month calendars,** click the up or down triangle located at the top of the mini-month list.

Return to today's date

There are several easy ways **to get back to the current date** after jumping to future dates in iCal. Do one of the following:

The mini-month pane.

▼ In the mini-month pane, click the diamond-shaped icon at the top of the list (between the up and down triangles).

▼ **Or** from the View menu, choose "Go To Today."

▼ **Or** press Command T.

Create a New Calendar

Keep track of the schedules of selected family, friends, and colleagues. If you share the same user account on your Mac with other family members, you can view their individual calendars in your iCal application.

Use this pop-up menu to assign calendar color.

To create a new calendar, click the "plus" button in the bottom-left corner, then enter a name for the calendar and choose a color (see below).

To change the color of a calendar, select the calendar (click once on its name) in the Calendars list, click the Show Info button (the letter "i"), then choose a color from the pop-up menu in the Calendar Info drawer that opens (shown on the left).

To change a calendar name, double-click a name in the Calendars list, then type a new name.

When iCal is in Day or Week view, any item selection highlights all other items from that same calendar.

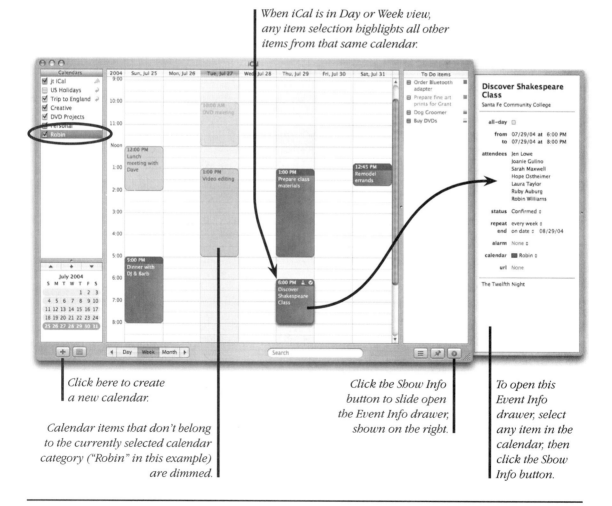

Click here to create a new calendar.

Calendar items that don't belong to the currently selected calendar category ("Robin" in this example) are dimmed.

Click the Show Info button to slide open the Event Info drawer, shown on the right.

To open this Event Info drawer, select any item in the calendar, then click the Show Info button.

Create a New Event in a Calendar

Items that you enter into an iCal calendar are called **events.** An event can be an appointment, a party, a reminder, an all-day class, or a week-long seminar. Or anything else that's in your schedule.

To create an event:

1. Click on a calendar in the Calendars list to select it. If none of the calendars in the list seems appropriate for the new event you want to add, create a new calendar as explained on the previous page.

2. In the Calendar View pane, press-and-drag vertically in the time slot in which you want to place an event.

   Or double-click the time slot in which you want to place a new event. Once you've created the event, you can drag it to any other position in the calendar.

   Or click once in a time slot, then from the File menu choose "New Event."

3. When you create a new event, the text "New Event" is already selected (highlighted), so all you have to do is start typing a description of your event.

   Or click the Calendar Info button to open the Info drawer (shown on the right), then click on the text at the top of the drawer and type a description there.

4. Add other relevant information for the event to the Info drawer.

To see all the information about an event, select the event in the Calendar View pane, then click the Info button in the bottom-right corner of the window. The Event Info drawer opens to show the event information.

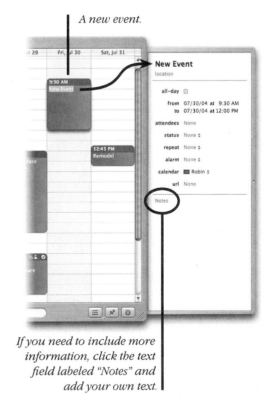

A new event.

If you need to include more information, click the text field labeled "Notes" and add your own text.

Create an all-day event or a multiple-day event

All-day and **multiple-day events** are represented by rounded rectangles that
stretch the width of the event duration. In Day or Week view, they appear in
a row at the top of the calendar in order to leave more room for other items
in the main window and to avoid overlapping too many events in the same
column (see the example below, left).

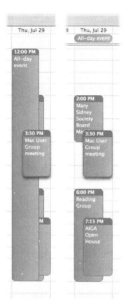

A multiple-day event. *A two-day event.* *An all-day event.*

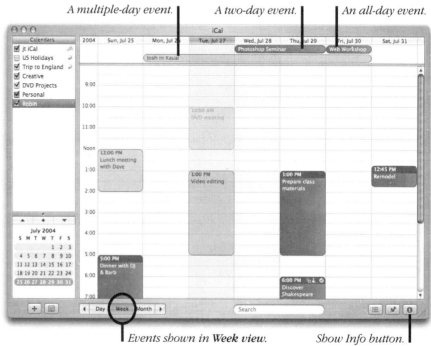

*Events shown in **Week view**.* *Show Info button.*

*Above-left: An all-day
event created by drag-
ging the bottom edge
of the event item to fill
the day's column. This
technique crowds the
other items.*

*Above-right: The same
event designated as
an all-day event in
the Event Info drawer.
This technique moves
the all-day event to the
top, out of the way.*

*iCal's **Month view** shows all-day events as
an event bar that stretches across one or
more days within the main calendar grid.*

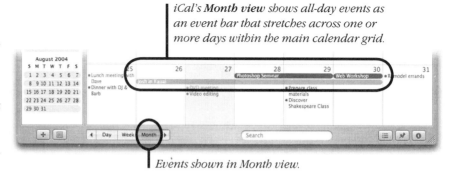

Events shown in Month view.

To create an all-day event:

1. Create a new event in the iCal window, as explained on page 321.

   Or select an existing event that you want to change to an all-day event.

2. Click the Show Info button to open the Event Info drawer (on the right).

3. In the Event Info drawer, click the "all-day" checkbox.

4. Press Return on your keyboard to apply your settings.

To create a multiple-day event:

1. Create a new event as explained on page 321, or select an existing event.

2. Click the Show Info button to open the Info drawer.

3. Click the "all-day" checkbox.

4. Set the "from" and "to" buttons to show the duration of the event. Click on the "to" date, then press the Up or Down arrow on your keyboard to change the date.

5. Press the Return key.

To create recurring events:

1. Click an event in iCal to select it.

2. Click the Show Info button to open the Info drawer.

3. Click the "repeat" pop-up menu in the Event Info drawer, as shown on the right, and choose one of the frequency options listed.

4. For more options, select "Custom" from the pop-up menu and make additional choices as shown below.

5. Click OK to apply your settings.

These options are available when you select "Custom" from the "repeat" pop-up menu.

iCal provides a visual indication of **schedule conflicts.** The example below shows three calendar items with overlapping times. If the items belong to *different* calendars (from the Calendars list), the color coding will indicate to which calendar an item belongs.

All-day and multiple-day events.

*iCal's **Week view** overlaps conflicting events. Click on an event to bring it to the foreground.*

***To reschedule an event to another time,** just drag the event to any position in the calendar grid.*

Multiple-day event.

*This is how **Day view** shows different events that are scheduled in overlapping time slots.*

***To see an overview of your appointments,** use the **Week** view. Switch to **Day** view to see a more detailed, less cluttered calendar.*

Delete an event

To manually delete an event, select it, then press the Delete key on your keyboard. To select multiple events at once, Shift-select two or more events, then press Delete. **Or** from the Edit menu, choose Delete.

To automatically delete events that have passed:

1. From the iCal menu, choose "Preferences...."

2. Click the checkbox labeled "Delete events and To Do items after X days" in the "Events and To Do items" section, then enter the number of days after which events are to be deleted.

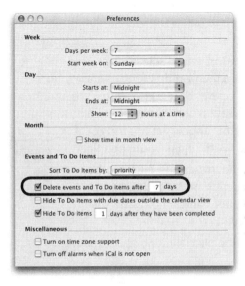

When you select this option, an event is deleted after it occurs in the calendar. A To Do item is deleted after you mark it as **completed** *in the To Do pane by clicking its checkbox.*

To keep iCal and the To Do pane from becoming cluttered with old events and tasks, automatically delete events and To Do items (as described above). However, if you want to keep a record of schedules, appointments, and events, uncheck this checkbox and let iCal store your information.

Tip: If you have more than one email account, you can specify which account is the default: Open the Mail preferences and click the Accounts icon. The account name at the top of the list is the default. To change it, drag another account name to the top of the list.

Invite people to an event

iCal uses Mail and your Address Book to invite people to an event (if you have more than one account, Mail uses the *default* email account).

To invite people:

1. Select an event in the View pane and click the "Show Info" button.

2. In the Event Info drawer, click next to the "attendees" label and enter the name of a person to invite. If the person is in your Address Book, iCal will autofill the rest of the name. Press Return to finish or continue entering names until all the attendees have been added.

   Or click on the "attendees" label and select "Open Address Book" from the pop-up menu as shown on the left. When the Address Book opens, drag contacts from the Address Book window and drop them on top of the attendees field.
   A small "people" icon (right) appears at the top of an event item when you invite one or more people.

3. When you're ready to send invitations, click on the "attendees" label and select "Send Invitations" from the pop-up menu. Mail opens and sends email messages to all the people in the attendees list.

4. The recipient gets a message like the one shown below.

Recipients that have iCal, or some other calendar application that can read .ics files, will receive an invitation in addition to an email. Other recipients will get the email message about the event.

Recipients can put the event in one of their own iCal calendars.

5. When the recipient clicks on the link, it opens an invitation with a response. If she checks "Mail your answer" and clicks "Accept," you get a response, and iCal automatically updates the attendee status in your iCal Event Info window. If the recipient has iCal, the event automatically appears in her iCal in the selected destination calendar.

Move an event

To move an event to another day or time, drag the event to a new location in the calendar window. If the date is not visible in your current view, change to another view. For instance, in Month view you can drag an event anywhere in the month.

To move an event to another month or year:

1. Single-click the event to select it.

2. Click the Show Info button to open the Event Info drawer.

3. Change the date and time information to the new event date.

Click the month, day, or year field to select it, then type in a new value, or use the Up and Down arrow keys to change the value.

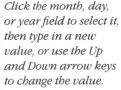

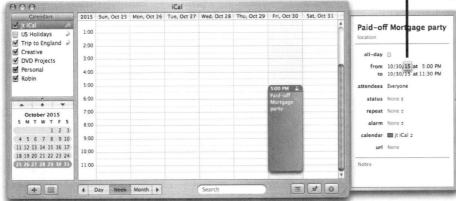

To move an event to another calendar:

When you move an event to a different calendar, nothing changes except the color of the item in the calendar grid (and some invisible iCal reorganization).

Control-click on an event to open the pop-up menu, choose "Calendar," then from the submenu choose a calendar to assign to the event.

▾ **Either:** Control-click the event, then choose a calendar from the pop-up menu that appears, as shown below. The event will change to the color associated with the other calendar category.

▾ **Or** select an event, click the Show Info button, then from the Event Info drawer (shown above) choose a calendar from the "calendar" pop-up menu.

Let iCal notify you of an upcoming event

There's no need to worry that you'll forget an important event in your calendar. iCal can notify you of upcoming events with three different alarm types, even if the iCal application is not active.

To set an Event Alarm:

1. Click on an iCal event to select it, then click the Show Info button to open the Event Info drawer.

2. Click next to the "alarm" label in the Event Info drawer, and choose one of the alarm options: "Message," "Message with Sound," "Email," or "Open File."

3. Depending on the alarm option you choose, specify the relevant options that appear in the alarm field.

4. Enter the number of minutes, hours, or days before or after an event that you want to be notified.

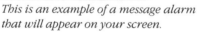

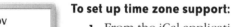

This is an example of a message alarm that will appear on your screen.

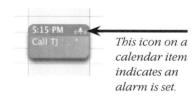

This icon on a calendar item indicates an alarm is set.

Work with different time zones

iCal makes it easy to globalize your schedules by letting you set up different time zones for different events, regardless of the time zone your computer is using.

To set up time zone support:

1. From the iCal application menu, select "Preferences…."

2. Place a check next to the item "Turn on time zone support" in the Miscellaneous category, then close the Preferences window.

   When time zone support is turned on, a time zone pop-up menu appears in the Event Info drawer, as shown on the left.

3. Click the time zone field and select "Other" to change to a different time zone than your current setting. "Other" displays a world map, allowing you to click a region and change the time zone. iCal recognizes the difference between your own time zone and the event's time zone and coordinates any alarms you create accordingly.

iCal Search

Use iCal's **search** feature to locate any event in any calendar.

To search for an event:

1. In the text entry field at the bottom of the calendar, type a keyword or phrase. All possible matches to your text entry will appear in the Search Results pane. The list of possible matches is narrowed as you continue to type.

2. When you finish typing, click the item you want. iCal shows the selected item in the Calendar View pane.

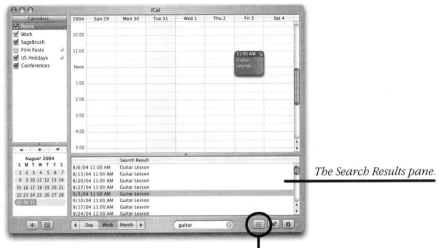

The Search Results pane.

To show or hide the Search Results pane, click this button.

To open the Show Info window for a found item, double-click the item in the Search Results pane. **Or** double-click the title bar of the event in the Calendar View pane.

To change the information for an event, double-click the text in the event item, then type your changes. **Or** click an event to select it, then click the Show Info button (the "i" icon) to open the Event Info drawer. Make changes to the text in the drawer, then press Return.

Create a To Do List

Use iCal to keep a reminder list of things you need to do.

To create a To Do list:

1. Select a calendar in the Calendars list.

   Note: When you create a To Do item, it is automatically color-coded to match the *selected* calendar. If you need to switch the To Do item to a different calendar, Control-click on the item and choose another calendar from the pop-up menu that appears.

2. Click the To Do button in the bottom-right corner of the iCal window (the pushpin icon) to show the To Do items pane.

   To resize the panel, drag the tiny dot on the left edge of the panel.

3. Control-click inside of the To Do items pane and select "New To Do" from the pop-up menu. The new To Do item is automatically selected, allowing you to type a name for it.

4. To open the To Do Info drawer, select a To Do item, then click the Show Info button (the "i" at the bottom of the window).

5. Type a description of your To Do item, and choose other options in the To Do Info drawer. Close the drawer when you're done.

After a To Do task is completed, click the little checkbox to mark it as completed. **Or** click the *completed* checkbox in the To Do Info drawer.

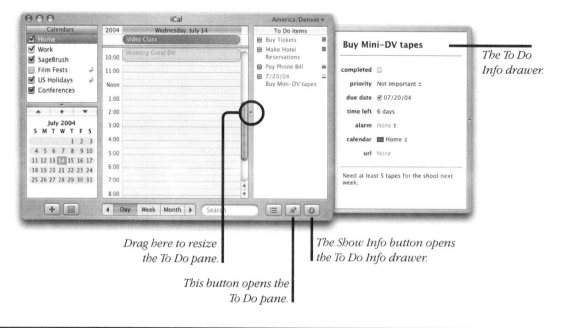

Drag here to resize
the To Do pane.

The Show Info button opens
the To Do Info drawer.

This button opens the
To Do pane.

The To Do
Info drawer.

Rate the importance of a To Do item

You can **assign priorities** to To Do items, rating them as "Very Important," "Important," or "Not Important."

A "Very Important" item is marked with a small icon of three horizontal bars; an "Important" item has two horizontal bars; a "Not Important" item has one horizontal bar. Multiple items with the same priority are listed alphabetically within that priority group. All items that do not have a priority assigned are listed alphabetically below the prioritized items.

1. Click on a To Do item to select it.

2. Click the Show Info button to open the To Do Info drawer.

3. From the "priority" pop-up menu (above-right) choose a priority. Close the drawer.

To choose how to sort To Do items, Control-click in the To Do pane. The "Summary" option (shown on the right) alphabetizes the items.

The To Do Info drawer

The "To Do Info" drawer also has several other uses. You can:

▼ Make editing changes to a task's description.

▼ Check off a task as "completed." You can also do this in the To Do pane by clicking the checkbox next to a task.

▼ Set a "due date" that will appear above the task in the To Do pane.

▼ Assign a selected To Do item to a different calendar (from the "calendar" pop-up menu, choose a different calendar).

▼ Assign a URL (a web site address) to accompany the To Do item.

▼ Display a lengthy task description that is too long to show in the To Do pane (open its "To Do Info" drawer, where the entire description appears).

Print a To Do list

When you print a calendar, you can include its To Do list (see page 333).

Hide or show various To Do lists

To Do items from different calendars all share the same To Do list. They are color-coded to match the calendar to which they belong. When you hide a calendar (uncheck its box in the Calendars list), all the To Do items associated with that calendar are also hidden. If you have a lot of items in your To Do list, hiding some of them can make finding others easier.

A To Do item's priority is indicated by the number of horizontal bars in the icon next to it.

Click directly on the icon to change the number of bars and the priority rating.

If all three bars are gray (instead of the item's calendar color), a priority is not assigned.

iCal Preferences

To customize the appearance of iCal calendars and some of their settings, use the iCal Preferences.

1. From the iCal application menu, choose "Preferences...."

2. In the "Week" section of the Preferences window, choose how many days a calender shows and on which day of the week to start a calendar.

3. In the "Day" section, choose the hours that a calendar shows.

4. In the "Month" section, select "Show time in month view" to include the time an event is scheduled in the event description.

The "Show time in month view" option adds the item's start time.

5. In the "Events and To Do items" and "Miscellaneous" sections, make choices for the settings listed.

If you want iCal **to store your past schedules and appointments, uncheck** the first checkbox, "Delete events and To Do items after X days."

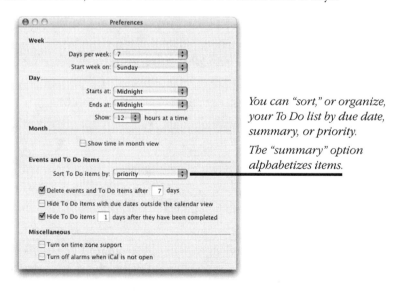

You can "sort," or organize, your To Do list by due date, summary, or priority.

The "summary" option alphabetizes items.

Print Your iCal Calendar

No matter how convenient the digital lifestyle may be, sometimes you need an old-fashioned paper printout. **To print a calendar:**

1. Select the calendar you want to print in the Calendars list.

2. From the File menu, choose "Print...."

3. From the pop-up menu (shown below), choose "iCal" to show iCal's printing options.

4. Select the checkboxes of items you want to print, then select calendar dates and a time range to print. Click in the day, month, or year field, then click the Up or Down triangle to change values. Do the same in the hours and minutes field.

5. Click "Preview" to see how the page will look when printed.

6. Click "Print."

By default, the Preview is in color. Click the "Soft Proof" checkbox to simulate how it will look when printed on your printer. If you have a black-and-white printer, the Preview will change to black and white.

iCal's Preview.

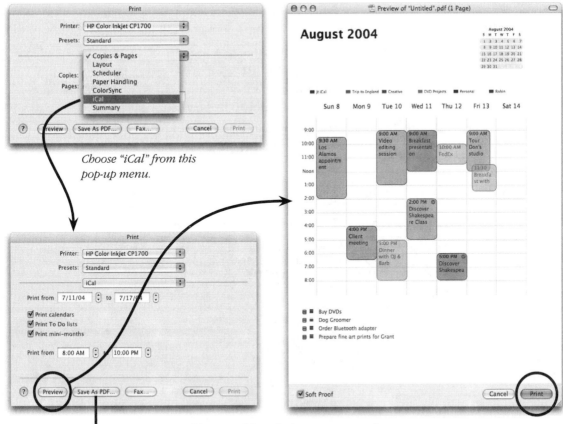

Choose "iCal" from this pop-up menu.

To create a printable copy of the info that you can send to anyone on any computer, click here to create a PDF.

The broadcast icon indicates a published calendar.

When you choose "Publish" from the Calendar menu, this Publish Calendar sheet drops down in front of the iCal window.

Publish Your iCal Calendar

If you want to **make your calendar available to others on the Internet,** you can *publish* it. Anyone can view published calendars from any computer in the world using a web browser.

To publish your calendar (you must be connected to the Internet):

1. In iCal, select a calendar in your Calendars list.

2. From the Calendar menu in the top menu bar, choose "Publish...." The Publish Calendar sheet slides down into view.

3. Type a name for your published calendar and select the checkboxes to publish changes automatically and to choose which calendar items to publish. Select an option from the "Publish calendar" pop-up menu:

   ▼ Choose "on .Mac" to publish your calendar to the Apple server provided with your .Mac account.

   ▼ Choose "on a WebDAV server" if you plan to publish to a WebDAV server other than your .Mac account. See the sidebar on the opposite page for more information about WebDAV.

4. Click the "Publish" button.

5. When your calendar has uploaded to the server, the "Calendar Published" window opens to show the address where you or others can go to view or subscribe to that particular calendar.

   To see your calendar online, click "Visit Page" (circled below-left).
   To notify others that you've published a calendar, click "Send Mail."

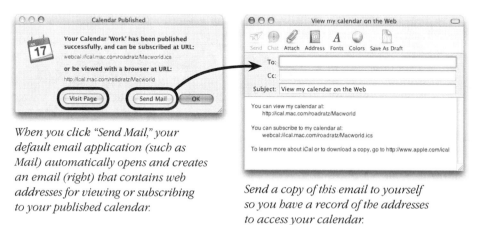

When you click "Send Mail," your default email application (such as Mail) automatically opens and creates an email (right) that contains web addresses for viewing or subscribing to your published calendar.

Send a copy of this email to yourself so you have a record of the addresses to access your calendar.

Password protection for a published calendar

To add password protection to a published calendar, you need access to a WebDAV server that supports password protection. Choose "Publish on a WebDAV server" in the Publish Calendar sheet. This option displays text fields for entering a WebDAV server address and for setting a login name and password.

For an alternative to publishing calendars on the .Mac site, check iCal Exchange at www.icalx.com. iCal Exchange offers free iCalendar publishing to its own WebDAV server.

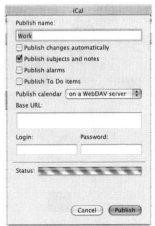

WebDAV (Web Distributed Authoring and Versioning) is a standard for collaborative authoring. Generally speaking, WebDAV servers enable web-based enterprise collaboration, such as a large corporation developing a business plan or a team of programmers creating software.

Most of us are content just to know that a WebDAV server allows us to share calendars that have been created using the industry-standard iCalendar specification (.ics).

Make changes to a published calendar

When you make changes to a calendar that has already been published, you can update the published calendar in several ways.

- ▼ **Either** select a calendar from the Calendars list, then from the Calendar menu at the top of your screen, choose "Refresh."

- ▼ **Or** select a calendar from the Calendars list, then from the Calendar menu at the top of your screen, choose "Publish." Give the calendar the exact same name as the existing published one. This new, updated calendar will replace the old one.

- ▼ **Or** select a calendar from the Calendars list, then click the Show Info button. Click next to the "auto-publish" field in the Info drawer and select "after each change" from the pop-up menu (shown right).

- ▼ **Or** when you first publish a calendar, set iCal to automatically update changes: From the Calendar menu at the top of your screen, choose "Publish," then select "Publish changes automatically" in the Publish Calendar sheet (see the previous page). If you have a full-time Internet connection, iCal **automatically** uploads the changes. (If you don't have a full-time connection, *don't* choose this option; instead, dial up and publish changes when necessary.)

Unpublish an iCal calendar

If you decide **to unpublish a published calendar,** it's easy to do: Make sure you're connected to the Internet. Select the name of a published calendar in the Calendars list, then from the Calendar menu choose "Unpublish."

You still have the original copy of the calendar on your computer, but it's no longer available for viewing by others.

Subscribe to iCal Calendars

You can **subscribe to calendars** that have been published by family, friends, colleagues, or total strangers. You do not have to have a .Mac account to sub-scribe to a calendar that's hosted on .Mac or other WebDAV servers.

To subscribe to any iCal calendar:

1. From the Calendar menu at the top of your screen, choose "Subscribe...."

2. In the sheet that appears, enter the URL (web address) that was given to you or that you may have received in an email from the publisher of the calendar.

   Or if you know the web address of a site that offers iCalendars for subscription (such as http://apple.com/ical/library), use your browser to visit the site and click one of the available calendar links. A sheet will drop down in front of the iCal window with that particular calen-dar address entered in the "Calendar URL" field, as shown below.

3. Use the checkboxes to set your preferences for the options listed. The "Refresh" option assumes you have a full-time Internet connec-tion such as cable, DSL, T1, etc.—don't bother to check it if you have a dial-up modem.

4. If subscription to the calendar requires a password, you'll be pre-sented with the "Authentication" dialog window shown below. Enter the appropriate user name and password and click OK to continue.

5. The subscribed calendar appears in the Calendars list in your iCal application. Select it to show the calendar in the main viewing area.

Other calendars available for subscription

In addition to subscribing to the calendars of friends, family, and colleagues, there are many special-interest calendars available online to which you can subscribe. It's quite amazing—there are public calendars that list graphic design and typographic events, hundreds of athletic games, school calendars, religious events, sci-fi events, movies, television, and so many more. Visit these sites to see some of the possibilities:

www.apple.com/ical/library

www.iCalshare.com

Refresh calendars

To make sure that you **see the most current version** of a subscribed calendar, you can refresh it. Refresh downloads the current calendar from the server, ensuring that you have the latest published information. If you don't have a full-time connection, make sure you dial up to connect to the Internet before you choose to refresh.

1. Select a subscribed calendar in the Calendars list.

2. From the Calendar menu at the top of your screen, choose "Refresh."

If you have a full-time Internet connection, you can set up an automatic schedule that determines how often your subscribed calendar is updated:

1. From the Calendar menu, choose "Subscribe...."

2. Click the "Refresh" checkbox, then from that pop-up menu, choose a time interval (every 15 minutes, every hour, every day, or every week) to set how often your computer downloads a new version of the subscribed calendar.

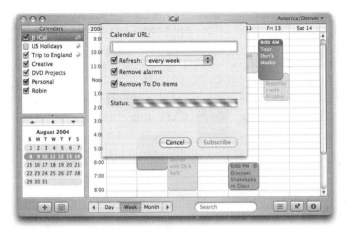

Import Calendars

An iCal file is actually a text file (.ics) that can be sent as an email attachment. iCal can import other iCal files and vCal files (iCal and vCal are similar calendar/scheduling formats) that you may have received from someone.

Kauai_calendar.ics

This is an iCal file.

To import a calendar file:

1. From the File menu, choose "Import…" to open the Import window, shown below.

2. Click the "Import" button to open the "iCal: Import" Finder window. Locate and select the calendar file you want to import.

3. Click "Import" to place the calendar in iCal's Calendars list. Click the checkbox next to the imported calendar to show it in iCal.

   Or simply drag a calendar file (an iCal file or a vCal file) from the Finder to the Calendars list in the iCal window.

Large calendars can take several minutes to import, so be patient.

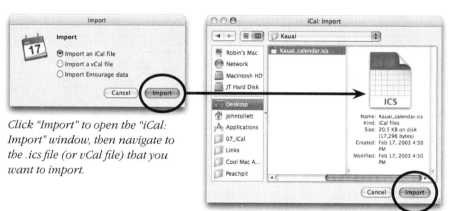

Click "Import" to open the "iCal: Import" window, then navigate to the .ics file (or vCal file) that you want to import.

If you plan to import Microsoft Entourage events, make sure the events are set for the same time zone as your iCal. If the Entourage events are set for a different time zone, their scheduled times may change. If this happens, drag the imported Entourage events to the correct time slots, or change your iCal time zone setting to match the original Entourage events' time zone. See the following page to learn about resetting iCal's time zone.

Export Calendars

You can export a calendar as an ".ics" file, a standard calendar format. The exported .ics file can then be imported to a calendar on another computer, attached to an email for someone else to import into their iCal, or imported into another device such as a Palm or iPod.

To export a calendar:

1. Select a calendar in the Calendars list.

2. From the File menu, choose "Export." The "iCal: Export" window opens.

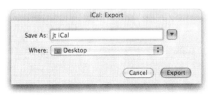

3. Type a name for your exported calendar in the "Save As" field.

4. From the "Where" pop-up menu, choose the location where you want to save the exported .ics file.

5. Click "Export." The .ics extension will be automatically added to the file name.

iCal's time zone setting shows here.

Change iCal's Time Zone Setting

iCal uses the time zone information in your System Preferences to set the time zone for your calendars. You can change iCal's time zone setting.

To reset iCal's time zone setting:

1. Open iCal Preferences. Select "Turn on time zone support" to show the time zone in the top-right corner of the iCal window (circled, top-right).

2. Click the time zone text in the top-right corner of the iCal window (circled, middle-right) to open a pop-up menu. Choose "Other…" from the pop-up menu. In the "Change time zone" window that opens (bottom-right), select a time zone. Use the "Closest City" pop-up menu to choose a time zone, or click on the map to set a time zone.

3. Click OK.

Once you've selected alternative time zones, they remain available in the time zone pop-up menu (circled, middle-right).

Back Up Your Calendars

If iCal is storing a lot of valuable information, don't forget to back up your calendars. Copy your calendars to an external drive or to some removable media, such as a CD, DVD, or Zip disk.

To find your calendars, which are saved as .ics files in the Calendars folder:

1. Go to your Home folder, open the Library folder, then locate the Calendars folder.

2. To make a backup copy, drag the Calendars folder to another drive, or drag it to an icon that represents any removable media that may be connected to your computer (Zip, CD, or DVD).

For detailed information about Backup, see Chapter 10.

Another way to back up calendars is to use **Backup,** an application provided with .Mac memberships. You can make backup copies of files locally or to your .Mac iDisk (storage space on Apple's computers that's provided with .Mac membership). Backup makes the process simple and easy.

1. Download Backup from the .Mac web site if you don't already have it on your computer.

2. Open Backup.

3. From the pop-up menu, choose where to put your backup copies. You can choose your iDisk or a local drive (Zip, CD, or DVD).

4. Click the checkbox next to "iCal calendars."

5. Click the "Backup Now" button. The Backup application knows where to find your calendars.

The checkmarks indicate which items are selected for backup.

Safari

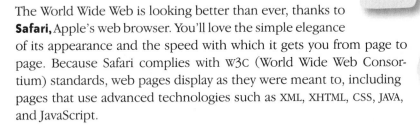
15

The World Wide Web is looking better than ever, thanks to **Safari,** Apple's web browser. You'll love the simple elegance of its appearance and the speed with which it gets you from page to page. Because Safari complies with W3C (World Wide Web Consortium) standards, web pages display as they were meant to, including pages that use advanced technologies such as XML, XHTML, CSS, JAVA, and JavaScript.

Safari makes text on web pages look its best with high-quality anti-aliasing (a technique to reduce the "jaggy" look text can have on a computer screen). Safari and Mac OS X work together to take advantage of Unicode, which makes it possible to display text on web pages in languages such as Japanese, Chinese, Arabic, and Korean.

In this chapter

Download Safari

If Safari is not already on your Mac, you can download it free from Apple's website: **www.apple.com/safari.**

Once you download Safari, your Software Update will automatically find and download the updates as they appear.

To download Safari, of course, you need to use another browser. You should have Internet Explorer on your Mac—just go to Apple's website and click the link to download, then follow the directions on the screen.

The Safari Window

Below is the basic Safari web browser window with just about everything explained either here or on the following pages. Such a nice, clean browser! If you don't see some of these items in your toolbar or if you want to add or delete any of them, see the following page.

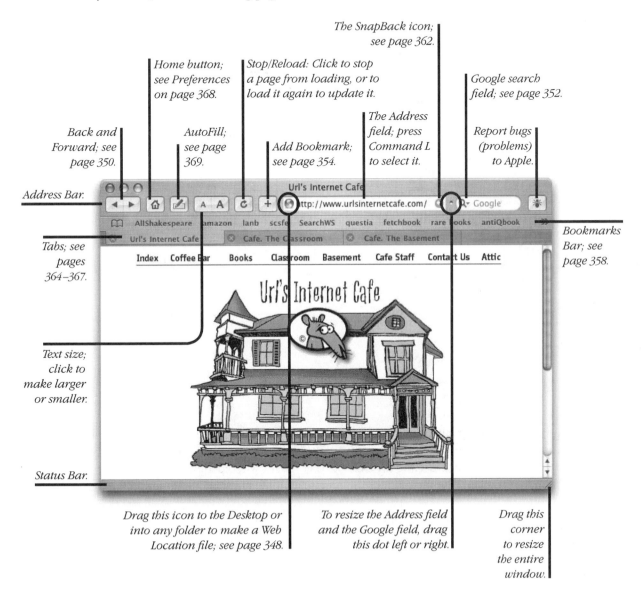

The SnapBack icon; see page 362.

Home button; see Preferences on page 368.

Stop/Reload: Click to stop a page from loading, or to load it again to update it.

Google search field; see page 352.

The Address field; press Command L to select it.

Back and Forward; see page 350.

AutoFill; see page 369.

Add Bookmark; see page 354.

Report bugs (problems) to Apple.

Address Bar.

Tabs; see pages 364–367.

Bookmarks Bar; see page 358.

Text size; click to make larger or smaller.

Status Bar.

Drag this icon to the Desktop or into any folder to make a Web Location file; see page 348.

To resize the Address field and the Google field, drag this dot left or right.

Drag this corner to resize the entire window.

Customize the Toolbar

You can choose which icons to display in the Safari toolbar. Go to the View menu and look under the gray "Show" heading (shown below). The items you see in the menu below are in the same order the items will appear, left to right, in the toolbar shown on the previous page.

The Bookmarks Bar appears under the Address Bar, and the Status Bar appears at the bottom of the window.

To remove items from the toolbar, you must uncheck them from the View menu; you can't drag or Command-drag them off, nor can you rearrange the icons.

Quick Tips

Here are just a few quick tips in Safari.

Scrolling tips

Scroll around a web page: Either click in the web page or hit the Tab key until the *page* (as opposed to the Address field or Google field) is selected. Then use the **arrow keys** to go up, down, or sideways.

Scroll farther: Use Option Arrowkeys.

Scroll DOWN a window screen at a time: Hit the Spacebar.

Scroll UP a window screen at a time: Press Shift Spacebar.

Bigger or smaller text on the web page

Depending on how the web designer designed the page, it is often possible for you to make the reading text larger or small. This will not affect any text in graphics, however.

Make text bigger: Command +

Make text smaller: Command –

Or if you have the "Text Size" button displayed in your Safari toolbar, as shown on page 343, click the large or small A icon.

Death to pop-up windows!

Do you hate those annoying little advertisement windows that pop up without your permission? Press **Command K** to prevent their appearance. If you decide you want them, press Command K again to allow their presence. You'll find this command in the Safari menu.

Web address tips

If a web address ends in **.com,** all you need to type is the main name, such as **apple, toyota,** or **NFL,** then hit Return. That is, you never have to type **http://** or **.com.** To go to a website that ends in anything besides **.com,** you will need to type that part (such as **.org, .edu,** or any country code).

You'll notice **as you type a web address** that previous and similar addresses appear below the Address field. When you see the correct address appear, stop typing, then use the DownArrow key to select the address you want to go to. When it's highlighted, hit the Return key and off you'll go.

*This is one of my favorite features: Just double-click in the domain name between **www** and **com,** and **only that one word,** the one you need to change, is selected. No more trying to press-and-drag across that tiny word in the tiny Address field to select it!*

Email a link

It's easy to send an email link to someone. Just open the email message, then drag the tiny icon to the left of a web address in the Address Bar, and drop it in the email message.

Drag this icon to an email message and drop it in the message at the point where you want it to appear.

Links tips

Sometimes you want to open several links at once without losing the page you're on.

To open a link in a new window, Command-click on it (that is, hold down the Command key and click on the link). The page will open in a separate window.

To open a link in a new window that is *behind* the current window, Shift-Command–click on it. This is one of my favorite features—I can go to a search results page and open a dozen windows in five seconds, then go see what they are about.

To get a contextual menu of options, as shown below, Control-click on a link. The options that appear in the menu depend on what kind of item you Control-click on.

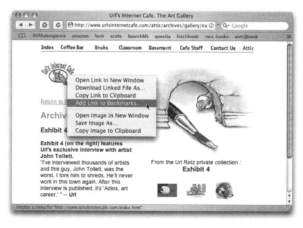

View a link's location in the Status Bar

If the **Status Bar** in Safari is showing, you can position your mouse over a link (don't click), and the address of where the link will take you is visible in the Status Bar.

To show the Status Bar, go to the View menu and choose "Status Bar," *or* press Command \. (The backslash is right above the Return key.)

Status bar.

*The **progress bar** slides right across the web address as the new page loads. Watch for it. When the bar stops progressing, the page is fully loaded.*

Notice the mouse is positioned over the link to the "Art Gallery." In the Status Bar, you can see the address where that link will take you if you click it.

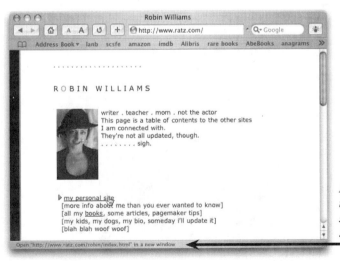

If the link will open the new page in a new, separate window, Safari's Status Bar will tell you so.

Make a Web Location of any link

A **Web Location** is a tiny file that will open your browser (if it isn't already) and go to that web page. The advantage of a Web Location over a bookmark is that you don't have to have the browser already open before you can use a Web Location—double-click a Web Location icon (.webloc) and it will automatically open Safari and go straight to that page.

To make a Web Location, just drag a link off of a web page and drop it on the Desktop.

Louvre.webloc

This is what a Web Location file looks like.

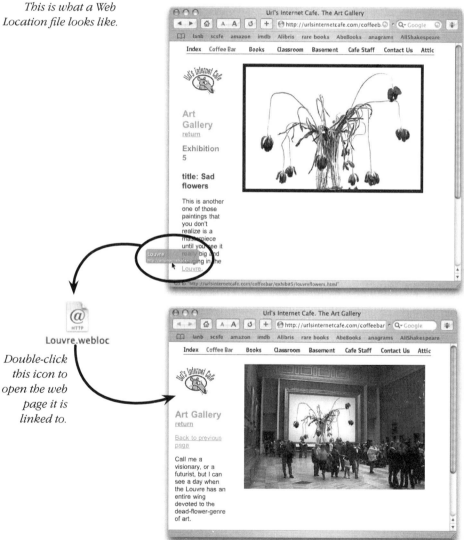

Louvre.webloc

Double-click this icon to open the web page it is linked to.

Open a Web Location icon

Once you've made a Web Location icon, as described on the opposite page, there are several things you can do with it.

Louvre.webloc

Put the location in the Dock: Drag it to the right side of the dividing line (on the side where the Trash basket is). When you click on this icon in the Dock, that web page will open in a new, separate browser window (meaning it won't replace any existing browser windows that are already open).

Open that web page in a new and separate window: Double-click this icon.

Open the page in a window that's already open on your screen: Drag this icon and drop it in the middle of the window (*not* in the Address field). The new page will *replace* the existing one.

You can send a folder full of Web Location files to friends so they can access your favorite sites with the click of a button.

Back and Forward Menus

As you may already know, you can *press* on the Back or Forward button and you'll get a menu showing the pages you can go back to, or pages you have come from that you can go forward to, as shown below.

*Press on the Back or Forward button to get a menu of the pages you've been to. The menu displays the **page names** (what the designers named the pages).*

But did you know that if you hold the Option key down while you press on either the Back or Forward button, you will **see the actual web addresses** of the pages you have been to?

*Option-press on the Back or Forward button to see the **actual web addresses** displayed in the menu.*

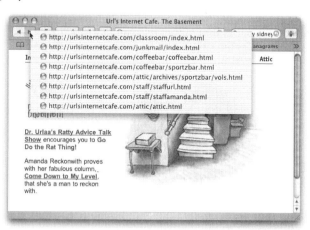

Address Book

If you have entered web addresses for people in your **Address Book** (see Chapter 16), you can access those websites directly from the Bookmarks Bar in Safari, as shown below.

These are the people in my Address Book whose contact page includes a web address.

To put the Address Book item in your Bookmarks Bar:

1. Open the Safari Preferences (go to the Safari menu and choose "Preferences…").

2. Click the "Bookmarks" icon in the toolbar. You'll get the little window shown below.

3. Check the box to "Include Address Book." Close the Preferences.

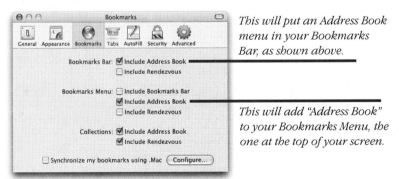

This will put an Address Book menu in your Bookmarks Bar, as shown above.

This will add "Address Book" to your Bookmarks Menu, the one at the top of your screen.

Tip: If you don't want to take up the space in your Bookmarks Bar with the Address Book, don't forget that you can always access the Address Book in the Bookmarks window; see page 355. Or you can add it to your main Bookmarks Menu, the one at the top of your screen.

Google Search

If you've ever used **Google** as your search engine, you know how amazing it is. If you haven't yet, once you do you might never use anything else. Because it's so great (it even figures out if you've misspelled something you're looking for), Apple has included it in your Safari toolbar. Use it just as you would if you went directly to the **Google.com** site. Here are a few extra tips for searching (these tips apply to any search tool, actually).

If you don't see the Google search field in your toolbar, go to the View menu and choose "Google search."

Type your search term in this little field.

To delete whatever is in there, click the X.

Put quotation marks around words that should be found together, as explained below.

With quotation marks *around a phrase, Google will find only those pages where those two words are next to each other.*

With quotation marks, Google found 33 pages.

Without quotation marks, *Google displays 88 pages because it finds every page that has the word "brenda" on it and the word "euland," whether they are next to each other or not.*

Limit your search even more

Use **Boolean operators** to limit your search. That is, put a **+** sign in front of any word or phrase (in quotation marks) that you want to make sure Google finds; put a **−** sign in front of any word that you do not want to appear on a page. Do not put a space after the + or −.

For all the details about this very useful SnapBack button that you see in the Google field, see pages 362–363.

▼ A search for just the word **safari** gave me 7,500,000 results.

▼ A search for **safari +apple −africa** gave me "only" 771,000 results, and pages about Apple's Safari were right at the top.

▼ A search for **safari +browser +apple −africa** gave me "only" 262,000 results, again with Apple's Safari at the very top.

Extra tips

Here are a couple of handy menus for Google.

▼ Click on the tiny magnifying tool and triangle in the Google field and you'll get a menu listing the **last ten searches** you did in Google, as shown to the right.

Safari maintains this list no matter how many windows you open or even if you quit Safari.

▼ Select a word or phrase on any web page, then Control-click on that word. A **contextual menu** will appear with the option to do a "Google Search," as shown to the right. Choose it and the new results will appear instantly.

Bookmarks

Click this icon to show the Bookmarks window or to hide it.

Make a **bookmark** of a page that you want to return to anytime in the future; this bookmark will then be available in the Bookmarks Menu at the top of your screen. Just choose that page from the menu to go directly to it. Bookmarks, of course, are the handiest features of any browser.

The biggest problem with bookmarks is they are *so* handy you end up making hundreds of them, and then it can be difficult to find the one you want (which defeats the purpose of a bookmark in the first place). All browsers allow you to create folders and to store collections of bookmarks in those folders, but Safari has made it more convenient.

To bookmark a web page:

1. Go to the web page that you want to bookmark.

2. **Either:** Click the **+** button in the toolbar, if it's there (if the **+** is not in your toolbar and you want it, see page 344).

   Or: Press Command D.

   Or: Go to the Bookmarks Menu and choose "Add Bookmark...."

Tip: To add a page to the Bookmarks Menu *without* displaying the drop-down sheet asking you to rename and file it, press **Command Shift D.**

3. A small "sheet" drops down from the title bar of the window, as shown below. This sheet offers the opportunity to **change the name of the bookmark**—just edit as you would anything else.

From the menu in the sheet, you can also choose to **store this bookmark in an existing folder** that you previously made (see the following page), *or* in the main Bookmarks Menu, *or* in the Bookmarks Bar (the thin bar beneath the toolbar, shown below).

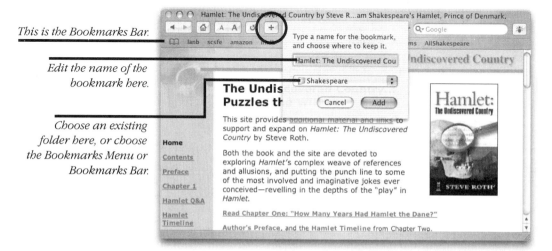

This is the Bookmarks Bar.

Edit the name of the bookmark here.

Choose an existing folder here, or choose the Bookmarks Menu or Bookmarks Bar.

The Bookmarks window

Below you see the **Bookmarks window.** On the left side is the **Collections pane,** which holds your entire assortment of bookmarks. You can have "collections" (folders) of bookmarks that *do not* show up in the Bookmarks Menu; this gives you the option to keep your menu short, sweet, and useful instead of two yards long and difficult to wade through.

Hide or show the Bookmarks window.

This is what my Bookmarks Menu looks like, both in the menu itself (above) and in the Bookmarks window (left).

The "Bookmarks Menu" is selected, and to its right is a display of all the bookmarks I have created and stored in the Bookmarks Menu. As you can see, most of my bookmarks are organized into folders.

If you see a little checkbox in an "Auto-Tab" column, see page 366.

Bookmarks Bar: Anything you put in the Bookmarks Bar will appear in the bar itself, as explained more fully on the following page. This gives you instant access to your most-visited web pages.

Bookmarks Menu: Anything in here will appear in the list that drops down from the Bookmarks Menu at the top of your screen, as shown above, right.

Address Book: Any websites you have added to any contacts in your Address Book (see Chapter 16) will appear here. Also see page 351.

Rendezvous: Websites for printers, routers, webcams, or administrative sites on your network will automatically appear here.

History: Every web page you have visited for the past week is here; see page 359 for details.

Folders: *Folders in the Collections pane do not appear in the Bookmarks Menu.* This is a good place to keep bookmarks you don't need often, like those for a specific client or project. See the following pages.

Organize your bookmarks

You can create as many folders as you like and store as many bookmarks in those folders as you like. You can choose to have folders appear in the Bookmarks Menu or not, or you can put an entire folder of bookmarks into the Bookmarks Bar.

To make a new folder in the Collections pane:

1. Click the **+** sign at the bottom of the Collections pane.

2. The new folder appears and is ready for you to name it, as shown below—just type.

*This is a new Collections folder. It will appear in the drop-down sheet menu when you make a new bookmark, but as long as it is sitting in this Collections pane, **it will not appear** in the Bookmarks Menu.*

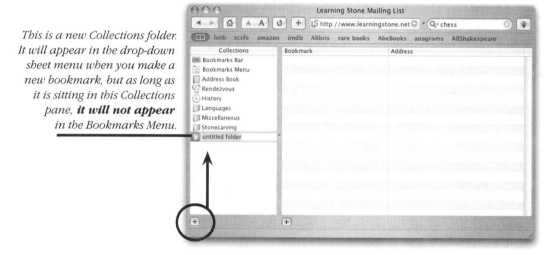

To put a NEW bookmark into the new folder in the Collections pane:

1. Make a new bookmark as usual (as described on page 354).

2. In the sheet that drops down (as shown on page 354), press on the little menu and you will see the new folder you just made. Choose it and the new bookmark will be stored inside that folder.

To move an EXISTING bookmark into a new folder in the Collections pane:

1. Click on any other collection in the Collections pane, such as History, Bookmarks Menu, or any other folder. The existing bookmarks that are stored in that collection will appear on the right.

2. Drag a bookmark from the *right* side of the window and drop it into the new folder in the Collections pane, as shown at the top of the opposite page.

To move a COPY of an existing bookmark, Option-drag it.

I made a new collections folder and named it "Chess."

Then I clicked on the "Bookmarks Menu" collection to display the bookmarks I made earlier.

*I found the chess bookmark I had made, and here you can see me dragging it from the right side over to the folder on the left. When I drop it, that bookmark will **move** into the new folder.*

All of the folders and single bookmarks shown on the right side of this window are the ones that are stored in the Bookmarks Menu; you can see that "Bookmarks Menu" is the selected collection.

To make a new folder inside an existing collection (such as the Bookmarks Menu collection):

1. Select a collection in the Collections pane, such as "Bookmarks Menu." (To select it, click once on its name.) *Any bookmarks and folders stored in the Bookmarks Menu collection will appear in the Bookmarks Menu at the top of the screen.*

2. On the *right* side of the window, click the **+** sign at the bottom. This will make a new, untitled folder on the *right* side, which means it is stored inside the selected collection.

3. Make new bookmarks and choose this folder to store them in, or drag existing bookmarks from the same collection into other folders. For instance, in the example above, I should make a new folder and drag the English castle bookmarks into it.

The Bookmarks Bar

The **Bookmarks Bar** is where you can store your most visited websites. You can put folders in the Bookmarks Bar as well as individual links.

To add a bookmark to the Bookmarks Bar:

If the Bookmarks Bar is not showing in your browser window, press Command B.

▾ **Either:** When you are at the page you want to bookmark, **drag the tiny icon** in the Address field and drop it on the Bookmarks Bar.

▾ **Or:** Press Command D to get the drop-down sheet. Edit the bookmark so its name is short, then from the menu in the sheet, choose "Bookmarks Bar."

▾ **Or:** Open the Bookmarks window (click the tiny icon on the far left of the Bar). Select the collection on the left that contains a bookmark you want in the Bar. Find the bookmark on the right side of the window, then drag it into the "Bookmarks Bar" collection on the left.

This will *move* the bookmark from the existing collection to the Bar. **To put a copy in the Bar** instead, hold down the Option key and drag.

▾ **Or:** Open the Bookmarks window, as described above. Find a bookmark in any collection. From the right side of the window, drag the bookmark directly into the Bar itself (as opposed to the collection on the left). This will also put the bookmark into the Bookmarks Bar collection. Option-drag to put a copy in the Bar.

▾ **Or:** Open the Bookmarks window. Drag any **folder** from the Collections pane on the left and drop it directly in the Bookmarks Bar *or* into the Bookmarks Bar collection.

The Bookmarks Bar.

*If you put a **folder** in the Bookmarks Bar, you will have access to every bookmark in the folder. This example shows a folder with subfolders stored in the Bookmarks Bar.*

To rearrange the bookmarks in the Bar:

▾ Drag the bookmarks left or right in the Bar.

*Control-click on any bookmark in the Bar to get this **contextual menu** where you can **edit** the name or address, **delete** the bookmark, or **open** it in a new, separate window.*

To REMOVE a bookmark from the Bar:

▼ Drag the bookmark off the TOP of the bar (not sideways or down). **IMPORTANT NOTE:** This will **DELETE** the bookmark, not just remove it from the Bar! If you drag a folder off the Bar, *it will delete every bookmark in that folder!*

▼ **To remove an individual bookmark** from the Bookmarks Bar and still **KEEP THE BOOKMARK,** open the Bookmarks window. Select the Bookmarks Bar collection on the left, then drag the bookmark you want to remove and drop it into any other collection.

▼ **To remove a bookmark folder,** open the Bookmarks window, select the Bookmarks Bar collection, drag the folder from the right side of the window, and drop it into the Collections pane on the left.

The History menu

The History menu keeps track of every website you've visited for the past week: Use the History menu or the Bookmarks window, as shown below. Click any History page like a bookmark to go back to that page. After about a week, the pages you've visited will disappear from the History menu.

To clear all the pages out at once whenever you feel like it, go to the History menu and choose "Clear History." **Or** in the Bookmarks window, select the "History" collection, click in the Bookmark pane on the right, press Command A to select all, then hit the Delete key.

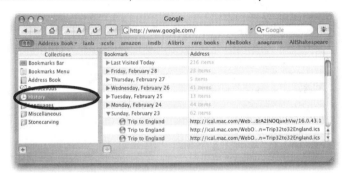

To save any History page as a permanent bookmark, drag it from the right side of this window and drop it into a collection on the left.

Import bookmarks from Internet Explorer

If you've been using **Internet Explorer** as your browser, any "Favorites" you made in that program will automatically be imported into Safari. You'll find them in the Bookmarks window, in the Collections pane; there will be a folder called "Imported IE Favorites."

As explained on page 355, folders in the Collections pane will not appear in the Bookmarks Menu. You can either move the bookmarks from this folder into the "Bookmarks Menu" collection, as described below, or double-click on any link in the Bookmarks window to go there.

To move Internet Explorer bookmarks into your Bookmarks Menu:

1. Open the Bookmarks window (click on the tiny book icon in the Bookmarks Bar *or* press Command Option B).

2. Click once on the folder in the Collections pane named "Imported IE Favorites." Its bookmarks will appear on the right.

3. Drag the bookmarks from the right side of the window and drop them into the collection of your choice on the left side.

   To make all of these imported bookmarks appear in the menu at the top of the screen: Click on the right side of the Bookmarks window, press Command A to select all, then drag them all into the "Bookmarks Menu" collection.

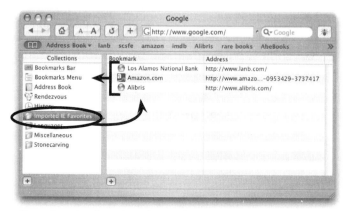

Drag these bookmarks either to the "Bookmarks Menu"
or to another Collections folder. Once the IE Favorites folder
is empty, select it and hit the Delete key to remove it.

Import bookmarks from other browsers

Importing bookmarks from browsers other than Internet Explorer is not as straightforward as described on the opposite page. You can use the method below, however, to get your bookmarks from Netscape into Safari:

1. Find your bookmark file; it should be in the path shown below.

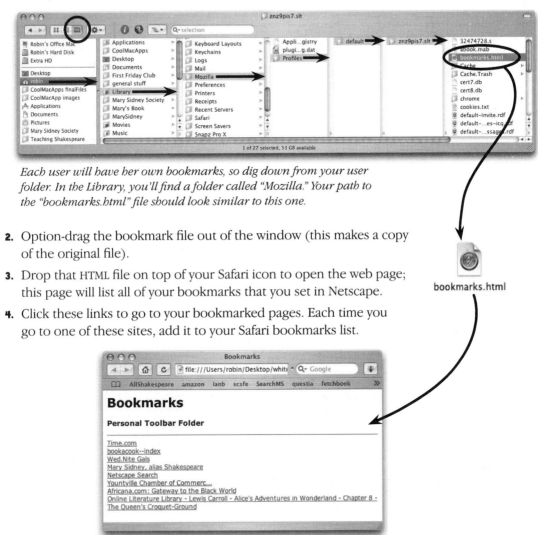

Each user will have her own bookmarks, so dig down from your user folder. In the Library, you'll find a folder called "Mozilla." Your path to the "bookmarks.html" file should look similar to this one.

2. Option-drag the bookmark file out of the window (this makes a copy of the original file).

3. Drop that HTML file on top of your Safari icon to open the web page; this page will list all of your bookmarks that you set in Netscape.

4. Click these links to go to your bookmarked pages. Each time you go to one of these sites, add it to your Safari bookmarks list.

bookmarks.html

SnapBack

This is the icon you'll often see in the Address field or in the Google field.

SnapBack

The **SnapBack** button is a great feature. How often have you gone to a page you enjoyed, wandered off the path into the wilderness of the Internet, then tried to find that original page again? SnapBack can take you right back to where you started. Keep in mind that SnapBack is a *temporary* marker.

There are three ways to use SnapBack:

▼ **Google search results:** When you do a search in Google, the search results page from which you choose a link is set as the SnapBack page. That is, you might click a link on the *first* page of the search results, then wander through four or five pages. The SnapBack icon in the Google field will take you back to that *first* page.

If you go to the *fourth* page of Google results and click a link from there, the SnapBack icon will take you back to that *fourth* page.

Note: If you open different windows to use Google, the SnapBack button in each window will return you to the search results for that window.

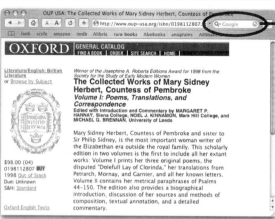

Because I got to this web page by following links from the Google search results page, this SnapBack will return me to the original results page, above.

▼ **Choose a page:** When you type a new URL (web address), **or** choose a bookmark, **or** choose a page from the History menu, **or** open a new window, *the SnapBack is applied to that page.*

You won't see the SnapBack button until you leave the marked page and go to another.

As soon as you leave the marked page, the SnapBack button will appear. It will stay there, linked to that page, until you enter a new web address, choose a different bookmark, or choose a page from the History menu.

If you open a new window, the new page in that new window will have its own SnapBack button. The SnapBack in the previous window will remain active for the contents of that window.

▼ **Assign SnapBack to a page:** You can go to the History menu and choose "Mark Page for SnapBack" for any open page (or press Command Option K). This will override the automatic SnapBack that was applied to a page.

This assigned SnapBack **will only last** until you do one of the things mentioned above: enter a new URL, choose a bookmark, choose a page from the History menu, **or** click the Back or Forward button.

If a link opens to a new window, you lose the SnapBack because it belongs with the other window.

Tabbed Browsing

Safari has a feature you can turn on or off called **Tabbed Browsing**. When Tabbed Browsing is turned on, you can choose to have a number of pages open in the same window instead of separate windows, and each page is accessible by clicking a tab, as shown below. One advantage of Tabbed Browsing is that pages can load in the background while you peruse other pages.

The tiny square indicates this is a collection of bookmarks with Auto-Tab turned on; see page 366.

*Click the **x** to close that tabbed page without having to open it.*

*Option-click the **x** to close all other pages **except** this one.*

A spinning wheel indicates that page is still loading.

Each one of these tabs is an open page. The light-color tab indicates the page in front of you. Single-click a tab to display that page.

When you use various keyboard shortcuts (as explained on the opposite page), the Status Bar will tell you whether that page will open in a new tab, a new window, or some other possibility.

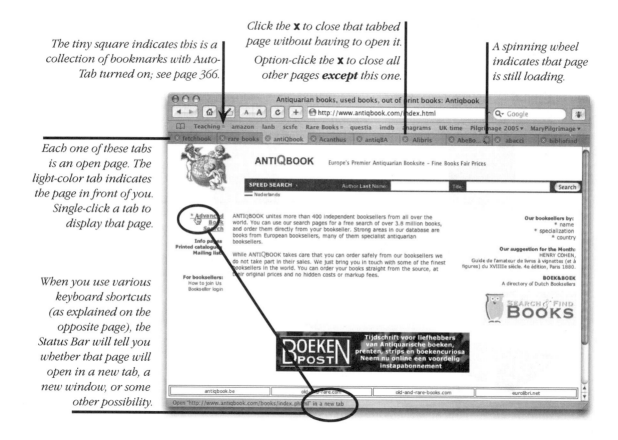

When you click on a link, the new page that opens **replaces** the one you are currently looking at—it does not automatically create a new tabbed page. Depending on the preferences you choose (see the opposite page), you can Command-click or Command-Shift-click a link to create a new tabbed page for that link. Also see the tips on page 367.

Preferences for Tabbed Browsing

Go to the Safari menu and choose "Preferences…," then click the "Tabs" button so you can turn on Tabbed Browsing and make some choices about how to work with it. Notice in the preferences windows below that the keyboard shortcuts change depending on whether or not you choose the second checkbox.

 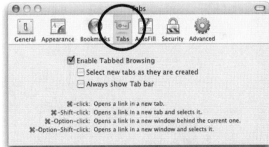

- ▼ **Enable Tabbed Browsing:** Obviously, this turns the feature on or off.

- ▼ **Select new tabs as they are created:** With this checked, as soon as you create a tabbed page (Command-click on a link), Safari will display that window instead of hiding it in the row of tabs.

- ▼ **Always show Tab bar:** This makes the Tab bar visible whether or not you have a tabbed page open.

  If this is unchecked, the Tab bar appears only when you have more than one page chosen as a tabbed page or when you click on a *folder* in your Bookmarks Bar that is set to open as tabbed pages.

  If this is checked, the Tab bar is always visible in your window, even if there is only one tab in which all your pages open, as shown below.

Read the options in the preferences window carefully to see what they do! If you like Tabbed Browsing, choose one shortcut and learn it well, then come back and learn another.

If you choose to always show the Tab bar, you will always see at least one tab.

If you do not choose to open other links in separate tabs, every page will just open in this one tab, as if you weren't even using Tabbed Browsing.

The Auto-Tab feature

If you have a slow dial-up connection, it's not a good idea to open a lot of links with Auto-Tab because your connection will have to go to every page and load it.

If you have put collections (folders) of bookmarks in your Bookmarks Bar, you can set them to **Auto-Tab.** This means when you single-click on a folder's link in the Bookmarks Bar, every bookmarked page in that collection will open, each page with a tab for instant access.

You will know if a folder has been set to Auto-Tab because the tiny triangle you would normally see in the bar becomes a tiny square, as shown below.

When set to Auto-Tab, you'll see this tiny square.

*When a folder is **not** set to Auto-Tab, it displays a tiny triangle.*

Command-click any single link in the Bookmarks Bar to open that page in a new tab.

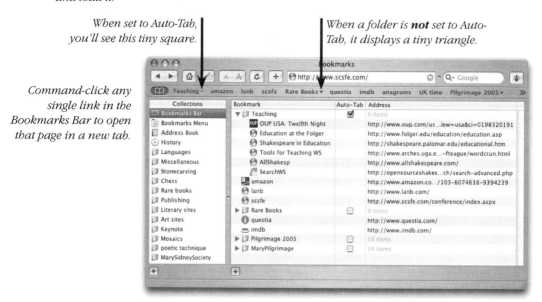

To set a folder (collection) of bookmarks to Auto-Tab:

1. Make sure you have enabled "Tabbed Browsing" in the Safari preferences, as described on the previous page.

2. Click the small book icon in the Bookmarks Bar to open the Bookmarks window. (If the Bookmarks Bar is not showing, press Command B to make it visible, or choose "Bookmarks Bar" from the View menu.)

3. If you don't have a folder of bookmarks, create one as explained on page 356.

4. In the Collections pane on the left, single-click "Bookmarks Bar." This will display, on the right, all the links you have put into your Bookmarks Bar, as shown above.

5. Only folders will have a checkbox in the Auto-Tab column. Simply click a checkbox to turn that feature on for that folder.

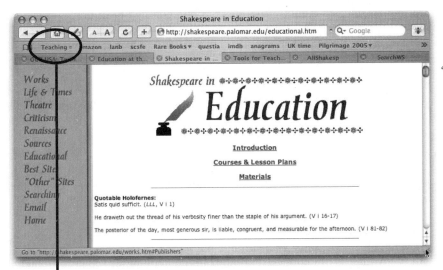

I single-clicked the "Teaching" link in the Bookmarks Bar and Safari opened every link in that folder and gave each one a tab. Each page is already loaded so I can click any tab and that page instantly displays in this same window.

To open individual pages *in a folder that has been set to Auto-Tab, Option-click the folder link in the Bookmarks Bar and you'll get a regular menu of bookmarks.*

A few other tips

▼ If you have more than a few bookmarks, DO NOT go to the Bookmarks Menu and choose "Open in Tabs" (it's the last item in the Bookmarks list) because that will load every bookmarked page in your entire list! Guess how I discovered *that* feature.

▼ In the Bookmarks window shown on the opposite page, you can open an entire folder in tabs: In the Collections pane, select "Bookmarks Bar." Control-click any folder in the Bookmark pane (not the Collections pane) and the pop-up menu will have an option to "Open in Tabs."

▼ If Tabbed Browsing is enabled, when you click on links in other applications, such as in an email program or on a PDF, that link will open in a new tab in the existing window.

▼ To open a new page in a new tab, press Command T, then type the URL in the Address field that appears. **Or** go to the File menu and choose "New Tab."

▼ If you choose a page from your Bookmarks or History list, the page opens in whatever tab is showing on your screen. If you want it to open in its own tab, first press Command T, *then* choose the page.

▼ Each tab has its own memory for the Back and Forward buttons. This means you can go to any number of pages in each tabbed window and go Back and Forward through those pages.

Safari Preferences

The preferences for Safari are pretty simple and self-explanatory. Click each item in the toolbar to set preferences for that feature.

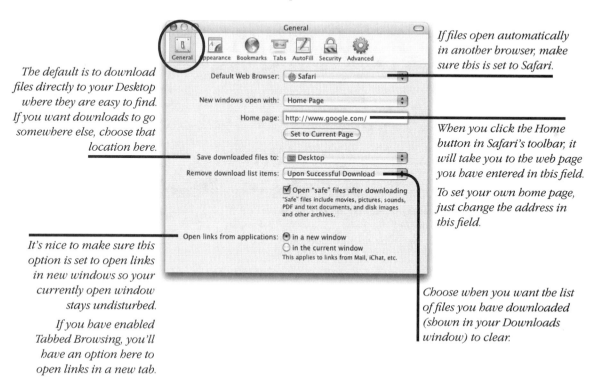

The default is to download files directly to your Desktop where they are easy to find. If you want downloads to go somewhere else, choose that location here.

If files open automatically in another browser, make sure this is set to Safari.

When you click the Home button in Safari's toolbar, it will take you to the web page you have entered in this field.

To set your own home page, just change the address in this field.

It's nice to make sure this option is set to open links in new windows so your currently open window stays undisturbed.

If you have enabled Tabbed Browsing, you'll have an option here to open links in a new tab.

Choose when you want the list of files you have downloaded (shown in your Downloads window) to clear.

If you have a very slow connection, you can choose to turn off the graphics.

Unless you know you want a different encoding, leave this setting.

Choose which fonts you want web pages to display in. The two choices here are nice and readable.

Many web pages will override your choices!

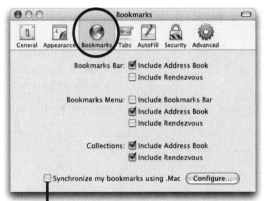

Checking any box will do just what it says: It will put that item in that location so you can access it from there. For information about the Bookmarks Bar, Menu, and Collections, see pages 354–359.

For details about synchronizing your bookmarks with your .Mac account, see Chapter 11.

These preferences are explained on pages 364–367. The keyboard shortcuts change depending on whether or not you click the option to "Select new tabs as they are created."

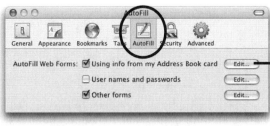

If you check "User names and passwords," Safari will take notice next time you fill them in on a web page, such as eBay or Amazon.com, and ask if you want AutoFill to remember them for you. You'll have a choice of "Never for this Website," "Not Now," or "Yes."

The **next** time you go to that site, Safari will have filled in the name and password. Only choose this option if no one else uses your computer!

If you choose to AutoFill forms, when you go to a web page with a form you need to fill out, Safari will automatically fill out as many fields as it can for you. It gets the information from your Address Book card (see Chapter 16).

Click the **Edit buttons** to edit your Address Book card or to delete any websites that you have told Safari to AutoFill.

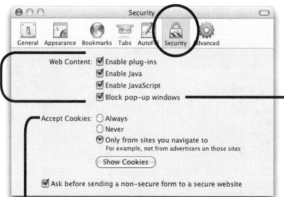

Unless you have a good reason to uncheck these, leave them checked so content on web pages will appear properly.

You can also block or unblock pop-up windows with the keyboard shortcut Command K.

Cookies are little pieces of code that websites send to your computer to get certain information. For instance, when you go to Amazon.com and it knows it's you, that's because of cookies. It's okay to accept cookies from websites that you know, love, and trust.

Never accepting cookies will limit what you can do on some sites. However, it's a good idea to check the box to only accept cookies from sites you navigate to (choose to go to) to avoid getting junk thrown at you from advertisers you didn't choose to use.

Universal Access can help people who have one sort of difficulty or other with web pages.

The first option will try to make all text larger on the screen.

The next option lets you choose links without using the mouse. Hit the Tab key and it will select the next "link" on the page. "Link" refers to the location box where you can type the web address, plus all the links you might have in your Bookmarks Bar, plus every graphic on a page that is a link. Once a link is highlighted, hit Return or Enter to go to that link.

You can leave this option off and still use Option-Tab to highlight links.

*If you have a **web page style sheet** you like, you can choose to override a website's style sheet with one of your own. If you don't know what style sheets are, ignore this.*

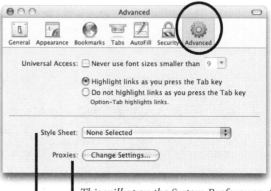

This will open the System Preferences for the Network settings, where it will display the Proxies pane. If you know what proxies are and when and why to change them, go ahead. Otherwise, leave it alone.

If you do make changes, be sure to click the "Apply Now" button in Network preferences so your changes take effect.

Mail & Address Book 16

With Mail you can write, send, and receive email messages. Mail also has many useful tools for organizing, formatting, searching, and filtering email.

The **Address Book** is a separate application that works with Mail. Save your favorite email addresses and contact information, enter an address with the click of the mouse, make a mailing list to send a message to a number of people at once, and much more.

In this chapter

The **basic** things you will be doing in **Mail** are checking messages, replying to messages, and composing new messages. On these first few pages are directions for how to do just that. If you haven't created an email account yet so you can use Mail, jump ahead to pages 397–401 to learn how to create accounts.

You must have an Internet connection already set up, and you must have **already set up an email account** with your .Mac account (or with any other email provider). If you haven't set up a .Mac account yet, and you want one (you don't have to have one), see page 233.

You cannot get your AOL mail through any other client except AOL or their website.

The Viewer Window

Mail opens up to the **Viewer window.** If you open Mail and don't see this window (shown below), press Command Option N. **Or** go to the File menu and choose "New Viewer Window."

Mailboxes drawer. The number in parentheses indicates unread messages.

Status Bar.

Toolbar. Control-click in the toolbar to get a few options.

Message List. A blue dot means you have not yet read that message.

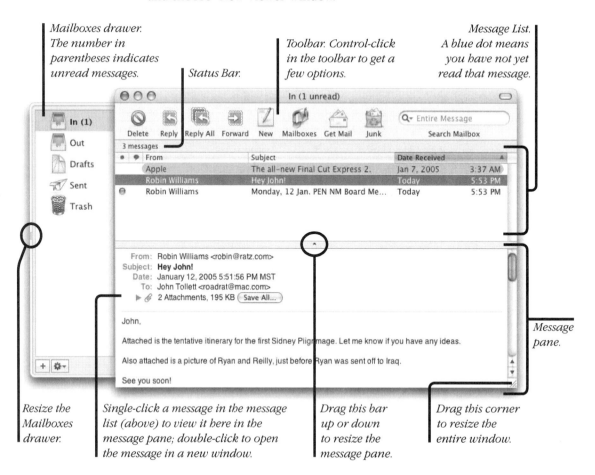

Message pane.

Resize the Mailboxes drawer.

Single-click a message in the message list (above) to view it here in the message pane; double-click to open the message in a new window.

Drag this bar up or down to resize the message pane.

Drag this corner to resize the entire window.

Basic Features

Here are the basic features of using Mail.

Read a message: *If the message pane is visible,* just **single-click** any email message in the list in the top portion of the Viewer window. The email will open in the message pane. Resize the pane if necessary, or use the scroll bar to see the rest of the message.

If the message pane is not visible, or if you want to open the email in its own window, **double-click** any email message in the list.

Hide the message pane: Sometimes you may find that you want to delete email messages without having to read them first, but if the message pane is visible, the message pops up in that pane the instant you select a message, before you can delete it. To solve this problem, press on the tiny dot in the dividing bar (circled on the opposite page) and drag the bar *all the way to the bottom.* When the message pane is hidden, you can single-click to select any message, then click the Delete button. **To read a message,** double-click it.

Have your mail read out loud to you: Select the entire letter (press Command A) *or* press-and-drag the mouse over the text you want read out loud. Control-click anywhere in the message to open a contextual menu, slide down to "Speech," and choose "Start Speaking." Mail will read your letter out loud using the default computer voice chosen in the Speech system preferences. To make it stop speaking, Control-click again and choose "Stop Speaking."

Tip: In any open message, press Control S (not Command S) and a voice will tell you the sender's name and the subject.

Select a range of text, then Control-click anywhere in the message pane to open the contextual menu shown here.

New

To write and send a NEW message:

1. Click "New" in the toolbar to open a "New Message" window, as shown below.

2. Click in the "To" area (called a field) and type an email address. You can type more than one address in here, as long you type a comma and space after each one. Mail is so smart that as soon as you type the comma, it inserts the space.

An email address must have an @ symbol, and there must be a dot followed by a "domain name," such as "ratz.com," "aol.com," or "comcast.net," etc.

If the person you are sending email to is in your Address Book or Previous Recipients list, Mail will replace the email address with that person's name as soon as you type it.

Click here to send your message.

If you can't apply formatting to the selected text, such as bold, italic, or color, perhaps your mail is set up as "Plain Text." From the Format menu, choose "Make Rich Text."

If you need to change or edit that name, single-click on the name and a little menu will pop up; choose the action you want to take (as shown below). If the recipient is in your Address Book and has more than one email address, the pop-up menu also shows all available email addresses; choose the address you want to use.

If Mail finds the recipient's name in Address Book or in the Previous Recipients list, it creates a Smart Address, as shown here. A Smart Address is an "object" that you can drag and drop in other locations.

You can drag a Smart Address object between the To, Cc, and Bcc fields. You can also drag a Smart Address to an email message pane, to a text document, or to your Desktop. Double-click a Smart Address that's on your Desktop to open a new email message window addressed to that recipient.

Hover the pointer over a Smart Address to see the email address associated with it. If you prefer to include the address in the "To" field (as shown below), from the View menu choose "Addresses," then choose "Show name and address."

3. If you want to send a copy of this same letter to someone, click in the "Cc" field and type an address. You can type more than one address, separated by a comma and space.

4. Click in the "Subject" field and type a personalized message description so the recipient knows your message is not junk mail. Avoid using phrases that spammers use, such as "Hi," "I missed you," or "We need to talk."

5. Click in the empty message pane and type a message.

6. Connect to the Internet if you're not already connected.

7. Click the "Send" icon in the toolbar (shown on the right).

   A copy of the sent message will be stored in the "Sent" folder in the Mailboxes drawer.

Send

To save a message as a draft: To finish a message later, click "Save As Draft" in the toolbar, or press Command S. The message will be saved in the Drafts folder within your Mailboxes drawer. You will only see this button when you're writing a new message.

Save As Draft

Mail **automatically** creates a draft for you whenever you're writing a lengthy letter—in case something happens and your computer goes down, you won't lose the entire letter. But to make sure, press Command S regularly, as you would in any document.

To open the draft ("restore" it) later for editing, select the "Drafts" icon in the Mailboxes drawer, then double-click the desired draft in the list.

To address a message using the Address Pane: Click the "Address" button in the "New Message" toolbar to open a limited version of your Address Book, called the Address Pane. Double-click a name in your list to address your message to that person.

Address

To send the same message to more than one person, hold down the Command key to select multiple names in the Address Pane, then click the "To" button (or just double-click on each person's name and they will be added one at a time). You'll only see this "Address" button when you're writing a new message or if you customize Mail's toolbar to include the Address Book icon (page 394).

Get Mail

Reply   Reply All

To check for messages:

1. Connect to the Internet if you're not already connected.

2. Click once on the Mail icon in the Dock to open Mail.

3. Click the "Get Mail" icon in Mail's toolbar.

   Next to the Inbox in the Mailboxes drawer (and in the Dock, as shown top-left) you might see a number in bold—that number indicates how many unread messages are in your Inbox.

4. Your messages will appear in the Message List. Single-click a message to display its contents in the message pane.

To reply to the sender of a message:

1. If the message is not already open, select it in the Viewer window, then click the "Reply" button in the toolbar.

2. A message window opens that contains the original sender's address in the "To" field, and the original message formatted as a quote. Type your reply above the quote, then click the "Send" button in the toolbar.

   If you select a portion of the text before you click "Reply," just that portion of text will be copied into the new email message!

To reply to ALL recipients of a message:

Tip: When you select a message and choose "Reply" or "Reply All" from the toolbar, the Reply window that opens also has a "Reply" button in its toolbar. Click the button to toggle it between "Reply" (reply to message sender only) and "Reply to All" (reply to all message recipients).

Mail that you receive may have been sent to multiple recipients, either directly as a Carbon copy (Cc) (or "Courtesy copy" since it's no longer on carbon paper), or secretly as a Blind carbon copy (Bcc). You can choose to reply to all recipients with one email (the reply will *not* include anyone in the hidden Bcc list).

1. If the message is not already open, select the message in the Viewer window, then click the "Reply All" button in the toolbar.

2. Type your reply above the original quoted message, then click the "Send" button in the toolbar.

To send a Bcc (blind courtesy copy):

1. Address and write your message as usual.

2. From the View menu, choose "Bcc Header." This puts a new field in the address area. Any address(es) you type in this field will *not* be seen by anyone whose address is in the "To" or "Cc" field.

The Bcc field.

To:	Mary Sidney
Cc:	Andrew Aguecheek
Subject:	Malvolio's strange behavior
Bcc:	Sir Toby ▾

To forward a message:

1. Select or open a message in the Viewer window, then click the "Forward" button in the toolbar.

2. Type any comments above the original quoted message, then click the "Send" button in the toolbar. *PLEASE remove all the names and addresses of everyone else in the forwarded list before you send it!*

To attach a file:

1. Click the "Attach" button in the toolbar (if it's not in the toolbar, you can add it—see page 394).

   Or go to the File menu and choose "Attach File...."

2. The standard Open dialog sheet appears. Find the file you wish to attach. Select it, then click "Choose File." (See page 413 for a tip on attachments for Windows users.)

Tip: **To make sure others can see your photos,** use photos in the *JPEG* format.

Use standard file-naming conventions (no special characters such as ! or ?).

Make sure the file name has the extension *.jpg* at the end.

You can also drag a file's icon from wherever it is on your Mac and drop it in the "New Message" window. This means you need to go to the Desktop and either arrange an open window to the side of your screen or drag that file out of its folder and let it sit on the Desktop. When you are in Mail, drag the file into the message window to attach it, as shown below.

To remove an attachment from a message, select the attachment in the "New Message" window (click once on it), then press the Delete key.

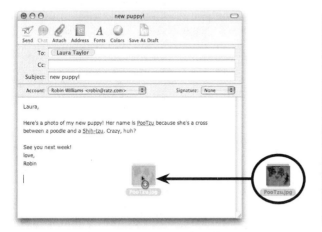

I put the photograph I want to send on the Desktop. Then I opened Mail and wrote my message. Now I can just drag the photo and drop it directly in the message, as shown above.

This is what the attachment looks like in the message area. The recipient can usually just double-click on the image to open it or drag it to the Desktop first, and then open it.

If your attachment is not an image, the recipient will see a file icon with a link.

Message List

The **Message List** displays a list of all messages in the currently selected Mailbox. The list is divided into several columns. The Message List provides different organizations and views of a list, depending on which *column* is selected and whether or not you choose to *organize by thread.*

View message threads

A group of *related* messages and replies are called **message threads.** If you reply to an email whose subject field is labeled "Page edits," the default subject field is labeled "Re: Page edits." Mail identifies messages that have identical subject fields as being in the *same thread* and highlights *all* of the messages in a thread when any related message is selected, as shown on the left. You can turn off this highlighting or change the highlight color in Mail preferences (see page 404).

To organize messages by thread, from the View menu choose "Organize by Thread." All related messages are now grouped together and highlighted in the Message List, as shown below. This is a convenient and easy way to find all the correspondence related to a particular subject.

All of the messages in a thread are highlighted when you select any related message. **To select every message thread, or just the next one,** *go to the View menu and use the "Select" command.*

Click the small disclosure triangle to the left of a message thread to **expand** the thread and *show* all its related messages. Click the triangle again to **collapse** the thread and *hide* the related messages.

To expand all threads: From the View menu, choose "Expand All Threads."

To collapse all threads: From the View menu, choose "Collapse All Threads."

The Thread column icon.

These highlighted messages are organized by thread. Click the small triangle to show the other messages in the thread (below).

The expanded thread shows the related messages. Click the triangles to collapse the thread down to a single visible message.

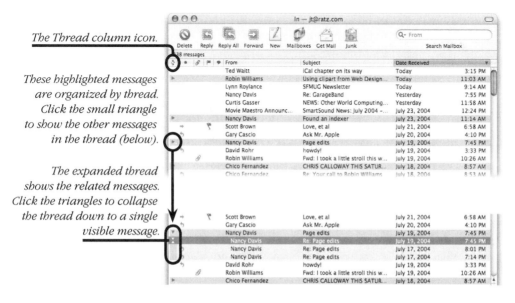

The columns of information

In addition to the default headings that appear in your Viewer window, you can choose to show a number of other **columns.** The function of most columns is obvious—the ones that aren't so obvious are explained on the following pages.

From the View menu you can choose to **hide** any column you don't want to see—just uncheck it from the list.

To change the column widths, position the pointer over the gray dividing line in the column headings, then press-and-drag the column left or right.

To rearrange (sort) the list according to the column heading, single-click the heading at the top of a column. The column heading that is blue is the one that items are currently arranged by. For instance, I like to keep my email organized by date received with the newest email at the top of the list, as shown below. But sometimes I want to find an old email from a particular *person,* so I click the "From" column to alphabetize the names; then I can quickly skim through the collection of email from each person.

To move columns, position the pointer over a column heading, then press-and-drag the column left or right. As you drag a column on top of another column, the column underneath moves over to leave an empty area for you. When you let go, the column snaps into the new position.

These are the column headings.
Click a heading to sort the messages by that column.

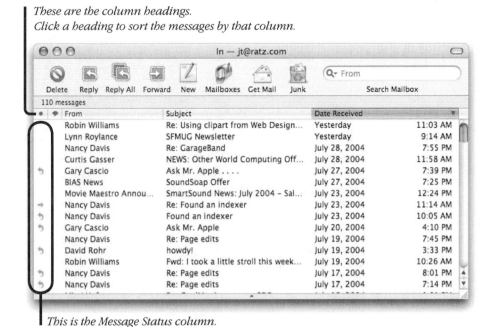

This is the Message Status column.

Message Status column (●): uses different icons to indicate if you've read the message, replied to it, forwarded it, or redirected it. These icons show up automatically when one of those actions takes place.

You can also manually mark an email that you've already read as "unread." Use this as a reminder to go back and read a message again, or to make a message stand out: Select one or more messages, then from the Message menu, select "Mark As Unread."

Click the Message Status column heading (●) to group similar categories, such as unread or returned messages, together in the list. Click again in the column heading to reverse the order of the list.

Message Status **icons** give visual clues to the status of messages.

Blue orb: message has not been read.

Curved arrow: message was replied to.

Right arrow: message was forwarded.

Segmented arrow: message was redirected.

The Message Status column. Click the Status column head to organize status categories together in groups. Click the column head again to reverse the sort order of the column.

Number column: In a series of email exchanges, it may be useful to know in what order messages were received. The Number column keeps track of the order for you. Click the **#** symbol in the column heading to arrange messages by order. Click again in the column heading to reverse the order of the list.

Flags column: Mark a message as flagged when you want it to stand out in the list or if you want to temporarily tag a group of related messages. **To search for flagged files** in a list, click the "Flag" column heading; all flagged messages will move to the top of the list. Click the heading again to reverse the order and put flagged messages at the bottom of the list.

Subject column: The Subject column shows what the sender typed into the Subject header of their email message. Click the column heading to show the subjects in alphabetical order; click again to reverse the order of the list.

Date Received column: The Date Received column shows when you received a message. Click the heading of the column to show messages in the time sequence they were received; click again to reverse the order of the list.

Flags column.   *Subject column.*   *Date Received column.*

Buddy Availability column: If you have a Buddy List set up in iChat (see Chapter 17), this column will display a green orb when a Buddy is online and a yellow orb when he is online but idle (perhaps his computer has gone to sleep). When you see a Buddy is online, you can double-click the green "Chat" orb to open a new iChat instant message window and start a chat with him.

Well, it will display the colored orbs if you haven't turned off that feature in the preferences; see page 404.

Or customize the toolbar (see page 394) to include a Chat button (shown below). Select an *online* Buddy in the Message List, then click the "Chat" button to open iChat and start an instant message.

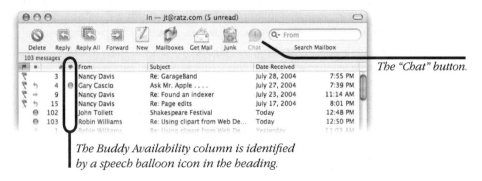

The "Chat" button.

The Buddy Availability column is identified by a speech balloon icon in the heading.

Mailboxes Drawer

The **Mailboxes drawer** slides out from the side of the Viewer window. The drawer might slide out from *either side* of the Viewer window, depending on how much screen space is available to the left or right.

To open the drawer, click the Mailboxes button in the toolbar. **To close the drawer,** click the Mailboxes button again, or drag the edge of the drawer in toward the main window. The pointer turns into a double arrow icon when you hover over the drawer's edge (circled below, left).

To make the drawer appear on one side or the other, drag a message from the Viewer window off to the side on which you want the drawer. When the drawer appears, put the letter back where it was.

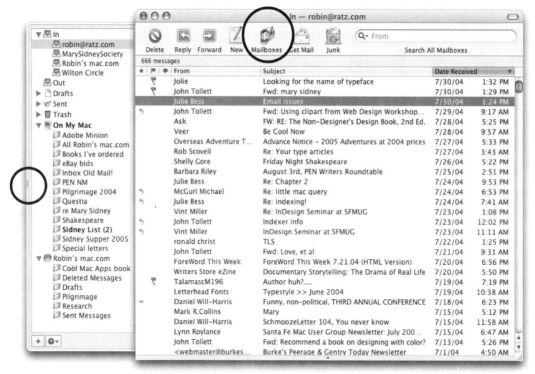

This is the Mailboxes drawer where all of her email is neatly organized.

This is Robin's working Mail program. Above you see her list of mostly unanswered mail, and in the drawer to the left you see her collection of folders (mailboxes) into which a lot of her mail is automatically sorted using the Rules in the Mail preferences.

Make new mailboxes (folders)

You can make as many mailboxes as you like in which to sort your different types of mail. You can use the Rules feature to have incoming mail automatically placed into certain mailboxes (as described on pages 408–411).

Here are a couple of different ways to make new mailboxes.

To make a new mailbox (folder):

1. From the Mailbox menu, choose "New...."

2. Choose where you want this mailbox located:

    On My Mac: This puts the actual folder on your hard disk. All messages in folders on your Mac are literally stored on your computer.

    .Mac account: If you have a .Mac account, your account name will be listed in this pop-up menu. All messages in these folders are actually stored on Apple's servers, which means you can read anything in these folders from any browser anywhere in the world. In the Mailboxes drawer, these folders will be under a blue magic globe icon, as shown below, right.

3. Name the mailbox and click OK.

Tip: You can create a folder within a folder in this dialog box: Type the name of the first folder, type a slash, then type the name of the folder you want *inside* the first one. For instance, Clients/Acme Inc.

This blue globe indicates the folders beneath it are actually on Apple's computers, not yours.

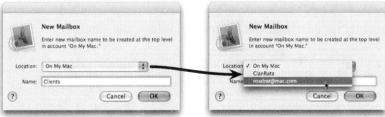

Choose "On My Mac" to create a folder that is on your local hard disk.

Or choose to create a folder on Apple's computers in your .Mac email account.

Notice in the examples above, the dialog box tells you this new mailbox will be created at the top level of the chosen account. You can also choose **to make a mailbox inside an existing mailbox:**

1. Click once on an existing folder in the Mailboxes drawer. Then:

    Either: Click the "New Folder" button at the bottom of the drawer (shown on the right).

    Or Control-click on that folder and choose "New...."

2. The dialog box shown above will appear with a message that this new mailbox will be created "as a child of" the selected folder.

3. Click OK. The "parent" folder will have a disclosure triangle next to it to indicate there is a "child" folder inside.

New Folder button.

Delete or rename existing mailboxes

You can always rename mailboxes or delete them altogether. Keep in mind that *when you delete a mailbox, you delete all the messages stored within it.*

1. In the Mailboxes drawer, single-click to select the mailbox you want to rename or delete.

2. Go to the Mailbox menu and choose either "Rename…" or "Delete…," **or** Control-click on the mailbox you want to rename or delete.

3. In the dialog box that appears, rename the mailbox or click the "Delete" button.

The easiest thing to do is Control-click on the mailbox you want to rename or delete.

Icons in the drawer

Here is an explanation of the various **icons** you might see in your Mailboxes drawer. As you make and delete folders and change your preferences, your arrangement of icons in the drawer will change, so don't worry if you don't see all of these or if you see more than I have listed here.

▼ The **number in parentheses** is the number of unread messages in that folder. The *first-level* folder (the In box in the example to the right) shows you the **total** number of messages in all accounts, while the *second-level* folders (for the accounts "jt" and "roadrat" in the example) show you specifically how many messages are in that particular account.

▼▣ In (4)
    ▣ jt@ratz.com (3)
    ▣ roadrat (1)

▼ Single-click the main folder (first level) to show a list in the Viewer window of *all* messages of that sort for *all* accounts. For instance, click the "In" box to see all mail in all accounts; click the "Sent" icon to see all messages you have sent from any account; etc.

▼ Click *one* of the individual folders to see messages for just that selected account.

▼ If you have many email accounts and want to check for messages from several of them at once, Command-click the accounts to make a multiple selection, then click the "Get Mail" button.

In box: At the top of the drawer you can tell if you have received any email, as described above. Messages contained in these "In" boxes are stored on your computer if they are POP accounts; for IMAP accounts, you can choose for them to be stored on your Mac or not; see page 400.

▣ In (4)

Out box: Stores messages temporarily while waiting to be sent. If you're not connected to the Internet at the moment (you're working "offline" or your connection is down), messages you send are stored in the "Out" box until an online connection is established.

▣ Out

Drafts folder: Stores unfinished messages that you're composing. If you have multiple Mail accounts set up, you'll have separate "Drafts" folders for each account. The messages in the "Drafts" folders are stored on your computer.

▣ **Drafts (1)**

Sent folder: Contains copies of messages that you sent to other people. If you have multiple email accounts, the "Sent" folder contains a "Sent" folder for each account you've set up. The messages in the "Sent" folders are stored on your computer.

✓ Sent

Junk (8)

Junk folder: This Junk folder is automatically created when you change the Junk Mail mode from "Training" to "Automatic" in the Mail menu (as explained on pages 389–393). It stores messages that have been identified by Mail as junk mail. The number in parentheses tells you how many junk messages have not been read.

Trash (2)

Red circle Trash folder: Contains messages you have deleted. If you have multiple accounts, the main "Trash" folder contains a separate "Trash" folder for each of your accounts. Messages in these "red circle" Trash folders are stored on your computer—they are not *really* thrown away until you choose to empty the Trash.

Use the Mail preferences to set up your Trash **to empty automatically** at certain times: In the Accounts pane, select an account name, then click the "Special Mailboxes" button and make your Trash choice.

If you do not set up Mail to empty the Trash at certain times, make sure to **empty all your Trash mailboxes** occasionally. If you have an IMAP account (like Mac.com), you must empty your Trash or your mailbox on the IMAP server may get too full and you won't get any more mail.

To empty all messages in the Trash, select the topmost Trash icon in the Mailboxes drawer. From the Mailbox menu, choose "Erase Deleted Messages," then from the submenu choose "In All Accounts" (or press Command K). You can also select a specific account in this submenu (if you have more than one) to empty only trashed messages from that account.

On My Mac
 ADC newsletters
▶ Book feedback
 DVD Workshop
 Online receipts
 Reply ASAP
 Shakespeare

On My Mac: Contains *custom folders* that you create for storing and organizing your messages. If you use Rules (see pages 408–411), you can make certain messages automatically go to one of these folders. All messages in these folders are stored on your computer.

You might not see the actual little computer icon called "On My Mac" or the Internet account icon until you create a custom folder (mailbox) as described on page 383.

Internet icon: If you choose to make a new mailbox on your **.Mac account** (see page 383), the blue crystal ball appears, as well as folders labeled "Sent Messages," "Deleted Messages," and "Drafts." **These folders and the files inside of them are stored on Apple's server.** Any folders in this section will also appear in your .Mac webmail, as described in Chapter 9, and any folders you make in your .Mac webmail account will appear here in Mail. Messages in this account are stored on Apple's servers in your email allotment of 15 megabytes (you can buy up to 200 megabytes).

roadrat@mac.com
Deleted Messages
Research
Sent Messages
Travel folder

You can drag other messages from any account into these folders and into any other folders you create in your .Mac account. You'll have access to the messages in this Mailbox from any computer in the world—just open any browser, go to **www.mac.com,** click the Mail icon, and sign in.

In the Mail preferences, you can set up Rules (see pages 408–411) that tell certain types of email to go into certain folders, including these .Mac folders so those messages will be available online.

If you delete all of the folders in this mailbox, the entire Mailbox and crystal ball will disappear.

If you want it back, make a new Mailbox as described on page 383. Or go to **www.mac.com,** log in to Mail, make a new folder online, and it will appear here in Mail on your Mac. Amazing.

Email accounts

You might get email at several different addresses, each coming from a different server. **Mail can check all of your email accounts at once.** When you answer email, or compose a new message, you can choose to have it answered from any of your accounts. **To set up your other accounts** so Mail can check them all, see pages 397–401.

If you have more than one account in the Mailboxes drawer, a "New Message" window provides a pop-up **Account menu** that contains the names of any accounts you've set up, as shown to the right. From the "Account" pop-up menu, choose the account that you want the message sent from.

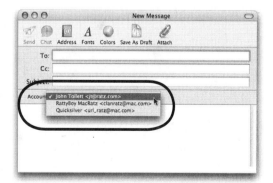

When I receive an email to my ratz.com account, I can answer it with a return address from any of my other accounts.

Contextual Menus

Mail makes extensive use of **contextual menus:** Control-click on a message, the toolbar, or an item in the Mailboxes drawer to open a pop-up menu that offers various commands, as shown below. If you have a two-button mouse, right-click on an item to show a contextual menu.

Using contextual menus is just a convenient way to access menu commands—there is nothing in a contextual menu that you can't find in the main menu bar across the top of your screen.

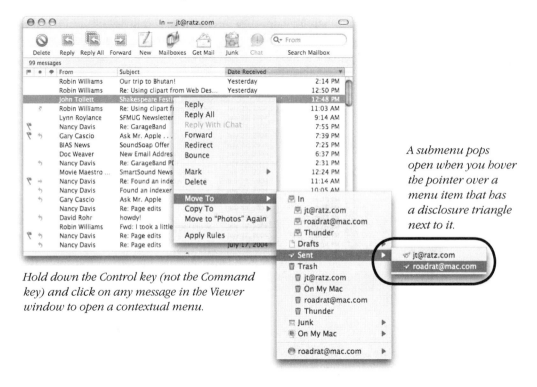

A submenu pops open when you hover the pointer over a menu item that has a disclosure triangle next to it.

Hold down the Control key (not the Command key) and click on any message in the Viewer window to open a contextual menu.

Junk Mail Filter!

Okay, this is really incredible. You can set Mail so it **automatically deletes junk mail without you ever having to see it.** Or if you are a little more cautious, you can have all the junk mail sent to a folder where you can check through it in case something you want accidentally ended up in the junk pile. And this really works—even though it's not 100 percent effective, it does make a dramatic difference in how much junk mail gets through.

To turn the Junk Mail feature on or off:

1. Go to the Mail menu and choose "Preferences...."

2. Click the "Junk Mail" button.

3. Check or uncheck the box "Enable Junk Mail filtering."

Set up your window

First of all, make sure your Viewer window is set up as shown on the following page. This has nothing to do with the junk filter, but it will prevent the following from happening: When you single-click on a junk message to delete it, the message appears in the bottom pane. This does two things—it displays the message, which sometimes can take valuable time, and it often sends back a message to the despicable junk mailer confirming that this is a valid email address, which means you'll get more email from them and they'll sell your address to other evil junkheads (also known as spammers)! So you don't want to give them the satisfaction of even *opening* junk mail.

Get rid of the bottom pane, as explained on the following page, and when you want to **read a message,** *double-click* the message name in the Viewer and it will open in its own window.

—continued

To prevent having to open every piece of mail to delete it, follow the one step shown below. When you want to read a message, double-click it anywhere in the message line.

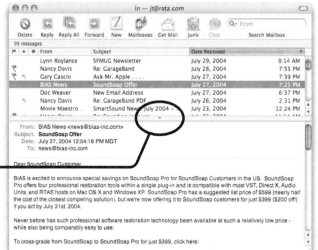

When both panes are showing, as in this example, the entire email appears in the bottom pane when you click on a message—even if you want to delete it.

To prevent this, *drag this bar all the way to the bottom.*

When the bottom pane is gone, you can select one, several, or all email messages and delete them (hit the Delete key) without having to open them first.

To read a message, *double-click it and a separate window will open.*

Automatic junk mail detection

Mail automatically analyzes incoming messages and identifies what it thinks is **junk mail** by highlighting the message in brown. If your "Flags" column is showing in the Viewer window, you'll see a junk mail icon (a brown mail bag) in that column.

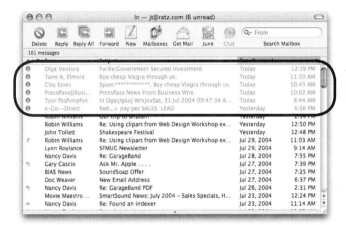

Mail's default is to turn junk mail brown.

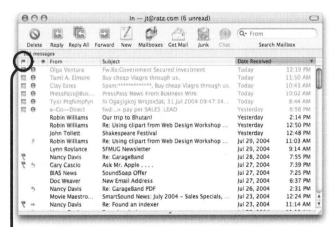

To make the Flags column visible, from the View menu choose "Columns," then from the submenu choose "Flags."

Train Mail to find junk more accurately

You can **train Mail to be more accurate** in identifying junk:

1. From the Mail menu, choose "Preferences…."

2. Check the box to "Enable Junk Mail filtering."

3. From the options titled "When Junk Mail arrives," choose "Leave it in my Inbox, but indicate it is Junk Mail (Training)."

4. When you receive a new email message, check to see if Mail has correctly identified it.

▼ If the new message is **unwanted junk mail, but Mail did not mark it** as such: Single-click the message, then click the "Junk" icon in the toolbar to mark it as junk mail.

Or from the Message menu, choose "Mark," then from the submenu choose "As Junk Mail."

Or press Command Shift J.

▼ **If Mail *incorrectly* identifies** a message as junk mail, you can correct it: Select the message incorrectly marked and notice the "Junk" icon in the toolbar has changed to "Not Junk." Click the "Not Junk" icon to correctly identify the message.

5. Continue training Mail in this way for a couple of weeks, or until most incoming messages seem to be correctly identified.

When you're ready to **let Mail automatically handle junk mail,** go to the Mail preferences, click the "Junk Mail" button, then choose "Move it to the Junk mailbox (Automatic)." Mail will create a Junk mailbox (in the Mailboxes drawer) to store all your unwanted mail. You might want to occasionally review the messages in this mailbox to make sure mail is being correctly identified.

When you're satisfied that Mail is accurately finding junk mail, you may want to change your setting so **Junk mail is instantly deleted** (see the next page). Be careful with this! If you choose this option, you will never see the mail, nor can you undo the action or find it in any "Trash" mailbox—it's gone. And good riddance.

Instantly delete junk mail

You can have Mail delete junk before you ever see it—spam will be instantly deleted and you won't even be able to find it.

To delete junk mail before it ever appears in your box:

1. From the Mail menu, choose "Preferences…," then click the "Rules" button.

2. Click the "Add Rule" button. A sheet slides down from the title bar in which you set the conditions and actions for email messages.

For more details about making Rules, see pages 408–411.

Tip: If you buy airline tickets online, the email confirmation might be considered spam and thus deleted. I set up a special rule (see pages 408–411) that allows mail from places like Southwest or Delta to stay in my inbox.

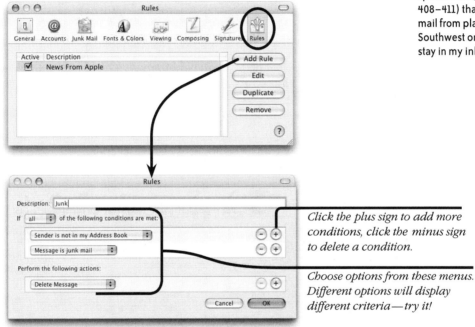

Click the plus sign to add more conditions, click the minus sign to delete a condition.

Choose options from these menus. Different options will display different criteria—try it!

In the example above, you can see how I've set up my Mail preferences so junk is deleted before it ever lands in my box. Remember, you have to be very confident that you're not getting any real mail mixed up in your junk mail. (Personally, if something gets accidentally labeled as junk and disappears, that's too bad—it's not worth it to me to sort through hundreds of pieces of junk mail to see if there's one good message.)

The Toolbar

The buttons in the **toolbar** are duplicates of some of the commands that are also available in the menu bar at the top of the screen. You can customize this toolbar just like you customize the one in the Finder window.

Control-click on the toolbar to open this contextual menu.

To add additional tool buttons to the toolbar, go to the View menu and choose "Customize Toolbar…." **Or** Control-click in the toolbar, then choose "Customize Toolbar" from the contextual menu that opens. A sheet of buttons slides down from the toolbar; the buttons represent various functions, as shown below. Drag any of these icons to the toolbar, then click "Done."

To remove a button from the toolbar, Command-drag it off the bar.

To rearrange a button, Command-drag it to another position.

Command-click this button at any time to switch the toolbar between large icons with text, small icons with text, large icons, small icons, or just text.

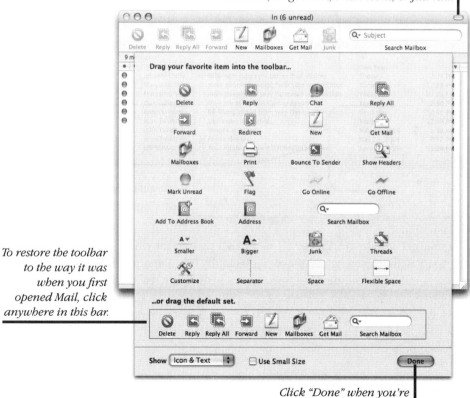

To restore the toolbar to the way it was when you first opened Mail, click anywhere in this bar.

Click "Done" when you're finished to put this sheet away.

Other buttons that don't have obvious functions are "Bounce To Sender" and "Redirect."

Bounce To Sender is meant to discourage unwanted email: Select an unwanted message, then from the Message menu, choose "Bounce To Sender" (or click the button in your toolbar, if it's there). The sender receives a reply that says your email address is invalid and the message was not delivered; the recipient cannot tell if the message has been read. The unwanted message is moved to your Trash folder. Unfortunately, this does not work for most junk email because spam return addresses are usually fake (to prevent spammers' lives from being threatened).

Redirect is similar to "Forward," except that redirected mail shows the *original* sender's name in the "From" column instead of yours, and shows the time the message was originally composed. When you redirect mail, your name is at the top of the message so the new recipient knows you received the message and redirected it.

Notice a redirected message tells the recipient who originated the message, and if it was modified.

Mail Search

You can search a specific account, mailbox/folder, or all mailboxes at once.

To search a *specific* account or folder, single-click an account or folder in the Mailboxes drawer, then click the triangle next to the magnifying glass in the Search field. From the pop-up menu, use the top group of search criteria. Choose whether to search entire messages or just one of the header fields (From, To, or Subject). Type a search term in the Search field.

To search *multiple* folders and mailboxes, Command-click items in the Mailboxes drawer to search, then set the search criteria as explained above.

To search *all* mailboxes, from the Search pop-up menu, choose a search criteria under the heading "In All Mailboxes."

Choose a search category from this group to search a folder (mailbox) that's selected in the drawer.

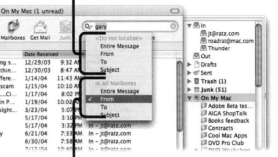

Choose a search category from this group to search all mailboxes. The Viewer window shows the search results; the far-right column tells you which folder a selected message is in.

IMAP vs. POP

Apple's Mail program can handle two types of incoming mail "protocol": **IMAP** and **POP** (or POP3, to be specific). A protocol is a particular set of standards or rules having to do with communications between computers. You can set up IMAP or POP accounts in Mail; see the following pages.

Email from a POP account is stored "locally," which means on your hard disk.

POP3 (Post Office Protocol 3) is a protocol in which the server automatically downloads the mail to your computer when you check mail, then *deletes* the mail from the server. With POP you cannot read mail until it has been downloaded to your computer. POP works best for users who always use one computer on which the email files are stored and managed.

You can choose to leave your mail on the POP server after it has been downloaded to your Mac (see page 401), but check with your service provider before you do that—it might make them mad to have all of your email clogging up space on their server.

Email from an IMAP account is stored on a remote server (although you can keep copies on your hard disk).

IMAP (Internet Message Access Protocol) is a protocol that receives and *holds* email on a server for a certain amount of time, typically thirty days. IMAP allows you to view email before deciding whether or not to download it to your computer.

One advantage of IMAP is that you can manage your email from multiple computers because the email files are kept on the IMAP server for storage and manipulation; this means you can check your mail on a computer while you're on holiday in Glasgow, and when you come home, you'll still have the same messages at home that you read in Glasgow.

Another advantage is that you can choose *not* to download emails that have large attachments or email from people you don't want to hear from. You can wait until it's convenient, until you know who an attachment is from, or you can just delete unwanted or unsolicited email and attachments before they ever get to your computer.

America Online uses an IMAP server. That's why you can choose whether or not to download a file, and your email disappears automatically after thirty days whether you like it or not.

When you sign up for a Mac.com email service through .Mac, you're assigned a fifteen-megabyte mailbox on Apple's IMAP mail server. All unread messages within an account, *even deleted messages,* are stored on Apple's server. If you have more than fifteen megabytes of mail and attachments, people will not be able to send you any more email at that account until you clear it out. See Section 2 for more information about .Mac accounts.

Set Up a New Account or Edit an Existing Account

Use **Mail Preferences** to create new mail accounts, edit existing accounts, and customize Mail's behavior. You may have more than one email account in your life. For instance, you might have one that is strictly for business, one for friends and family, one for your lover, and one for your research. Mail can manage them all for you.

To open Preferences and get the Accounts pane:

1. From the Mail menu, choose "Preferences…," then click **Accounts.**

2. The **Accounts** list will show all the email accounts you've created.

   To **create** a new account, click the + button at the bottom of the Accounts pane, then name it something you will recognize.

   To **edit** an existing account, single-click the account in the list, then see the following pages for detailed descriptions of the options.

*Mail cannot get your AOL email. Nothing can get AOL email except AOL (although you can use any browser anywhere in the world and go to **www.aol.com** to get your mail).*

Before you set up an account, this is a pop-up menu with the options POP, IMAP, .Mac, and Exchange.

(If you need to create an Exchange account, talk to your Exchange system administrator.)

***To remove an account,** select its name in the Accounts pane, then click the − sign. Or instead, you could make an account inactive; see page 400 or 401.*

3. Choose an **Account Type** from the pop-up menu.

   Choose ".Mac" if you're setting up an email account that you created using the Mac.com website.

   If you're setting up an account that comes from some other service provider, they can tell you if they use POP or IMAP (most likely POP).

4. In the **Description** field, type a name that will identify the account in the Mailboxes drawer. You can name it anything, such as "Lover Boy," "Research Mailing List," "earthlink," etc.

5. Enter your full email address in the **Email Address** field. If you're setting up a .Mac account, this will be automatically filled in with your email address at Mac.com.

—continued

6. **Incoming Mail Server:** If your account type is .Mac, the host name is automatically filled in with "mail.mac.com."

   If you're setting up another account type, the mail service provider can tell you what name to use. Tell them you need the "incoming" mail server name, also known as the "POP address." (It's probably something like "mail.domainname.com," where "domainname" is the name in your email address, such as mail.ratz.com.)

7. If you're setting up a .Mac account, **User Name** and **Password** are the same ones you chose when you signed up for your account. You should have received an email from Apple verifying this information.

   If you're setting up a POP account, your user ID and password may have been assigned by your provider, or they may have been chosen by you. *These are not necessarily the same user ID and password that you use to access your email.* If necessary, ask your provider for the user ID and password information.

8. **Outgoing Mail Server:** No matter where your email account *comes* from, the outgoing mail server (the SMTP Host) for every account is always the one you're paying money to for your Internet service—it's your Internet Service Provider's name, such as "mail.providername. com" because that's how your email is going *out*. Mac.com is *not* the SMTP host for your Mac.com account.

   If "smtp.provider.com" or "mail.provider.com" don't work, call your provider and ask them what their SMTP Host is called.

My friend Joannie made up a great mnemonic for SMTP: Send Money To Person.

Next, click the **Special Mailboxes** tab of the window. The items in this tab change depending on whether you're creating an IMAP account (such as .Mac) or a POP account (most others).

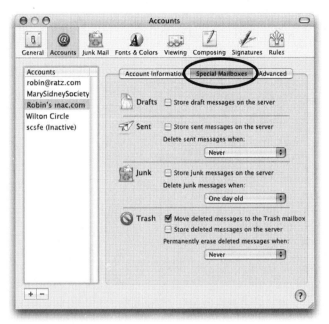

These are the IMAP options. The advantage to storing items on the server is that you can access them from anywhere in the world; they're not stored on your computer. If you have a .Mac email acount, you can go to www.mac.com and log into your account on any computer that has a browser and an Internet connection.

These are the POP options. These refer to the messages that are in the Mail program and stored on your Mac, not on a remote server.

—continued

*See the opposite page
for the POP options.*

If you're creating an IMAP account, the following options are shown in the Advanced pane:

Enable this account: Check to make the account active. Uncheck it to make the account **inactive,** which does not delete the account—it just tells Mail to ignore it for now.

Include when automatically checking for new mail: UNcheck this box when you want to prevent Mail from checking email at this address. This is useful if you have several email addresses and you choose not to check some accounts as often as others. You can always manually check for messages in any account—use the "Get New Mail" option in the Mailboxes menu.

Compact mailboxes automatically: When you select and delete messages on an IMAP server, they don't really get deleted—they get placed in a "Deleted" folder on the server. The server stores these deleted files for a user-specified length of time before they are erased. Apple doesn't give you a choice about this with your .Mac email account—the files you delete will be erased immediately when you quit the Mail application; this frees up your email space on their server.

Keep copies of messages for offline viewing: This menu offers options for copying email messages from an IMAP server onto your own Mac.

"All messages and their attachments" will copy all of your email, plus any attachments you were sent, to your hard disk.

"All messages, but omit attachments" will copy the body of the email messages, but not attachments.

"Only messages I've read" will only copy and store messages if you've read them. You can mark a letter as "Unread" or "Read" whether you really have or not—use the Message menu.

"Don't keep copies of any messages" will not copy any of your mail to your hard disk. This option provides you with extra security and privacy if other people have access to your computer. If you choose this option, be aware that some IMAP servers will eventually erase messages that have been stored for a user-specified length of time (thirty days, generally), whether you've read them or not.

If you're creating a POP account, the following options are shown in the Advanced tab:

See the opposite page for the IMAP options.

Enable this account: Check to make the account active. Uncheck it to make the account **inactive,** which does not delete the account—it just tells Mail to ignore it for now.

Include when automatically checking for new mail: UNcheck this box to prevent Mail from checking email at this address. This is useful if you have several accounts and you choose not to check some email as often as others. You can always manually check for messages in any account—use the "Get New Mail" option in the Mailboxes menu.

Remove copy from server after retrieving a message:
POP servers prefer that you choose the option to delete a message from the server as soon as it is downloaded to your Mac. Uncheck it only when you need to temporarily keep a copy of your mail on the server. In the pop-up menu you'll find several options for lengths of time to store messages.

Prompt me to skip messages over __ KB: When checking for mail, you can choose to skip over messages that are larger than you want to receive. This can eliminate unsolicited attachments. Enter the maximum file size that you'll permit Mail to download. A typical text email message with no attachments is about 1 to 10 KB (kilobytes). Messages in HTML format (the fancy ones with nice type and graphics) might be 30 to 60 KB.

All done?

When all the "Accounts" preferences are set, click the red Close button; a sheet will drop down and ask if you want to save the changes. Your new account will appear in the Mailboxes drawer, under the "In" icon. If you don't see it, perhaps the In box is closed up—single-click the disclosure triangle to display the accounts, as shown below.

This In box is closed; notice the triangle is pointing to the right. Click the triangle.

With the triangle pointing down, the accounts are displayed.

Mail Preferences

As usual in a Mac application, you have a lot of preferences to set up Mail to suit how you work.

General

In this preference pane, tell other applications to use Mail for email links and when to check for new messages.

To open Preferences and get the General pane:

▼ From the Mail menu, choose "Preferences…," then click **General.**

Default Email Reader: Choose "Mail" in this menu so when you go to a web page or a PDF and click an email link, it will open a pre-addressed email compose window for you.

Check for new mail: Set how often you want to check for new mail. This only works if Mail is open (if the triangle is under its icon in the Dock). If you don't have a full-time, always-on connection to the Internet (such as DSL or cable modem), you'll probably want to select "Manually" from this pop-up menu to avoid having your modem dialing and trying to connect when you least expect it.

New mail sound: Choose various sounds (or "None") to alert you when new mail appears in your In box. If you create various rules that filter your mail, you can have different sounds for each of the rules so you know exactly when junk mail has been deleted, a letter from your lover has arrived, or mail for your family has gone into the Family mailbox; see pages 408–411.

Play sounds for other mail actions: Also plays a tiny sound when mail has been sent, when it checked for mail and there wasn't any, or when there was a problem fetching mail.

Index decrypted messages for searching: If you know what encryption is and you're using it, this will add encrypted messages to Mail's database of files it has indexed for searching.

Fonts & Colors

Select **fonts, font sizes,** and **text colors** for various parts of your messages.

To open Preferences and get the Fonts & Colors pane:

▼ From the Mail menu, choose "Preferences…," then click the icon at the top, **Fonts & Colors.**

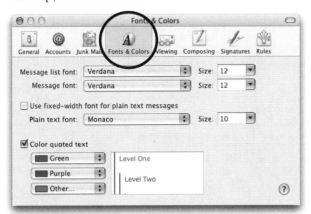

Message list font is the font used in the list of messages on your Mac.

Message font is the font in which you will type your email messages. If you choose a font that your recipients do not have installed on their computers, this font you choose will turn into their default fonts.

Use fixed-width font for plain text messages: When you choose to receive or write messages in "plain text," which is totally without formatting or other typefaces, this is the pop-up menu of fonts that are suitable.

Color quoted text: Email replies often contain quotes from previous emails. Color coding and indenting the quotes helps visually organize the message in a hierarchy of responses. To apply color to quoted messages, check the box, then choose colors.

In this example, you can see how each message is indented and colored. This makes it easy to keep track of what's going on in a continuing message.

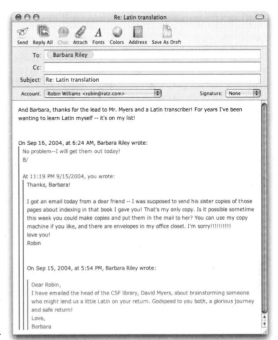

Viewing

Viewing

The **Viewing** preferences affect the information you see in the main Viewer window and in the body of email messages.

To open Preferences and get the Viewing pane:

▼ From the Mail menu, choose "Preferences…," then click **Viewing.**

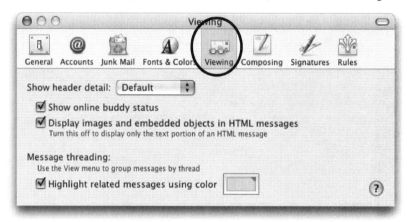

Show header detail: This menu lets you choose how much, if any, header information (all that to/from/date stuff) shows at the top of emails. This can be handy when you want to check for fraudulent emails, like those from scumbags pretending to need your eBay account information; check to show "All" headers and look for suspicious data, like return addresses that are different from the one that appears in your In box.

Choose "Custom…" to customize what information appears in the headers. "Default" means the simple, basic stuff you usually see.

Show online buddy status: Click this to display the Buddy Availability column in your Viewer window. When someone in your Buddy List is online, a green dot appears in this column; a yellow dot is displayed if they are online but idle. See page 381.

Display images and embedded objects in HTML messages: If it makes you crazy when you get big, complex web pages through your email messages, uncheck this box so only the text will appear, not all the fancy graphics and fonts.

Highlight related messages using color: For an explanation of message threading, please see page 378. Click the color box to choose a color for message threads.

Composing

The **Composing** pane applies to email messages as you write them.

To open Preferences and get the Composing pane:

▼ From the Mail menu, choose "Preferences…," then click **Composing.**

Format: "Rich Text" allows you to stylize messages with fonts and formatting, but not everyone will be able to see these features, depending on their computer and mail program. The other option in this pop-up menu, "Plain Text," can be seen by everyone but does not show any color and style formatting. Choose the format you'll use most often; you can change individual messages to the other format when necessary (choose it from the Format menu in the main menu bar).

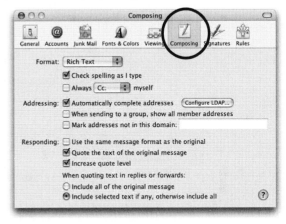

Check spelling as I type: Check this to catch spelling errors immediately. When Mail doesn't recognize a word, it underlines the word with a dotted red line. If you need help with the correct spelling, Control-click on a misspelled word and you'll get a pop-up menu with alternative spellings to choose from. Or from the Edit menu choose "Spelling," then choose "Spelling…" from the submenu.

Always Cc myself to send a copy of outgoing messages to yourself. From this same menu you can also choose **Always Bcc myself** to send yourself a copy without the recipient knowing it.

Automatically complete addresses: As you type a few letters in the "To" field, Mail will add the rest of the address for you. If there is more than one match, you'll get a list to choose from. If the correct one is the one in the Address field, just hit Return. If you get a list of possible addresses, use the DownArrow to move down the list, selecting each one; hit Return or Enter when the proper address is chosen.

When sending to a group, show all member addresses: When you send a message to a group (mailing list, as explained on pages 423–426), Mail will display everyone's address. Unless you have a specific reason to do this, UNcheck this box so the actual addresses are hidden.

The other options in this pane are self-explanatory.

Tip: If you select some text in an email message and hit the Reply button, only the selected text will appear in the reply as a quoted message.

Signatures

A **signature** is a blurb of prepared information about you or your company that can be added to the end of a message, either manually or automatically, as shown on the opposite page. You can create different signatures that include different types of information for various types of messages. For instance, in addition to a signature for personal mail that may include your address and phone number, you may want to create a different business signature that doesn't include personal information.

To open Preferences and get the Signatures pane:

▼ From the Mail menu, choose "Preferences…," then click **Signatures.**

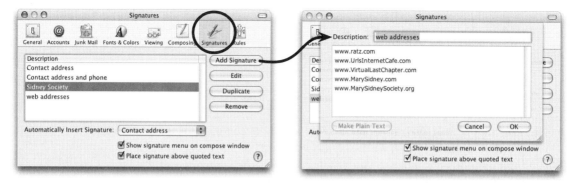

To create a signature, click the "Add Signature" button; a sheet will drop down from the title bar, as shown above.

In the "Description" field, enter a name for the signature that is descriptive to you. In the big text field, enter any information you want to include in the signature.

To add a photograph or graphic image to your signature, drag it into the big text field. The image format should be JPEG (.jpg). If your message is going to another Mac, other formats will work, such as TIFF, PICT, or PNG, but JPEG is still the recommended format.

Click OK when you're done.

To create a new signature that's similar to an existing signature, select the signature you want to use as a model, then click the "Duplicate" button. This duplicate now shows up in the list of signatures; select it, then click the "Edit" button. Make necessary changes to the signature, change its name in the "Description" field, and click OK.

To edit the information in a signature, choose a signature name in the Description list, then click the "Edit" button (or double-click the signature name). Make changes in the signature file, then click OK.

To remove a signature from the list, select it, then click the "Remove" button.

To choose a default signature, select its name in the "Automatically Insert Signature" pop-up menu. This signature will be used in all messages unless you override it by choosing another signature or "None" from the pop-up menu (discussed below) when you're writing a new email.

Show signature menu on compose window: Check this to install a pop-up menu in the "New Message" window that contains all of your signatures, as shown below. Then in any email message, just choose the one you want to include at the end of that message.

Place signature above quoted text: This puts your signature at the end of *your message,* not at the end of all the quoted information that might be in the letter.

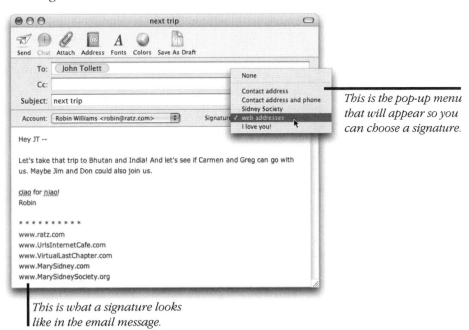

This is the pop-up menu that will appear so you can choose a signature.

This is what a signature looks like in the email message.

Rules

Use **Rules** to manage and organize your messages automatically. Rules act as filters that sift through your messages and put them in their proper mailboxes, delete them, forward them, or follow other actions, according to your directions. You might belong to a mailing list about pack rats, so you can have every email that comes in from that mailing list automatically delivered to the Pack Rat mailbox. Or you might want to delete every email with a subject that contains the words "mortgage," "enlargement," "babes," "hot," "insurance," or other obvious junk-mail words.

To open Preferences and get the Rules pane:

▼ From the Mail menu, choose "Preferences…," then click **Rules.**

This rule is probably already in your list. It highlights email from Apple with a color. Feel free to delete it if you like— nothing bad will happen.

To create a new Rule:

1. Click the "Add Rule" button. You'll get the dialog box shown below (except yours isn't filled in yet).

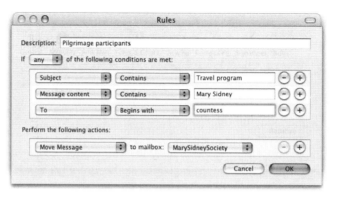

2. The **Description** field contains a default name, such as "Rule #1." Change this name to something that describes your intended rule. In the example below, I want to keep track of messages about a travel adventure I'm going on, so I want messages relating to that to go into the "Bhutan trip" folder (mailbox) that I created.

3. In the **following conditions** section, specify which elements of an email message are to be searched and what the subject of the search will be.

   The first pop-up menu contains types of message **headers** that usually are included with an incoming message, such as To, From, Subject, etc., *or* you can choose to find text in the body of the message.

   Then choose a "modifier" from the second pop-up menu, such as "Contains," "Does not contain," or others.

   Type an appropriate word or words into the text field. The rule below will search for messages whose "Subject" field "Contains" the word "Bhutan."

—continued

Click on each one of these pop-up menus to see your options!

When you choose a different option in this first pop-up menu, the other two options in this row change to match. Try it.

Be sure to check this menu carefully to see the kinds of things you can do with specified messages! See the following page for details.

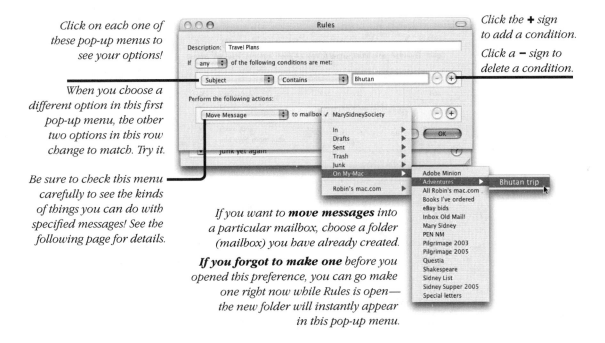

Click the + sign to add a condition.

Click a – sign to delete a condition.

*If you want to **move messages** into a particular mailbox, choose a folder (mailbox) you have already created.*

***If you forgot to make one** before you opened this preference, you can go make one right now while Rules is open— the new folder will instantly appear in this pop-up menu.*

4. **Perform the following actions:** Determines what actions will be applied to messages that match the criteria you specified. You can check as many or as few of these actions as you like.

> **Move Message:** Select an existing mailbox or make one while Rules is open (see page 383) to move the messages into.
>
> **Copy Message:** This will put a copy wherever you want it to go, and leave the original where it is.
>
> **Set Color of Message:** Choose a color for highlighting messages that match the criteria. Then you can quickly identify various categories of filtered email that may appear in a message list.
>
> **Play Sound:** Choose a sound that will alert you when you receive a message that matches the criteria.
>
> **Bounce Icon in Dock:** When certain mail comes in, your Mail icon in the Dock will bounce up and down, even if you hide the Dock.
>
> **Reply to Message:** This opens a text box in which you can type a message that will be automatically sent.
>
> **Forward Message:** To forward certain incoming mail to another email address, check and enter an email address in the text field that you want the forwarded mail sent to. After you choose this you will get a little button, "Message…"; click it to enter a message that will appear at the beginning of the forwarded email.
>
> **Redirect Message:** *Forwarded* mail shows *your* name in the "From" column of the email, plus the date and time you forwarded it. *Redirected* mail shows the *original* sender's name in the "From" column, and the original time it was sent. When you redirect mail, your name shows up in a "Resent from" field so the new recipient knows you received the message and redirected it.
>
> **Delete Message:** Removes any message that meets the criteria. This does not put the message in the Trash folder—it just disappears.
>
> **Mark as Read:** Removes the blue dot from the Message Status column (if it's showing) even if you didn't really open and read it.
>
> **Mark as Flagged:** Puts a little flag marker in the Flags column (if it's showing) to call your attention to this message.
>
> **Run AppleScript:** If you have created an AppleScript, you can choose it.
>
> **Stop evaluating Rules:** Just like it says.

5. **OK:** Click OK and the rule is made. All incoming mail will now be searched and sorted using the criteria you just created.

Rules are listed in an order and will be applied in that order. **Change the priority order** by dragging a rule to another position in the list.

To edit a rule, select it in the list, then click the "Edit" button, *or* double-click the rule name in the list.

Duplicate a rule if you want to create a new rule that is similar to an existing one. Select an existing rule in the list, click "Duplicate," then select and edit that new rule.

To remove a rule, select it in the rule list, then click the "Remove" button or press the "Delete" key on your keyboard.

Instead of removing a rule that might have taken some time to create, you can make it **inactive:** Uncheck the box in the **Active** column. When you want to use the rule again, it's still there and can be activated.

Rules affect new messages that are received *after* a rule was created. **To apply rules to messages you've already received,** select the messages in the main Viewer window. From the "Message" menu, choose "Apply Rules." **Or** Control-click on one of the selected messages and choose "Apply Rules" from the pop-up menu.

Tips: If you won't be able to respond to your mail for a while, set up an **autoresponder** that will automatically return a message saying you are away and will respond later:

Choose "If sender is in my Address Book," and "Reply to message," then click the button to enter your message. You might say something like, "Thank you for your email. When I return from the Amazon on October 27, I will answer your lovely message."

Or **forward** all of your own email to yourself at another address.

Menu Commands

Following are some of the items in the **menus** that aren't explained elsewhere.

File menu

New Viewer Window: If you've closed the main Viewer window and realize that you need it back, use this command, or press Command Option N.

You can't import AOL mailboxes (not because of Mail's limitations, but because of AOL's prohibitions).

Import Mailboxes: Mail can import the mailboxes of many popular email applications. If you have custom mailboxes already set up in another email application, from the File menu, choose "Import Mailboxes…." Select one of the email clients in the list, then click the right arrow button for instructions. Mail will open a directory window so you can navigate to the appropriate mailbox file and import it. You might also want to try using the AppleScript "Import Addresses"; see page 416.

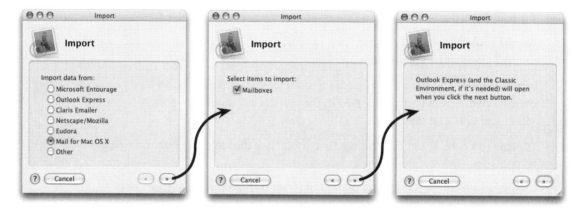

To print an email message: Double-click a message to open it. Click the "Print" icon in the open message's toolbar to open the Print dialog box. **Or** select a message in the Message List pane, go to the File menu and choose "Print…." Make the appropriate selections and click "Print."

To print multiple email messages: From the Message List, select multiple messages. From the File menu, choose "Print…." All selected messages, including header information, will print out in continuous fashion—it will not print a separate page for each message.

Save Attachment: Open any message that has attachments included. Choose "Save Attachment…" and you can choose where you want the files saved.

Edit menu

Paste As Quotation: Use this command when you want to paste text from another document into an email message as a quotation. In Mail, a quotation is styled with indentation, a vertical bar, and a user-specified color, as explained on page 403.

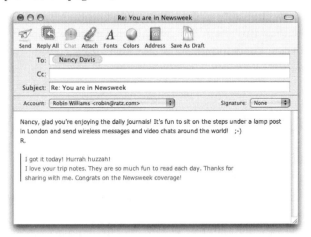

Append Selected Messages: This will add entire email messages you have received onto the end of a different message you compose. Compose your message, then go to the Viewer window, select the email message you want to append, and choose this command from the Edit menu.

Paste in Current Style: This is a nice feature. When you copy and paste text from another message or another document, it drops in with its own font and size which usually doesn't match your chosen font in the message you're writing. But if you copy text and then choose this command, the text will paste in using the font and size that is already in your message.

Attachments: You have two options here. You can choose to **Include Original Attachments in Reply,** which does just what it says—when you reply, any photos or other files that came to you will be sent back to that person. Only do this if you have a reason to do so. The other option in this menu, **Always Send Windows Friendly Attachments,** will try to make sure your attachments can be read by people using Windows machines. However, this can mess up files for Mac users, so I don't recommend you turn on this feature from this menu because it will apply to every file you send. You can always choose to make **individual files** Windows friendly: Use the Attach button in a new message window so you get the Open dialog box. At the bottom of that dialog box is a checkbox where you can choose to "Send Windows Friendly Attachments." This will apply only to the attachment you select.

View menu

Display Selected Messages Only: Select messages (Command-click to select more than one), then choose this option so *only* those messages will be visible in the Message List. To show all of the messages again, go back to the View menu and choose "Display All Messages."

Hide Status Bar or **Show Status Bar:** The Status Bar is located just below the toolbar. The left side of the Status Bar provides information about your Internet connection when checking for mail, and it displays the number of messages in the current Mailbox.

Mailbox menu

Online Status: If you have a dial-up account that ties up your phone line while you're connected to the Internet, you can "Go Offline." This disconnects you from the Internet, but leaves Mail open. Before you go offline, transfer any messages you want to read to another folder (just drag them over and drop them in). Then go offline, read your mail, compose messages, print them, etc. Messages you compose while offline are stored in the Outbox in the Mailboxes drawer, where you can open and edit them. When you're ready to send mail, from the Mailbox menu, choose "Online Status" and then select either an individual account to take online, or "Go Online" in general.

Get New Mail: If you have more than one account in Mail, go to this menu to selectively check the mail in just a single account.

Rebuild: If messages come in garbled or with some strange font, try using the Rebuild command. If your hard disk is really full, clear some room before you try this because it needs hard disk space to do its rebuilding.

Window menu

Activity Viewer: The right side of the Status Bar displays a revolving wheel when connecting to a remote server to send or receive mail. Click that revolving wheel (or click where it would be) to open the **Activity Viewer,** as shown below, and see what's going on as it connects.

Click the revolving wheel again to close the Activity Viewer, or click the red Close button. Click any "stop sign" to stop that particular activity.

Format menu

In the Format menu, under "Font," there is a command to make the selected text **Bigger**. The menu says the keyboard shortcut is Command +, but that doesn't work—use **Shift Command +**.

Make Plain Text changes messages from "Rich Text" format to "Plain Text" format, which will strip out all of the formatting, different fonts, colors, etc. If the message is already in Plain Text, this command appears as "Make Rich Text." This will *not* restore any formatting that was removed.

Quote Level: To format text as a Mail-style quote or to increase the existing quote level, click within a line of text, choose "Quote Level," and then choose "Increase." Choose the command again to further increase the quote level, as shown below. Of course, choose "Decrease" to take the text back towards normal.

The operation is much easier and faster if you learn the keyboard shortcuts: Click within the appropriate text, then type Command ' (that's the typewriter apostrophe, just to the left of the Return key) to increase the quote level, or type Option Command ' to decrease the quote level.

You can choose the colors for the quoted sections in the Fonts & Colors preferences; see page 403.

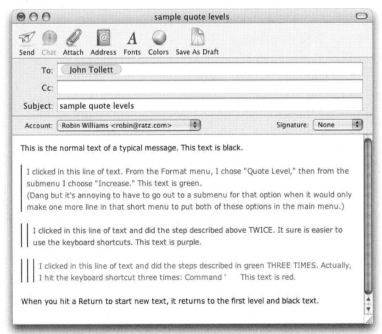

Each of these quoted sections has been increased one more level than the one above it.

Scripts menu

An **AppleScript** is a small piece of code that makes something happen. If you know how to write them, you can do all kinds of great things. Mail provides you with a list of several useful and useless scripts here in the Scripts menu (which doesn't actually say "Scripts" in the menu bar but has a little icon that looks like a parchment scroll).

Feel free to experiment with these scripts—just choose one and let it run. Check out the "Crazy Message Text" script.

For full details about AppleScript, go to the website at **www.apple.com/ applescript.**

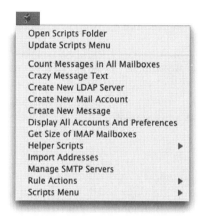

The **Address Book** works both independently and with Mail to create Address Cards that store contact information for individuals or groups. When *Mail* is open, you can automatically create an Address Book entry for anyone who sent mail to you. When you open the *Address Book* from a new message you're writing, you can automatically address email to an individual or an entire group.

The Address Book icon is in your Dock, your Applications folder, and in the Mail "New Message" toolbar.

*Edit a card, then double-click here to open the box where you can choose an image to apply (TIF, GIF, or JPG; not EPS format). **Or** drag an image from your Desktop and drop it in this space.*

Once you add an image, it will appear in a chat session with this person.

Switch between this full-column view and the card-only view.

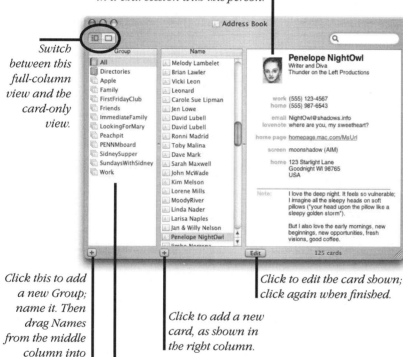

Click this to add a new Group; name it. Then drag Names from the middle column into this Group.

Click to add a new card, as shown in the right column.

Click to edit the card shown; click again when finished.

Organize your cards into Groups. Then you can address email to the Group name and the message will go to everyone in the entire Group.

Add any Name into any number of different Groups; every Name will always appear in the "All" list.

If you **add** a Name directly into a **Group**, it is automatically added to the All list.

When you **delete** a Name from a Group, it is not deleted from the "All" list.

> The "card" in the right column is called a **vcard**, or virtual card.
>
> A Group of addresses is a **Group card**.

Add New Names and Addresses

There are several ways to **add a new card of information** or just a name and email address to the Address Book, depending on whether you are using Address Book or Mail at the moment.

To add a new address card while using Address Book:

1. Single-click the **+** sign at the bottom of the "Name" column (or at the bottom of the visible card if you are viewing by card only).

2. This makes a new card automatically appear and the name of the person is already selected for you, waiting for you to type.

   Type the person's first name, then hit the Tab key. Type the last name, then hit Tab, etc. Continue to fill in all the information you know.

3. If a label is changeable, you'll see two tiny arrows. For instance, maybe you want to change the label "mobile" to "cell." Single-click the tiny arrows and you'll get a little pop-up menu, as shown below. Either choose one of the pre-named labels, or choose "Custom…" and type in the name of the label you want.

4. Click the green **+** sign to add another label and field; click the red **−** sign to delete the label and field to its right.

Tip: You can use Services to make a Sticky note out of the text in any field.

Just select the text in a field (press Command A to select all of the text, even if you can't see it all).

From the Address Book menu, choose "Services," then choose "Make New Sticky Note."

Or press Command Shift Y instead of going to the menu at all.

> This man is brilliantly talented. And so nice, too.

This is a Sticky note made from the Note field in the Address Card.

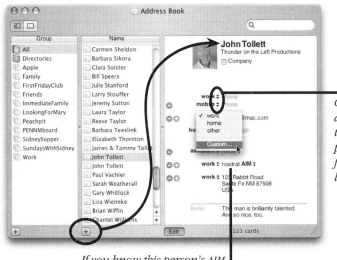

Click the tiny double arrows to get different pop-up menus for different labels, as shown.

*If you know this person's AIM name, Buddy name, or Mac.com email address, enter it here so you can use it in **iChat**.*

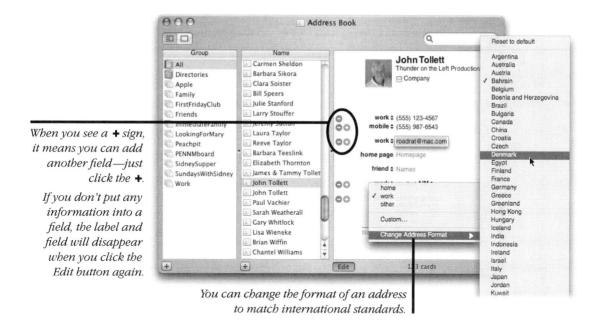

When you see a + sign, it means you can add another field—just click the +.

If you don't put any information into a field, the label and field will disappear when you click the Edit button again.

You can change the format of an address to match international standards.

To add a sender's email address to your Address Book instantly:

1. In the **Mail** program, either single-click on a message in your list, or open an email message.

2. From the Message menu in the menu bar across the top of your screen, choose "Add Sender To Address Book," *or* press Command Y. The Address Book will not open, but the sender's address will be added.

   Check on that address later, though, because if a person's first and last names are not included in their own email address, you'll find the new address in your Address Book at the very top of the "Name" column as <No Name>. Edit that card to add the person's name so he is sorted in the list properly.

Click on a sender's email in your list, then press Command Y.

—continued

To add someone's address from your "Previous Recipients" list:

1. In the **Mail** program, go to the Window menu and choose "Previous Recipients." This brings up a window, shown below, that has kept track of everyone you have sent email to (not everyone who has sent *you* email because then you'd have thousands of junk mail addresses).

If an address has a card icon to its left, that name and address is already in your Address Book.

2. Single-click the name of someone whose address you want to add to your Address Book, then click the button "Add to Address Book."

Ta da. You won't see anything happen on your screen, but that address has been added.

Have you noticed that when you start typing some addresses, Mail fills in the rest for you? Mail gets that information from this list.

Remove any names you don't think you'll be needing anymore.

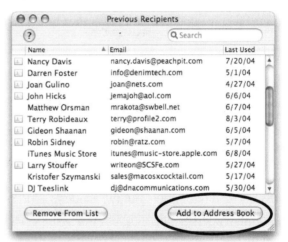

Note: If you scroll down to the bottom of the Previous Recipients list, you'll find all the people you have emailed but whose actual names are not shown. If you add one of *those* addresses to your Address Book, it will show up in the Name column in your Address Book at the top of the list as <No Name>.

To fix this, open your Address Book and select <No Name> to display its card. Click the Edit button and add the person's name to the card.

Send email to someone in your Address Book

Open your Address Book and find the person you want to **send email** to. Click on the *label* that's to the left of the email address. A menu will pop up, as shown below. Choose "Send Email," and a new message window will appear with that person's address in the "To" field.

Also see page 375 about using the Address Pane while in the Mail program.

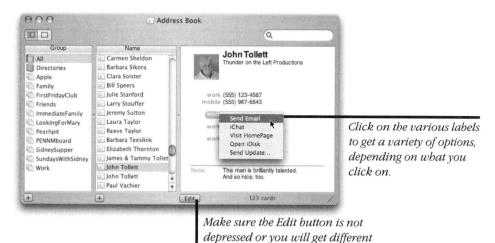

Click on the various labels to get a variety of options, depending on what you click on.

Make sure the Edit button is not depressed or you will get different pop-up menus!

Label Options

The various entries in a card each have different **options,** as shown below. Single-click on each entry *label* (the bold word on the left, not the entry data) and see what the options are.

Experiment with the options to become familiar with them. If you see pop-up menus that say things like "work" and "home," that means you're still in Edit mode—click the Edit button again to get out of Edit mode.

See a fax number from across the room

You can choose to see phone and fax numbers in type large enough to fill your screen so you can see it across the room when you fax someone. Try it. (Or type a love note instead of a phone number and flash it to your sweetheart on the other side of the room.)

Send an email (and other options)

You will see more or fewer options here depending on whether the person is a .Mac member or not.

Regardless, you can always click on their email address to open an email message pre-addressed to this person.

Go to a web page or open a chat

Go directly to a person's web page, if you included their web address in the card.

Click on his Instant Message name to open a chat with him (as explained in Chapter 17).

Create and Use a Group Mailing List

You can make a **Group** in the Address Book, which not only helps organize your address list, but also acts as a **mailing list;** that is, you can send an email message to the Group name and the one message will go to everyone in that list. You can put the same name in more than one list.

To make a Group mailing list:

1. In the Address Book, make sure you see all three columns, as shown below, left. (If you only see one panel, the "Card" panel, click the "View Card and Column" button shown below, right.)

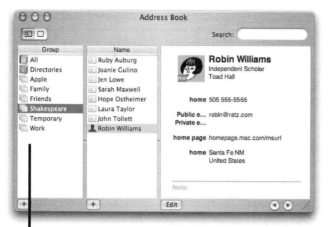 

In the left column you see the Groups I have made, and the "Shakespeare" Group is currently selected. In the center column are all the people in that selected Group.

If you only see one card, click this button.

2. Under the Group column, click the **+** sign. A "Group Name" will appear in the Group column, selected and ready for you to type a new name, as shown below. Just type to replace the selected name *(but do not type a space in the name or it won't work as an address!).* When done, hit the Enter key.

I'm going to name this new group "PENNMwriters."

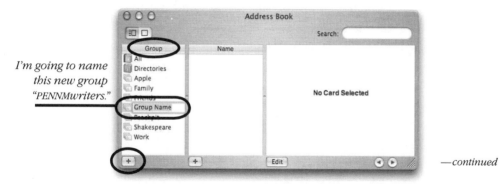

—continued

3. Now you can do one of two things: **Either** in the "Name" column, click the **+** sign and add a new address; this new address will be added to your "All" group *and* to the new Group that you just made (which is still selected, right?).

   Or click the "All" Group so you see all of the addresses in your book, then drag an existing address and drop it on the Group name, as shown below.

"All" contains the name of every person in every Group, as well as those who are in no Group at all. Each Group actually contains "aliases" to the one address card.

Now Denise is in the "All" list, as well as in the "PENNMwriters" Group. You can put the same person in any number of Groups.

Shortcut to make a Group

Here's an **even faster way** to make a Group:

1. Hold down the Command key and click on all the names in the list that you want to put into a new Group.

2. Let go of the Command key.

3. Go to the File menu, and choose "New Group From Selection."

4. Change the name of the Group (but don't put a space in the name), as shown on the previous page.

Send email to an entire Group

Once you've made a Group mailing list, you can send a message to everyone in that list simply by sending the email to the Group name.

To send an email message simultaneously to every person in a Group:

1. You don't have to have the Address Book open. In **Mail,** start a new email message.

2. In the "To" box, type the name of the Group. That's all—write your letter and send it and it will go to everyone in the Group.

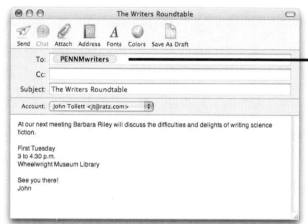

Enter the name of the Group here and the email message will be delivered to everyone in that Group.

If you see a list of all the individual names of the Group in this field instead of the Group name, see the following page.

Suppress the address list when sending mail to a Group

It's polite to **suppress the address list** when sending to a Group. For one thing, it's *really* annoying to have to scroll through a long list of addresses to get to the message. For another, *some* people don't want their private email address broadcast to everyone else on the list.

To suppress the Group list of addresses:

1. In the Mail program (not the Address Book), open the Mail preferences (go to the Mail menu and choose "Preferences…").

2. Click the "Composing" icon in the Toolbar, as shown below.

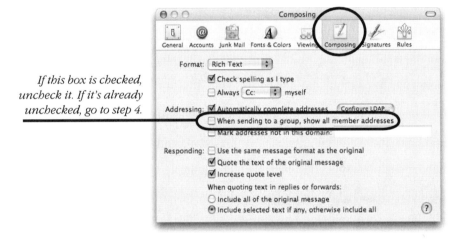

If this box is checked, uncheck it. If it's already unchecked, go to step 4.

3. UNcheck the box (if it's checked) "When sending to a group, show all member addresses."

4. Put the Preferences away (click the red Close button).

Export an Address or a Group of Addresses

You can **export** a single address, a collection of selected addresses, or a Group. Once exported, any other Address Book users can import the addresses into their application. There are two simple ways to export:

▼ Drag a Group, a name, or a collection of names from the Address Book and drop them on the Desktop or inside any Finder window. It will make an icon like the ones shown below.

Drag a selection of cards to the Desktop and the Mac will create this icon.

vCards

Drag a Group to the Desktop and the Mac will create an icon for you with the name of the Group.

Family

▼ Select the Group, a name, or a collection of names in the Address Book. From the File menu, choose "Export card…" or "Export Group card…." You will be asked where you want to save the exported card. An icon like the ones shown above will appear in the location where you chose to save it.

Important tip: What you **don't** want to do now is double-click this icon! I know, it's almost irresistible. But if you double-click it, it will look like nothing happened. So you'll probably double-click again. And maybe a third time just to make sure you didn't miss something. Every time you double-click, the addresses in the file are added to your Address Book! So if you double-click three times, you'll have each person's address in your book four times! So let's say you open your Address Book and delete three of those extra names — if any of those names were in a Group, you could be deleting them from their Group because only one of those four duplicates are actually in the Group — but which one? Sigh. How do you think I know this?

You can **send this file** to anyone with the current version of Address Book—they double-click the file **(once)** and those addresses are now in their Address Book.

Save your Address Book

If you plan to reformat your hard disk, **save a copy of your Address Book** file onto another disk so you can place it in the same location after you reinstall Mac OS X. To find the Address Book file, open your Home folder, then open the "Library" folder, then the "Application Support" folder. The address book folder is located here, named **AddressBook**.

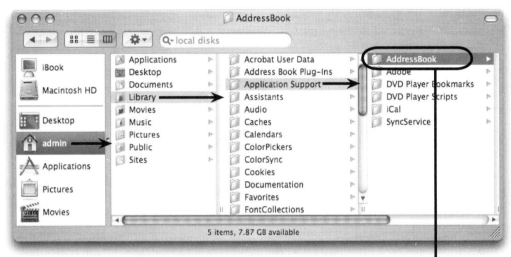

This is the AddressBook folder that contains your list of email addresses and contact information. Before you do anything that might change it, drag a copy of this original file into another folder, like your Documents folder: Hold down the Option key and drag it to another folder.

Save it to another disk if you plan to reformat your hard disk.

Email Etiquette

Many people use email everyday without being aware of **email etiquette** and without realizing that they're **1)** annoying co-workers, friends, and relatives; **2)** making themselves look naive and amateurish in the email world; and **3)** turning themselves into junk mailers, albeit well-intentioned.

If no one has complained about your email etiquette, you're probably in good shape. Or it could be that family members and friends do not want to risk embarrassing you. To be safe, consider the following suggestions and see if your email manners are up to date.

1. Get permission before you add someone to a mailing list.
You may be well-intentioned, but most people get so much spam and junk mail that they'd rather not receive the inspirational messages that someone sent you—especially since they probably received five other copies already. Not everyone is a curmudgeon about getting email like this, but it's polite, professional, and considerate to ask for permission before putting someone on your mailing list. And please, don't take it personally if they decline. Privacy on the Internet is hard to come by, and many people try to keep their email address off as many mailing lists as possible. When you add someone's address to your mailing list without their permission, you're publishing private information without permission.

2. Clean up the email headers.
Even if someone wants to be on your mailing list, it's extremely annoying to get email that has dozens (or hundreds) of lines of header information before the message. This happens when you receive an email message that was sent to a list (a Group), then someone sent it to their list, then someone else sent it to their list. This kind of email makes the sender look like the clueless amateur they are. Before you send a forwarded message like this, delete all that header stuff so the recipient can see the message at a glance without having to scroll through pages of junk. (To delete the header information, click the Forward button to forward the message, then select all those email addresses and other stuff, and hit the Delete button.)

Tip: If you're using Mail, select the good part of the message you want to forward, **then** forward the letter. Mail will put just the good part in the new message.

3. Hide the mailing list addresses.
When you send a message to your mailing list (called a "Group" in Mail), you are essentially providing every reader of the message with the email addresses of all your friends and relations. Then if those people forward your message, all of their recipients have the email addresses of all your friends and relations. Not many people appreciate that. Not only is it neater to hide these addresses, it is more polite to everyone involved.

—continued

To hide the addresses of a Group in Mail, go to the Mail Preferences, click "Composing," and make sure there is NO checkmark in the option "When sending to a group, show all member addresses."

4. Take the time to personalize your email.

If you send well-intentioned junk email to an acquaintance, friend, or relative, it will be appreciated if you take the time to add a personal note to the forwarded message, such as "Hi Jay, I thought you might enjoy this." To receive an unsolicited, unsigned, almost-anonymous forwarded email makes me wonder when I can expect to start receiving the rest of the sender's postal service junk mail and Sunday supplements.

5. Identify your email attachments.

Tip: If you want to send photographs as email attachments to a wide variety of computer users on all different sorts of computers, follow these guidelines:

Make sure the file is in the *JPEG format.* (If it came from your digital camera, it probably is.)

Name the file with a short name with no special characters such as ! ? / or : .

The file must have the *extension .jpg* at the end.

When you attach a file to an email message, don't make the recipient guess what kind of file it is or what program might open it. Include a description of the attachment and the file type, or what program is needed to open it. Say something like, "Barbara, the attached file is a photograph that I saved as a .tif in Photoshop CS on a Mac." Dealing with attachments can be confusing, and any helpful information is usually appreciated.

6. Don't fall for the urban legends and hoaxes that travel around the Internet.

When you get a panic-stricken email from a friend warning you of an apocalyptic virus and to "Please forward this email to everyone you know," do not forward it to anyone you know. This email message usually contains the words "THIS IS NOT A HOAX!" That means that this is a hoax. These messages float around the Internet constantly and some of them are many years old. If there's a deadly virus about to destroy the world as we know it, you're more likely to hear about it from the national news services and online news sites than from your cousin who's been using email for three months.

And anyway, your Mac doesn't get these viruses.

Also, do not forward the email messages that tell you Microsoft will pay you one dollar every time you use Hotmail or visit the Microsoft website. And don't forward the warning that the postal service is going to start charging us for every email, or that the phone company is going to tax every message, and that little boy in the hospital who is waiting for your postcard went home years ago.

And make darn sure your email recipient has *begged* you to send all those messages that say "Send this to at least ten other people. Do not break this chain!"

iChat AV and Rendezvous

17

If you've ever used a chat program or "instant messaging" program, such as AOL Instant Messenger or ICQ, you'll love **iChat AV.** In addition to text messaging that other chat apps offer, iChat AV also delivers audio and video conferencing as well. Audio chats require a microphone (most newer Macs have a built-in microphone), and video chats require a video camera with a FireWire connection (Apple's iSight camera includes a built-in microphone).

While iChat makes it easy (and free) to have conversations over the Internet with buddies anywhere in the world, Rendezvous makes it incredibly easy to chat or share files over a local area network.

In a legal issue over the rights to use the name Rendezvous, Apple will soon change the Rendezvous name to **OpenTalk.**

iChat AV requires a computer with Mac OS X installed, and a .Mac account or an AIM account (AOL Instant Messaging).

Text messaging needs only a low bandwidth connection, such as a dial-up modem.

Audio and video conferencing requires a broadband connection, such as cable or DSL.

iChat AV also requires a lot of processing power. For audio or video conferencing you need at least a G3 computer with a 600 MHz processor or faster. Any G4 should work very well, and G5s are more than capable.

Set Up iChat

The first time you click the **iChat** icon in the Dock, a Welcome window opens. Click the "Continue" button to proceed to the next window where you enter information to set up a new iChat account (shown below). The "Account Type" pop-up menu lets you choose between using your .Mac account (if you have one) *or* an existing AOL Instant Messenger account (called AIM; go to **www.aim.com** to get a *free* account; you don't have to subscribe to AOL to get a free AIM account).

If the iChat icon isn't in the Dock, you'll find it in the Applications folder.

If you don't have a .Mac account and you want one, you can click the "Get an iChat Account" button to sign up for it right now. Otherwise, enter your information, and click OK.

Your iChat "Buddy name" (Account Name) is the same as your .Mac membership name (or your AIM Buddy name). Your online buddies will use that name to find you and send Instant Messages or files. You can even have both an AOL Instant Messenger Buddy name and your Mac.com Buddy name and switch between them (only one can be *active* at a time).

Note: You must be connected to the Internet to use iChat!

If you are connected to other computers in your office, you can use Rendezvous to chat, even when you're not online. See page 462.

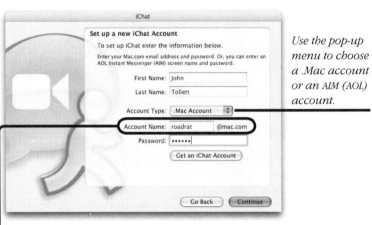

Use the pop-up menu to choose a .Mac account or an AIM (AOL) account.

This is your "Buddy" name. For a .Mac account, your Buddy name is your .Mac email address (including "@mac.com," which is added automatically).

For an AOL or AIM account, enter your AOL Buddy name (without the "@aol.com" part).

After you enter the information to set up a new iChat account, click "Continue." Another window opens to ask if you want to use Rendezvous messaging. If you have two or more computers connected to each other on a local network, choose "Use Rendezvous messaging" to make sharing files (or network chatting) easy and convenient (see pages 460–464).

Create a Buddy List

No matter what kind of chat you plan to do (text, audio, or video), the first thing you need to do is create a Buddy List. If you plan to chat often with certain people, **add them to your Buddy List** so you can easily see when they're online, and with the click of a button you can start a chat of any kind or send a file.

This is a typical Buddy List. The people in the list that have a green orb next to their names are online and you can start a chat with them. The dimmed out names are offline and unavailable at the moment.

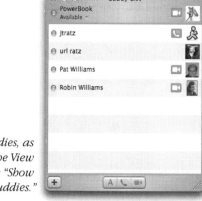

To hide offline buddies, as shown here, in the View menu uncheck "Show Offline Buddies."

To open your Buddy List and add people to it:

1. Click the iChat icon in the Dock, if iChat is not already open. If you don't see your Buddy List, press Command 1 (the number "one"), **or** go to the Window menu and choose "Buddy List."

2. In the Buddy List window that opens, click the **+** button (circled, above). A "sheet" will drop down from the top of the window, as shown below.

3. The sheet that drops down in front of the Buddy List window contains all of your Address Book contacts (as shown above).

—continued

If the person you want to add is in your Address Book, select that contact, then click the "Select Buddy" button. The new Buddy can now be seen in the Buddy list.

If you have not put that person's AIM name (Buddy name or .Mac email address) in your Address Book yet, you'll get another sheet like the one shown below.

If the Buddy you want to add is NOT in your Address Book, click the "New Person" button in the Address Book panel, which will bring down a different sheet, as shown below.

To remove a buddy from the Buddy List, select the buddy, then press Delete.

4. From the "Account Type" pop-up menu, select "Mac.com" *if* the new person uses their Mac.com account for instant messaging.

 Or choose "AIM" if the new person uses an AOL or AIM screen name.

5. Enter the "Address Book Information" if you want this person to be added to your Address Book as well.

6. To make a photo or custom icon appear next to a *new* Buddy's name, drag an image on top of the Buddy Icon window in the New Person panel (the photo or image must be a JPEG, GIF, or TIFF file). This picture will appear in your Address Book, in the Buddy List, and in Chat windows.

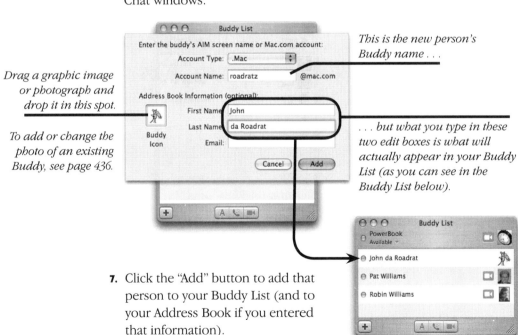

Drag a graphic image or photograph and drop it in this spot.

To add or change the photo of an existing Buddy, see page 436.

This is the new person's Buddy name . . .

. . . but what you type in these two edit boxes is what will actually appear in your Buddy List (as you can see in the Buddy List below).

7. Click the "Add" button to add that person to your Buddy List (and to your Address Book if you entered that information).

Status and messages in your Buddy List

Your name appears in the top-left corner of the **Buddy List.** The **colored status buttons** indicate the online status of you and your Buddies: Green means "Available," red means "Unavailable," and yellow means "Idle," which usually means that person's computer has gone to sleep due to inactivity.

A status message indicates your **availability:** "Available," "Away," or any *custom* message that you create. *It's not just a message—it actually changes whether people can see you or not.* When you choose any message with a red dot, no one can send you messages.

Tip: If you're colorblind between red and green, go to the Preferences (see page 452) and choose to have the availability buttons displayed as flat, unshaded squares and circles. They'll still be red and green, but at least you'll be able to tell which is which.

To change the status message, click the existing message ("Available" or "Away") that is located under your Buddy name, then from the pop-down menu (shown below-left) choose another message.

To create a *custom* status message, click the existing message ("Available" or "Away"), then from the pop-down menu choose "Custom…" and type your message in the text field (below, middle).

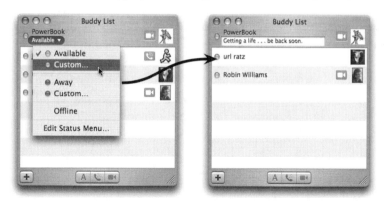

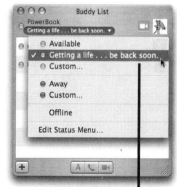

After you create custom status messages, they appear in this list.

Your custom status message will appear in the Buddy List of other iChat users, as shown below.

A custom status message.

Photos in your Buddy List

If you've put a **photo or image** for someone (or yourself) in your Address Book, it will appear in your Buddy List and iChat windows. If your AOL Buddy has added a photo or image in AOL, or in their own iChat application, their photo or image will appear instead of the one you placed.

But perhaps you don't like the image your friend uses. **To override his image,** select his Buddy name in your Buddy List, then "Get Info" for that Buddy:

1. From the Buddies menu, choose "Get Info."
   Or press Command Shift I.

2. An Info window opens, shown below-left. From the "Show" pop-up menu choose "Address Card." Drag a photo to the "Picture" well. If the photo you place is larger than 62 x 62 pixels, the "Buddy Picture" window (below-right) opens so you can resize it. **Or** instead of dragging a photo to the well, you can double-click the well to open the "Buddy Picture" window (below-right).

3. If you dragged a photo into the well in Step 2, it appears here. If the image area is empty, click the "Choose" button to make a Finder sheet slide down in which you can locate the photo you want to use, then click an "Open" button to place it here. **Or** you can drag a photo into this window (shown below-right).

4. Use the size slider (the blue dot) to adjust the photo size. Press on the image and drag it around to adjust the cropping.

5. Click "Set" to attach the photo to the buddy in your Buddy List.

6. Back in the Info window (below-left), click OK.

You can drag a photo to the "Picture" well.

Check "Always use this picture" if you want iChat to ignore the photo set by your buddy.

To remove a picture, click on the "Picture" box and hit the Delete key.

To add or change your picture, use the Address Book (see page 417).

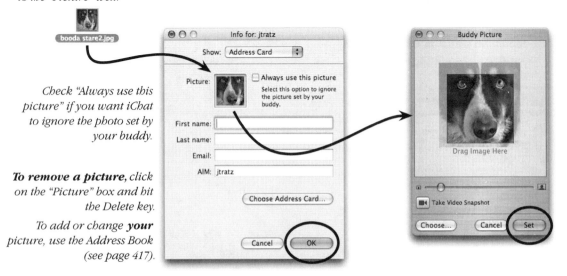

Create actions for a selected Buddy

Every Buddy has "actions" associated with it. You can have iChat announce that your Buddy has arrived or left (logged on or logged off), if you got a new message from him, or if he finally sent you a reply, etc.

To create actions for a selected Buddy, select his name in your Buddy List, then "Get Info" for that Buddy: From the Buddies menu choose "Get Info." **Or** press Command Shift I ("i" for "info"). The Info box *for that Buddy* opens. From the Show menu, choose "Actions," then set your preferences. In the example below, when jtratz becomes available (logs in), my Mac says out loud to me, "who's your buddy."

The voice used is the one you last chose in the Speech preferences: Click the "System Preferences" icon in the Dock, then click the "Speech" icon on the bottom row. Click the "Default Voice" button and choose a voice.

Store information about a selected Buddy

You can store information about a buddy in the same Information window described above.

1. Select a buddy in the Buddy List.

2. From the Buddies menu choose "Get Info" (or press Command Shift I).

3. In the Info window, choose the name of your Buddy's account in the "Show" pop-up menu. If the buddy has written a profile in America Online or AIM, it will appear here. You can also type additional notes about this person in the lower area, as shown on the right.

4. Click OK.

To see information about a buddy, or to add information, select the buddy's chat account from the "Show" pop-up menu.

Text, Audio, and Video Chats

For now, a text chat is the only way iChat can include more than one buddy at a time. However, the next major version of Mac OS X (Tiger) will allow multiple buddies to participate in audio and video chats.

After you create a Buddy List, you can select a buddy name in the list that's online, then start chatting. You can chat using text-based messaging, audio (page 456), or video (page 458), depending on the connection speed and the hardware available to both of you.

Text messaging may sound low-tech, but it has some advantages that make it a popular option. It's much more private than talking aloud during an audio or video chat. Text messaging lets you send files to others as you chat. You can include HTML web address links within a message. And you can chat with groups of people instead of just one at a time.

iChat Text Messaging

Below is a typical iChat text message window and how it basically works: You type a message to someone that's online—they type back to you.

The icon next to a buddy photo indicates what kind of chat is possible. A *camera icon* means the buddy has a video camera attached and can use text, audio or video to chat. A *phone icon* means the buddy has a mic attached or built in and can use text or audio to chat. *No icon* means the buddy can only use text messages to chat.

Click on the name that shows here. It toggles between the name in Address Book designated as "Me" and your iChat account login name. I set my Address Book name (the one designated as "Me") to be "Mr Powerbook" so I can easily identify which of my computers is showing up in a Buddy List or in Rendezvous.

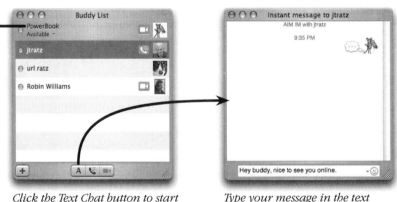

Click the Text Chat button to start a text chat with a selected buddy.

Type your message in the text box, then press Return or Enter.

To start a text chat:

1. Select a buddy in the Buddy List.

2. Click the Text Chat button (the letter "A") at the bottom of the iChat window to open a message window like the one shown above-right.

3. Type a message in the text box of the message window, then press Return. When your buddy answers you, his messages and yours are staggered in the window and tagged with the photos that were set in the chat software (iChat or AIM).

4. When you receive an instant message, a message window
   (as shown above-left) opens on your Desktop. The top of
   the window identifies the buddy sending you a message.
   Click on the window to expand it (above-middle) and
   choose "Decline" or "Accept." If you accept, the window
   expands again (above-right). Type a reply in the text box,
   then press Return.

A typical message window is shown below.

You can customize the color of your bubble, the typeface, and the color of the typeface for both yourself and your participants. See page 453.

*Each person in the window has their own talk bubble and an icon that represents them. You can **customize the icon** for yourself or for others; see page 436.*

When either you or a buddy starts to type, a thought cloud appears to let the other person know a message is on its way.

When a web address is typed into an iChat message, it becomes an active link to that web page.

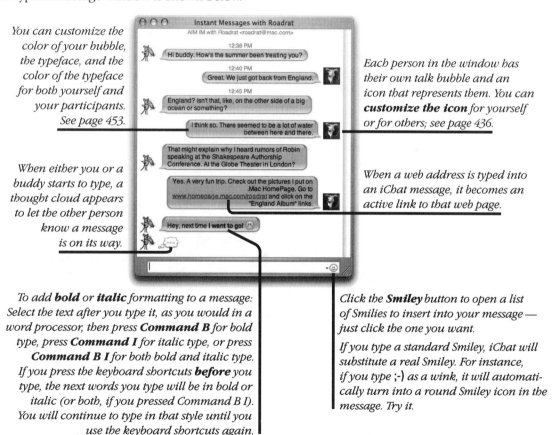

*To add **bold** or **italic** formatting to a message: Select the text after you type it, as you would in a word processor, then press **Command B** for bold type, press **Command I** for italic type, or press **Command B I** for both bold and italic type. If you press the keyboard shortcuts **before** you type, the next words you type will be in bold or italic (or both, if you pressed Command B I). You will continue to type in that style until you use the keyboard shortcuts again.*

*Click the **Smiley** button to open a list of Smilies to insert into your message — just click the one you want.*

If you type a standard Smiley, iChat will substitute a real Smiley. For instance, if you type ;-) as a wink, it will automatically turn into a round Smiley icon in the message. Try it.

Instant Message, Direct Message, Group Chat, and Rendezvous

With iChat *text messaging,* you can communicate with others in **four different ways:** Instant Messages, Direct Messages, group chats, and Rendezvous. Each method is different from the others and each has its own advantages.

An **Instant Message** opens a small window in which you can "talk" back and forth with *one other person,* and your talk is private (unless someone is looking over your shoulder). You must be connected to the Internet.

The easiest way to start a text Instant Message is to double-click a buddy in the Buddy List.

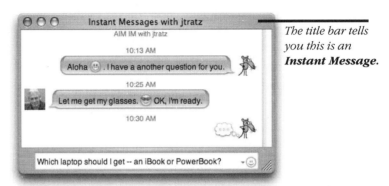

The title bar tells you this is an Instant Message.

To see information about your buddy as you chat: From the View menu choose "Show Chat Participants." A "Participants" drawer slides open (as shown on the next page). Click the buddy name, then from the Buddies menu choose "Get Info" (see pages 436–437).

A **Direct Message** looks just like an Instant Message and is even more private. Instant Messages go through a central messaging server on the Internet, while a Direct Message goes directly to *one other person's computer,* bypassing the central server. Some network or firewall security settings will not allow Direct Messages to be sent or delivered. You must be connected to the Internet.

A Direct Message is between two people —you cannot invite anyone else to join you.

The title bar says it's an Instant Message...

...but inside the window you can see you have actually started a Direct Message session.

A **Group Chat** is a public "room" where you can invite *any number of people*. These people might be spread all over the world, but you can all gab together. People can come and go as they please and the room stays open until the last person leaves. You can name the Group Chat, allowing anyone who knows the chat name to join in. You must be connected to the Internet. Learn more about groups on pages 444–447.

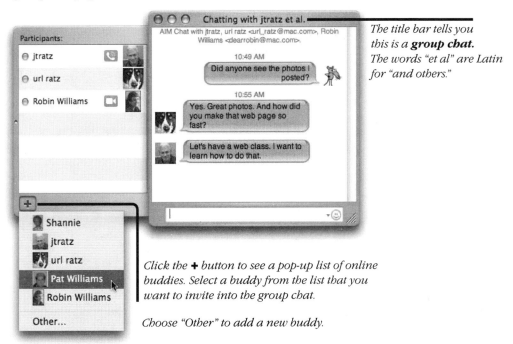

*The title bar tells you this is a **group chat**. The words "et al" are Latin for "and others."*

Click the ✚ button to see a pop-up list of online buddies. Select a buddy from the list that you want to invite into the group chat.

Choose "Other" to add a new buddy.

A **Rendezvous message** does not go through the Internet—it goes through your local network directly to another computer on the same network. Rendezvous automatically detects and connects other computers on your local network. You do not have to be connected to the Internet to send Rendezvous messages or to transfer files to another computer. See pages 460–464 for details about Rendezvous.

*This **Rendezvous** Instant Message looks just like any other instant message except for this small line that identifies it as a Rendezvous IM (Instant Message).*

To see who's available on your local network, press Command 2 to open this Rendezvous window. Select a name and click the Text Chat button ("A") to send a message.

The iChat File Menu

You can also start a chat from the **iChat File menu.**

From the File menu, choose **"New Chat"** to open a Chat window such as the one shown below. The chat becomes an Instant Message, a Direct Message, or a Group Chat, depending on which "Chat Option" is set for that particular window, as explained below.

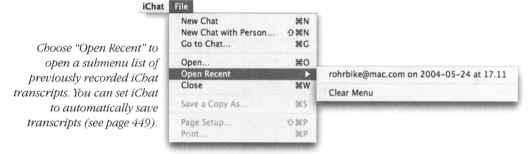

Choose "Open Recent" to open a submenu list of previously recorded iChat transcripts. You can set iChat to automatically save transcripts (see page 449).

Chat options

To set Chat Options for a "New Chat":

1. From the File menu, choose "New Chat."

2. Before you start a message to anyone, go to the View menu and choose "Chat Options...."

3. Press on the "Mode" pop-up menu, as shown below-right. Choose "Instant Message" for a one-on-one message session. Choose "Direct IM" to start a Direct Message session. Choose "Chat" to start a Group Chat.

4. Click OK.

You can only change the mode if you haven't yet sent a message. Once you start a dialog, the window is set in the selected mode and can't be changed.

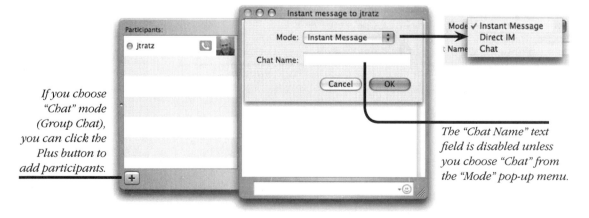

If you choose "Chat" mode (Group Chat), you can click the Plus button to add participants.

The "Chat Name" text field is disabled unless you choose "Chat" from the "Mode" pop-up menu.

From the File menu, choose **"New Chat with Person..."** to open a **new Instant Message** window with a drop-down sheet, as shown below. Type the Buddy name of the person with whom you want to chat, then click OK.

From the File menu, choose **"Go To Chat..."** to open a **Group Chat** window in which you can invite more than one buddy. Learn more about Groups on pages 444–447.

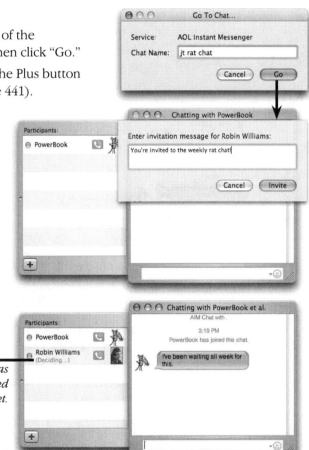

1. Type a name in the "Chat Name" field of the "Go To Chat..." window (right-top), then click "Go."

2. In the chat window that opens, click the Plus button to add participants (as shown on page 441). When you add a participant, an invitation message sheet slides down (right-middle).

3. Type an invitation message in the text field, then click "Invite." As you add participants, the same sheet opens. Click the "Invite" button for each buddy, or you can customize the invitation for some buddies if necessary.

4. To leave a Group Chat, click the red Close button in the top-left corner of the window.

This invited participant has not declined or accepted her invitation yet.

More about Group Chats

A **Group Chat** is different from an Instant or Direct Message in that you can have a number of people around the world in the same "chat room" (which looks amazingly like an Instant Message window) all chatting at once.

You can **create a new Group Chat** with a unique name and invite a large number of people to join you, as explained on page 443. .Mac members, AOL members, and AIM users can all be invited into the chat.

You can **join an existing Group Chat** that another iChat or AIM user has created if you know the exact name of the Group Chat, as explained below.

1. From the File menu, choose "Go to Chat...."

2. In the "Go To Chat" window, type in the name of the Group Chat you want to join (shown bottom-left).

3. Click the "Go" button. If other buddies are already there, you will join them. If you're the first one there, type a greeting and wait for a response from others as they join in.

   Note: If you enter the name of a Group Chat that other .Mac users in the world have already set up, you will land in their room! So you want to be sure to type the correct name of the room you want to join. Caps and lowercase don't matter when typing the name of a Group Chat.

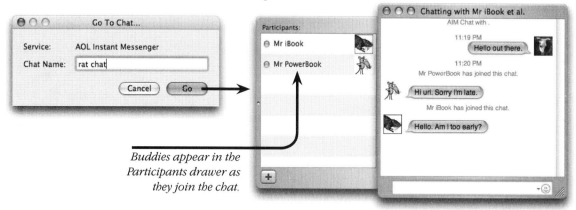

Buddies appear in the Participants drawer as they join the chat.

An easy way to start a group chat

You can quickly **start a new group chat** without having to type an invitation as described on page 443. First, make a multiple selection of buddies by *Command*-clicking on people in your Buddy List that you want to invite to a group chat. Then *Control*-click on any selected Buddy in the list, and choose "Invite to Chat..." from the contextual menu that pops up. A new message window will open and every selected Buddy will receive an invitation in the form of an iChat window popping open on their Desktop.

Create and organize chat groups

iChat lets you create *groups* of Buddies so that you see only the buddies you want to see in your Buddy List. iChat automatically creates a default list called "Buddies" which includes all buddies in your list.

You can create any number of groups. **To add a buddy to a group,** drag the buddy from the Buddy List to the Group in the drawer. When you do this, it *moves* the buddy from the Buddy List to the group. If you then delete the buddy from the group, the buddy is removed from iChat completely. Instead of *moving* buddies around, you can *copy* them to a group: *Option-drag* a buddy from the Buddy List to a group in the drawer, or from one group to another group. One buddy can be in multiple groups. A buddy that you delete from one group will remain in other groups.

To create groups in Buddy List:

1. From the iChat menu, choose "Preferences…."
2. Click the "General" button in the Preferences toolbar to show the General Preferences pane.
3. Click the "Use groups in Buddy List" checkbox.

The drawer opens from the side of the Buddy List. If your Buddy list doesn't open the Groups drawer, go to the View menu and choose "Show Groups."

A new pop-down menu also appears just above the buddy names. This menu contains a list of all groups that you create, plus the default "Buddies" group.

To *move* a buddy to a group: Drag a buddy from the Buddy List to another group in the Groups drawer. The buddy is *removed* from its original group.

To *copy* a buddy to a group: Option-drag a buddy from the Buddy List to another group in the Groups drawer. The buddy *remains* in its original group.

To add offline buddies to a group: From the View menu, choose "Show Offline Buddies," then drag dimmed-out buddies from the Buddy List to a group.

To delete a group: Select the group in the drawer, then press Delete. But remember that you'll also be deleting the buddies in that group. If those buddies are not in another group, you'll have to manually add them again later if you want them in your Buddy List.

To hide groups completely: Go back to the General pane of iChat preferences and *uncheck* "Use groups in Buddy List."

From this menu you can choose groups without opening the drawer on the left. Select "Groups" from this menu to open or close the drawer.

This button closes the drawer.

Click here to add a new group to the drawer.

Another way to create a Group Chat and invite others to join you:

1. From the File menu, choose "New Chat."

2. A new message window appears. *Before you type anything or choose anyone to invite,* go to the View menu and choose "Chat Options...."

3. From the pop-up "Mode" menu, choose "Chat," as shown below.

4. If iChat supplies a Chat Name for you, you can change it. If you change it, be sure to enter a name that no one else in the world would be using at this moment or you might end up in someone else's Chat. (How do you think I know this?) Click OK.

Caps and lowercase don't matter in a Chat Name, nor do spaces; that is, "tea room" is the same as "TeaRoom."

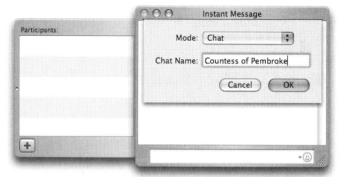

5. **To invite one or more of your buddies** to the new chat, drag them from the Buddy list to the chat's Participants drawer (shown below). **Or** click the **+** button at the bottom of the Participants drawer, then choose people from your list who are online at the moment.

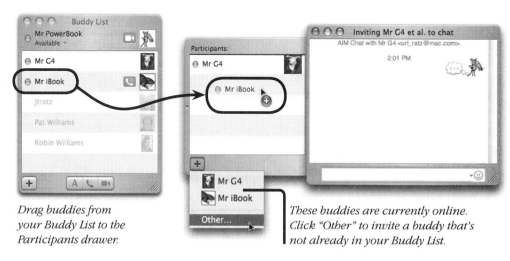

Drag buddies from your Buddy List to the Participants drawer.

These buddies are currently online. Click "Other" to invite a buddy that's not already in your Buddy List.

6. **To invite someone who is not on your Buddy List,** click the **+** button at the bottom of the drawer, then choose "Other...." Type the buddy chat name in the invitation sheet that slides down from the top of the message window (shown below), then click OK. An invited buddy must be online already.

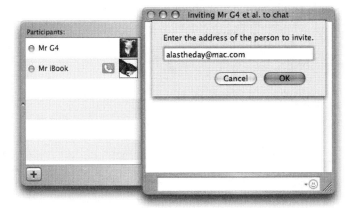

7. Once you have added the participants to the list, type a message into the text field at the bottom of the window, hit Return, and that message will go out to everyone on your list.

You can always add more people at any time, and anyone in the world can enter your Chat Room name and drop in to your window. For instance, if someone is not yet online when you send out an invitation, you can send them an email telling them to join you in that particular room as soon as they are online.

8. All of your participants will get a message on their screens inviting them. As soon as they respond, they will appear in your window.

Join an existing Chat Room

You can **join an existing Group Chat** that another Mac.com member started if you know its name. You cannot join a chat that an AOL user started in AOL.

1. From the File menu, choose "Go To Chat...."

2. In the "Go To Chat..." window, type in the exact name of the Group Chat you wish to join, then click "Go."

If a Chat Room by this name exists somewhere in the world, you will appear in it and it will appear on your screen.

If there is no such existing room, an "Empty chat room" will open on your screen. People can join you there if they know the chat name.

Send or Receive Files through iChat

You may want to **send a picture or some other file** to a Buddy in your list. This technique only works if your Buddy is also an iChat user. If he is an AOL user, you'll have to send the file as an email attachment.

To send a file to another iChat Buddy on your list:

1. Drag a file icon and drag it on top of a Buddy's name in the Buddy List.

2. A panel appears on your Desktop that asks you to cancel or send the file. Click "Send."

On the recipient's computer (assuming it's an iChat user, not an AOL user), an alert panel appears warning of an incoming file, as shown below-left.

1. Click anywhere in the white alert panel to transform it into the "Incoming File Transfer" window (below-right) which identifies the sender, the file name, the file type, and the file size.

2. Based on the information in the "Incoming File Transfer" window, you can choose to "Decline" the transfer, or click the "Save File" button and download it. If you save the file, it will appear on your Desktop.

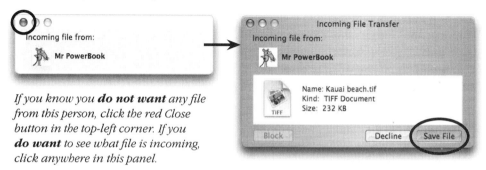

*If you know you **do not want** any file from this person, click the red Close button in the top-left corner. If you **do want** to see what file is incoming, click anywhere in this panel.*

Save Transcripts of Chats

You can save a transcript of any text chat—Instant Messages, Direct Messages, and Group Chats—to document a conversation, read later, or store in your digital box of love letters.

To save an individual chat:

1. Make sure the chat you want to save is the "active" window on the screen—click once on it to make sure.

2. From the File menu, choose "Save a Copy As...."

3. Name the document and choose a folder in which to store it. Click "Save."

To automatically save all chat transcripts:

1. From the iChat menu, choose "Preferences...."

2. Click the "Messages" icon in the Preferences toolbar.

3. Check the box to "Automatically save chat transcripts" (see page 453). This creates a new folder inside your Documents folder, called "iChats." Every conversation you have in iChat will automatically be recorded and stored in this folder—you don't ever have to choose to "Save."

Instant Messages
with Mr G4

The file icon of a saved chat transcript looks like this.

To open the most recently saved chat transcripts:

▼ From the File menu choose "Open Recent," then choose a file from the submenu.

To read any saved chat:

▼ Double-click the chat file icon. The file will open in a chat window. When you open a saved chat transcript you can scroll through it just like you can an active chat window.

To print a chat:

1. Start a text chat, or open a saved chat transcript.

2. From the iChat File menu, choose "Print...."

3. In the Print dialog box, click the "Preview" button to see what your document will look like.

4. Click the "Print" button in the Preview window.

A saved chat transcript.

Customize the Chat Background

You can **customize the background** of any chat window by adding a picture or graphic. This comes in handy when you've got several chats going on and don't want to get confused about who is in which window.

This image will appear only on *your* computer—the person you are chatting with will not see it. As soon as you close this chat window, that background disappears and will not automatically re-appear anywhere.

To customize a chat window:

1. Click anywhere in a chat window to select that window.

2. From the View menu, choose "Set Chat Background...."

3. In the dialog box that appears, select an image file that's on your computer, then click "Open."

   Or simply drag any image file from your Desktop and drop it directly into an empty space in the chat window.

Small images will "tile" (repeat over and over) to fill the window space. Large images will display full-sized, cropping off the image where necessary.

Simple or subdued background images are best for readability.

To remove a background, click once in the chat window, then go to the View menu and choose "Clear Background."

Set Up Additional iChat Accounts

In addition to your .Mac account, you can also set up an existing AOL Instant Messenger Account (AIM), additional .Mac accounts, or use your AOL screen name as a different account. No matter how many different accounts you have, though, only *one* can be *active* at any time. Each account you create has its own Buddy List.

To set up another iChat account:

1. From the iChat menu, choose "Preferences…."

2. Click the "Accounts" icon in the toolbar.

3. Type in a new "Screen Name" (buddy name).

    Either: This would be another .Mac account name you own, which would be your email address including the "@mac.com" part. Click the menu arrow to get a menu where you can choose to "Create a new .Mac account…" (shown below-right).

    Or: Use an existing AIM account name that you got at **www.aim.com**.

    Or: Use your AOL name if you have an AOL account. Do *not* include "@aol.com."

4. Enter the login password you chose when you set up that particular account.

5. Hit Return to add the new account to the "Screen Name" pop-up menu.

6. Close the Preferences window.

7. From the iChat menu, choose "Log Into AIM" to go online with the currently selected screen name.

Switch to a different account

Once you have set up different accounts, as explained on the previous page, you can switch from one to the other.

To switch to a different iChat account:

1. From the iChat menu, choose "Preferences...."

2. Click the "Accounts" icon in the toolbar.

3. From the "Screen Name" pop-up menu, choose a different account that you previously set up (see the previous page). Close the Preferences window.

4. From the iChat menu, choose "Log Into AIM" to go online with the currently selected screen name.

Preferences

Most of the options in **Preferences** are self-explanatory, but here are a few tips:

Accounts: If you have several accounts set up, as described on the previous page, you may want to select a particular account *before* you actually go online. You can save a couple of steps if you do this:

1. Open the iChat Preferences, then click the **General** icon.

2. In the General Preferences pane, **uncheck** the box, "When iChat opens, automatically log in." Close the window.

3. The next time you open iChat, you will not be logged in, so open Preferences and choose an account from the "AIM Screen Name" pop-up menu. Close Preferences.

4. Go to the iChat menu, and choose "Log Into AIM."

This technique lets you open iChat without being actually logged in, which means no one will know you are online under the previous account.

*You can choose to see the red and green status lights as circles and squares, in case you are **colorblind** between red and green.*

Messages: Use the Messages pane to customize many features of your Chat windows, such as the color of your balloon and the balloons of other people, the font you use and they use, and the colors of the fonts. As you make choices, your choices will be shown in the little window space, as you can see below.

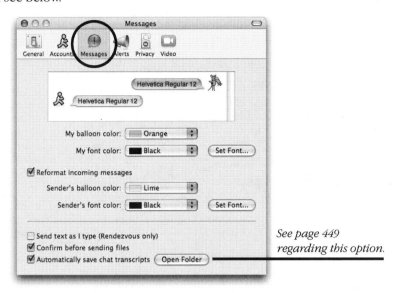

See page 449 regarding this option.

Click "Repeat" if you want the action to happen each time the event occurs. Deselect "Repeat" if you want the action to happen only the next time the event occurs.

Alerts: In the Alerts pane, you can have certain actions happen as the result of certain events. For instance, you can make sure your computer tells you how wonderful you look every time you log in, just in case no one else in your office tells you so.

Choose an event from the top pop-up menu, then choose the actions you want to happen upon that event.

After you choose an event (shown above), you can choose a sound to play when that event occurs. Quit and reopen iChat for changes to take effect.

Privacy: If you want to be **invisible** to certain people, or you want to be **visible only** to certain people, click the "Privacy" icon in the Preferences toolbar, then from the Privacy Level pop-up menu, choose a setting.

To allow or block specific people, choose "Allow Specific People" **or** "Block Specific People." In either case, a sheet slides down (shown below) in which you can add specific chat names. Click the Add button (the plus sign) to add a name. To remove a name from the list, select it, then click the Remove button (the minus sign).

If you choose to "Allow people in my Buddy List," it automatically limits who can see you online to the people you know well enough to have in your List.

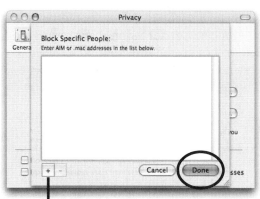

Click this button, then type a screen name (chat name) that you want blocked in the space above.

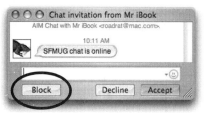

If you click the "Block" button when you receive a chat invitation, the sender's buddy name is added to the list of blocked users.

Video: This Preferences pane lets you preview your video camera picture and adjust a few settings.

Use the **Microphone** pop-up menu to choose a source for audio. From the "Microphone" pop-up menu, choose an option.

- ▾ **Choose "iSight Built-in"** if you have an Apple iSight camera connected. If you have some other FireWire video camera connected, the camera name or model number appears in this pop-up menu.

- ▾ **Choose "Internal microphone"** if you want to use the built-in internal microphone that came with your computer.

- ▾ **Choose "Line In"** if you have an external microphone connected to your computer through the Line In port.

Use the **Bandwidth Limit** pop-up menu to set limits for how much bandwidth to use when doing Video Chats. A low bandwidth selection is best for slower connections, but the video quality is compromised to a degree.

- ▾ **Choose 100 Kbps** or **200 Kbps** (kilobits per second) if you have a relatively slow broadband connection.

- ▾ **Choose 500 Kbps** for a good, average broadband connection.

- ▾ **Choose None** or **1 Mbps** or **2 Mbps** (megabits per second) if you have a really fast broadband connection.

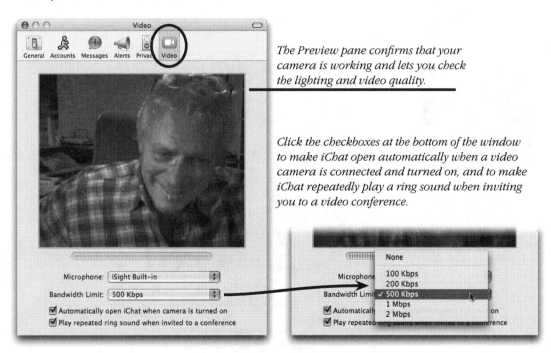

The Preview pane confirms that your camera is working and lets you check the lighting and video quality.

Click the checkboxes at the bottom of the window to make iChat open automatically when a video camera is connected and turned on, and to make iChat repeatedly play a ring sound when inviting you to a video conference.

Audio Chats

You can audio chat with other iChat users that have a microphone connected or built in to their computer. Since iChat uses the Internet, that means you can make long distance phone calls to buddies anywhere in the world for free. We carry a laptop with us when we travel and do all kinds of chats (text, audio, and video) with friends and family back home. Pretty amazing.

Tip: You need a broadband connection (not a dial-up modem connection) to audio or video chat. Travelers will be pleased to know that many hotels and lodges around the world provide broadband connections. The broadband wireless connections (Wi-Fi) that many coffee shops provide work very well.

Extra tip for frequent travelers: Sign up for a T-mobile Hot Spot wireless account. Starbucks all over the world provide Hot Spot connections. And, as we learned in London, the connection stays on 24/7, even when Starbucks is closed.

Robin on the steps of a closed Starbucks, across the street from Shakespeare's Globe Theatre, sending messages back home.

Set up for audio chats

Audio chats require almost no setup. In fact, the settings below are automatic and you don't need to change them unless you have a problem connecting.

1. Make sure you have a microphone connected or built in to your Mac.

2. Open iChat. From the iChat menu choose "Preferences...," then click the "Video" icon in the toolbar to open the Video Preferences pane.

3. From the "Microphone" pop-up menu, choose a source for audio. **Choose "iSight Built-in"** if you have an Apple iSight camera connected. If you have some other FireWire video camera connected, the camera name or model number appears in this pop-up menu. **Choose "Internal microphone"** if you want to use the built-in internal microphone that came with your computer. **Choose "Line In"** if you have an external microphone connected to your computer through the Line In port.

Start an audio chat

1. Open iChat.

2. Select a buddy in the iChat window that shows an "Audio Chat" icon (a telephone) to the right of the buddy name. You can also audio chat with a buddy that shows a "Video Chat" icon (a video camera), in case you're still in your pajamas. Or not.

3. To start an audio chat, click the "Audio Chat" icon next to the buddy name, or click the "Audio Chat" button at the bottom of the Rendez-vous window (shown on the right).

4. An audio panel opens on your Desktop, waiting for your buddy to accept the invitation, as shown below.

5. On the buddy's Desktop, the audio chat invitation appears. When he clicks on the invitation, it opens into the audio chat panel shown below, where he can choose to "Decline" or "Accept" the invitation. He can also choose a "Text Reply."

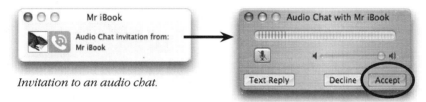

Invitation to an audio chat.

6. Once the audio chat invitation has been accepted, you can talk back and forth just as if you were using a telephone. The audio chat panel shows an animated sound level meter and provides a volume slider so you can adjust the chat volume.

End an audio chat

To end an audio chat, just click the red Close button in the top-left corner of the "Audio Chat" panel. Either party can end an audio chat at any time. When a buddy leaves the audio chat, your "Audio Chat" panel notifies you with a message.

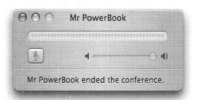

Video Chats

iChat makes video chats so easy that it's just unbelievable. In addition to iChat, you need a broadband connection to the Internet and a FireWire-enabled video camera. Apple sells a great little camera, called iSight, for $149. If you already own a more expensive digital video camera with FireWire, you can use that too.

Set up a video chat

▼ Make sure you have a FireWire-enabled video camera connected to your Mac and turned on. Make sure the videocam is in *Camera* or *Record* mode. An Apple iSight camera is automatically set to record.

Start a video chat

1. Open iChat. From the iChat menu choose "Preferences...," then click the "Video" icon in the toolbar to open the Video preferences pane. Choose video settings as described on page 455.

2. Select a buddy in the Buddy List whose name has a "Video Chat" icon (a video camera) next to it.

3. Click the "Video Chat" icon next to the buddy name, or click the "Video Chat" button (the one with a video camera icon) at the bottom of the Buddy List window.

4. A video chat window opens on your Desktop, as shown below. The video Preview pane shows what your own camera sees (you) while you wait for a response from your buddy.

Tip: You can take a snapshot of a buddy as you video chat, then use that photo in Address Book to make buddy identification fast and easy. From the Video menu, choose "Take Snapshot." The snapshot is placed on your Desktop.

This is what you see on your Desktop while waiting for your buddy to click the "Accept" button (shown on the next page).

5. When your buddy responds by clicking anywhere in the invitation panel (below-left), a video chat window opens on her Desktop with the option to "Decline" or "Accept" (below-right). She can also choose to respond with a "Text Reply."

This is what the buddy sees on her Desktop.

Your buddy receives an invitation like this one. If she clicks anywhere on it (except the red Close button), a video chat window opens on her Desktop, like the one shown on the right.

6. When the buddy clicks the "Accept" button in her invitation window (shown on the right), the thumbnail video preview image in *your* video chat window shrinks and zooms to a corner of the window, as shown below-right. To change the position of the inset thumbnail preview, press-and-drag it anywhere in the pane. To resize the thumbnail, press-and-drag its bottom-right corner.

7. Start chatting. If you're using a laptop with a wireless connection, you can roam around and give a tour of your house.

Start a one-way video chat

If you have a video camera and your buddy doesn't, you can still do a one-way video chat.

1. Open iChat and select a buddy in the Buddy List.

2. From the Buddies menu, choose "Invite to One-Way Video Chat."

3. Your buddy receives an invitation (shown on the right). When the buddy clicks the "Accept" button, you'll appear in a video chat window on the buddy's Desktop.

This is what you see on your Desktop after your buddy clicks the "Accept" button.

Mute the audio.   *Show video chat in full-screen mode.*

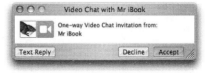

Rendezvous

iChat

Rendezvous is part of the **iChat** software in Mac OS X. If you have two or more Macs connected together on a local area network (ethernet, wireless, or a combination of both), Rendezvous automatically detects and connects the other computers on your network. You can send Instant Messages or files to other computers on the network. You can also have audio or video chats with others on the network if a mic or digital video camera is connected.

To use Rendezvous, you don't need to have a Mac.com account, or an AIM account, as you must to use iChat. Any computer that you want to connect through Rendezvous needs to have iChat installed (which automatically includes Rendezvous) and must be connected through some sort of network (ethernet, wireless, or a combination of the two).

To set up Rendezvous:

1. Open iChat: Either single-click on its icon in the Dock, or double-click its icon in the Applications window.

2. The first time you open iChat, the series of dialogs opens to set up iChat and Rendezvous (see page 432).

3. One of the dialogs (shown below) is titled "Set up Rendezvous Messaging." All you have to do is choose "Use Rendezvous messaging" and you're all set up.

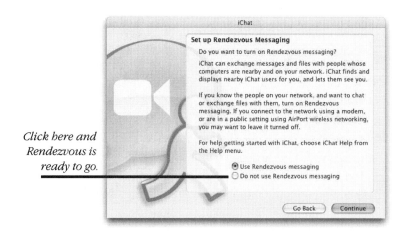

Click here and Rendezvous is ready to go.

It's not too late to set up Rendezvous

If you previously opened iChat and set it up but did not turn on Rendezvous, **or** if you want to change any of the settings (**or** turn off Rendezvous), use the iChat preferences:

1. While iChat is open, go to the iChat menu and choose "Preferences…."

2. In the "Accounts" pane, as shown below, check the box to "Enable local Rendezvous messaging."

*Check this box to
turn on Rendezvous;
uncheck it to turn it off.*

Just about everything that applies to **iChat** (preferences, images, opening and closing, changing your availability message, what all the icons indicate, etc.) also applies to **Rendezvous.** So if you haven't already, read the other pages in this chapter about iChat to answer questions about Rendezvous.

Chat through Rendezvous

Rendezvous is an easy and instant way to communicate and exchange files with other people on your local network. Depending on the hardware available you can use Rendezvous for text messaging, audio chats, and even video chats. Video chats are also referred to as video conferencing, but that will seem more appropriate when the next version of iChat supports multiple video connections at one time.

Select a buddy on the network, then click the Text Chat button.

Text messaging

1. Open iChat, which will activate Rendezvous.

2. If the Rendezvous window (left) doesn't appear, press Command 2, **or** go to the Window menu and choose "Rendezvous." Other users on your network who also have iChat installed will appear in the Rendezvous window.

3. In the Rendezvous window, select the user to whom you want to send a file, then click the Text Chat button (the "A" icon). An Instant Message window opens.

4. Type a message in the text box, then press Return to send it.

Audio chats

When you see someone in the Rendezvous window you want to invite to an audio chat, click their name, then click the telephone icon button at the bottom of the window. If the telephone icon is dimmed out, it means the other person does not have a microphone connected or built in. If a video camera icon appears next to a name, that person can either audio chat or video chat (video chat includes audio).

An audio chat in Rendezvous works exactly the same as in iChat (see pages 456–459), except for a couple of Rendezvous advantages. Working on a local network can provide faster connections than some Internet connections (iChat requires an Internet connection), and an audio chat invitation you send on a local network will not time-out if it's not responded to immediately.

Icons not dimmed out indicate the types of chat you can do with that person.

Video chats

A video chat in Rendezvous also works the same as in iChat: Select a name in the Rendezvous window, then click the video chat icon (a video camera) next to the name, or click the video icon button at the bottom of the window. Rendezvous video chats have the same advantages mentioned above for audio chats. If a name in the list shows a video camera icon, you can invite them to any type of chat.

Read pages 456–459 for more information about video and audio chats.

Send a file through Rendezvous to another computer

You can send a file to any other user on your network with just a drag-and-drop. It's the best.

To send a file to another computer on your local network:

1. Open iChat, which will activate Rendezvous.

2. If the Rendezvous window (shown below, left) doesn't appear, press Command 2, **or** go to the Window menu and choose "Rendezvous." Other users who also have Rendezvous set up and running will appear in your Rendezvous window.

3. To send *one* file or a *folder* containing several files, drag it to the Rendezvous window and drop it on a computer user's name. You will be asked to cancel or send the file.

4. The other computer will get an "Incoming file" notification message, shown below. When that user clicks "Save File," the file will be sent from one machine to another. Now that was pretty easy.

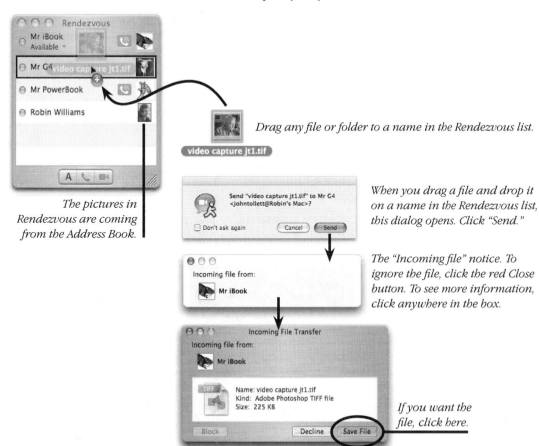

Drag any file or folder to a name in the Rendezvous list.

The pictures in Rendezvous are coming from the Address Book.

When you drag a file and drop it on a name in the Rendezvous list, this dialog opens. Click "Send."

The "Incoming file" notice. To ignore the file, click the red Close button. To see more information, click anywhere in the box.

If you want the file, click here.

Send a file through a Rendezvous Instant Message
Another way to send a file through Rendezvous:

1. Open iChat, which will activate Rendezvous.

2. If the Rendezvous window (shown on the left) doesn't appear, press Command 2, **or** go to the Window menu and choose "Rendezvous." Other users on your network who also have iChat installed will appear in the Rendezvous window.

3. In the Rendezvous window, select the user to whom you want to send a file, then click the Text Chat button (the "A" icon), shown on the left. An Instant Message (IM) window opens (below-left).

4. Type a message in the text box, then press Return to send it. The recipient receives an Instant Message notice (shown below as the borderless panel titled "Mr PowerBook").

5. When you're ready to send a file, drag a file icon (or a folder of files) from any Finder window to the text box at the bottom of the Rendezvous window.

6. The file name and icon appears in a message bubble. When the recipient clicks once on the file name, it downloads to his Desktop.

Select a buddy on the network, then click the Text Chat button.

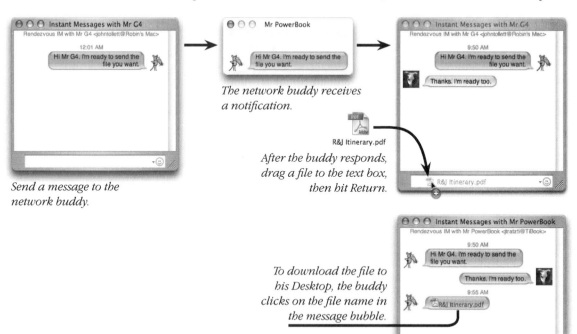

Send a message to the network buddy.

The network buddy receives a notification.

R&J Itinerary.pdf

After the buddy responds, drag a file to the text box, then hit Return.

To download the file to his Desktop, the buddy clicks on the file name in the message bubble.

Section four

Index